Java 9 Programming Blueprints

Implement new features such as modules, the process
handling API, REPL, and many more to build end-to-end
applications in Java 9

Jason Lee

BIRMINGHAM - MUMBAI

Java 9 Programming Blueprints

First published: July 2017

Production reference: 1250717

Published by Packt Publishing Ltd.
Livery Place
35 Livery Street
Birmingham
B3 2PB, UK.

ISBN 978-1-78646-019-6

www.packtpub.com

Credits

Author
Jason Lee

Reviewer
Dionisios Petrakopoulos

Commissioning Editor
Kunal Parikh

Acquisition Editor
Chaitanya Nair

Content Development Editor
Lawrence Veigas

Technical Editor
Abhishek Sharma

Copy Editor
Zainab Bootwala

Project Coordinator
Prajakta Naik

Proofreader
Safis Editing

Indexer
Rekha Nair

Graphics
Abhinash Sahu

Production Coordinator
Nilesh Mohite

About the Author

Jason Lee has been writing software professionally for over 20 years, but his love for computers started over a decade earlier, in the fourth grade, when his dad brought home a Commodore 64. He has been working with Java for almost his entire career, with the last 12+ years focused primarily on Enterprise Java. He has written in-house web applications and libraries, and also worked on large, more public projects, such as the JavaServer Faces reference implementation Mojarra, GlassFish, and WebLogic Server.

Jason is currently the President of the Oklahoma City Java Users Group, and is an occasional speaker at conferences. Ever the technology enthusiast, his current interests include cloud computing, mobile development, and emerging JVM languages.

Apart from work, Jason enjoys spending time with his wife, Angela, and his two sons, Andrew and Noah. He is active in the music ministry of his local church, and enjoys reading, running, martial arts, and playing his bass guitar.

Everyone told me that writing a book is hard, and they weren't kidding! There's no way I could have done this without the love and support of my beautiful wife, Angela, who was patient and supportive during all of my late nights and long weekends, and was kind enough to read through every last page, helping me clean things up.

My two awesome sons, Andrew and Noah, also deserve huge thanks. There were certainly many nights when I was locked away in my office instead of spending time with you. I appreciate your understanding and patience during this project, and I hope this is something we can all be proud of together.

Angela, Andrew, and Noah, this is for you. I love you all!

About the Reviewer

Dionisios Petrakopoulos has worked in several companies using different technologies and programming languages, such as C, C++, Java SE, Java EE, and Scala, as a senior software engineer for the past 15 years. His main interest is the Java ecosystem and the various facets of it. His other area of interest is information security, especially cryptography. He holds a BSc degree in computer science and an MSc degree in information security, both from Royal Holloway, University of London. He is also the technical reviewer of the book *Learning Modular Java Programming* by Packt.

I would like to thank my wife Anna for her support and love.

www.PacktPub.com

For support files and downloads related to your book, please visit www.PacktPub.com.

Did you know that Packt offers eBook versions of every book published, with PDF and ePub files available? You can upgrade to the eBook version at www.PacktPub.com and as a print book customer, you are entitled to a discount on the eBook copy. Get in touch with us at service@packtpub.com for more details.

At www.PacktPub.com, you can also read a collection of free technical articles, sign up for a range of free newsletters and receive exclusive discounts and offers on Packt books and eBooks.

https://www.packtpub.com/mapt

Get the most in-demand software skills with Mapt. Mapt gives you full access to all Packt books and video courses, as well as industry-leading tools to help you plan your personal development and advance your career.

Why subscribe?

- Fully searchable across every book published by Packt
- Copy and paste, print, and bookmark content
- On demand and accessible via a web browser

Customer Feedback

Thanks for purchasing this Packt book. At Packt, quality is at the heart of our editorial process. To help us improve, please leave us an honest review on this book's Amazon page at `https://www.amazon.com/dp/178646019X`.

If you'd like to join our team of regular reviewers, you can e-mail us at `customerreviews@packtpub.com`. We award our regular reviewers with free eBooks and videos in exchange for their valuable feedback. Help us be relentless in improving our products!

Table of Contents

Preface

The world has been waiting for Java 9 for a long time. More specifically, we've been waiting for the Java Platform Module System, and Java 9 is finally going to deliver it. If all goes as planned, we'll finally have true isolation, giving us, potentially, smaller JDKs and more stable applications. That's not all that Java 9 is offering of course; there is a plethora of great changes in the release, but that's certainly the most exciting. That said, this book is not a book about the module system. There are plenty of excellent resources that can give you a deep dive into the Java Platform Module System and its many implications. This book, though, is a much more practical look at Java 9. Rather than discussing the minutiae of the release, as satisfying as that can be, what we'll do over the next few hundred pages is look at different ways all of the great changes in recent JDK releases--especially Java 9--can be applied in practical ways.

When we're done, you'll have ten different projects that cover a myriad of problem areas, from which you can draw usable examples as you work to solve your own unique challenges.

What this book covers

Chapter 1, *Introduction*, gives a quick overview of the new features in Java 9, and also covers some of the major features of Java 7 and 8 as well, setting the stage for what we'll be using in later chapters.

Chapter 2, *Managing Process in Java*, builds a simple process management application (akin to Unix's top command), as we explore the new OS process management API changes in Java 9.

Chapter 3, *Duplicate File Finder*, demonstrates the use of the New File I/O APIs in an application, both command line and GUI, that will search for and identify duplicate files. Technologies such as file hashing, streams, and JavaFX are heavily used.

Chapter 4, *Date Calculator*, shows a library and command-line tool to perform date calculations. We will see Java 8's Date/Time API exercised heavily.

Chapter 5, *Sunago - A Social Media Aggregator*, shows how one can integrate with third-party systems to build an aggregator. We'll work with REST APIs, JavaFX, and pluggable application architectures.

Chapter 6, *Sunago - An Android Port*, sees us return to our application from Chapter 5, *Sunago - A Social Media Aggregator*.

Chapter 7, *Email and Spam Management with MailFilter*, builds a mail filtering application, explaining how the various email protocols work, then demonstrates how to interact with emails using the standard Java email API--JavaMail.

Chapter 8, *Photo Management with PhotoBeans*, takes us in a completely different direction when we build a photo management application using the NetBeans Rich Client Platform.

Chapter 9, *Taking Notes with Monumentum*, holds yet another new direction. In this chapter, we build an application--and microservice--that offers web-based note-taking similar to several popular commercial offerings.

Chapter 10, *Serverless Java*, moves us into the cloud as we build a Function as a Service system in Java to send email and SMS-based notifications.

Chapter 11, *DeskDroid - A Desktop Client for Your Android Phone*, demonstrates a simple approach for a desktop client to interact with an Android device as we build an application to view and send text messages from our desktop.

Chapter 12, *What's Next?*, discusses what the future might hold for Java, and also touches upon two recent challengers to Java's preeminence on the JVM--Ceylon and Kotlin.

What you need for this book

You need the Java Development Kit (JDK) 9, NetBeans 8.2 or newer, and Maven 3.0 or newer. Some chapters will require additional software, including Scene Builder from Gluon and Android Studio.

Who this book is for

This book is for beginner to intermediate developers who are interested in seeing new and varied APIs and programming techniques applied in practical examples. Deep understanding of Java is not required, but a basic familiarity with the language and its ecosystem, build tools, and so on is assumed.

Conventions

In this book, you will find a number of text styles that distinguish between different kinds of information. Here are some examples of these styles and an explanation of their meaning.

Code words in text, database table names, folder names, filenames, file extensions, pathnames, dummy URLs, user input, and Twitter handles are shown as follows: "The Java architects have introduced a new file, `module-info.java`, similar to the existing `package-info.java` file, found at the root of the module, for example at `src/main/java/module-info.java`."

A block of code is set as follows:

```
module com.steeplesoft.foo.intro {
    requires com.steeplesoft.bar;
    exports com.steeplesoft.foo.intro.model;
    exports com.steeplesoft.foo.intro.api;
}
```

Any command-line input or output is written as follows:

```
$ mvn -Puber install
```

New terms and **important words** are shown in bold. Words that you see on the screen, for example, in menus or dialog boxes, appear in the text like this: "In the **New Project** window, we select **Maven** then **NetBeans Application**."

Warnings or important notes appear like this.

Tips and tricks appear like this.

Reader feedback

Feedback from our readers is always welcome. Let us know what you think about this book-what you liked or disliked. Reader feedback is important for us as it helps us develop titles that you will really get the most out of.

To send us general feedback, simply e-mail `feedback@packtpub.com`, and mention the book's title in the subject of your message.

If there is a topic that you have expertise in and you are interested in either writing or contributing to a book, see our author guide at `www.packtpub.com/authors`.

Customer support

Now that you are the proud owner of a Packt book, we have a number of things to help you to get the most from your purchase.

Downloading the example code

You can download the example code files for this book from your account at `http://www.packtpub.com`. If you purchased this book elsewhere, you can visit `http://www.packtpub.com/support` and register to have the files e-mailed directly to you.

You can download the code files by following these steps:

1. Log in or register to our website using your e-mail address and password.
2. Hover the mouse pointer on the **SUPPORT** tab at the top.
3. Click on **Code Downloads & Errata**.
4. Enter the name of the book in the **Search** box.
5. Select the book for which you're looking to download the code files.
6. Choose from the drop-down menu where you purchased this book from.
7. Click on **Code Download**.

Once the file is downloaded, please make sure that you unzip or extract the folder using the latest version of:

- WinRAR / 7-Zip for Windows
- Zipeg / iZip / UnRarX for Mac
- 7-Zip / PeaZip for Linux

The code bundle for the book is also hosted on GitHub at `https://github.com/PacktPubl` `ishing/Java-9-Programming-Blueprints`. We also have other code bundles from our rich catalog of books and videos available at `https://github.com/PacktPublishing/`. Check them out!

Downloading the color images of this book

We also provide you with a PDF file that has color images of the screenshots/diagrams used in this book. The color images will help you better understand the changes in the output. You can download this file from `https://www.packtpub.com/sites/default/files/down` `loads/Java9ProgrammingBlueprints_ColorImages`.

Errata

Although we have taken every care to ensure the accuracy of our content, mistakes do happen. If you find a mistake in one of our books-maybe a mistake in the text or the code-we would be grateful if you could report this to us. By doing so, you can save other readers from frustration and help us improve subsequent versions of this book. If you find any errata, please report them by visiting `http://www.packtpub.com/submit-errata`, selecting your book, clicking on the **Errata Submission Form** link, and entering the details of your errata. Once your errata are verified, your submission will be accepted and the errata will be uploaded to our website or added to any list of existing errata under the Errata section of that title.

To view the previously submitted errata, go to `https://www.packtpub.com/books/content/support` and enter the name of the book in the search field. The required information will appear under the **Errata** section.

Piracy

Piracy of copyrighted material on the Internet is an ongoing problem across all media. At Packt, we take the protection of our copyright and licenses very seriously. If you come across any illegal copies of our works in any form on the Internet, please provide us with the location address or website name immediately so that we can pursue a remedy.

Please contact us at `copyright@packtpub.com` with a link to the suspected pirated material.

We appreciate your help in protecting our authors and our ability to bring you valuable content.

Questions

If you have a problem with any aspect of this book, you can contact us at
`questions@packtpub.com`, and we will do our best to address the problem.

1
Introduction

In the process of erecting a new building, a set of blueprints helps all related parties communicate--the architect, electricians, carpenters, plumbers, and so on. It details things such as shapes, sizes, and materials. Without them, each of the subcontractors would be left guessing as to what to do, where to do it, and how. Without these blueprints, modern architecture would be almost impossible.

What is in your hands--or on the screen in front of you--is a set of blueprints of a different sort. Rather than detailing exactly how to build your specific software system, as each project and environment has unique constraints and requirements, these blueprints offer examples of how to build a variety of Java-based systems, providing examples of how to use specific features in the **Java Development Kit**, or **JDK**, with a special focus on the new features of Java 9 that you can then apply to your specific problem.

Since it would be impossible to build an application using only the new Java 9 features, we will also be using and highlighting many of the newest features in the JDK. Before we get too far into what that entails, then, let's take a brief moment to discuss some of these great new features from recent major JDK releases. Hopefully, most Java shops are already on Java 7, so we'll focus on version 8 and, of course, version 9.

In this chapter, we will cover the following topics:

- New features in Java 8
- New features in Java 9
- Projects

New features in Java 8

Java 8, released on March 8, 2014, brought arguably two of the most significant features since Java 5, released in 2004--lambdas and streams. With functional programming gaining popularity in the JVM world, especially with the help of languages such as Scala, Java adherents had been clamoring for more functional-style language features for several years. Originally slated for release in Java 7, the feature was dropped from that release, finally seeing a stable release with Java 8.

While it can be hoped that everyone is familiar with Java's lambda support, experience has shown that many shops, for a variety of reasons, are slow to adopt new language versions and features, so a quick introduction might be helpful.

Lambdas

The term lambda, which has its roots in lambda calculus, developed by Alonzo Church in 1936, simply refers to an anonymous function. Typically, a function (or method, in more proper Java parlance), is a statically-named artifact in the Java source:

```
public int add(int x, int y) {
   return x + y;
}
```

This simple method is one named `add` that takes two `int` parameters as well as returning an `int` parameter. With the introduction of lambdas, this can now be written as follows:

```
(int x, int y) → x + y
```

Or, more simply as this:

```
(x, y) → x + y
```

This abbreviated syntax indicates that we have a function that takes two parameters and returns their sum. Depending on where this lambda is used, the types of the parameters can be inferred by the compiler, making the second, even more concise format possible. Most importantly, though, note that this method is no longer named. Unless it is assigned to a variable or passed as a parameter (more on this later), it can not be referenced--or used--anywhere in the system.

This example, of course, is absurdly simple. A better example of this might be in one of the many APIs where the method's parameter is an implementation of what is known as a **Single Abstract Method** (**SAM**) interface, which is, at least until Java 8, an interface with a single method. One of the canonical examples of a SAM is `Runnable`. Here is an example of the pre-lambda `Runnable` usage:

```
Runnable r = new Runnable() {
  public void run() {
    System.out.println("Do some work");
  }
};
Thread t = new Thread(r);
t.start();
```

With Java 8 lambdas, this code can be vastly simplified to this:

```
Thread t = new Thread(() ->
  System.out.println("Do some work"));
t.start();
```

The body of the `Runnable` method is still pretty trivial, but the gains in clarity and conciseness should be pretty obvious.

While lambdas are anonymous functions (that is, they have no names), Java lambdas, as is the case in many other languages, can also be assigned to variables and passed as parameters (indeed, the functionality would be almost worthless without this capability). Revisiting the `Runnable` method in the preceding code, we can separate the declaration and the use of `Runnable` as follows:

```
Runnable r = () {
  // Acquire database connection
  // Do something really expensive
};
Thread t = new Thread(r);
t.start();
```

This is intentionally more verbose than the preceding example. The stubbed out body of the `Runnable` method is intended to mimic, after a fashion, how a real-world `Runnable` may look and why one may want to assign the newly-defined `Runnable` method to a variable in spite of the conciseness that lambdas offer. This new lambda syntax allows us to declare the body of the `Runnable` method without having to worry about method names, signatures, and so on. It is true that any decent IDE would help with this kind of boilerplate, but this new syntax gives you, and the countless developers who will maintain your code, much less noise to have to parse when debugging the code.

Any SAM interface can be written as a lambda. Do you have a comparator that you really only need to use once?

```
List<Student> students = getStudents();
students.sort((one, two) -> one.getGrade() - two.getGrade());
```

How about `ActionListener`?

```
saveButton.setOnAction((event) -> saveAndClose());
```

Additionally, you can use your own SAM interfaces in lambdas as follows:

```
public <T> interface Validator<T> {
  boolean isValid(T value);
}
cardProcessor.setValidator((card)
card.getNumber().startsWith("1234"));
```

One of the advantages of this approach is that it not only makes the consuming code more concise, but it also reduces the level of effort, such as it is, in creating some of these concrete SAM instances. That is to say, rather than having to decide between an anonymous class and a concrete, named class, the developer can declare it inline, cleanly and concisely.

In addition to the SAMs Java developers have been using for years, Java 8 introduced a number of functional interfaces to help facilitate more functional style programming. The Java 8 Javadoc lists 43 different interfaces. Of these, there are a handful of basic function **shapes** that you should know of, some of which are as follows:

`BiConsumer<T,U>`	This represents an operation that accepts two input arguments and returns no result
`BiFunction<T,U,R>`	This represents a function that accepts two arguments and produces a result
`BinaryOperator<T>`	This represents an operation upon two operands of the same type, producing a result of the same type as the operands
`BiPredicate<T,U>`	This represents a predicate (Boolean-valued function) of two arguments
`Consumer<T>`	This represents an operation that accepts a single input argument and returns no result
`Function<T,R>`	This represents a function that accepts one argument and produces a result

`Predicate<T>`	This represents a predicate (Boolean-valued function) of one argument
`Supplier<T>`	This represents a supplier of results

There are a myriad of uses for these interfaces, but perhaps the best way to demonstrate some of them is to turn our attention to the next big feature in Java 8--Streams.

Streams

The other major addition to Java 8, and, perhaps where lambdas shine the brightest, is the new **Streams API**. If you were to search for a definition of Java streams, you would get answers that range from the somewhat circular **a stream of data elements** to the more technical **Java streams are monads**, and they're probably both right. The Streams API allows the Java developer to interact with a stream of data elements via a **sequence of steps**. Even putting it that way isn't as clear as it could be, so let's see what it means by looking at some sample code.

Let's say you have a list of grades for a particular class. You would like to know what the average grade is for the girls in the class. Prior to Java 8, you might have written something like this:

```
double sum = 0.0;
int count = 0;
for (Map.Entry<Student, Integer> g : grades.entrySet()) {
  if ("F".equals(g.getKey().getGender())) {
    count++;
    sum += g.getValue();
  }
}
double avg = sum / count;
```

We initialize two variables, one to store the sums and one to count the number of hits. Next, we loop through the grades. If the student's gender is female, we increment our counter and update the sum. When the loop terminates, we then have the information we need to calculate the average. This works, but it's a bit verbose. The new Streams API can help with that:

```
double avg = grades.entrySet().stream()
  .filter(e -> "F".equals(e.getKey().getGender())) // 1
  .mapToInt(e -> e.getValue()) // 2
  .average() // 3
  .getAsDouble(); //4
```

This new version is not significantly smaller, but the purpose of the code is much clearer. In the preceding pre-stream code, we have to play computer, parsing the code and teasing out its intended purpose. With streams, we have a clear, declarative means to express application logic. For each entry in the map do the following:

1. Filter out each entry whose `gender` is not F.
2. Map each value to the primitive int.
3. Average the grades.
4. Return the value as a double.

With the stream-based and lamba-based approach, we don't need to declare temporary, intermediate variables (grade count and total), and we don't need to worry about calculating the admittedly simple average. The JDK does all of the heavy-lifting for us.

The new java.time package

While lambdas and streams are extremely important game-changing updates, with Java 8, we were given another long-awaited change that was, at least in some circles, just as exciting: a new date/time API. Anyone who has worked with dates and times in Java knows the pain of `java.util.Calendar` and company. Clearly, you can get your work done, but it's not always pretty. Many developers found the API too painful to use, so they integrated the extremely popular Joda Time library into their projects. The Java architects agreed, and engaged Joda Time's author, Stephen Colebourne, to lead JSR 310, which brought a version of Joda Time (fixing various design flaws) to the platform. We'll take a detailed look at how to use some of these new APIs in our date/time calculator later in the book.

Default methods

Before turning our attention to Java 9, let's take a look at one more significant language feature: default methods. Since the beginning of Java, an interface was used to define how a class looks, implying a certain type of behavior, but was unable to implement that behavior. This made polymorphism much simpler in a lot of cases, as any number of classes could implement a given interface, and the consuming code treats them as that interface, rather than whatever concrete class they actually are.

One of the problems that have confronted API developers over the years, though, was how to evolve an API and its interfaces without breaking existing code. For example, take the ActionSource interface from the JavaServer Faces 1.1 specification. When the JSF 1.2 expert group was working on the next revision of the specification, they identified the need to add a new property to the interface, which would result in two new methods--the getters and setters. They could not simply add the methods to the interface, as that would break every implementation of the specification, requiring the maintainers of the implementation to update their classes. Obviously, this sort of breakage is unacceptable, so JSF 1.2 introduced ActionSource2, which extends ActionSource and adds the new methods. While this approach is considered ugly by many, the 1.2 expert group had a few choices, and none of them were very good.

With Java 8, though, interfaces can now specify a default method on the interface definition, which the compiler will use for the method implementation if the extending class does not provide one. Let's take the following piece of code as an example:

```
public interface Speaker {
  void saySomething(String message);
}
public class SpeakerImpl implements Speaker {
  public void saySomething(String message) {
    System.out.println(message);
  }
}
```

We've developed our API and made it available to the public, and it's proved to be really popular. Over time, though, we've identified an improvement we'd like to make: we'd like to add some convenience methods, such as sayHello() and sayGoodbye(), to save our users a little time. However, as discussed earlier, if we just add these new methods to the interface, we'll break our users' code as soon as they update to the new version of the library. Default methods allow us to extend the interface and avoid the breakage by defining an implementation:

```
public interface Speaker {
  void saySomething(String message);
  default public void sayHello() {
    System.out.println("Hello");
  }
  default public void sayGoodbye() {
    System.out.println("Good bye");
  }
}
```

Now, when users update their library JARs, they immediately gain these new methods and their behavior, without making any changes. Of course, to use these methods, the users will need to modify their code, but they need not do so until--and if--they want to.

New features in Java 9

As with any new version of the JDK, this release was packed with a lot of great new features. Of course, what is most appealing will vary based on your needs, but we'll focus specifically on a handful of these new features that are most relevant to the projects we'll build together. First up is the most significant, the Java Module System.

Java Platform Module System/Project Jigsaw

Despite being a solid, feature-packed release, Java 8 was considered by a fair number to be a bit disappointing. It lacked the much anticipated **Java Platform Module System (JPMS)**, also known more colloquially, though not quite accurately, as Project Jigsaw. The Java Platform Module System was originally slated to ship with Java 7 in 2011, but it was deferred to Java 8 due to some lingering technical concerns. Project Jigsaw was started not only to finish the module system, but also to modularize the JDK itself, which would help Java SE scale down to smaller devices, such as mobile phones and embedded systems. Jigsaw was scheduled to ship with Java 8, which was released in 2014, but it was deferred yet again, as the Java architects felt they still needed more time to implement the system correctly. At long last, though, Java 9 will finally deliver this long-promised project.

That said, what exactly is it? One problem that has long haunted API developers, including the JDK architects, is the inability to hide implementation details of public APIs. A good example from the JDK of private classes that developers should not be using directly is the `com.sun.*`/`sun.*` packages and classes. A perfect example of this--of private APIs finding widespread public use--is the `sun.misc.Unsafe` class. Other than a strongly worded warning in Javadoc about not using these internal classes, there's little that could be done to prevent their use. Until now.

With the JPMS, developers will be able to make implementation classes public so that they may be easily used inside their projects, but not expose them outside the module, meaning they are not exposed to consumers of the API or library. To do this, the Java architects have introduced a new file, `module-info.java`, similar to the existing `package-info.java` file, found at the root of the module, for example, at `src/main/java/module-info.java`. It is compiled to `module-info.class`, and is available at runtime via reflection and the new `java.lang.Module` class.

So what does this file do, and what does it look like? Java developers can use this file to name the module, list its dependencies, and express to the system, both compile and runtime, which packages are exported to the world. For example, suppose, in our preceding stream example, we have three packages: `model`, `api`, and `impl`. We want to expose the models and the API classes, but not any of the implementation classes. Our `module-info.java` file may look something like this:

```
module com.packt.j9blueprints.intro {
    requires com.foo;
    exports com.packt.j9blueprints.intro.model;
    exports com.packt.j9blueprints.intro.api;
}
```

This definition exposes the two packages we want to export, and also declares a dependency on the `com.foo` module. If this module is not available at compile-time, the project will not build, and if it is not available at runtime, the system will throw an exception and exit. Note that the `requires` statement does not specify a version. This is intentional, as it was decided not to tackle the version-selection issue as part of the module system, leaving that to more appropriate systems, such as build tools and containers.

Much more could be said about the module system, of course, but an exhaustive discussion of all of its features and limitations is beyond the scope of this book. We will be implementing our applications as modules, though, so we'll see the system used--and perhaps explained in a bit more detail--throughout the book.

 Those wanting a more in-depth discussion of the Java Platform Module System can search for the article, *The State of the Module System*, by Mark Reinhold.

Process handling API

In prior versions of Java, developers interacting with native operating system processes had to use a fairly limited API, with some operations requiring resorting to native code. As part of **Java Enhancement Proposal (JEP)** 102, the Java process API was extended with the following features (quoting from the JEP text):

- The ability to get the pid (or equivalent) of the current Java virtual machine and the pid of processes created with the existing API.
- The ability to enumerate processes on the system. Information on each process may include its pid, name, state, and perhaps resource usage.

- The ability to deal with process trees; in particular, some means to destroy a process tree.
- The ability to deal with hundreds of subprocesses, perhaps multiplexing the output or error streams to avoid creating a thread per subprocess.

We will explore these API changes in our first project, the Process Viewer/Manager (see the following sections for details).

Concurrency changes

As was done in Java 7, the Java architects revisited the concurrency libraries, making some much needed changes, this time in order to support the reactive-streams specification. These changes include a new class, java.util.concurrent.Flow, with several nested interfaces: Flow.Processor, Flow.Publisher, Flow.Subscriber, and Flow.Subscription.

REPL

One change that seems to excite a lot of people isn't a language change at all. It's the addition of a **REPL** (**Read-Eval-Print-Loop**), a fancy term for a language shell. In fact, the command for this new tool is jshell. This tool allows us to type or paste in Java code and get immediate feedback. For example, if we wanted to experiment with the Streams API discussed in the preceding section, we could do something like this:

```
$ jshell
|  Welcome to JShell -- Version 9-ea
|  For an introduction type: /help intro

jshell> List<String> names = Arrays.asList(new String[]{"Tom", "Bill",
"Xavier", "Sarah", "Adam"});
names ==> [Tom, Bill, Xavier, Sarah, Adam]

jshell> names.stream().sorted().forEach(System.out::println);
Adam
Bill
Sarah
Tom
Xavier
```

This is a very welcome addition that should help Java developers rapidly prototype and test their ideas.

Projects

With that brief and high-level overview of what new features are available to use, what do these blueprints we'll cover look like? We'll build ten different applications, varying in complexity and kind, and covering a wide range of concerns. With each project, we'll pay special attention to the new features we're highlighting, but we'll also see some older, tried and true language features and libraries used extensively, with any interesting or novel usages flagged. Here, then, is our project lineup.

Process Viewer/Manager

We will explore some of the improvements to the process handling APIs as we implement a Java version of the age old Unix tool--**top**. Combining this API with JavaFX, we'll build a graphical tool that allows the user to view and manage processes running on the system.

This project will cover the following:

- Java 9 Process API enhancements
- JavaFX

Duplicate File Finder

As a system ages, the chances of clutter in the filesystem, especially duplicated files, increases exponentially, it seems. Leveraging some of the new File I/O libraries, we'll build a tool to scan a set of user-specified directories to identify duplicates. Pulling JavaFX back out of the toolbox, we'll add a graphical user interface that will provide a more user-friendly means to interactively process the duplicates.

This project will cover the following:

- Java File I/O
- Hashing libraries
- JavaFX

Date Calculator

With the release of Java 8, Oracle integrated a new library based on a redesign of Joda Time, more or less, into the JDK. Officially known as JSR 310, this new library fixed a longstanding complaint with the JDK--the official date libraries were inadequate and hard to use. In this project, we'll build a simple command-line date calculator that will take a date and, for example, add an arbitrary amount of time to it. Consider the following piece of code for example:

```
$ datecalc "2016-07-04 + 2 weeks"
2016-07-18
$ datecalc "2016-07-04 + 35 days"
2016-08-08
$ datecalc "12:00CST to PST"
10:00PST
```

This project will cover the following:

- Java 8 Date/Time APIs
- Regular expressions
- Java command-line libraries

Social Media Aggregator

One of the problems with having accounts on so many social media networks is keeping tabs on what's happening on each of them. With accounts on Twitter, Facebook, Google+, Instagram, and so on, active users can spend a significant amount of time jumping from site to site, or app to app, reading the latest updates. In this chapter, we'll build a simple aggregator app that will pull the latest updates from each of the user's social media accounts and display them in one place. The features will include the following:

- Multiple accounts for a variety of social media networks:
  - Twitter
  - Pinterest
  - Instagram
- Read-only, rich listings of social media posts
- Links to the appropriate site or app for a quick and easy follow-up
- Desktop and mobile versions

This project will cover the following:

- REST/HTTP clients
- JSON processing
- JavaFX and Android development

Given the size and scope of this effort, we'll actually do this in two chapters: JavaFX in the first, and Android in the second.

Email filter

Managing email can be tricky, especially if you have more than one account. If you access your mail from more than one location (that is, from more than one desktop or mobile app), managing your email rules can be trickier still. If your mail system doesn't support rules stored on the server, you're left deciding where to put the rules so that they'll run most often. With this project, we'll develop an application that will allow us to author a variety of rules and then run them via an optional background process to keep your mail properly curated at all times.

A sample `rules` file may look something like this:

```
[
  {
    "serverName": "mail.server.com",
    "serverPort": "993",
    "useSsl": true,
    "userName": "me@example.com",
    "password": "password",
    "rules": [
       {"type": "move",
          "sourceFolder": "Inbox",
          "destFolder": "Folder1",
          "matchingText": "someone@example.com"},
       {"type": "delete",
          "sourceFolder": "Ads",
          "olderThan": 180}
    ]
  }
]
```

This project will cover the following:

- JavaMail
- JavaFX
- JSON Processing
- Operating System integration
- File I/O

JavaFX photo management

The Java Development Kit has a very robust assortment of image handling APIs. In Java 9, these were augmented with improved support for the TIFF specification. In this chapter, we'll exercise this API in creating an image/photo management application. We'll add support for importing images from user-specified locations into the configured official directory. We'll also revisit the duplicate file finder and reuse some of the code developed as a part of the project to help us identify duplicate images.

This project will cover the following:

- The new `javax.imageio` package
- JavaFX
- NetBeans Rich Client Platform
- Java file I/O

A client/server note application

Have you ever used a cloud-based note-taking application? Have you wondered what it would take to make your own? In this chapter, we'll create such an application, with complete front and backends. On the server side, we'll store our data in the ever popular document database, MongoDB, and we'll expose the appropriate parts of the business logic for the application via REST interfaces. On the client side, we'll develop a very basic user interface in JavaScript that will let us experiment with, and demonstrate how to use, JavaScript in our Java project.

This project will cover the following:

- Document databases (MongoDB)
- JAX-RS and RESTful interfaces
- JavaFX
- JavaScript and Vue 2

Serverless Java

Serverless, also known as **function as a service** (**FaaS**), is one of the hottest trends these days. It is an application/deployment model where a small function is deployed to a service that manages almost every aspect of the function--startup, shutdown, memory, and so on, freeing the developer from worrying about such details. In this chapter, we'll write a simple serverless Java application to see how it might be done, and how you might use this new technique for your own applications.

This project will cover the following:

- Creating an Amazon Web Services account
- Configuring AWS Lambda, Simple Notification Service, Simple Email Service, and DynamoDB
- Writing and deploying a Java function

Android desktop synchronization client

With this project, we'll change gears a little bit and focus specifically on a different part of the Java ecosystem: Android. To do this, we'll focus on a problem that still plagues some Android users--the synchronization of an Android device and a desktop (or laptop) system. While various cloud providers are pushing us to store more and more in the cloud and streaming that to devices, some people still prefer to store, for example, photos and music directly on the device for a variety of reasons, ranging from cost for cloud resources to unreliable wireless connectivity and privacy concerns.

In this chapter, we'll build a system that will allow users to synchronize music and photos between their devices and their desktop or laptop. We'll build an Android application that provides the user interface to configure and monitor synchronization from the mobile device side as well as the Android Service that will perform the synchronization in the background, if desired. We will also build the related components on the desktop--a graphical application to configure and monitor the process from the desktop as well as a background process to handle the synchronization from the desktop side.

This project will cover the following:

*   Android
*   User interfaces
*   Services
*   JavaFX
*   REST

Getting started

We have taken a quick look at some of the new language features we will be using. We have also seen a quick overview of the projects we will be building. One final question remains: what tools will we be using to do our work?

The Java ecosystem suffers from an embarrassment of riches when it comes to development tools, so we have much to choose from. The most fundamental choice facing us is the build tool. For our work here, we will be using Maven. While there is a strong and vocal community that would advocate Gradle, Maven seems to be the most common build tool at the moment, and seems to have more robust, mature, and native support from the major IDEs. If you do not have Maven already installed, you can visit `http://maven.apache.org` and download the distribution for your operating system, or use whatever package management system is supported by your OS.

For the IDE, all screenshots, directions, and so forth will be using NetBeans--the free and open source IDE from Oracle. There are, of course, proponents of both IntelliJ IDEA and Eclipse, and they're both fine choices, but NetBeans offers a complete and robust development out-of-the-box, and it's fast, stable, and free. To download NetBeans, visit `http://netbeans.org` and download the appropriate installer for your operating system. Since we are using Maven, which IDEA and Eclipse both support, you should be able to open the projects presented here in the IDE of your choice. Where steps are shown in the GUI, though, you will need to adjust for the IDE you've chosen.

At the time of writing, the latest version of NetBeans is 8.2, and the best approach for using it to do Java 9 development is to run the IDE on Java 8, and to add Java 9 as an SDK. There is a development version of NetBeans that runs on Java 9, but, as it is a development version, it can be unstable from time to time. A stable NetBeans 9 should ship at roughly the same time as Java 9 itself. In the meantime, we'll push forward with 8.2:

1. To add Java 9 support, we will need to add a new Java platform, and we will do that by clicking on **Tools | Platforms**.
2. This will bring up the **Java Platform Manager** screen:

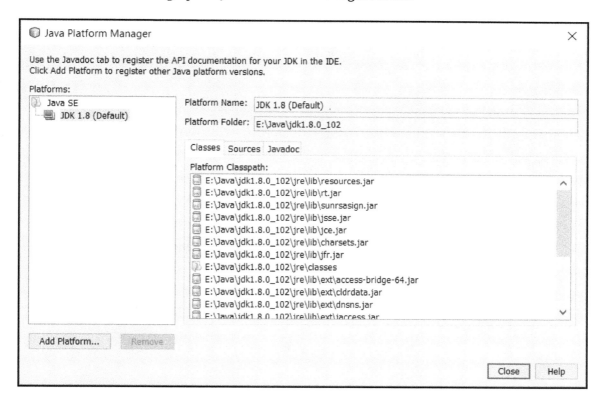

3. Click on **Add Platform...** on the lower left side of your screen.

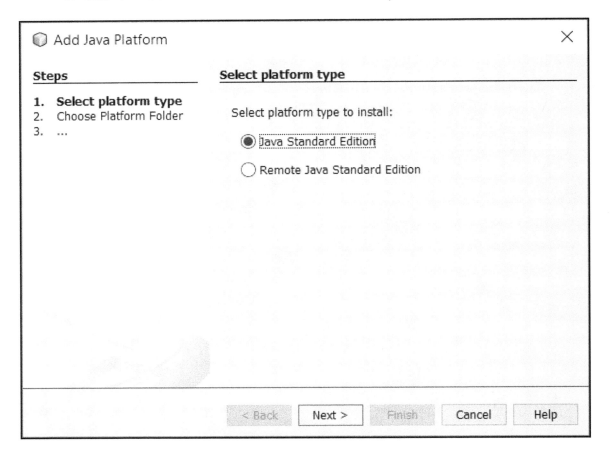

4. We want to add a **Java Standard Edition** platform, so we will accept the default and click on **Next**.

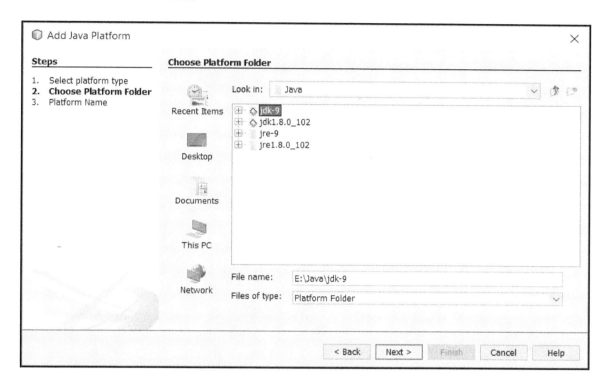

5. On the **Add Java Platform** screen, we will navigate to where we've installed Java 9, select the JDK directory, and click on **Next**.

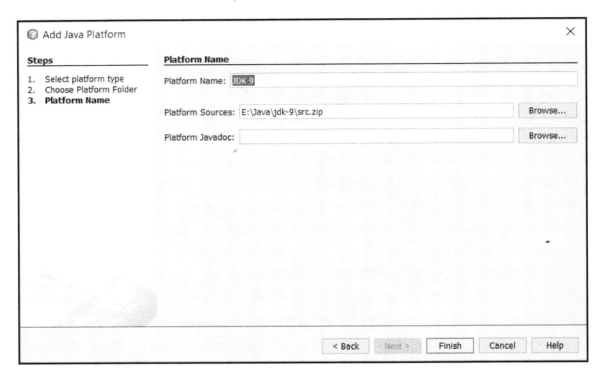

6. We need to give the new Java Platform a name (NetBeans defaults to a very reasonable JDK 9) so we will click on **Finish** and can now see our newly added Java 9 option.

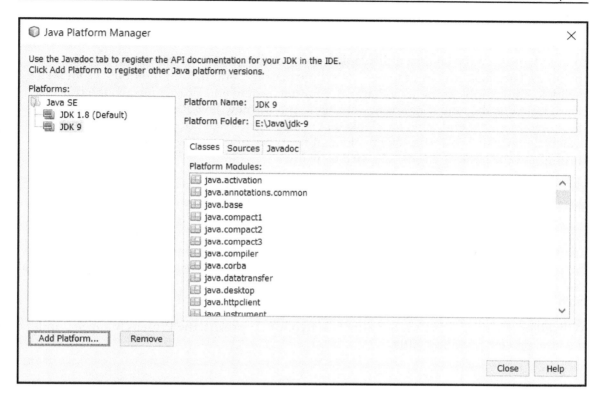

With the project SDK set, we're ready to take these new Java 9 features for a spin, which we'll start doing in `Chapter 2`, *Managing Processes in Java*.

> If you do run NetBeans on Java 9, which should be possible by the time this book is published, you will already have Java 9 configured. You can, however, use the preceding steps to configure Java 8, should you need that version specifically.

Summary

In this chapter, we've taken a quick look at some of the great new features in Java 8, including lambdas, streams, the new date/time package, and default methods. From Java 9, we took a quick look at the Java Platform Module System and Project Jigsaw, the process handling APIs, the new concurrency changes, and the new Java REPL. For each, we've discussed the what and why, and looked at some examples of how these might affect the systems we write. We've also taken a look at the types of project we'll be building throughout the book and the tools we'll be using.

Before we move on, I'd like to restate an earlier point--every software project is different, so it is not possible to write this book in such a way that you can simply copy and paste large swathes of code into your project. Similarly, every developer writes code differently; the way I structure my code may be vastly different from yours. It is important, then, that you keep that in mind when reading this book and not get hung up on the details. The purpose here is not to show you the one right way to use these APIs, but to give you an example that you can look at to get a better sense of how they might be used. Learn what you can from each example, modify things as you see fit, and go build something amazing.

With all of that said, let's turn our attention to our first project, the Process Manager, and the new process handling APIs.

2
Managing Processes in Java

With a very quick tour through some of the big new features of Java 9, as well as those from a couple of previous releases, let's turn our attention to applying some of these new APIs in a practical manner. We'll start with a simple process manager.

While having your application or utility handle all of your user's concerns internally is usually ideal, occasionally you need to run (or **shell out to**) an external program for a variety of reasons. From the very first days of Java, this was supported by the JDK via the `Runtime` class via a variety of APIs. Here is the simplest example:

```
Process p = Runtime.getRuntime().exec("/path/to/program");
```

Once the process has been created, you can track its execution via the `Process` class, which has methods such as `getInputStream()`, `getOutputStream()`, and `getErrorStream()`. We have also had rudimentary control over the process via `destroy()` and `waitFor()`. Java 8 moved things forward by adding `destroyForcibly()` and `waitFor(long, TimeUnit)`. Starting with Java 9, these capabilities will be expanded. Quoting from the **Java Enhancement Proposal (JEP)**, we see the following reasons for this new functionality:

Many enterprise applications and containers involve several Java virtual machines and processes and have long-standing needs that include the following:

- *The ability to get the pid (or equivalent) of the current Java virtual machine and the pid of processes created with the existing API.*
- *The ability to enumerate processes on the system. Information on each process may include its pid, name, state, and perhaps resource usage.*
- *The ability to deal with process trees, in particular, some means to destroy a process tree.*
- *The ability to deal with hundreds of sub-processes, perhaps multiplexing the output or error streams to avoid creating a thread per sub-process.*

In this chapter, we'll build a simple process manager application, akin to **Windows Task Manager** or *nix's top. There is, of course, little need for a process manager written in Java, but this will be an excellent avenue for us to explore these new process handling APIs. Additionally, we'll spend some time with other language features and APIs, namely, JavaFX and `Optional`.

The following topics are covered in this chapter:

- Creating the project
- Bootstrapping the application
- Defining the user interface
- Initializing the user interface
- Adding menus
- Updating the process list

With that said, let's get started.

Creating a project

Typically speaking, it is much better if a build can be reproduced without requiring the use of a specific IDE or some other proprietary tool. Fortunately, NetBeans offers the ability to create a Maven-based JavaFX project. Click on **File** | **New Project** and select `Maven`, then **JavaFX Application**:

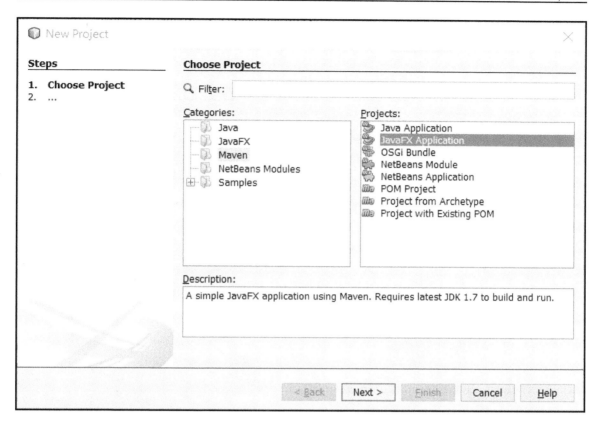

Next, perform the following steps:

1. Click on **Next**.
2. Enter **Project Name** as ProcessManager.
3. Enter **Group ID** as com.steeplesoft.
4. Enter **Package** as com.steeplesoft.processmanager.
5. Select **Project Location**.
6. Click on **Finish**.

Consider the following screenshot as an example:

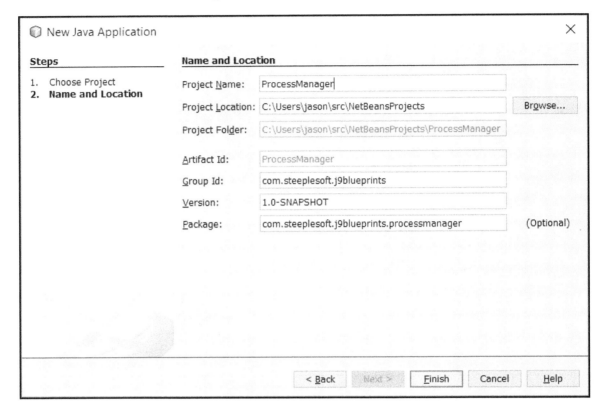

Once the new project has been created, we need to update the Maven pom to use Java 9:

```
<build>
  <plugins>
    <plugin>
      <groupId>org.apache.maven.plugins</groupId>
      <artifactId>maven-compiler-plugin</artifactId>
      <version>3.6.1</version>
      <configuration>
        <source>9</source>
        <target>9</target>
      </configuration>
    </plugin>
  </plugins>
</build>
```

Now, with both NetBeans and Maven configured to use Java 9, we're ready to start coding.

Bootstrapping the application

As noted in the introduction, this will be a JavaFX-based application, so we'll start by creating the skeleton for the application. This is a Java 9 application, and we intend to make use of the Java Module System. To do that, we need to create the module definition file, `module-info.java`, which resides in the root of our source tree. This being a Maven-based project, that would be `src/main/java`:

```
module procman.app {
  requires javafx.controls;
  requires javafx.fxml;
}
```

This small file does a couple of different things. First, it defines a new `procman.app` module. Next, it tells the system that this module `requires` two JDK modules: `javafx.controls` and `javafx.fxml`. If we did not specify these two modules, then our system, which we'll see below, would not compile, as the JDK would not make the required classes and packages available to our application. These modules are part of the standard JDK as of Java 9, so that shouldn't be an issue. However, that may change in future versions of Java, and this module declaration will help prevent runtime failures in our application by forcing the host JVM to provide the module or fail to start. It is also possible to build custom Java runtimes via the **J-Link** tool, so missing these modules is still a possibility under Java 9. With our module configured, let's turn to the application.

The emerging standard directory layout seems to be something like `src/main/java/<module1>`, `src/main/java/<module2>`, and so on. At the time of writing this book, while Maven can be coaxed into such a layout, the plugins themselves, while they do run under Java 9, do not appear to be module-aware enough to allow us to organize our code in such a manner. For that reason, and for the sake of simplicity, we will treat one Maven module as one Java module and maintain the standard source layout for the projects.

The first class we will create is the `Application` descendant, which NetBeans created for us. It created the `Main` class, which we renamed to `ProcessManager`:

```
public class ProcessManager extends Application {
  @Override
  public void start(Stage stage) throws Exception {
    Parent root = FXMLLoader
      .load(getClass().getResource("/fxml/procman.fxml"));
    Scene scene = new Scene(root);
    scene.getStylesheets().add("/styles/Styles.css");
    stage.setTitle("Process Manager");
```

```
        stage.setScene(scene);
        stage.show();
    }

    public static void main(String[] args) {
        launch(args);
    }
}
```

Our `ProcessManager` class extends the JavaFX base class, `Application`, which provides a variety of functionality to start and stop the application. We see in the `main()` method that we simply delegate to `Application.launch(String[])`, which does the heavy lifting for us in starting our new application.

The more interesting part of this class is the `start()` method, which is where the JavaFX life cycle calls back into our application, giving us the opportunity to build the user interface, which we'll do next.

Defining the user interface

When building the user interface for a JavaFX application, you can do it in one of two ways: code or markup. To keep our code smaller and more readable, we'll build the user interface using FXML--the XML-based language created specifically for JavaFX to express user interfaces. This presents us with another binary choice--do we write the XML by hand, or do we use a graphical tool? Again, the choice is a simple one--we'll use a tool, **Scene Builder**, which is a WYSIWYG tool originally developed by Oracle and now maintained and supported by Gluon. We will, however, also be looking at the XML source so that we can understand what's being done, so if you don't like using a GUI tool, you won't be left out.

Installing and using Scene Builder is, as you would expect, pretty straightforward. It can be downloaded from `http://gluonhq.com/labs/scene-builder/`. Once installed, you need to tell NetBeans where to find it, which can be done in the Settings window, under **Java | JavaFX**, as you can see in the following screenshot:

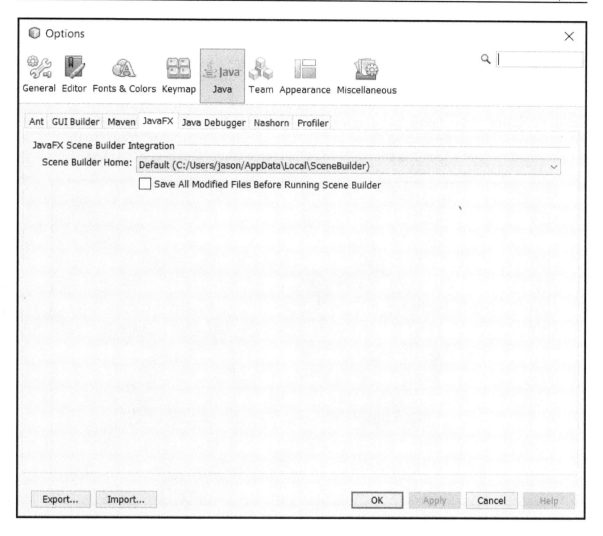

We are now ready to create the FXML file. Under the `resources` directory in the Project View, create a new folder called `fxml`, and in that folder, create a file called `procman.fxml`, as follows:

```
<BorderPane xmlns="http://javafx.com/javafx/8.0.60"
    xmlns:fx="http://javafx.com/fxml/1"
    fx:controller="com.steeplesoft.procman.Controller">
</BorderPane>
```

BorderPane is a container that defines five regions--top, bottom, left, right, and center, giving us a fairly coarsely-grained control over where on the form the controls should appear. Typically, with BorderPane, each area uses a nested container to provide the finer-grained control often necessary. For our needs, this level of control will be perfect.

The primary concern of the user interface is the list of processes, so we'll start with the controls for that. From Scene Builder, we want to click on the Controls section on the accordion on the left, then scroll down to TableView. Click on this and drag it to the CENTER region on the form, as shown here in this screenshot from Scene Builder:

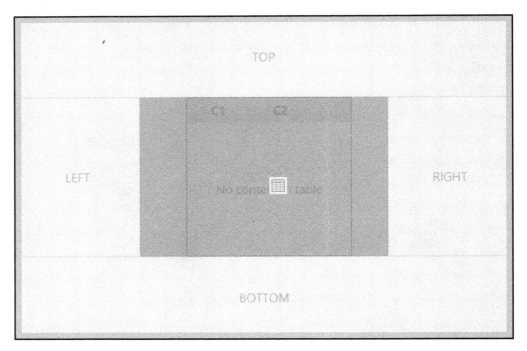

The resulting FXML should look something like this:

```
<center>
    <TableView fx:id="processList"
            BorderPane.alignment="CENTER">
    </TableView>
</center>
```

With no components in the other areas, TableView will expand to fill the window's full area, which is what we want for now.

Initializing the user interface

While the FXML defines the structure of the user interface, we do need some Java code to initialize various elements, respond to actions, and so forth. This class, referred to as the controller, is simply a class that extends `javafx.fxml.Initializable`:

```
public class Controller implements Initializable {
    @FXML
    private TableView<ProcessHandle> processList;
    @Override
    public void initialize(URL url, ResourceBundle rb) {
    }
}
```

The `initialize()` method comes from the interface, and is used by the JavaFX runtime to initialize the controller when it is created in the call to `FXMLLoader.load()` from the preceding `Application` class. Note the `@FXML` annotation on the instance variable `processList`. When JavaFX initializes the controller, before the `initialize()` method is called, the system looks for FXML elements that specify an `fx:id` attribute, and assigns that reference to the appropriate instance variable in the controller. To complete this connection, we must make one more change to our FXML file:

```
<TableView fx:id="processList" BorderPane.alignment="CENTER">
...
```

The change can also be made in Scene Builder as seen in this screenshot:

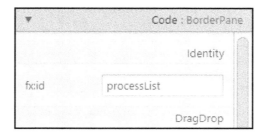

The value of the **fx:id** attribute must match the name of an instance variable that has been annotated with `@FXML`. When `initialize` is called, `processList` will have a valid reference to `TableView` that we can manipulate in our Java code.

The value of **fx:id** can be set via Scene Builder as well. To set the value, click on the control in the form editor, then expand the **Code** section in the accordion on the right. In the **fx:id** field, type in the name of the desired variable name.

The final piece of the puzzle is specifying the controller for the FXML file. In the XML source, you can set this via the `fx:controller` attribute on the root element of the user interface:

```
<BorderPane  xmlns="http://javafx.com/javafx/8.0.60"
    xmlns:fx="http://javafx.com/fxml/1"
    fx:controller="com.steeplesoft.procman.Controller">
```

This can also be set via Scene Builder. In the **Document** section of the accordion on the left, expand the **Controller** section and enter the desired fully-qualified class name in the **Controller class** field:

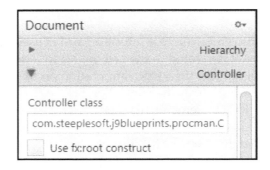

With those pieces in place, we can begin the work of initializing `TableView`, which gets us back to our primary interest, the process handling APIs. Our starting point is `ProcessHandles.allProcesses()`. From the Javadoc, you learn that this method returns **a snapshot of all processes visible to the current process**. From each `ProcessHandle` in the stream, we can get information about the process ID, its state, children, parents, and so on. Each `ProcessHandle` also has a nested object, `Info`, that contains a snapshot of information about the process. Since not all information is available across the various supported platforms and it is limited by the privileges of the current process, the properties on the `Info` object are the `Optional<T>` instances, indicating that the values may or may not be set. It's probably worth the time to take a quick look at what `Optional<T>` is.

The Javadoc describes `Optional<T>` as a **container object which may or may not contain a non-null value**. Inspired by Scala and Haskell, `Optional<T>` was introduced in Java 8 to allow API authors to provide a more null-safe interface. Prior to Java 8, a method on `ProcessHandle.Info` may be defined like this:

```
public String command();
```

To consume the API, the developer would likely write something like this:

```
String command = processHandle.info().command();
if (command == null) {
  command = "<unknown>";
}
```

If the developer fails to check for null explicitly, `NullPointerException` is almost certain to occur at some point. By using `Optional<T>`, the API author signals to the user that the return value may be null and should be handled carefully. The updated code, then, may look like this:

```
String command = processHandle.info().command()
  .orElse("<unknown>");
```

Now, in one concise line, we can get the value, if it is present, or a default if it is not. The `ProcessHandle.Info` API makes extensive use of this construct as we'll see later.

What else does `Optional` afford us as developers? There are a number of instance methods that can help clarify null-handling code:

- `filter(Predicate<? super T> predicate)`: With this method, we filter the contents of `Optional`. Rather than using an `if...else` block, we can pass the `filter()` method a `Predicate` and do the test inline. A `Predicate` is a `@FunctionalInterface` that takes an input and returns a Boolean. For example, some uses of the JavaFX `Dialog` may return `Optional<ButtonType>`. If we wanted to do something **only** if the user clicked a specific button, say, OK, we could filter `Optional` like this:

  ```
  alert.showAndWait()
    .filter(b -> b instanceof ButtonType.OK)
  ```

- `map(Function<? super T,? extends U> mapper)`: The `map` function allows us to pass the contents of `Optional` to a function, which will perform some processing on it, and return it. The return from the function, though, will be wrapped in an `Optional`:

  ```
  Optional<String> opts = Optional.of("hello");
  Optional<String> upper = opts.map(s ->
    s.toUpperCase());
  Optional<Optional<String>> upper2 =
    opts.map(s -> Optional.of(s.toUpperCase()));
  ```

Note the double wrapping in `Optional` for `upper2`. If `Function` returns `Optional`, it will be wrapped in another `Optional`, giving us this odd double wrap, which is less than desirable. Fortunately, we have an alternative.

- `flatMap(Function<? super T,Optional<U>> mapper)`: The `flatMap` function combines two functional ideas--maps and flatten. If the result of `Function` is an `Optional` object, rather than double wrapping the value, it is flattened to a single `Optional` object. Revisiting the preceding example, we get this:

```
Optional<String> upper3 = opts.flatMap(s ->
 Optional.of(s.toUpperCase()));
```

Note that `upper3`, unlike `upper2`, is a single `Optional`:

- `get()`: This returns the wrapped value, if present. If there is no value, a `NoSuchElementException` error is thrown.
- `ifPresent(Consumer<? super T> action)`: If the `Optional` object contains a value, it is passed to the `Consumer`. If there is no value present, nothing happens.
- `ifPresentOrElse(Consumer<? super T> action, Runnable emptyAction)`: Like `ifPresent()`, this will pass the value to the `Consumer` if there is one present. If no value is present, the `Runnable emptyAction` is executed.
- `isPresent()`: This simply returns true if the `Optional` object contains a value.
- `or(Supplier<Optional<T>> supplier)`: If the `Optional` object has a value, the `Optional` is described. If there is no value present, an `Optional` object produced by the `Supplier` is returned.
- `orElse(T other)`: If the `Optional` object contains a value, it is returned. If there is no value, `other` is returned.
- `orElseGet(Supplier<? extends T> supplier)`: This works just like `orElse()` mentioned earlier, but, if no value is present, the result of the `Supplier` is returned.

- `orElseThrow(Supplier<? extends X> exceptionSupplier)`: If there is a value present, it is returned. If there is no value, the `Exception` provided by the `Supplier` is thrown.

`Optional` also has several static methods that facilitate the creation of the `Optional` instances, some of which are as follows:

- `empty()`: This returns an empty `Optional` object.
- `of(T value)`: This returns an `Optional` object describing the non-null value. If the value is null, a `NullPointerException` is thrown.
- `ofNullable(T value)`: This returns an `Optional` object describing the value. If the value is null, an empty `Optional` is returned.

With that very brief introduction to `Optional<T>` under our belts, let's see how its presence affects our application.

Returning our attention to the `initialize()` method, then, our first step is to get the list of processes to display. The streams API makes this extremely simple:

```
ProcessHandle.allProcesses()
  .collect(Collectors.toList());
```

The `allProcesses()` method returns `Stream<ProcessHandle>`, which allows us to apply the new stream operations to our problem. In this case, we just want to create a `List` of all of the `ProcessHandle` instances, so we call `collect()`, which is a stream operation that takes in a `Collector`. There are a number of options from which we could choose, but we want a `List`, so we use `Collectors.toList()`, which will collect each item in the stream and eventually return a `List` when the stream terminates. Note that the parameterized type of `List` will match that of `Stream`, which is `ProcessHandle` in this case.

This one line, then, gets us a `List<ProcessHandle>` of every process on the system that the current process can see, but that only gets us halfway. The `TableView` API doesn't accept a `List<T>`. It only supports `ObservableList<T>`, but what is that? Its Javadoc defines it very simply--*A list that allows listeners to track changes when they occur*. To put it another way, when this list changes, `TableView` will be told about it automatically and will redraw itself. Once we associate `TableView` with this list, all we have to worry about is the data, and the control will handle the rest. Creating `ObservableList` is pretty straightforward:

```
@FXML
private TableView<ProcessHandle> processView;
```

```
final private ObservableList<ProcessHandle> processList =
  FXCollections.observableArrayList();
// ...
processView.setItems(processList);
processList.setAll(ProcessHandle.allProcesses()
  .collect(Collectors.toList()));
```

In our case, the `TableView` instance is injected by the runtime (included here for clarity), and we create the `ObservableList` via `FXCollections.observableArrayList()`. In `initialize()`, we set the `ObservableList` on the `TableView` via `setItems()`, then populate the `ObservableList` via `setAll()`. With that, our `TableView` has all the data it needs to render itself. Almost. It has the **data** to render, but **how** does it do it? Where does each field of `ProcessHandle.Info` go? To answer that, we have to define the columns on the table, and tell each column where to get its data.

To do that, we need to create several `TableColumn<S, T>` instances. The `TableColumn` is responsible for displaying not only its column heading (as appropriate), but also the value of each cell. However, you have to tell it **how** to display the cell. That is done via a cell value factory. Under Java 7, that API would get us code like this:

```
TableColumn<ProcessHandle, String> commandCol =
 new TableColumn<>("Command");
commandCol.setCellValueFactory(new
  Callback<TableColumn.CellDataFeatures<ProcessHandle, String>,
   ObservableValue<String>>() {
     public ObservableValue<String> call(
      TableColumn.CellDataFeatures<ProcessHandle,
       String> p) {
         return new SimpleObjectProperty(p.getValue()
          .info()
          .command()
          .map(Controller::afterLast)
          .orElse("<unknown>"));
      }
   }
);
```

I'll go ahead and say it for you: that's really ugly. Fortunately, we can put lambdas and type inference to work for us, to make that a lot more pleasant to read:

```
TableColumn<ProcessHandle, String> commandCol =
 new TableColumn<>("Command");
commandCol.setCellValueFactory(data ->
 new SimpleObjectProperty(data.getValue().info().command()
  .map(Controller::afterLast)
  .orElse("<unknown>")));
```

That's fourteen lines of code replaced by six. Much prettier. Now, we just have to do that five more times, once for each column. As improved as the preceding code may be, there's still quite a bit of repeated code. Again, Java 8 functional interfaces can help us clean the code up a bit more. For each column, we want to specify the header, a width, and what to extract from ProcessHandle.Info. We can encapsulate that with this method:

```
private <T> TableColumn<ProcessHandle, T>
  createTableColumn(String header, int width,
    Function<ProcessHandle, T> function) {
      TableColumn<ProcessHandle, T> column =
        new TableColumn<>(header);

      column.setMinWidth(width);
      column.setCellValueFactory(data ->
        new SimpleObjectProperty<T>(
          function.apply(data.getValue())));
      return column;
}
```

The Function<T,R> interface is FunctionalInterface, which represents a function that takes in one type, T, and returns another, R. In our case, we're defining this method as one that takes as parameters a String, an int, and a function that takes in ProcessHandle and returns a generic type. That may be hard to picture, but with this method defined, we can replace the preceding code and the others like it with calls to this method. The same preceding code can now be condensed to this:

```
createTableColumn("Command", 250,
  p -> p.info().command()
  .map(Controller::afterLast)
  .orElse("<unknown>"))
```

Now we just need to add these columns to the control, which we can do with this:

```
processView.getColumns().setAll(
  createTableColumn("Command", 250,
  p -> p.info().command()
   .map(Controller::afterLast)
   .orElse("<unknown>")),
  createTableColumn("PID", 75, p -> p.getPid()),
  createTableColumn("Status", 150,
   p -> p.isAlive() ? "Running" : "Not Running"),
  createTableColumn("Owner", 150,
   p -> p.info().user()
    .map(Controller::afterLast)
    .orElse("<unknown>")),
  createTableColumn("Arguments", 75,
   p -> p.info().arguments().stream()
```

```
.map(i -> i.toString())
.collect(Collectors.joining(", "))));
```

Note that every method we're using on `ProcessHandle.Info` returns the `Optional<T>` we looked at in the preceding code. Since it does this, we have a very nice and clean API to get the information we want (or a reasonable default) without the specter of a `NullPointerException` in production.

If we run the application now, we should get something like this:

Command	PID	Status	Owner	Arguments
svchost.exe	11772	Running	jason	
taskhostw.exe	6332	Running	jason	
RuntimeBroker.exe	10900	Running	jason	
<unknown>	8032	Not Running	<unknown>	
ETDIntelligent.exe	9656	Running	jason	
explorer.exe	3204	Running	jason	
igfxEM.exe	11676	Running	jason	
igfxHK.exe	8536	Running	jason	
igfxTray.exe	3948	Running	jason	
NvBackend.exe	12016	Running	jason	
ShellExperienceHost.exe	10260	Running	jason	
<unknown>	12212	Not Running	<unknown>	
RAVCpl64.exe	5472	Running	jason	
RAVBg64.exe	6452	Running	jason	
RAVBg64.exe	2512	Running	jason	
RAVBg64.exe	5632	Running	jason	
utility.exe	7824	Running	jason	
StagelightUpdate.exe	9496	Running	jason	
DolbyDAX2TrayIcon.exe	1472	Running	jason	

It's looking good so far, but it's not quite ready yet. We want to be able to start new processes as well as kill existing ones. Both of those will require menus, so we'll add those next.

Adding menus

Menus in JavaFX start with a component called `MenuBar`. We want this menu to be at the top of the window, of course, so we add the component to the `top` section of our `BorderPane`. If you use Scene Builder, you will end up with something like this in your FXML file:

```
<MenuBar BorderPane.alignment="CENTER">
  <menus>
    <Menu mnemonicParsing="false" text="File">
      <items>
        <MenuItem mnemonicParsing="false" text="Close" />
      </items>
    </Menu>
    <Menu mnemonicParsing="false" text="Edit">
      <items>
        <MenuItem mnemonicParsing="false" text="Delete" />
      </items>
    </Menu>
    <Menu mnemonicParsing="false" text="Help">
      <items>
        <MenuItem mnemonicParsing="false" text="About" />
      </items>
    </Menu>
  </menus>
</MenuBar>
```

We won't be needing the edit menu, so we can remove that section from the FXML file (or by right-clicking on the second `Menu` entry in Scene Builder and clicking on **Delete**). To create the menu items we do want, we add the appropriate `MenuItem` entries to the `item` element under the `File` element:

```
<Menu mnemonicParsing="true" text="_File">
  <items>
    <MenuItem mnemonicParsing="true"
      onAction="#runProcessHandler"
      text="_New Process..." />
    <MenuItem mnemonicParsing="true"
      onAction="#killProcessHandler"
      text="_Kill Process..." />
    <MenuItem mnemonicParsing="true"
      onAction="#closeApplication"
      text="_Close" />
  </items>
</Menu>
```

Each of these `MenuItem` entries has three attributes defined:

- `mnemonicParsing`: This instructs JavaFX to use any letter prefixed with an underscore as a keyboard shortcut
- `onAction`: This identifies the method on the controller that will be called when `MenuItem` is activated/clicked
- `text`: This defines the label of `MenuItem`

The most interesting part is `onAction` and its relationship with the controller. JavaFX, of course, already knows that this form is backed by `com.steeplesoft.procman.Controller`, so it will look for a method with the following signature:

```
@FXML
public void methodName(ActionEvent event)
```

`ActionEvent` is a class that is used in a number of scenarios by JavaFX. In our case, we have methods specifically for each menu item, so the event itself isn't too terribly interesting. Let's take a look at each handler, starting with the simplest-- `closeApplication`:

```
@FXML
public void closeApplication(ActionEvent event) {
  Platform.exit();
}
```

There's nothing much to see here; when the menu item is clicked, we exit the application by calling `Platform.exit()`.

Next up, let's see how to kill a process:

```
@FXML
public void killProcessHandler(final ActionEvent event) {
  new Alert(Alert.AlertType.CONFIRMATION,
  "Are you sure you want to kill this process?",
  ButtonType.YES, ButtonType.NO)
    .showAndWait()
    .filter(button -> button == ButtonType.YES)
    .ifPresent(response -> {
    ProcessHandle selectedItem =
     processView.getSelectionModel()
      .getSelectedItem();
    if (selectedItem != null) {
      selectedItem.destroy();
      processListUpdater.updateList();
    }
```

```
    });
  }
```

We have quite a bit going on here. The first thing we do is to create an `Alert` box of type `CONFIRMATION`, which asks the user to confirm the request. The dialog has two buttons: `YES` and `NO`. Once the dialog has been created, we call `showAndWait()`, which does as its name implies--it shows the dialog and waits for the user's response. It returns `Optional<ButtonType>`, which holds the type of the button that the user clicked on, which will either be `ButtonType.YES` or `ButtonType.NO`, given the type of `Alert` box we've created. With `Optional`, we can apply `filter()` to find only the type of button that we're interested in, which is `ButtonType.YES`, the result of which is another `Optional`. If the user clicked on yes, `ifPresent()` will return true (thanks to our filter), and the lambda we passed in will be executed. Very nice and concise.

The next area of interest is that lambda. Once we've identified **that** the user would like to kill a process, we need to identify **which** process to kill. To do that, we ask `TableView` which row is selected via `TableView.getSelectionModel().getSelectedItem()`. We do need to check for null (alas, there's no `Optional` here) in the event that the user has not actually selected a row. If it is non-null, we can call `destroy()` on the `ProcessHandle` the `TableView` gives us. We then call `processListUpdater.updateList()` to refresh the UI. We'll take a look at that later.

Our final action handler has to run the following command:

```
@FXML
public void runProcessHandler(final ActionEvent event) {
    final TextInputDialog inputDlg = new TextInputDialog();
    inputDlg.setTitle("Run command...");
    inputDlg.setContentText("Command Line:");
    inputDlg.setHeaderText(null);
    inputDlg.showAndWait().ifPresent(c -> {
      try {
        new ProcessBuilder(c).start();
      } catch (IOException e) {
          new Alert(Alert.AlertType.ERROR,
            "There was an error running your command.")
          .show();
      }
    });
  }
```

This is, in many ways, similar to the preceding `killProcessHandler()` method--we create a dialog, set some options, call `showAndWait()`, then process `Optional`. Unfortunately, the dialog doesn't support the builder pattern, meaning we don't have a nice, fluid API to build the dialog, so we do it in several discrete steps. Processing `Optional` is also similar. We call `ifPresent()` to see if the dialog returned a command line (that is, the user entered some text **and** pressed **OK**), and pass that to the lambda if present.

Let's take a quick look at the lambda. This is another example of a multiline lambda. Whereas most lambdas we've seen so far have been simple, one-line functions, remember that a lambda **can** span multiple lines. All that needs to be done to support that is to wrap the block in curly braces as we've done, and it's business as usual. Care must be taken with multiline lambdas like this, as any gains in readability and conciseness that lambdas give us can be quickly obscured or erased by a lambda body that grows too large. In those instances, extracting the code out to a method and using a method reference might be the wise thing to do. Ultimately, the decision is yours, but remember the words of Uncle Bob Martin--*Clarity is king*.

One final item on the topic of menus. To be even more useful, the application should provide a context menu that will allow the user to right-click on a process and kill it from there, as opposed to clicking on the row, moving the mouse to the `File` menu, and more. Adding a context menu is a simple operation. All we need to do is modify our `TableView` definition in FXML like this:

```
<TableView fx:id="processView" BorderPane.alignment="CENTER">
  <contextMenu>
    <ContextMenu>
      <items>
        <MenuItem onAction="#killProcessHandler"
           text="Kill Process..."/>
      </items>
    </ContextMenu>
  </contextMenu>
</TableView>
```

Here, we are adding a `contextMenu` child to our `TableView`. Much like its sibling, `MenuBar`, `contextMenu` has an `items` child, which, in turn, has 0 or more `MenuItem` children. In this case, the `MenuItem` for `Kill Process...` looks remarkably like that under `File`, with the only difference being the `mnemonicProcessing` information. We're even reusing the `ActionEvent` handler, so there's no extra coding, and the behavior for killing a process is always the same, regardless of which menu item you click on.

Updating the process list

If the application started and showed a list of processes, but never updated that list, it wouldn't be very useful at all. What we then need is a way to update the list periodically, and for that, we'll use a `Thread`.

As you may or may not know, a `Thread` is roughly a means to run a task in the background (the Javadoc describes it as a *thread of execution in a program*). A system can be single or multithreaded, depending on the needs and runtime environment of the system. And multithreaded programming is hard to get right. Luckily, our use case here is fairly simple, but we must still exercise caution, or we'll see some really unexpected behavior.

Ordinarily, the advice you would get when creating a `Thread` is to implement a `Runnable` interface, which you will then pass to the thread's constructor, and that's very good advice, as it makes your class hierarchy much more flexible, since you're not tied to a concrete base class (`Runnable` is an `interface`). In our case, however, we have a relatively simple system that has little to gain from that approach, so we'll extend `Thread` directly and simplify our code a little as well as encapsulating our desired behavior. Let's take a look at our new class:

```java
private class ProcessListUpdater extends Thread {
  private volatile boolean running = true;

  public ProcessListRunnable() {
    super();
    setDaemon(true);
  }

  public void shutdown() {
    running = false;
  }

  @Override
  public void run() {
    while (running) {
      updateList();
      try {
        Thread.sleep(5000);
      } catch (InterruptedException e) {
        // Ignored
      }
    }
  }

  public synchronized void updateList() {
```

```
processList.setAll(ProcessHandle.allProcesses()
  .collect(Collectors.toList()));
processView.sort();
  }
}
```

We have a pretty basic class, which we've given a reasonable and meaningful name that extends `Thread`. In the constructor, note that we call `setDaemon(true)`. This will allow our application to exit as expected and not block, waiting for the thread to terminate. We've also defined a `shutdown()` method, which we'll use from our application to stop the thread.

 The `Thread` class does have various state control methods, such as `stop()`, `suspend()`, `resume()`, and more, but these have all been deprecated as they are considered inherently unsafe. Search for the article, Why are `Thread.stop`, `Thread.suspend`, and `Thread.resume` deprecated? If you would like more details; however, the suggested best practice now is to use a control flag, like we've done with `running`, to signal to the `Thread` class that it needs to clean up and shut down.

Finally, we have the heart of our `Thread` class, `run()`, which loops infinitely (or until `running` becomes false), sleeping for five seconds after performing its work. The actual work is done in `updateList()`, which builds the list of processes, updates `ObservableList` we discussed earlier, and then instructs `TableView` to re-sort itself, based on the user's sort selection, if any. This is a public method, allowing us to call this at need, as we did in `killProcessHandler()`. That leaves us with the following block of code to set it up:

```
@Override
public void initialize(URL url, ResourceBundle rb) {
  processListUpdater = new ProcessListUpdater();
  processListUpdater.start();
  // ...
}
```

The following code will shut it down, which we've already seen in `closeHandler()`:

```
processListUpdater.shutdown();
```

The eagle-eyed will notice that `updateList()` has the `synchronized` keyword on it. This is to prevent any sort of race condition that might be caused by calling this method from multiple threads. Imagine the scenario where the user decides to kill a process and clicks on **OK** on the confirmation dialog at the exact moment the thread wakes up (this type of thing happens more often than you might think). We could conceivably have two threads calling `updateList()` at the same time, resulting in the first thread hitting `processView.sort()` just as the second is hitting `processList.setAll()`. What happens when `sort()` is called while another thread is rebuilding the list? It's hard to say for sure, but it could be catastrophic, so we want to disallow that. The `synchronized` keyword instructs the JVM to allow only one thread to execute the method at a time, causing all others to queue up, waiting their turn (note that their execution order is non-deterministic, so you can't base any expectations on the order in which threads get to run a `synchronized` method). This avoids the potential for a race condition, and ensures that our program doesn't crash.

While appropriate here, care must be taken with `synchronized` methods, as acquiring and releasing the locks can be expensive (though much less so with modern JVMs) and, more importantly, it forces threads to run sequentially when they hit this method call, which can cause a very undesirable lag in the application, especially in GUI applications. Keep that in mind when writing your own multithreaded applications.

Summary

With that in place, our application is complete. While not a terribly complex application, it does include several interesting technologies such as JavaFX, Lambdas, Streams, `ProcessHandle` plus related classes, and Threads.

In the next chapter, we'll build a simple command-line utility to find duplicate files. Through that, we'll get hands-on experience with the new File I/O APIs, the Java Persistence API (JPA), file hashing, and some more JavaFX.

3
Duplicate File Finder

Any system that's been running for a while starts to suffer from hard drive clutter. This is especially true, for example, with large music and photo collections. Except for the most fastidious files getting copied and moved, we end up with a copy here and a copy there. The question is, though, which of these are duplicates and which are not? In this chapter, we'll build a file-walking utility that will scan a set of directories looking for duplicate files. We'll be able to specify whether the duplicates should be deleted, **quarantined**, or simply reported.

In this chapter, we will cover the following topics:

- The Java Platform Module System
- The Java NIO (New I/O) File APIs
- File hashing
- **Java Persistence API (JPA)**
- The new Java Date/Time API
- Writing command-line utilities
- More JavaFX

Getting started

This application, while conceptually fairly simple, is a bit more complex than what we looked at in the last chapter, in that we will have both, a command line and a graphical interface. The experienced programmer is likely to immediately see the need to share the code between these two interfaces, as **DRY (Don't Repeat Yourself)** is one of the many hallmarks of a well-designed system. To facilitate this sharing of code, then, we will want to introduce a third module, which provides a library that can be consumed by the other two projects. We will call these modules `lib`, `cli`, and `gui`. Our first step in setting up the project is to create the various Maven POM files to describe the project's structure. The parent POM will look something like this:

```
<?xml version="1.0" encoding="UTF-8"?>
<project xmlns="http://maven.apache.org/POM/4.0.0"
   xmlns:xsi="http://www.w3.org/2001/XMLSchema-instance"
   xsi:schemaLocation="http://maven.apache.org/POM/4.0.0
   http://maven.apache.org/xsd/maven-4.0.0.xsd">
   <modelVersion>4.0.0</modelVersion>

   <groupId>com.steeplesoft.dupefind</groupId>
   <artifactId>dupefind-master</artifactId>
   <version>1.0-SNAPSHOT</version>
   <packaging>pom</packaging>

   <modules>
      <module>lib</module>
      <module>cli</module>
      <module>gui</module>
   </modules>

   <name>Duplicate Finder - Master</name>
</project>
```

This is a fairly typical POM file. We will start by identifying the project's parent that lets us inherit a number of settings, dependencies, and so on, and avoid having to repeat them in this project. Next, we will define the Maven coordinates for the project. Note that we don't define a version for this project, allowing the parent's version to cascade down. This will allow us to increase the version as needed in one place, and update all of the subprojects implicitly.

The last interesting part of this POM, for those who haven't seen a multi-module project before, is the `modules` section. The only thing to note here, for those who are new to this, is that each `module` element refers to a directory name, which is a direct child of the current directory, and should be declared in the order in which they are needed. In our case, the CLI and GUI both depend on the library, so `lib` goes first. Next, we'll need to create the POM files for each module. Each of these are typical POMs of type jar, so there's no need to include them here. There will be varying dependencies in each, but we'll cover those as the need arises.

Building the library

The foundational piece of this project is the library which both the CLI and the GUI will consume, so it makes sense to start here. When designing the library--its inputs, outputs, and general behavior--it helps to understand what exactly do we want this system to do, so let's take some time to discuss the functional requirements.

As stated in the introduction, we'd like to be able to search for duplicate files in an arbitrary number of directories. We'd also like to be able to restrict the search and comparison to only certain files. If we don't specify a pattern to match, then we want to check every file.

The most important part is how to identify a match. There are, of course, a myriad of ways in which this can be done, but the approach we will use is as follows:

- Identify files that have the same filename. Think of those situations where you might have downloaded images from your camera to your computer for safekeeping, then, later, perhaps you forgot that you had already downloaded the images, so you copied them again somewhere else. Obviously, you only want one copy, but is the file, for example, `IMG_9615.JPG`, in the temp directory the same as the one in your picture backup directory? By identifying files with matching names, we can test them to be sure.
- Identify files that have the same size. The likelihood of a match here is smaller, but there is still a chance. For example, some photo management software, when importing images from a device, if it finds a file with the same name, will modify the filename of the second file and store both, rather than stopping the import and requiring immediate user intervention. This can result in a large number of files such as `IMG_9615.JPG` and `IMG_9615-1.JPG`. This check will help identify these situations.

- For each match above, to determine whether the files are actually a match, we'll generate a hash based on the file contents. If more than one file generates the same hash, the likelihood of those files being identical is extremely high. These files we will flag as potential duplicates.

It's a pretty simple algorithm and should be pretty effective, but we do have a problem, albeit one that's likely not immediately apparent. If you have a large number of files, especially a set with a large number of potential duplicates, processing all of these files could be a very lengthy process, which we would like to mitigate as much as possible, which leads us to some non-functional requirements:

- The program should process files in a concurrent manner so as to minimize, as much as possible, the amount of time it takes to process a large file set
- This concurrency should be bounded so that the system is not overwhelmed by processing the request
- Given the potential for a large amount of data, the system must be designed in such a way so as to avoid using up all available RAM and causing system instability

With that fairly modest list of functional and non-functional requirements, we should be ready to begin. Like the last application, let's start by defining our module. In `src/main/java`, we will create this `module-info.java`:

```
module com.steeplesoft.dupefind.lib {
    exports com.steeplesoft.dupefind.lib;
}
```

Initially, the compiler--and the IDE--will complain that the `com.steeplesoft.dupefind.lib` package does not exist and won't compile the project. That's fine for now, as we'll be creating that package now.

The use of the word **concurrency** in the functional requirements, most likely, immediately brings to mind the idea of threads. We introduced the idea of threads in `Chapter 2`, *Managing Java Processes*, so if you are not familiar with them, review that section in the previous chapter.

Our use of threading in this project is different from that in the last, in that we will have a body of work that needs to be done, and, once it's finished, we want the threads to exit. We also need to wait for these threads to finish their work so that we can analyze it. In the `java.util.concurrent` package, the JDK provides several options to accomplish this.

Concurrent Java with a Future interface

One of the more common and popular APIs is the `Future<V>` interface. `Future` is a means to encapsulate an asynchronous calculation. Typically, the `Future` instance is returned by `ExecutorService`, which we'll discuss later. The calling code, once it has the reference to `Future`, can continue to work on other tasks while `Future` runs in the background in another thread. When the caller is ready for the results of `Future`, it calls `Future.get()`. If `Future` has finished its work, the call returns immediately with the results. If, however, `Future` is still working, calls to `get()` will block until `Future` completes.

For our uses, though, `Future` isn't the most appropriate choice. Looking over the non-functional requirements, we see the desire to avoid crashing the system by exhausting the available memory explicitly listed out. As we'll see later, the way this will be implemented is by storing the data in a lightweight on-disk database, and we will implement that--again, as we'll see later-by storing the file information as it is retrieved rather than by gathering the data, then saving it in a post-process method. Given that, our `Future` won't be returning anything. While there is a way to make that work (defining `Future` as `Future<?>` and returning `null`), it's not the most natural approach.

Perhaps the most appropriate approach is `ExecutorService`, which is `Executor` that provides additional functionality, such as the ability to create a `Future`, as discussed earlier, and manage termination of the queue. What, then, is `Executor`? `Executor` is a mechanism to execute `Runnable` that is more robust than simply calling `new Thread(runnable).start()`. The interface itself is very basic, consisting only of the `execute(Runnable)` method, so its value is not immediately apparent just from looking at the Javadoc. If, however, you look at `ExecutorService`, which is the interface that all `Executor` provided by the JDK implement, as well as the various `Executor` implementations, their value easily becomes more apparent. Let's take a quick survey now.

Looking at the `Executors` class, we can see five different types of `Executor` implementations: a cached thread pool, a fixed-size thread pool, a scheduled thread pool, a single thread executor, and a work-stealing thread pool. With the single thread `Executor` being the only exception, each of these can be instantiated directly (`ThreadPoolExecutor`, `ScheduledThreadPoolExecutor`, and `ForkJoinPool`), but users are urged by the JDK authors to use the convenience methods on the `Executors` class. That said, what are each of these options and why might you choose one?

- `Executors.newCachedThreadPool()`: This returns `Executor` that provides a pool of cached threads. As tasks come in, `Executor` will attempt to find an unused thread to execute the task with. If one cannot be found, a new `Thread` is created and the work begins. When a task is complete, `Thread` is returned to the pool to await reuse. After approximately 60 seconds, unused threads are destroyed and removed from the pool, which prevents resources from being allocated and never released. Care must be taken with this `Executor`, though, as the thread pool is unbounded, which means that under heavy use, the system could be overwhelmed by active threads.

- `Executors.newFixedThreadPool(int nThreads)`: This method returns an `Executor` similar to the one previously mentioned, with the exception that the thread pool is bounded to at most `nThreads`.

- `Executors.newScheduledThreadPool(int corePoolSize)`: This `Executor` is able to schedule tasks to run after an optional initial delay and then periodically, based on the delay and `TimeUnit` value. See, for example, the `schedule(Runnable command, long delay, TimeUnit unit)` method.

- `Executors.newSingleThreadExecutor()`: This method will return an `Executor` that will use a single thread to execute the tasks submitted to it. Tasks are guaranteed to be executed in the order in which they were submitted.

- `Executors.newWorkStealingExecutor()`: This method will return a so-called **work stealing** `Executor`, which is of type `ForkJoinPool`. The tasks submitted to this `Executor` are written in such a way as to be able to divide up the work to additional worker threads until the size of the work is under a user-defined threshold.

Given our non-functional requirements, the fixed-size `ThreadPoolExecutor` seems to be the most appropriate. One configuration option we'll need to support, though, is the option to force the generation of hashes for every file found. Based on the preceding algorithm, only files that have duplicate names or sizes will be hashed. However, users may want a more thorough analysis of their file specification and would like to force a hash on every file. We'll implement this using the work-stealing (or fork/join) pool.

With our threading approach selected, let's take a look at the entry point for the library, a class we'll call `FileFinder`. Since this is our entry point, it will need to know where we want to search and what we want to search for. That will give us the instance variables, `sourcePaths` and `patterns`:

```
private final Set<Path> sourcePaths = new HashSet<>();
private final Set<String> patterns = new HashSet<>();
```

We're declaring the variables as `private`, as that is a good object-oriented practice. We're also declaring them `final`, to help avoid subtle bugs where these variables are assigned new values, resulting in the unexpected loss of data. Generally speaking, I find it to be a good practice to mark variables as `final` by default to prevent such subtle bugs. In the case of instance variables in a class like this, a variable can only be declared `final` if it is either immediately assigned a value, as we are doing here, or if it is given a value in the class' constructors.

We also want to define our `ExecutorService` now:

```
private final ExecutorService es =
    Executors.newFixedThreadPool(5);
```

We have somewhat arbitrarily chosen to limit our thread pool to five threads, as it seems to be a fair balance between providing a sufficient number of worker threads for heavy requests, while not allocating a large number of threads that may not be used in most cases. In our case, it is probably a minor issue overblown, but it's certainly something to keep in mind.

Next, we need to provide a means to store any duplicates found. Consider the following lines of code as an example:

```
private final Map<String, List<FileInfo>> duplicates =
    new HashMap<>();
```

We'll see more details later, but, for now, all that we need to note is that this is a `Map` of `List<FileInfo>` objects, keyed by the file hash.

The final variable to make note of is something that might be a bit unexpected--an `EntityManagerFactory`. You might be asking yourself, what is that? The `EntityManagerFactory` is an interface to interact with a persistence unit as defined by the **Java Persistence API (JPA)**, which is part of the Java Enterprise Edition Specification. Fortunately, though, the specification was written in such a way to mandate that it be usable in a **Standard Edition (SE)** context like ours.

So, what are we doing with such an API? If you'll look back at the non-functional requirements, we've specified that we want to make sure that the search for duplicate files doesn't exhaust the available memory on the system. For very large searches, it is quite possible that the list of files and their hashes can grow to a problematic size. Couple that with the memory it will take to generate the hashes, which we'll discuss later, and we can very likely run into out-of-memory situations. We will, therefore, be using JPA to save our search information in a simple, light database (SQLite) that will allow us to save our data to the disk. It will also allow us to query and filter the results more efficiently than iterating over in-memory structures repeatedly.

Before we can make use of those APIs, we need to update our module descriptor to let the system know that we now require the persistence modules. Consider the following code snippet as an example:

```
module dupefind.lib {
    exports com.steeplesoft.dupefind.lib;
    requires java.logging;
    requires javax.persistence;
}
```

We've declared to the system that we require both `javax.persistence` and `java.logging`, which we'll be using later. As we discussed in Chapter 2, *Managing Processes in Java*, if any one of these modules are not present, the JVM instance will fail to start.

Perhaps the more important part of the module definition is the `exports` clause. With this line (there can be 0 or more of them), we're telling the system that we are exporting all of the types in the specified package. This line will allow our CLI module, which we'll get into later, to use the classes (as well as interfaces, enums, and so on, if we were to add any) in that module. If a type's package does not `export`, consuming modules will be unable to see the type, which we'll also demonstrate later.

With that understanding, let's take a look at our constructor:

```
public FileFinder() {
    Map<String, String> props = new HashMap<>();
    props.put("javax.persistence.jdbc.url",
      "jdbc:sqlite:" +
      System.getProperty("user.home") +
      File.separator +
      ".dupfinder.db");
    factory = Persistence.createEntityManagerFactory
      ("dupefinder", props);
    purgeExistingFileInfo();
}
```

To configure the persistence unit, JPA typically uses a `persistence.xml` file. In our case, though, we'd like a bit more control over where the database file is stored. As you can see in the preceding code, we are constructing the JDBC URL using the `user.home` environment variable. We then store that in a `Map` using the JPA-defined key to specify the URL. This `Map` is then passed to the `createEntityManagerFactory` method, which overrides anything set in `persistence.xml`. This allows us to put the database in the home directory appropriate for the user's operating system.

With our class constructed and configured, it's time to take a look at how we'll find duplicate files:

```
public void find() {
  List<PathMatcher> matchers = patterns.stream()
    .map(s -> !s.startsWith("**") ? "**/" + s : s)
    .map(p -> FileSystems.getDefault()
    .getPathMatcher("glob:" + p))
    .collect(Collectors.toList());
```

Our first step is to create a list of the `PathMatcher` instances based on the patterns specified by the user. A `PathMatcher` instance is a functional interface that is implemented by objects that attempt to match files and paths. Our instances are retrieved from the `FileSystems` class.

When requesting `PathMatcher`, we have to specify the globbing pattern. As can be seen in the first call to `map()`, we have to make an adjustment to what the user specified. Typically, a pattern mask is specified simply as something like `*.jpg`. However, a pattern mask like this won't work in a way that the user expects, in that it will only look in the current directory and not walk down into any subdirectories. To do that, the pattern must be prefixed with `**/`, which we do in the call to `map()`. With our adjusted pattern, we request the `PathMatcher` instance from the system's default `FileSystem`. Note that we specify the matcher pattern as `"glob:" + p` because we need to indicate that we are, indeed, specifying a `glob` file.

With our matchers prepared, we're ready to start the search. We do that with this code:

```
sourcePaths.stream()
  .map(p -> new FindFileTask(p))
  .forEach(fft -> es.execute(fft));
```

Using the `Stream` API, we map each source path to a lambda that creates an instance of `FindFileTask`, providing it the source path it will search. Each of these `FileFindTask` instances will then be passed to our `ExecutorService` via the `execute()` method.

The `FileFindTask` method is the workhorse for this part of the process. It is a `Runnable` as we'll be submitting this to the `ExecutorService`, but it is also a `FileVisitor<Path>` as it will be used in walking the file tree, which we do from the `run()` method:

```
@Override
public void run() {
  final EntityTransaction transaction = em.getTransaction();
  try {
    transaction.begin();
    Files.walkFileTree(startDir, this);
    transaction.commit();
  } catch (IOException ex) {
    transaction.rollback();
  }
}
```

Since we will be inserting data into the database via JPA, we'll need to start a transaction as our first step. Since this is an application-managed `EntityManager`, we have to manage the transaction manually. We acquire a reference to the `EntityTransaction` instance outside the `try/catch` block to simplify referencing it. Inside the `try` block, we start the transaction, start the file walking via `Files.walkFileTree()`, then commit the transaction if the process succeeds. If it fails--if an `Exception` was thrown--we roll back the transaction.

The `FileVisitor` API requires a number of methods, most of which are not too terribly interesting, but we'll show them for clarity's sake:

```
@Override
public FileVisitResult preVisitDirectory(final Path dir,
final BasicFileAttributes attrs) throws IOException {
  return Files.isReadable(dir) ?
    FileVisitResult.CONTINUE : FileVisitResult.SKIP_SUBTREE;
}
```

Here, we tell the system that if the directory is readable, then we continue with walking down that directory. Otherwise, we skip it:

```
@Override
public FileVisitResult visitFileFailed(final Path file,
 final IOException exc) throws IOException {
    return FileVisitResult.SKIP_SUBTREE;
}
```

The API requires this method to be implemented, but we're not very interested in file read failures, so we simply return a skip result:

```
@Override
public FileVisitResult postVisitDirectory(final Path dir,
  final IOException exc) throws IOException {
    return FileVisitResult.CONTINUE;
}
```

Much like the preceding method, this method is required, but we're not interested in this particular event, so we signal the system to continue:

```
@Override
public FileVisitResult visitFile(final Path file, final
  BasicFileAttributes attrs) throws IOException {
    if (Files.isReadable(file) && isMatch(file)) {
      addFile(file);
    }
    return FileVisitResult.CONTINUE;
}
```

Now we've come to a method we're interested in. We will check to make sure that the file is readable, then check to see if it's a match. If it is, we add the file. Regardless, we continue walking the tree. How do we test if the file's a match? Consider the following code snippet as an example:

```
private boolean isMatch(final Path file) {
  return matchers.isEmpty() ? true :
    matchers.stream().anyMatch((m) -> m.matches(file));
}
```

We iterate over the list of `PathMatcher` instances we passed in to the class earlier. If the `List` is empty, which means the user didn't specify any patterns, the method's result will always be `true`. However, if there are items in the `List`, we use the `anyMatch()` method on the `List`, passing a lambda that checks the `Path` against the `PathMatcher` instance.

Adding the file is very straightforward:

```
private void addFile(Path file) throws IOException {
  FileInfo info = new FileInfo();
  info.setFileName(file.getFileName().toString());
  info.setPath(file.toRealPath().toString());
  info.setSize(file.toFile().length());
  em.persist(info);
}
```

We create a `FileInfo` instance, set the properties, then persist it to the database via `em.persist()`.

With our tasks defined and submitted to `ExecutorService`, we need to sit back and wait. We do that with the following two method calls:

```
es.shutdown();
es.awaitTermination(Integer.MAX_VALUE, TimeUnit.SECONDS);
```

The first step is to ask `ExecutorService` to shut down. The `shutdown()` method will return immediately, but it will instruct `ExecutorService` to refuse any new tasks, as well as shut down its threads as soon as they are idle. Without this step, the threads will continue to run indefinitely. Next, we will wait for the service to shut down. We specify the maximum wait time to make sure we give our tasks time to complete. Once this method returns, we're ready to process the results, which is done in the following `postProcessFiles()` method:

```
private void postProcessFiles() {
  EntityManager em = factory.createEntityManager();
  List<FileInfo> files = getDuplicates(em, "fileName");
```

Modern database access with JPA

Let's stop here for a moment. Remember our discussion of the **Java Persistence API (JPA)** and database? Here is where we see that coming in. With the JPA, interactions with the database are done via the `EntityManager` interface, which we retrieve from the cleverly named `EntityManagerFactory`. It is important to note that the `EntityManager` instances are not thread-safe, so they should not be shared between threads. That's why we didn't create one in the constructor and pass it around. This is, of course, a local variable, so we need not worry about that too much until, and if, we decide to pass it as a parameter to another method, which we are doing here. As we will see in a moment, everything happens in the same thread, so we will not have to worry about thread-safety issues as the code stands now.

With our `EntityManager`, we call the `getDuplicates()` method and pass the manager and field name, `fileName`. This is what that method looks like:

```
private List<FileInfo> getDuplicates(EntityManager em,
  String fieldName) {
    List<FileInfo> files = em.createQuery(
      DUPLICATE_SQL.replace("%FIELD%", fieldName),
       FileInfo.class).getResultList();
    return files;
}
```

This is a fairly straightforward use of the Java Persistence API--we're creating a query and telling it that we want, and getting a `List` of `FileInfo` references back. The `createQuery()` method creates a `TypedQuery` object, on which we will call `getResultList()` to retrieve the results, which gives us `List<FileInfo>`.

Before we go any further, we need to have a short primer on the Java Persistence API. JPA is what is known as an **object-relational mapping (ORM)** tool. It provides an object-oriented, type-safe, and database-independent way of storing data in, typically, a relational database. The specification/library allows application authors to define their data models using concrete Java classes, then persist and/or read them with little thought about the mechanics specific to the database currently being used. (The developer isn't completely shielded from database concerns--and it's arguable as to whether or not he or she should be--but those concerns are greatly lessened as they are abstracted away behind the JPA interfaces). The process of acquiring a connection, creating the SQL, issuing it to the server, processing results, and more are all handled by the library, allowing a greater focus on the business of the application rather than the plumbing. It also allows a high degree of portability between databases, so applications (or libraries) can be easily moved from one system to another with minimal change (usually restricted to configuration changes).

At the heart of JPA is `Entity`, the business object (or domain model, if you prefer) that models the data for the application. This is expressed in the Java code as a **plain old Java object (POJO)**, which is marked up with a variety of annotations. A complete discussion of all of those annotations (or the API as a whole) is outside the scope of this book, but we'll use enough of them to get you started.

With that basic explanation given, let's take a look at our one and only entity--the `FileInfo` class:

```
@Entity
public class FileInfo implements Serializable {
  @GeneratedValue
  @Id
  private int id;
```

```
    private String fileName;
    private String path;
    private long size;
    private String hash;
}
```

This class has five properties. The only one that needs special attention is id. This property holds the primary key value for each row, so we annotate it with @Id. We also annotate this field with @GeneratedValue to indicate that we have a simple primary key for which we'd like the system to generate a value. This annotation has two properties: strategy and generator. The default value for strategy is GenerationType.AUTO, which we happily accept here. Other options include IDENTITY, SEQUENCE, and TABLE. In more complex uses, you may want to specify a strategy explicitly, which allows you to fine-tune how the key is generated (for example, the starting number, the allocation size, the name of the sequence or table, and so on). By choosing AUTO, we're telling JPA to choose the appropriate generation strategy for our target database. If you specify a strategy other than AUTO, you will also need to specify the details for the generator, using @SequenceGenerator for SEQUENCE and @TableGenerator for TABLE. You will also need to give the ID of the generator to the @GeneratedValue annotation using the generator attribute. We're using the default, so we need not specify a value for this attribute.

The next four fields are the pieces of data we have identified that we need to capture. Note that if we do not need to specify anything special about the mapping of these fields to the database columns, no annotations are necessary. However, if we would like to change the defaults, we can apply the @Column annotation and set the appropriate attribute, which can be one or more of columnDefinition (used to help generate the DDL for the column), insertable, length, name, nullable, precision, scale, table, unique, and updatable. Again, we're happy with the defaults.

JPA also requires each property to have a getter and a setter; the specification seems to be worded oddly, which has led to some ambiguity as to whether or not this is a hard requirement, and different JPA implementations handle this differently, but it's certainly safer to provide both as a matter of practice. If you need a read-only property, you can experiment with either no setter, or simply a no-op method. We haven't shown the getters and setters here, as there is nothing interesting about them. We have also omitted the IDE-generated equals() and hashCode() methods.

To help demonstrate the module system, we've put our entity in a
`com.steeplesoft.dupefind.lib.model` subpackage. We'll tip our hand a bit and go
ahead and announce that this class will be used by both our CLI and GUI modules, so we'll
need to update our module definition as follows:

```
module dupefind.lib {
    exports com.steeplesoft.dupefind.lib;
    exports com.steeplesoft.dupefind.lib.model;
    requires java.logging;
    requires javax.persistence;
}
```

That's all there is to our entity, so let's turn our attention back to our application logic. The
`createQuery()` call deserves a bit of discussion. Typically, when using JPA, queries are
written in what is called **JPAQL (Java Persistence API Query Language)**. It looks very
much like SQL, but has a more object-oriented feel to it. For example, if we wanted to query
for every `FileInfo` record in the database, we would do so with this query:

SELECT f FROM FileInfo f

I have put the keywords in all caps, with variable names in lower and the entity name in
camel case. This is mostly a matter of style, but while most identifiers are case-insensitive,
JPA does require that the case on the entity name matches that of the Java class it
represents. You must also specify an alias, or identification variable, for the entity, which
we simply call `f`.

To get a specific `FileInfo` record, you can specify a WHERE clause as follows:

SELECT f from FileInfo f WHERE f.fileName = :name

With this query, we can filter the query just as SQL does, and, just like SQL, we specify a
positional parameter. The parameter can either be a name, like we've done here, or simply a
`?`. If you use a name, you set the parameter value on the query using that name. If you use
the question mark, you must set the parameter using its index in the query. For small
queries, this is usually fine, but for larger, more complex queries, I would suggest using
names so that you don't have to manage index values, as that's almost guaranteed to cause a
bug at some point. Setting the parameter can look something like this:

```
Query query = em.createQuery(
    "SELECT f from FileInfo f WHERE f.fileName = :name");
query.setParameter("name", "test3.txt");
query.getResultList().stream() //...
```

With that said, let's take a look at our query:

```
SELECT f
FROM FileInfo f,
   (SELECT s.%FIELD%
     FROM FileInfo s
     GROUP BY s.%FIELD%
     HAVING (COUNT(s.%FIELD%) > 1)) g
WHERE f.%FIELD% = g.%FIELD%
AND f.%FIELD% IS NOT NULL
ORDER BY f.fileName, f.path
```

This query is moderately complicated, so let's break it down and see what's going on. First, in our SELECT query, we will specify only f, which is the identification variable of the entity for which we are querying. Next, we are selecting from a regular table and a temporary table, which is defined by the subselect in the FROM clause. Why are we doing it this way? We need to identify all of the rows that have a duplicate value (fileName, size, or hash). To do that, we use a HAVING clause with the COUNT aggregation function, HAVING (COUNT(fieldName > 1)) which says, in effect, give me all of the rows where this field occurs more than one time. The HAVING clause requires a GROUP BY clause, and once that's done, all of the rows with duplicate values are aggregated down to a single row. Once we have that list of rows, we will then join the real (or physical) table to those results to filter our physical table. Finally, we filter out the null fields in the WHERE clause, then order by fileName and path so that we don't have to do that in our Java code, which is likely to be less efficient than it would be if done by the database--a system designed for such operations.

You should also note the %FIELD% attribute in the SQL. We'll run the same query for multiple fields, so we've written the query once, and placed a marker in the text that we will replace with the desired field, which is sort of a *poor man's* template. There are, of course, a variety of ways to do this (and you may have one you find superior), but this is simple and easy to use, so it's perfectly acceptable in this environment.

We should also note that it is, generally speaking, a very bad idea to either concatenate SQL with values or do string replacements like we're doing, but our scenario is a bit different. If we were accepting user input and inserting that into the SQL this way, then we would certainly have a target for an SQL injection attack. In our use here, though, we aren't taking input from users, so this approach should be perfectly safe. In terms of database performance, this shouldn't have any adverse effects either. While we will require three different hard parses (one for each field by which we will filter), this is no different than if we were hardcoding the queries in our source file. Both of those issues, as well as many more, are always good to consider as you write your queries (and why I said the developer is mostly shielded from database concerns).

All of that gets us through the first step, which is identifying all of the files that have the same name. We now need to identify the files that have the same size, which can be done using the following piece of code:

```
List<FileInfo> files = getDuplicates(em, "fileName");
files.addAll(getDuplicates(em, "size"));
```

In our call to find duplicate filenames, we declared a local variable, `files`, to store those results. In finding files with duplicate sizes, we call the same `getDuplicates()` method, but with the correct field name, and simply add that to `files` via the `List.addAll()` method.

We now have a complete list of all of the possible duplicates, so we need to generate the hashes for each of these to see if they are truly duplicates. We will do that with this loop:

```
em.getTransaction().begin();
files.forEach(f -> calculateHash(f));
em.getTransaction().commit();
```

In a nutshell, we start a transaction (since we'll be inserting data into the database), then loop over each possible duplicate via `List.forEach()` and a lambda that calls `calculateHash(f)`, and then pass the `FileInfo` instance. Once the loop terminates, we commit the transaction to save our changes.

What does `calculateHash()` do? Let's a take a look:

```
private void calculateHash(FileInfo file) {
  try {
    MessageDigest messageDigest =
      MessageDigest.getInstance("SHA3-256");
    messageDigest.update(Files.readAllBytes(
      Paths.get(file.getPath())));
    ByteArrayInputStream inputStream =
      new ByteArrayInputStream(messageDigest.digest());
    String hash = IntStream.generate(inputStream::read)
      .limit(inputStream.available())
      .mapToObj(i -> Integer.toHexString(i))
      .map(s -> ("00" + s).substring(s.length()))
      .collect(Collectors.joining());
    file.setHash(hash);
  } catch (NoSuchAlgorithmException | IOException ex) {
    throw new RuntimeException(ex);
  }
}
```

This simple method encapsulates the work required to read the contents of a file and generate a hash. It requests an instance of MessageDigest using the SHA3-256 hash, which is one of the four new hashes supported by Java 9 (the other three being SHA3-224, SHA3-384, and SHA3-512). Many developers' first thought is to reach for MD-5 or SHA-1, but those are no longer considered reliable. Using the new SHA-3 should guarantee we avoid any false positives.

The rest of the method is pretty interesting in terms of how it does its work. First, it reads all of the bytes of the specified file and passes them to MessageDigest.update(), which updates the internal state of the MessageDigest object to give us the hash we want. Next, we create a ByteArrayInputStream that wraps the results of messageDigest.digest().

With our hash ready, we generate a string based on those bytes. We will do that by generating a stream via the IntStream.generate() method using the InputStream we just created as a source. We will limit the stream generation to the bytes available in the inputStream. For each byte, we will convert it to a string via Integer.toHexString(); then pad it with zero to two spaces, which prevents, for example, the single-digit hex characters E and F from being interpreted as EF; then collect them all into a string using Collections.joining(). Finally, we take that string value and update the FileInfo object.

The eagle-eyed might notice something interesting: we call FileInfo.setHash() to change the value of the object, but we never tell the system to persist those changes. This is because our FileInfo instance is a managed instance, meaning that we got it from JPA, which is keeping an eye on it, so to speak. Since we retrieved it via JPA, when we make any changes to its state, JPA knows it needs to persist those changes. When we call em.getTransaction().commit() in the calling method, JPA automatically saves those changes to the database.

 There's a catch to this automatic persistence: if you retrieve an object via JPA, then pass it across some sort of barrier that serializes the object, for example, across a remote EJB interface, then the JPA entity is said to be "detached". To reattach it to the persistence context, you will need to call entityManager. merge(), after which this behavior will resume. There is no need to call entityManager.flush() unless you have some need to synchronize the in-memory state of the persistence context with the underlying database.

Once we've calculated the hashes for the potential duplicates (at this point, given that they have duplicate SHA-3 hashes, they are almost certainly actual duplicates), we're ready to gather and report them:

```
getDuplicates(em, "hash").forEach(f -> coalesceDuplicates(f));
em.close();
```

We call the same `getDuplicates()` method to find duplicate hashes, and pass each record to the `coalesceDuplicates()` method, which will group these in a manner appropriate to report upstream to our CLI or GUI layers, or, perhaps, to any other program consuming this functionality:

```
private void coalesceDuplicates(FileInfo f) {
  String name = f.getFileName();
  List<FileInfo> dupes = duplicates.get(name);
  if (dupes == null) {
    dupes = new ArrayList<>();
    duplicates.put(name, dupes);
  }
  dupes.add(f);
}
```

This simple method follows what is likely a very familiar pattern:

1. Get a `List` from a `Map` based on the key, the filename.
2. If the map doesn't exist, create it and add it to the map.
3. Add the `FileInfo` object to the list.

This completes the duplicate file detection. Back in `find()`, we will call `factory.close()` to be a good JPA citizen, then return to the calling code. With that, we're ready to build our CLI.

Building the command-line interface

The primary means to interact with our new library will be the command-line interface we will now develop. Unfortunately, the Java SDK has nothing built in to help make sophisticated command-line utilities. If you've been using Java for any time, you've seen the following method signature:

```
public static void main(String[] args)
```

Clearly, there is *a* mechanism to process command-line arguments. The `public static void main` method is passed string arrays that represent arguments provided by the user on the command line, but that's about as far as it goes. To parse the options, the developer is required to iterate over the array, analyzing each entry. It might look something like this:

```
int i = 0;
while (i < args.length) {
  if ("--source".equals(args[i])) {
     System.out.println("--source = " + args[++i]);
  } else if ("--target".equals(args[i])) {
     System.out.println("--target = " + args[++i]);
  } else if ("--force".equals(args[i])) {
    System.out.println("--force set to true");
  }
  i++;
}
```

This is an effective solution, if very naive and error-prone. It assumes that whatever follows `--source` and `--target` is that argument's value. If the user types `--source --target /foo`, then our processor breaks. Clearly, something better is needed. Fortunately, we have options.

If you were to search for Java command-line libraries, you'll find an abundance of them (at least 10 at last count). Our space (and time) is limited here, so we obviously can't discuss all of them, so I'll mention the first three that I'm familiar with: Apache Commons CLI, Airline, and Crest. Each of these has some fairly significant differences from its competitors.

Commons CLI takes a more procedural approach; the list of available options, its name, description, whether or not it has arguments, and so forth, are all defined using Java method calls. Once the list of `Options` has been created, the command-line arguments are then manually parsed. The preceding example could be rewritten as follows:

```
public static void main(String[] args) throws ParseException {
  Options options = new Options();
  options.addOption("s", "source", true, "The source");
  options.addOption("t", "target", true, "The target");
  options.addOption("f", "force", false, "Force");
  CommandLineParser parser = new DefaultParser();
  CommandLine cmd = parser.parse(options, args);
  if (cmd.hasOption("source")) {
    System.out.println("--source = " +
      cmd.getOptionValue("source"));
  }
  if (cmd.hasOption("target")) {
    System.out.println("--target = " +
      cmd.getOptionValue("target"));
```

```
      }
      if (cmd.hasOption("force")) {
          System.out.println("--force set to true");
      }
    }
```

It's certainly more verbose, but it's also clearly, I think, more robust. We can specify long and short names for the option (`--source` versus `-s`), we can give it a description, and, best of all, we get built-in validation that an option has its required value. As much of an improvement as this is, I've learned from experience that the procedural approach here gets tedious in practice. Let's take a look at our next candidate to see how it fares.

Airline is a command-line library originally written as part of the airlift organization on GitHub. After languishing for some time, it was forked by Rob Vesse and given a new life (`http://rvesse.github.io/airline`). Airline's approach to command-line definition is more class-based--to define a command utility, you declare a new class, and mark it up appropriately with a number of annotations. Let's implement our preceding simple command line with Airline:

```
@Command(name = "copy", description = "Copy a file")
public class CopyCommand {
    @Option(name = {"-s", "--source"}, description = "The source")
    private String source;
    @Option(name = {"-t", "--target"}, description = "The target")
    private String target;
    @Option(name = {"-f", "--force"}, description = "Force")
    private boolean force = false;
    public static void main(String[] args) {
      SingleCommand<CopyCommand> parser =
        SingleCommand.singleCommand(CopyCommand.class);
      CopyCommand cmd = parser.parse(args);
      cmd.run();
    }

    private void run() {
      System.out.println("--source = " + source);
      System.out.println("--target = " + target);
      if (force) {
        System.out.println("--force set to true");
      }
    }
}
```

The options handling continues to grow in terms of code size, but we're also gaining more and more clarity as to what options are supported, and what they each mean. Our command is clearly defined via @Command on the class declaration. The possible options are delineated as @Option--annotated instance variables, and the business logic in run() is completely devoid of command-line parsing code. By the time this method is called, all the data has been extracted and we're ready to do our work. That looks very nice, but let's see what our last contender has to offer.

Crest is a library from Tomitribe, the company behind TomEE, the "all-Apache Java EE Web Profile certified stack" based on the venerable Tomcat Servlet container. Crest's approach to command definition is method based, where you define a method per command. It also uses annotations, and offers Bean Validation out of the box, as well as optional command discovery. Reimplementing our simple command, then, may look like this:

```
public class Commands {
  @Command
  public void copy(@Option("source") String source,
    @Option("target") String target,
    @Option("force") @Default("false") boolean force) {
    System.out.println("--source = " + source);
    System.out.println("--target = " + target);
    if (force) {
      System.out.println("--force set to true");
    }
  }
}
```

That seems to be the best of both worlds: it's nice and concise, and will still keep the actual logic of the command free from any CLI-parsing concerns, unless you're bothered by the annotations on the method. Although the actual logic-implementing code is free from such concerns. While Airline and Crest both offer things the other does not, Crest wins for me, so that's what we'll use to implement our command-line interface.

With a library chosen, then, let's take a look at what our CLI might look like. Most importantly, we need to be able to specify the path (or paths) we want to search. Likely, most files in those paths will have the same extension, but that certainly won't always be the case, so we want to allow the user to specify only the file patterns to match (for example, .jpg). Some users might also be curious about how long it takes to run the scan, so let's throw in a switch to turn on that output. And finally, let's add a switch to make the process a bit more verbose.

With our functional requirements set, let's start writing our command. Crest is method-based in its command declarations, but we'll still need a class to put our method in. If this CLI were more complicated (or, for example, if you were writing a CLI for an application server), you could easily put several CLI commands in the same class, or group similar commands in several different classes. How you structure them is completely your concern, as Crest is happy with whatever you choose.

We'll start with our CLI interface declaration as follows:

```
public class DupeFinderCommands {
  @Command
  public void findDupes(
    @Option("pattern") List<String> patterns,
    @Option("path") List<String> paths,
    @Option("verbose") @Default("false") boolean verbose,
    @Option("show-timings")
    @Default("false") boolean showTimings) {
```

Before we can discuss the preceding code, we need to declare our Java module:

```
module dupefind.cli {
  requires tomitribe.crest;
  requires tomitribe.crest.api;
}
```

We've defined a new module, which is named similarly to our library's module name. We also declared that we `require` two Crest modules.

Back to our source code, we have the four parameters that we discussed in our functional requirements. Note that `patterns` and `paths` are defined as `List<String>`. When Crest is parsing the command line, if it finds multiple instances of one of these (for example, `--path=/path/one--path=/path/two`), it will collect all of these values and store them as a `List` for you. Also, note that `verbose` and `showTimings` are defined as `boolean`, so we see a nice example of the type coercion that Crest will do on our behalf. We also have default values for both of these, so we're sure to have sane, predictable values when our method executes.

The business logic of the method is pretty straightforward. We will handle the verbose flag upfront, printing a summary of the operation requested as follows:

```
if (verbose) {
  System.out.println("Scanning for duplicate files.");
  System.out.println("Search paths:");
  paths.forEach(p -> System.out.println("\t" + p));
  System.out.println("Search patterns:");
  patterns.forEach(p -> System.out.println("\t" + p));
  System.out.println();
}
```

Then we will perform the actual work. Thanks to the work we did building the library, all of the logic for the duplicate search is hidden away behind our API:

```
final Instant startTime = Instant.now();
FileFinder ff = new FileFinder();
patterns.forEach(p -> ff.addPattern(p));
paths.forEach(p -> ff.addPath(p));
ff.find();

System.out.println("The following duplicates have been found:");
final AtomicInteger group = new AtomicInteger(1);
ff.getDuplicates().forEach((name, list) -> {
  System.out.printf("Group #%d:%n", group.getAndIncrement());
  list.forEach(fileInfo -> System.out.println("\t"
    + fileInfo.getPath()));
});
final Instant endTime = Instant.now();
```

This code won't compile at first, as we've not told the system we need it. We can do that now:

```
module dupefind.cli {
  requires dupefind.lib;
  requires tomitribe.crest;
  requires tomitribe.crest.api;
}
```

We can now import the `FileFinder` class. First, to demonstrate that the modules are, in fact, doing what they're supposed to do, let's try to import something that wasn't exported: `FindFileTask`. Let's create a simple class:

```
import com.steeplesoft.dupefind.lib.model.FileInfo;
import com.steeplesoft.dupefind.lib.util.FindFileTask;
public class VisibilityTest {
  public static void main(String[] args) {
    FileInfo fi;
    FindFileTask fft;
  }
}
```

If we try to compile this, Maven/javac will complain loudly with an error message like this:

```
[ERROR] Failed to execute goal org.apache.maven.plugins:maven-compiler-
plugin:3.6.1:compile (default-compile) on project cli: Compilation failure:
Compilation failure:
[ERROR] /C:/Users/jason/src/steeplesoft/DupeFinder/cli/src/main/java/com/
steeplesoft/dupefind/cli/VisibilityTest.java:[9,54]
com.steeplesoft.dupefind.lib.util.FindFileTask is not visible because
package com.steeplesoft.dupefind.lib.util is not visible
[ERROR] /C:/Users/jason/src/steeplesoft/DupeFinder/cli/src/main/java/com/
steeplesoft/dupefind/cli/VisibilityTest.java:[13,9] cannot find symbol
[ERROR] symbol:   class FindFileTask
[ERROR] location: class com.steeplesoft.dupefind.cli.VisibilityTest
```

We have successfully hidden our utility classes while exposing our public API. It may take some time for this practice to become widespread, but it should work wonders in preventing the crystallization of private APIs as pseudo-public.

Back on task, we create an instance of our `FileFinder` class, use `String.forEach` to pass our `paths` and `patterns` to the finder, then start the work with a call to `find()`. The work itself is threaded, but we've exposed a synchronous API, so our call here will block until the work has been completed. Once it returns, we start printing details to the screen. Since `FindFiles.getDuplicates()` returns `Map<String, List<FileInfo>>`, we call `forEach()` on the `Map` to iterate over each key, then we call `forEach()` on the `List` to print information about each file. We also use an `AtomicInteger` as the index, as the variable must be final or effectively final, so we just use a `final` instance of `AtomicInteger`. `BigInteger` may come to mind to more experienced developers, but it's immutable, so that makes it a poor choice for our use here.

The output of running the command will look something like this:

```
The following duplicates have been found:
Group #1:
    C:\some\path\test\set1\file5.txt
    C:\some\path\test\set2\file5.txt
Group #2:
    C:\some\path\test\set1\file11.txt
    C:\some\path\test\set1\file11-1.txt
    C:\some\path\test\set2\file11.txt
```

Next, we handle `showTimings`. I didn't call it out in the preceding code, though I will now, but we get an `Instant` instance (from the Java 8 date/time library in `java.time`) before and after processing. Only when `showTimings` is true do we actually do anything with them. The code that does that looks like this:

```
if (showTimings) {
  Duration duration = Duration.between(startTime, endTime);
  long hours = duration.toHours();
  long minutes = duration.minusHours(hours).toMinutes();
  long seconds = duration.minusHours(hours)
      .minusMinutes(minutes).toMillis() / 1000;
  System.out.println(String.format(
    "%nThe scan took %d hours, %d minutes, and %d seconds.%n",
      hours, minutes, seconds));
}
```

With our two `Instant`, we get a `Duration`, then start calculating hours, minutes, and seconds. Hopefully, this never runs more than an hour, but it can't hurt to be ready for it. And that's all there is to the CLI, in terms of code. Crest did the heavy lifting for our command-line parameter parsing, leaving us with a straightforward and clean implementation of our logic.

There's one last thing we need to add, and that's the CLI help. It would be very helpful for the end user to be able to find out how to use our command. Fortunately, Crest has support built in to provide that information. To add the help information, we need to create a file called `OptionDescriptions.properties` in the same package as our command class (remember that since we're using Maven, this file should be under `src/main/resource`), as follows:

```
path = Adds a path to be searched. Can be specified multiple times.
pattern = Adds a pattern to match against the file names (e.g.,
"*.png").
Can be specified multiple times.
show-timings= Show how long the scan took
verbose = Show summary of duplicate scan configuration
```

Doing so will produce an output like this:

```
$ java -jar cli-1.0-SNAPSHOT.jar help findDupes
Usage: findDupes [options]
Options:
  --path=<String[]>     Adds a path to be searched. Can be
                        specified multiple times.
  --pattern=<String[]> Adds a pattern to match against
                        the file names
                        (e.g., "*.png"). Can be specified
                        multiple times.
  --show-timings        Show how long the scan took
  --verbose             Show summary of duplicate scan configuration
```

You can be as verbose as you need to be without making your source code an unreadable mess.

With that, our CLI is feature-complete. Before we move on, we need to take a look at some build concerns for our CLI and see how Crest fits in. Obviously, we need to tell Maven where to find our Crest dependency, which is shown in the following piece of code:

```
<dependency>
    <groupId>org.tomitribe</groupId>
    <artifactId>tomitribe-crest</artifactId>
    <version>${crest.version}</version>
</dependency>
```

We also need to tell it where to find our duplicate finder library as follows:

```
<dependency>
    <groupId>${project.groupId}</groupId>
    <artifactId>lib</artifactId>
    <version>${project.version}</version>
</dependency>
```

Note `groupId` and `version`: since our CLI and library modules are part of the same parent multi-module build, we set `groupId` and `version` to that of the parent module, allowing us to manage that from a single location, which makes changing groups or bumping versions much simpler.

The more interesting part is the `build` section of our POM. First, let's start with `maven-compiler-plugin`. While we are targeting Java 9, `crest-maven-plugin`, which we'll look at in a moment, does not currently seem to like the classes generated for Java 9, so we instruct the compiler plugin to emit Java 1.8 bytecode:

```
<plugin>
  <groupId>org.apache.maven.plugins</groupId>
  <artifactId>maven-compiler-plugin</artifactId>
  <configuration>
    <source>1.8</source>
    <target>1.8</target>
  </configuration>
</plugin>
```

Next, we need to set up `crest-maven-plugin`. To expose our command classes to Crest, we have two options: we can use runtime scanning for the classes, or we can have Crest scan for commands at build time. In order to make this utility as small as possible, as well as reducing the startup time as much as possible, we will opt for the latter approach, so we will need to add another plugin to the build, as follows:

```
<plugin>
  <groupId>org.tomitribe</groupId>
  <artifactId>crest-maven-plugin</artifactId>
  <version>${crest.version}</version>
  <executions>
    <execution>
      <goals>
        <goal>descriptor</goal>
      </goals>
    </execution>
  </executions>
</plugin>
```

When this plugin runs, it will generate a file called `crest-commands.txt` that Crest will process to find classes when it starts. It may not save much time here, but it's definitely something to keep in mind for larger projects.

Finally, we don't want the user to have to worry about setting up the classpath (or module path!) each time, so we'll introduce the Maven Shade plugin, which will create a single, fat jar with all of our dependencies, transitive and otherwise:

```
<plugin>
  <artifactId>maven-shade-plugin</artifactId>
  <version>2.1</version>
  <executions>
    <execution>
      <phase>package</phase>
      <goals>
        <goal>shade</goal>
      </goals>
      <configuration>
        <transformers>
          <transformer implementation=
            "org.apache.maven.plugins.shade.resource
             .ManifestResourceTransformer">
            <mainClass>
              org.tomitribe.crest.Main
            </mainClass>
          </transformer>
        </transformers>
      </configuration>
    </execution>
  </executions>
</plugin>
```

After the build, we can then run a search with the following command:

```
java -jar target\cli-1.0-SNAPSHOT.jar findDupes \
  --path=../test/set1 --path=../test/set2 -pattern=*.txt
```

Clearly, it can still be improved, so we would want to ship that, say, with script wrappers (shell, batch, and so on), but the number of jars is cut down from 18 or so to 1, so that's a big improvement.

With our CLI done, let's make a simple GUI that consumes our library as well.

Building the graphical user interface

For our GUI, we'd like to expose the same type of functionality as the command line, but, obviously, with a nice graphical interface. For this, we'll again reach for JavaFX. We'll give the user a means to select, using a chooser dialog, the directories to be searched, and a field by which to add the search patterns. Once the duplicates have been identified, we will display them in a list for the user to peruse. All of the duplicate groups will be listed and, when clicked, the files in that group will be displayed in another list. The user can right-click on the list and choose to either view the file (or files) or delete it (or them). When we are finished, the application will look like this:

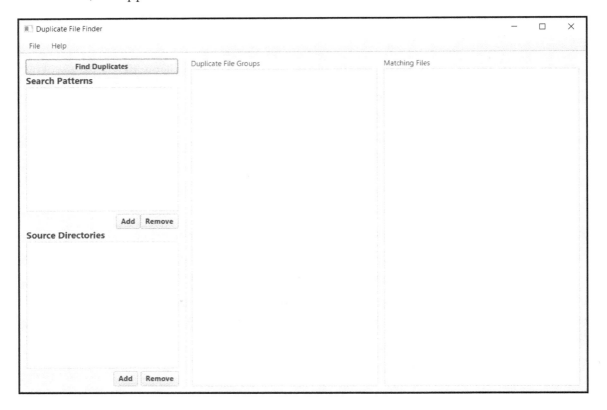

Let's start by creating our project. In NetBeans, go to **File | New Project** and select **Maven | JavaFX Application**. You can name it whatever you'd like, but we've used the name `Duplicate Finder - GUI`, groupId as `com.steeplesoft.dupefind`, and artifactId as `gui`.

Once you have your project, you should have two classes, `Main` and `FXMLController`, as well as the `fxml/Scene.fxml` resource. This may sound repetitive, but before we go any further, we need to set up our Java module as follows:

```
module dupefind.gui {
    requires dupefind.lib;
    requires java.logging;
    requires javafx.controls;
    requires javafx.fxml;
    requires java.desktop;
}
```

Then, to create the interface we saw, we will use `BorderPane`, to which we'll add `MenuBar` to the `top` section, as follows:

```
<top>
  <MenuBar BorderPane.alignment="CENTER">
    <menus>
      <Menu mnemonicParsing="false"
        onAction="#closeApplication" text="File">
        <items>
          <MenuItem mnemonicParsing="false" text="Close" />
        </items>
      </Menu>
      <Menu mnemonicParsing="false" text="Help">
        <items>
          <MenuItem mnemonicParsing="false"
            onAction="#showAbout" text="About" />
        </items>
      </Menu>
    </menus>
  </MenuBar>
</top>
```

When you add `MenuBar` with Scene Builder, it automatically adds several sample `Menu` entries for you. We've removed the unwanted entries, and tied the remaining to Java methods in the controller class. Specifically, the `Close` menu will call `closeApplication()` and `About` will call `showAbout()`. This looks just like the menu markup seen previously in the book, so there's not much to talk about.

The rest of the layout is a bit more complex. In the `left` section, we have a number of controls stacked vertically. JavaFX has a built-in container that makes that easy to do: `VBox`. We'll get to its contents in a moment, but its usage looks like this:

```
<VBox BorderPane.alignment="TOP_CENTER">
  <children>
```

```
            <HBox... />
            <Separator ... />
            <Label .../>
            <ListView ... />
            <HBox ... />
            <Label ... />
            <ListView... />
            <HBox ... />
        </children>
        <padding>
            <Insets bottom="10.0" left="10.0" right="10.0"
              top="10.0" />
        </padding>
    </VBox>
```

That's not valid FXML, so don't try to copy and paste that. I've omitted the details of the children for clarity. As you can see, VBox has a number of children, each of which will be stacked vertically, but, as we can see from the preceding screenshot, there are some we want to be lined up horizontally. To achieve that, we nest an HBox instance where needed. Its markup looks just like VBox.

There's not much of interest in this part of the FXML, but there are a couple of things to note. We want certain parts of the user interface to shrink and grow as the window is resized, namely ListView. By default, each component's various height and width properties--minimum, maximum, and preferred--will use the computed size, which means, roughly, that they'll be as big as they need to be to render themselves, and, in most cases, that's fine. In our situation, we want the two ListView instances to grow as much as possible inside their respective containers, which, in this case, is VBox we discussed earlier. To make that happen, we need to modify our two ListView instances like this:

```
    <ListView fx:id="searchPatternsListView" VBox.vgrow="ALWAYS" />
    ...
    <ListView fx:id="sourceDirsListView" VBox.vgrow="ALWAYS" />
```

With both the ListView instances set to ALWAYS grow, they will compete with each other for the available space, and end up sharing it. The available space, of course, is dependent on the height of the VBox instance, as well as the computed height of the other components in the container. With that property set, we can increase or decrease the size of the window, and watch the two ListView instances grow and shrink, while everything else remains the same.

For the rest of the user interface, we'll apply the same tactic to arrange components, but, this time, we'll start with an HBox instance, and divide that up as necessary. We have two ListView instances that we also want to fill all the available space with, so we mark those up in the same way we did the last two. Each ListView instance also has a Label, so we wrap each Label/ListView pair in a VBox instance to get our vertical distribution. In pseudo-FXML, this would look like this:

```
<HBox>
  <children>
    <Separator orientation="VERTICAL"/>
    <VBox HBox.hgrow="ALWAYS">
      <children>
        <VBox VBox.vgrow="ALWAYS">
          <children>
            <Label ... />
            <ListView ... VBox.vgrow="ALWAYS" />
          </children>
        </VBox>
      </children>
    </VBox>
    <VBox HBox.hgrow="ALWAYS">
      <children>
        <Label ... />
        <ListView ... VBox.vgrow="ALWAYS" />
      </children>
    </VBox>
  </children>
</HBox>
```

There is one item of interest in this part of the user interface, and that is the context menu we discussed earlier. To add a context to a control, you nest a contextMenu element in the target control's FXML like this:

```
<ListView fx:id="matchingFilesListView" VBox.vgrow="ALWAYS">
  <contextMenu>
    <ContextMenu>
      <items>
        <MenuItem onAction="#openFiles" text="Open File(s)..." />
        <MenuItem onAction="#deleteSelectedFiles"
          text="Delete File(s)..." />
      </items>
    </ContextMenu>
  </contextMenu>
</ListView>
```

We've defined a content menu with two MenuItem: "Open File(s)..." and "Deleted File(s)...". We've also specified the action for the two MenuItem using the onAction attribute. We'll look at these following methods.

This marks the end of our user interface definition, so now we turn our attention to the Java code, in which we will finish preparing the user interface for use, as well as implement our application's logic.

While we didn't show the FXML that accomplishes this, our FXML file is tied to our controller class: FXMLController. This class can be called anything, of course, but we've opted to use the name generated by the IDE. In a larger application, more care will need to be given in the naming of this class. To allow the injection of our user interface components into our code, we need to declare instance variables on our class, and mark them up with the @FXML annotation. Some examples include the following:

```
@FXML
private ListView<String> dupeFileGroupListView;
@FXML
private ListView<FileInfo> matchingFilesListView;
@FXML
private Button addPattern;
@FXML
private Button removePattern;
```

There are several others, but this should be sufficient to demonstrate the concept. Note that rather than declaring a plain ListView, we've parameterized our instances as ListView<String> and ListView<FileInfo>. We know this is what we're putting into the control, so specifying that the type parameter gets us a measure of type safety at compile time, but also allows us to avoid having to cast the contents every time we interact with them.

Next, we need to set up the collections that will hold the search paths and patterns that the user will enter. We'll use the ObservableList instances for that. Remember that with an ObservableList instance, the container can automatically rerender itself as needed when the Observable instance is updated:

```
final private ObservableList<String> paths =
  FXCollections.observableArrayList();
final private ObservableList<String> patterns =
  FXCollections.observableArrayList();
```

In the `initialize()` method, we can start tying things together. Consider the following code snippet as an example:

```
public void initialize(URL url, ResourceBundle rb) {
    searchPatternsListView.setItems(patterns);
    sourceDirsListView.setItems(paths);
```

Here, we associate our `ListView` instances with our `ObservableList` instances. Now, at any point that these lists are updated, the user interface will immediately reflect the change.

Next, we need to configure the duplicate file group `ListView`. The data coming back from our library is a `Map` of a `List<FileInfo>` object, keyed by the duplicate hashes. Clearly, we don't want to show the user a list of hashes, so, like the CLI, we want to denote each group of files with a more friendly label. To do that, we need to create a `CellFactory`, which will, in turn, create a `ListCell` that is responsible for rendering the cell. We will do that as follows:

```
dupeFileGroupListView.setCellFactory(
    (ListView<String> p) -> new ListCell<String>() {
        @Override
        public void updateItem(String string, boolean empty) {
            super.updateItem(string, empty);
            final int index = p.getItems().indexOf(string);
            if (index > -1) {
                setText("Group #" + (index + 1));
            } else {
                setText(null);
            }
        }
    }
});
```

While lambdas can be great, in that they tend to make code more concise, they can also obscure some details. In a non-lambda code, the lambda above might look like this:

```
dupeFileGroupListView.setCellFactory(new
    Callback<ListView<String>, ListCell<String>>() {
        @Override
        public ListCell<String> call(ListView<String> p) {
            return new ListCell<String>() {
                @Override
                protected void updateItem(String t, boolean bln) {
                    super.updateItem(string, empty);
                    final int index = p.getItems().indexOf(string);
                    if (index > -1) {
                        setText("Group #" + (index + 1));
                    } else {
                        setText(null);
```

```
                    }
                  }
                };
              }
          });
```

You certainly get more detail, but it's also much harder to read. The main point in including both here is twofold: to show why lambdas are often so much better, and to show the actual types involved, which helps the lambdas make sense. With that understanding of the lambdas under our belts, what is the method doing?

First, we call `super.updateItem()`, as that's simply good practice. Next, we find the index of the string being rendered. The API gives us the string (since it's a `ListView<String>`), so we find its index in our `ObservableList<String>`. If it's found, we set the text of the cell to `Group` # plus the index plus one (since indexes in Java are typically zero-based). If the string isn't found (`ListView` is rendering an empty cell), we set the text to null to ensure that the field is blank.

Next, we need to perform a similar procedure on `matchingFilesListView`:

```
matchingFilesListView.getSelectionModel()
  .setSelectionMode(SelectionMode.MULTIPLE);
matchingFilesListView.setCellFactory(
  (ListView<FileInfo> p) -> new ListCell<FileInfo>() {
    @Override
    protected void updateItem(FileInfo fileInfo, boolean bln) {
      super.updateItem(fileInfo, bln);
      if (fileInfo != null) {
        setText(fileInfo.getPath());
      } else {
        setText(null);
      }
    }
});
```

This is almost identical, but with a couple of exceptions. First, we're setting the selection mode of `ListView` to `MULTIPLE`. This will allow the user to control-click on items of interest, or shift-click on a range of rows. Next, we set up `CellFactory` in an identical fashion. Note that since the `ListView` instance's parameterized type is `FileInfo`, the types in the method signature of `ListCell.updateItem()` are different.

We have one last user interface setup step. If you look back at the screenshot, you will notice that the **Find Duplicates** button is the same width as `ListView`, unlike the other buttons, which are just wide enough to render their content. We do that by binding the width of the `Button` element to that of its container, which is an `HBox` instance:

```
findFiles.prefWidthProperty().bind(findBox.widthProperty());
```

We are getting the preferred width property, which is a `DoubleProperty`, and binding that to the width property (also a `DoubleProperty`) of `findBox`, the control's container. `DoubleProperty` is an `Observable` instance, just as `ObservableListView` is, so we're telling the `findFiles` control to observe its container's width property, and set its own value accordingly when the other changes. This lets us set the property, after a fashion, and then forget about it. Unless we want to break the binding between these two properties, we never again have to think about it, and we certainly don't need to manually watch one property to update the author. The framework does that for us.

Now, how about those buttons? How do we make them do something? We do that by setting the `onAction` property of the `Button` element to a method in our controller: `#someMethod` translates to `Controller.someMethod(ActionEvent event)`. We can handle this in one of at least two ways: we can create a separate handler method for each button, or, as we've done here, we can create one, then delegate to another method as appropriate; either is fine:

```
@FXML
private void handleButtonAction(ActionEvent event) {
  if (event.getSource() instanceof Button) {
    Button button = (Button) event.getSource();
    if (button.equals(addPattern)) {
      addPattern();
    } else if (button.equals(removePattern)) {
    // ...
```

We have to make sure we're actually getting a `Button` element, then we cast it and compare it to the instances that were injected. The actual handlers for each button are as follows:

```
private void addPattern() {
  TextInputDialog dialog = new TextInputDialog("*.*");
  dialog.setTitle("Add a pattern");
  dialog.setHeaderText(null);
  dialog.setContentText("Enter the pattern you wish to add:");

  dialog.showAndWait()
  .filter(n -> n != null && !n.trim().isEmpty())
  .ifPresent(name -> patterns.add(name));
}
```

To add a pattern, we create a `TextInputDialog` instance with the appropriate text, then call `showAndWait()`. The beauty of this method in JavaFX 8 is that it returns `Optional<String>`. If the user enters text in the dialog, and if the user clicks on OK, the `Optional` will have content. We identify that with the call to `ifPresent()`, passing it a lambda that adds the new pattern to `ObservableList<String>`, which automatically updates the user interface. If the user doesn't click on **OK**, the `Optional` will be empty. If the user didn't enter any text (or entered a bunch of spaces), the call to `filter()` will prevent the lambda from ever running.

Removing an item is similar, though we get to hide some of the details in a utility method, since we have two needs for the functionality. We make sure something is selected, then show a confirmation dialog, removing the pattern from the `ObservableList<String>` if the user clicks on **OK**:

```
private void removePattern() {
  if (searchPatternsListView.getSelectionModel()
  .getSelectedIndex() > -1) {
    showConfirmationDialog(
      "Are you sure you want to remove this pattern?",
      (() -> patterns.remove(searchPatternsListView
      .getSelectionModel().getSelectedItem())));
  }
}
```

Let's take a look at the `showConfirmationDialog` method:

```
protected void showConfirmationDialog(String message,
 Runnable action) {
  Alert alert = new Alert(Alert.AlertType.CONFIRMATION);
  alert.setTitle("Confirmation");
  alert.setHeaderText(null);
  alert.setContentText(message);
  alert.showAndWait()
  .filter(b -> b == ButtonType.OK)
  .ifPresent(b -> action.run());
}
```

Again, this is much like the dialogs earlier, and should be self-explanatory. The interesting part here is the use of a lambda as a method parameter that makes this, by the way, a higher order function--meaning it takes in a function as a parameter, returns a function as its result, or both. We pass in Runnable, as we want a lambda that takes in nothing and returns nothing, and Runnable is a FunctionalInterface that matches that description. After we show the dialog and get the user's response, we will filter for only responses where the button clicked on was OK, and, if present, we execute Runnable via action.run(). We have to specify b -> action.run() as ifPresent() takes a Consumer<? super ButtonType>, so we create one and ignore the value passed in, allowing us to shield our calling code from that detail.

Adding a path requires a DirectoryChooser instance:

```
private void addPath() {
    DirectoryChooser dc = new DirectoryChooser();
    dc.setTitle("Add Search Path");
    dc.setInitialDirectory(new File(lastDir));
    File dir = dc.showDialog(null);
    if (dir != null) {
        try {
            lastDir = dir.getParent();
            paths.add(dir.getCanonicalPath());
        } catch (IOException ex) {
            Logger.getLogger(FXMLController.class.getName()).log(
                Level.SEVERE, null, ex);
        }
    }
}
```

When creating the DirectoryChooser instance, we set the initial directory to the last directory used as a convenience for the user. When the application starts, this defaults to the user's home directory, but once a directory is successfully chosen, we set lastDir to the added directory's parent, allowing the user to start where he or she left off should there be a need to enter multiple paths. DirectoryChooser.showDialog() returns a file, so we get its canonical path and store that in paths, which, again, causes our user interface to be updated automatically.

Removing a path looks very similar to removing a pattern, as you can see in the following code snippet:

```
private void removePath() {
  showConfirmationDialog(
    "Are you sure you want to remove this path?",
    (() -> paths.remove(sourceDirsListView.getSelectionModel()
    .getSelectedItem()))));
}
```

Same basic code, just a different lambda. Aren't lambdas just the coolest?

The handler for the `findFiles()` button is a bit different, but looks a lot like our CLI code, as you can see here:

```
private void findFiles() {
    FileFinder ff = new FileFinder();
    patterns.forEach(p -> ff.addPattern(p));
    paths.forEach(p -> ff.addPath(p));

    ff.find();
    dupes = ff.getDuplicates();
    ObservableList<String> groups =
      FXCollections.observableArrayList(dupes.keySet());

    dupeFileGroupListView.setItems(groups);
}
```

We create our `FileFinder` instance, set the paths and patterns using streams and lambdas, then start the search process. When it completes, we get the list duplicate file information via `getDuplicates()`, then create a new `ObservableList<String>` instance using the keys of the map, which we then set on `dupeFileGroupListView`.

Now we need to add the logic to handle mouse clicks on the group list, so we will set the onMouseClicked property on ListView in the FXML file to #dupeGroupClicked, as you can see in the following code block:

```
@FXML
public void dupeGroupClicked(MouseEvent event) {
   int index = dupeFileGroupListView.getSelectionModel()
     .getSelectedIndex();
   if (index > -1) {
      String hash = dupeFileGroupListView.getSelectionModel()
      .getSelectedItem();
      matchingFilesListView.getItems().clear();
      matchingFilesListView.getItems().addAll(dupes.get(hash));
   }
}
```

When the control is clicked on, we get the index and make sure it is non-negative, so as to ensure that the user actually clicked on something. We then get the hash of the group by getting the selected item from ListView. Remember that while ListView may show something like Group #2, the actual content of that row is the hash. We just used a custom CellFactory to give it a prettier label. With the hash, we clear the list of items in matchingFilesListView, then get the control's ObservableList and add all of the FileInfo objects in the List keyed by the hash. And, again, we get an automatic user interface update, thanks to the power of Observable.

We also want the user to be able to navigate the list of duplicate groups using the keyboard to update the matching file list. We do that by setting the onKeyPressed attribute on our ListView to point to this rather simple method:

```
@FXML
public void keyPressed(KeyEvent event) {
   dupeGroupClicked(null);
}
```

It just so happens that we're not too terribly interested in the actual Event in either of these methods (they're never actually used), so we can naively delegate to the mouse-click method discussed earlier.

There are two more minor pieces of functionality we need to implement: viewing the matching files and deleting matching files.

We've already created the context menu and menu entries, so all we need to do is implement the handler methods as follows:

```
@FXML
public void openFiles(ActionEvent event) {
  matchingFilesListView.getSelectionModel().getSelectedItems()
  .forEach(f -> {
    try {
      Desktop.getDesktop().open(new File(f.getPath()));
    } catch (IOException ex) {
      // ...
    }
  });
}
```

The matching file list allows multiple selections, so we need to get `List<FileInfo>` from the selection model instead of the single object we've already seen. We then call `forEach()` to process the entry. We want to open the file in whatever application the user has configured in the operating system to handle that file type. To do this, we use an AWT class introduced in Java 6: `Desktop`. We get the instance via `getDesktop()`, then call `open()`, passing it `File` that points to our `FileInfo` target.

Deleting a file is similar:

```
@FXML
public void deleteSelectedFiles(ActionEvent event) {
  final ObservableList<FileInfo> selectedFiles =
    matchingFilesListView.getSelectionModel()
    .getSelectedItems();
  if (selectedFiles.size() > 0) {
    showConfirmationDialog(
      "Are you sure you want to delete the selected files",
      () -> selectedFiles.forEach(f -> {
        if (Desktop.getDesktop()
        .moveToTrash(new File(f.getPath()))) {
          matchingFilesListView.getItems()
          .remove(f);
          dupes.get(dupeFileGroupListView
          .getSelectionModel()
          .getSelectedItem()).remove(f);
        }
      }));
  }
}
```

Similarly to open files, we get all of the selected files. If there's at least one, we confirm the user's intent via `showConfirmationDialog()`, and pass in a lambda that handles the deleting. We do the actual file deletion using the `Desktop` class again to move the file to the trash can provided by the filesystem to provide the user with a safe delete option. If the file is successfully deleted, we remove its entry from `ObservableList`, as well as our cache duplicate file `Map`, so that it isn't shown should the user click on this file group again.

Summary

With that, our application is done. So, what have we covered? From the project description, this seemed like a pretty simple application, but as we started breaking down the requirements and delving into the implementation, we ended up covering a lot of territory-- a scenario that is not at all uncommon. We built another multi-module Maven project. We introduced Java concurrency, including basic `Thread` management and `ExecutorService` usage, as well as the Java Persistence API, showing basic `@Entity` definition, `EntityManagerFactory`/`EntityManager` usage, and JPAQL query authoring. We discussed creating file hashes using the `MessageDigest` classes, and demonstrated the new file I/O APIs, including the directory tree walking APIs. We also built a more complex user interface in JavaFX using nested containers, "linked" `ListView` instances, and bound properties.

That's quite a bit for such a "simple" project. Our next project will also be relatively simple, as we build a command-line date calculator that will allow us to explore the `java.time` package and see some of what this new date/time API offers.

4
Date Calculator

If you've been developing in Java for any serious length of time, you know one thing to be true--working with dates is awful. The `java.util.Date` class, with its related classes, shipped with 1.0, and `Calendar` and its related classes coming along in 1.1. Even early on, problems were apparent. For example, the Javadoc on `Date` says this--*Unfortunately, the API for these functions was not amenable to internationalization*. As a result, `Calendar` was introduced in 1.1. Sure, there have been other enhancements down through the years, but given Java's strict adherence to backwards compatibility, there's only so much the language architects can do. As much as they may want to fix those APIs, their hands are tied.

Fortunately, **Java Specification Request (JSR 310)** was filed. Led by Stephen Colebourne, an effort was begun to create a new API, based on the very popular open source library, Joda-Time. In this chapter, we'll take an in-depth look at this new API, then build a simple command-line utility to perform date and time math, which will give us an opportunity to see some of this API in action.

This chapter, then, will be covering the following topics:

- The Java 8 Date/Time API
- Revisiting command-line utilities
- Text parsing

Getting started

Like the project in Chapter 2, *Managing Processes in Java*, this project is fairly simple, conceptually. The end goal is a command-line utility to perform various date and time calculations. However, while we're at it, it would be very nice if the actual date/time work were to be put in a reusable library, so that's what we'll do. This leaves us with two projects, which we'll set up, like last time, as a multi-module Maven project.

The parent POM will look something like this:

```xml
<?xml version="1.0" encoding="UTF-8"?>
<project xmlns="http://maven.apache.org/POM/4.0.0"
  xmlns:xsi="http://www.w3.org/2001/XMLSchema-instance"
  xsi:schemaLocation="http://maven.apache.org/POM/4.0.0
  http://maven.apache.org/xsd/maven-4.0.0.xsd">
  <modelVersion>4.0.0</modelVersion>

  <artifactId>datecalc-master</artifactId>
  <version>1.0-SNAPSHOT</version>
  <packaging>pom</packaging>
  <modules>
    <module>datecalc-lib</module>
    <module>datecalc-cli</module>
  </modules>
</project>
```

If you read `Chapter 2`, *Managing Processes in Java*, or have worked with multi-module
Maven builds before, there's nothing new here. It's included simply for completeness. If this
is foreign to you, take a moment to review the first few pages of Chapter 2 before
continuing.

Building the library

Since we'd like to be able to reuse this tool in other projects, we'll start by building a library
that exposes its functionality. All of the functionality we'll need is built into the platform, so
our POM file is very simple:

```xml
<?xml version="1.0" encoding="UTF-8"?>
<project xmlns="http://maven.apache.org/POM/4.0.0"
  xmlns:xsi="http://www.w3.org/2001/XMLSchema-instance"
  xsi:schemaLocation="http://maven.apache.org/POM/4.0.0
  http://maven.apache.org/xsd/maven-4.0.0.xsd">
  <modelVersion>4.0.0</modelVersion>
  <parent>
    <groupId>com.steeplesoft</groupId>
      <artifactId>datecalc-master</artifactId>
      <version>1.0-SNAPSHOT</version>
  </parent>
  <artifactId>datecalc-lib</artifactId>
  <packaging>jar</packaging>
  <dependencies>
    <dependency>
      <groupId>org.testng</groupId>
```

```
      <artifactId>testng</artifactId>
      <version>6.9.9</version>
      <scope>test</scope>
    </dependency>
  </dependencies>
</project>
```

There are **almost** no external dependencies. The only dependency listed is on the testing library, TestNG. We didn't talk much about testing in the last chapter (rest assured, there are tests in the project). In this chapter, we'll introduce the topic of testing and show some examples.

Now we need to define our module. Remember that these are Java 9 projects, so we want to make use of the module functionality to help protect our internal classes from accidental public exposure. Our module is very simple. We need to give it a name, then export our public API package, as follows:

```
module datecalc.lib {
   exports com.steeplesoft.datecalc;
}
```

Since everything we need is already in the JDK, we have nothing to declare beyond what we export.

With our project set up, let's take a quick look at the functional requirements. Our intent with this project is to build a system that allows the user to provide an arbitrary string representing a date or time calculation expression and get a response. The string may look something like `"today + 2 weeks"` to find out the date 2 weeks from today, `"now + 3 hours 15 minutes"` to find out what time it is in 3 hours and 15 minutes, or `"2016/07/04 - 1776/07/04"` to find out how many years, months, and days are between the two dates. The processing of these expressions will be one line at a time, so the ability to pass in, for example, a text document with multiple expressions and get multiple results is explicitly excluded from the scope. This can be implemented easily enough, of course, by any consuming application or library.

So, now we have a project set up and ready to go, and we have a rough sketch of its fairly simple functional requirements. We're ready to start coding. Before we do that, let's take a quick tour of the new `java.time` package to get a better sense of what we'll be seeing in this project, as well as some of the functionality we **won't** be using in this simple project.

A timely interlude

Prior to Java 8, two primary date-related classes were `Date` and `Calendar` (and, of course, `GregorianCalendar`). The new `java.time` package offers several new classes, such as `Duration`, `Period`, `Clock`, `Instant`, `LocalDate`, `LocalTime`, `LocalDateTime`, and `ZonedDateTime`. There is a plethora of supporting classes, but these are the primary starting points. Let's take a quick look at each.

Duration

`Duration` is a **time-based unit of time**. While it may sound odd to phrase it that way, the wording was chosen to distinguish it from a date-based unit of time, which we'll look at next. In plain English, it's a measurement of time, such as **10 seconds**, **1 hour**, or **100 nanoseconds**. `Duration` is measured in seconds, but there are a number of methods to get a representation of the duration in other units of measure, which are as follows:

- `getNano()`: This is `Duration` in nanosecods
- `getSeconds()`: This is `Duration` in seconds
- `get(TemporalUnit)`: This is `Duration` in a unit of measure specified

There are also a variety of arithmetic methods, which are mentioned as follows:

- `add/minus (int amount, TemporalUnit unit)`
- `add/minus (Duration)`
- `addDays/minusDays(long)`
- `addHours/minusHours(long)`
- `addMillis/minusMillis(long)`
- `addMinutes/minusMinutes(long)`
- `addNanos/minusNanos(long)`
- `addSeconds/minusSeconds(long)`
- `dividedBy/multipliedBy`

We also have a number of convenient factory and extraction methods, such as the following:

- `ofDays(long)/toDays()`
- `ofHours(long)/toHours()`

- `ofMinutes(long)/toMinutes()`
- `ofSeconds(long)/toSeconds()`

A `parse()` method is also supplied. Unfortunately, perhaps, for some, the input for this method may not be what you might expect. Since we're dealing with a duration that is often, say, in hours and minutes, you might expect the method to accept something like "1:37" for 1 hour and 37 minutes. However, that will cause the system to throw `DateTimeParseException`. What the method expects to receive is a string in an ISO-8601 format, which looks like this--`PnDTnHnMn.nS`. That's pretty fantastic, isn't it? While it may be confusing at first, it's not too bad once you understand it:

- The first character is an optional + (plus) or – (minus) sign.
- The next character is `P` and can be either uppercase or lowercase.
- What follows is at least one of four sections indicating days (`D`), hours (`H`), minutes (`M`), and seconds (`S`). Again, case doesn't matter.
- They must be declared in this order.
- Each section has a numeric part that includes an optional + or – sign, one or more ASCII digits, and the unit of measure indicator. The seconds amount may be fractional (expressed as a floating point number) and may use a period or a comma.
- The letter `T` must come before the first instance of hours, minutes, or seconds.

Simple, right? It may not be very friendly to a non-technical audience, but that it supports encoding a duration in a string that allows unambiguous parsing is a huge step forward.

Period

`Period` is a date-based unit of time. Whereas `Duration` was about time (hours, minutes, seconds, and so on), `Period` is about years, weeks, months, and so forth. Like `Duration`, it exposes several arithmetic methods to add and subtract, though these deal with years, months, and days. It also offers `plus(long amount, TemporalUnit unit)` (and the equivalent `minus`) as well.

Also, like `Duration`, `Period` has a `parse()` method, which also takes an ISO-8601 format that looks like this--`PnYnMnD` and `PnW`. Based on the discussion earlier, the structure is probably pretty obvious:

- The string starts with an optional sign, followed by the letter `P`.

- After that, for the first form, come three sections, at least one of which must be present--years (Y), months(M), and days (D).
- For the second form, there is only one section--weeks (W).
- The amount in each section can have a positive or negative sign.
- The W unit can't be combined with the others. Internally, the amount is multiplied by 7 and treated as days.

Clock

Clock is an abstract class that provides access to the current instant (which we will see next), date, and time using a timezone. Prior to Java 8, we would have to call System.currentTimeInMillis() and TimeZone.getDefault() to calculate these values. Clock provides a nice interface to get that from one object.

The Javadoc states that the use of Clock is purely optional. In fact, the major date/time classes have a now() method that uses the system clock to get their value. If, however, you need to provide an alternate implementation (say, in testing, you need the LocalTime in another timezone), this abstract class can be extended to provide the functionality needed, and can then be passed to the appropriate now() method.

Instant

An Instant is a single, exact point in time (or **on the timeline**, you'll see the Javadoc say). This class offers arithmetic methods, much like Period and Duration. Parsing is also an option, with the string being an ISO-8601 instant format such as 1977-02-16T08:15:30Z.

LocalDate

LocalDate is a date without a timezone. While the value of this class is a date (year, month, and day), there are accessor methods for other values, which are as follows:

- getDayOfWeek(): This returns the DayOfWeek enum for the day of the week represented by the date.
- getDayOfYear(): This returns the day of the year (1 to 365, or 366 for leap years) represented by the date. This is a 1-based counter from January 1 of the specified year.
- getEra(): This returns the ISO era for the given date.

Local dates can be parsed from a string, of course, but, this time, the format seems much more reasonable--yyyy-mm-dd. If you need a different format, the `parse()` method has been overridden to allow you to specify the `DateTimeFormatter` that can handle the format of the string.

LocalTime

`LocalTime` is the time-based equivalent of `LocalDate`. It stores `HH:MM:SS`, but does **not** store the timezone. Parsing times requires the format above, but, just like `LocalDate`, does allow you to specify a `DateTimeFormatter` for alternate string representations.

LocalDateTime

`LocalDateTime` is basically a combination of the last two classes. All of the arithmetic, factory, and extraction methods apply as expected. Parsing the text is also a combination of the two, except that `T` must separate the date and time portions of the string--`'2016-01-01T00:00:00'`. This class **does not** store or represent a timezone.

ZonedDateTime

If you need to represent a date/time **and** a timezone, then `ZonedDateTime` is the class you need. As you might expect, this class' interface is a combination of `LocalDate` and `LocalTime`, with extra methods added for handling the timezone.

As shown at length in the overview of duration's API (and hinted at, though not as clearly shown in the other classes), one of the strong points of this new API is the ability to manipulate and process various date and time artifacts mathematically. It is precisely this functionality that we will spend most of our time with in this project as we explore this new library.

Back to our code

The first part of the process we need to tackle is parsing the user-provided string into something we can use programmatically. If you were to search for a parser generator, you would find a myriad of options, with tools such as Antlr and JavaCC showing up near the top. It's tempting to turn to one of these tools, but our purposes here are pretty simple, and the grammar is not all that complex. Our functional requirements include:

- We want to be able to add/subtract time to/from a date or a time

- We want to be able to subtract one date or time from another to get the difference between the two
- We want to be able to convert a time from one timezone to another

For something as simple as this, a parser is far too expensive, both in terms of complexity and binary size. We can easily write a parser using tools built into the JDK, which is what we'll do.

To set the stage before we get into the code, the plan is this--we will define a number of **tokens** to represent logical parts of a date calculation expression. Using regular expressions, we will break down the given string, returning a list of these tokens, which will then be processed **left to right** to return the result.

That said, let's make a list of the types of token we'll need. We'll need one for a date, a time, the operator, any numeric amount, the unit of measure, and the timezone. Obviously, we won't need each of these for every expression, but that should cover all of our given use cases.

Let's start with a base class for our tokens. When defining a type hierarchy, it's always good to ask whether you want a base class or an interface. Using an interface gives the developer extra flexibility with regard to the class hierarchy should the need arise to extend a different class. A base class, however, allows us to provide default behavior at the cost of some rigidity in the hierarchy of the type. To make our `Token` implementations as simple as possible, we'd like to put as much in the base class as possible, so we'll use a base class as follows:

```
public abstract class Token<T> {
  protected T value;
  public interface Info {
    String getRegex();
    Token getToken(String text);
  }
  public T getValue() {
    return value;
  }
}
```

Java 8 did introduce a means to provide default behavior from an interface, that being a **default methods**. A default method is a method on an interface that provides a concrete implementation, which is a significant departure from interfaces. Prior to this change, all interfaces could do was define the method signature and force the implementing class to define the body. This allows us to add methods to an interface and provide a default implementation so that existing implementations of the interface need not change. In our case, the behavior we're providing is the storing of a value (the instance variable `value`) and the accessor for it (`getValue()`), so an interface with a default method is not appropriate.

Note that we've also defined a nested interface, `Info`, which we will cover in more detail when we get to the parser.

With our base class defined, we can now create the tokens we will need as follows:

```
public class DateToken extends Token<LocalDate> {
   private static final String TODAY = "today";
   public static String REGEX =
      "\\d{4}[-/][01]\\d[-/][0123]\\d|today";
```

To start the class, we define two constants. TODAY is a special string that we will allow the user to specify today's date. The second is the regular expression we'll use to identify a date string:

```
"\\d{4}[-/][01]\\d[-/][0123]\\d|today"
```

It's no secret that regular expressions are ugly, and as these things go, this one's not too terribly complicated. We're matching 4 digits (`\\d{4}`), either a - or / (`[-/]`), a 0 or 1 followed by any digit (`[01]\\d`), another - or /, then a 0, 1, 2, or 3 followed by any digit. Finally, the last segment, `|today`, tells the system to match on the pattern that comes before, **or** the text `today`. All this regular expression can do is identify a string that **looks** like a date. In its current form, it can't actually ensure that it is valid. We can probably make a regex that can do exactly that, but the complexity that would introduce is just not worth it. What we can do though is let the JDK validate the string for us, which we'll do in the `of` method, as shown here:

```
public static DateToken of(String text) {
   try {
     return TODAY.equals(text.toLowerCase()) ?
       new DateToken(LocalDate.now()) :
       new DateToken(
         LocalDate.parse(text.replace("/", "-")));
   } catch (DateTimeParseException ex) {
       throw new DateCalcException(
         "Invalid date format: " + text);
```

```
            }
     }
```

Here, we've defined a static method to handle the creation of the `DateToken` instance. If the user provides the string `today`, we provide the value `LocalDate.now()`, which does what you think it might. Otherwise, we pass the string to `LocalDate.parse()`, changing any forward slashes to dashes, as that's what the method expects. If the user provided an invalid date, but the regular expression still matched it, we'll get an error here. Since we have built-in support to validate the string, we can content ourselves with letting the system do the heavy lifting for us.

The other tokens look very similar. Rather than showing each class, much of which would be very familiar, we'll skip most of those classes and just look at the regular expressions, as some are quite complex. Take a look at the following code:

```
public class IntegerToken extends Token<Integer> {
    public static final String REGEX = "\\d+";
```

Well, that one's not too bad, is it? One or more digits will match here:

```
public class OperatorToken extends Token<String> {
    public static final String REGEX = "\\+|-|to";
```

Another relatively simple one, which will match a +, a -, or the `to` text:

```
public class TimeToken extends Token<LocalTime> {
    private static final String NOW = "now";
    public static final String REGEX =
      "(?:[01]?\\d|2[0-3]):[0-5]\\d *(?:[AaPp][Mm])?|now";
```

The regular expression breaks down like this:

- `(?:`: This is a non-capturing group. We need to group some rules together, but we don't want them to show up as separate groups when we process this in our Java code.
- `[01]?`: This is a zero or a one. The `?` indicates that this should occur once or not at all.
- `|2[0-3]`: We either want to match the first half, **or** this section, which will be a 2 followed by a 0, 1, 2, or 3.
- `)`: This ends the non-capturing group. This group will allow us to match 12 or 24-hour times.
- `:`: This position requires a colon. Its presence is not optional.
- `[0-5]\\d`: Next, the pattern must match a digit of `0-5` followed by another digit. This is the minutes portion of the time.

- ' * ': It's hard to see, so I've added quotes to help indicate it, but we want to match 0 or more (as indicated by the asterisk) spaces.
- (?:: This is another non-capturing group.
- [AaPp] [Mm]: These are the A or P letters (of either case) followed by an M (also of either case).
-) ?: We end the non-capturing group, but mark it with a ? to indicate that it should occur once or not all. This group lets us capture any AM/PM designation.
- |now: Much like today above, we allow the user to specify this string to indicate the current time.

Again, this pattern may match an invalid time string, but we'll let LocalTime.parse() handle that for us in TimeToken.of():

```
public static TimeToken of(final String text) {
   String time = text.toLowerCase();
   if (NOW.equals(time)) {
   return new TimeToken(LocalTime.now());
   } else {
       try {
         if (time.length() <5) {
             time = "0" + time;
         }
         if (time.contains("am") || time.contains("pm")) {
           final DateTimeFormatter formatter =
             new DateTimeFormatterBuilder()
             .parseCaseInsensitive()
             .appendPattern("hh:mma")
             .toFormatter();
             return new
             TimeToken(LocalTime.parse(
                time.replaceAll(" ", ""), formatter));
         } else {
             return new TimeToken(LocalTime.parse(time));
         }
       } catch (DateTimeParseException ex) {
          throw new DateCalcException(
          "Invalid time format: " + text);
       }
   }
}
```

This is a bit more complex than others, primarily because of the default format expected by `LocalTime.parse()`, which is an ISO-8601 time format. Typically, time is specified in a 12-hour format with an am/pm designation. Unfortunately, that's not how the API works, so we have to make adjustments.

First, we pad the hour, if needed. Second, we look to see if the user specified `"am"` or `"pm"`. If so, we need to create a special formatter, which is done via `DateTimeFormatterBuilder`. We start by telling the builder to build a case-insensitve formatter. If we don't do that, `"AM"` will work, but `"am"` will not. Next, we append the pattern we want, which is hours, minutes, and am/pm, then build the formatter. Finally, we can parse our text, which we do by passing the string and the formatter to `LocalTime.parse()`. If all goes well, we'll get a `LocalTime` instance back. If not, we get an `Exception` instance, which we will handle. Note that we call `replaceAll()` on our string. We do that to strip any spaces out between the time and am/pm. Otherwise, the parse will fail.

Finally, we come to our `UnitOfMeasureToken`. This token isn't necessarily complex, but it's certainly not simple. For our units of measure, we want to support the words `year`, `month`, `day`, `week`, `hour`, `minute`, and `second`, all of which can be plural, and most of which can be abbreviated to their initial character. This makes the regular expression interesting:

```
public class UnitOfMeasureToken extends Token<ChronoUnit> {
    public static final String REGEX =
        "years|year|y|months|month|weeks|week|w|days|
        day|d|hours|hour|h|minutes|minute|m|seconds|second|s";
    private static final Map<String, ChronoUnit> VALID_UNITS =
        new HashMap<>();
```

That's not so much complex as ugly. We have a list of possible strings, separated by the logical OR operator, the vertical pipe. It is probably possible to write a regular expression that searches for each word, or parts of it, but such an expression will likely be very difficult to write correctly, and almost certainly hard to debug or change. Simple and clear is almost always better than clever and complex.

There's one last element here that needs discussion: `VALID_UNITS`. In a static initializer, we build a `Map` to allow looking up the correct `ChronoUnit`:

```
static {
    VALID_UNITS.put("year", ChronoUnit.YEARS);
    VALID_UNITS.put("years", ChronoUnit.YEARS);
    VALID_UNITS.put("months", ChronoUnit.MONTHS);
    VALID_UNITS.put("month", ChronoUnit.MONTHS);
```

And so on.

We're now ready to take a look at the parser, which is as follows:

```
public class DateCalcExpressionParser {
  private final List<InfoWrapper> infos = new ArrayList<>();

  public DateCalcExpressionParser() {
    addTokenInfo(new DateToken.Info());
    addTokenInfo(new TimeToken.Info());
    addTokenInfo(new IntegerToken.Info());
    addTokenInfo(new OperatorToken.Info());
    addTokenInfo(new UnitOfMeasureToken.Info());
  }
  private void addTokenInfo(Token.Info info) {
    infos.add(new InfoWrapper(info));
  }
```

When we build our parser, we register each of our `Token` classes in a `List`, but we see two new types: `Token.Info` and `InfoWrapper`. `Token.Info` is an interface nested inside the `Token` class:

```
public interface Info {
  String getRegex();
  Token getToken(String text);
}
```

We have added this interface to give us a convenient way to get the regular expression for a `Token` class, as well as the `Token`, without having to resort to reflection. `DateToken.Info`, for example, looks like this:

```
public static class Info implements Token.Info {
  @Override
  public String getRegex() {
    return REGEX;
  }

  @Override
  public DateToken getToken(String text) {
    return of(text);
  }
}
```

Since this is a nested class, we get easy access to members, including statics, of the enclosing class.

The next new type, `InfoWrapper`, looks like this:

```
private class InfoWrapper {
  Token.Info info;
  Pattern pattern;

  InfoWrapper(Token.Info info) {
    this.info = info;
    pattern = Pattern.compile("^(" + info.getRegex() + ")");
  }
}
```

This is a simple, private class, so some of the normal encapsulation rules can be set aside (although, should this class ever be made public, this would certainly need to be cleaned up). What we're doing, though, is storing a compiled version of the token's regular expression. Note that we're wrapping the regular expression with a couple of extra characters. The first, the caret (^), says that the match must be at the beginning of the text. We're also wrapping the regular expression in parentheses. However, this time this is a capturing group. We'll see why in the following parse method:

```
public List<Token> parse(String text) {
  final Queue<Token> tokens = new ArrayDeque<>();

  if (text != null) {
    text = text.trim();
    if (!text.isEmpty()) {
      boolean matchFound = false;
      for (InfoWrapper iw : infos) {
        final Matcher matcher = iw.pattern.matcher(text);
        if (matcher.find()) {
          matchFound = true;
          String match = matcher.group().trim();
          tokens.add(iw.info.getToken(match));
          tokens.addAll(
            parse(text.substring(match.length())));
          break;
        }
      }
      if (!matchFound) {
        throw new DateCalcException(
          "Could not parse the expression: " + text);
      }
    }
  }

  return tokens;
}
```

We start by making sure that `text` is not null, then `trim()` it, then make sure it's not empty. With the sanity checks done, we loop through the `List` of info wrappers to find a match. Remember that the pattern compiled is a capturing group looking at the start of the text, so we loop through each `Pattern` until one matches. If we don't find a match, we throw an `Exception`.

Once we find a match, we extract the matching text from `Matcher`, then, using `Token.Info`, we call `getToken()` to get a `Token` instance for the matching `Pattern`. We store that in our list, then recursively call the `parse()` method, passing a substring of text starting after our match. That removes the matched text from the original, then repeats the process until the string is empty. Once the recursion ends and things unwind, we return a `Queue` of tokens that represent the string the user provided. We use a `Queue` instead of, say, a `List`, as that will make processing a bit easier. We now have a parser, but our work is only half done. Now we need to process those tokens.

In the spirit of Separation of Concerns, we've encapsulated the processing of these tokens-- the actual calculation of the expression--in a separate class, `DateCalculator`, which uses our parser. Consider the following code:

```
public class DateCalculator {
    public DateCalculatorResult calculate(String text) {
        final DateCalcExpressionParser parser =
          new DateCalcExpressionParser();
        final Queue<Token> tokens = parser.parse(text);

        if (tokens.size() > 0) {
          if (tokens.peek() instanceof DateToken) {
            return handleDateExpression(tokens);
          } else if (tokens.peek() instanceof TimeToken) {
              return handleTimeExpression(tokens);
          }
        }
        throw new DateCalcException("An invalid expression
          was given: " + text);
    }
}
```

Each time `calculate()` is called, we create a new instance of the parser. Also, note that, as we look at the rest of the code, we pass the `Queue` around. While that does make the method signatures a bit bigger, it also makes the class thread-safe, as there's no state held in the class itself.

After our `isEmpty()` check, we can see where the `Queue` API comes in handy. By calling `poll()`, we get a reference to the next element in the collection, but--and this is important--**we leave the element in the collection**. This lets us look at it without altering the state of the collection. Based on the type of the first element in the collection, we delegate to the appropriate method.

For handling dates, the expression syntax is `<date>` `<operator>` `<date | number unit_of_measure>`. We can start our processing, then, by extracting a `DateToken` and an `OperatorToken`, as follows:

```
private DateCalculatorResult handleDateExpression(
  final Queue<Token> tokens) {
    DateToken startDateToken = (DateToken) tokens.poll();
    validateToken(tokens.peek(), OperatorToken.class);
    OperatorToken operatorToken = (OperatorToken) tokens.poll();
    Token thirdToken = tokens.peek();

    if (thirdToken instanceof IntegerToken) {
      return performDateMath(startDateToken, operatorToken,
        tokens);
    } else if (thirdToken instanceof DateToken) {
      return getDateDiff(startDateToken, tokens.poll());
      } else {
        throw new DateCalcException("Invalid expression");
      }
  }
```

To retrieve an element from a `Queue`, we use the `poll()` method, and we can safely cast that to `DateToken` since we checked that in the calling method. Next, we `peek()` at the next element and, via the `validateToken()` method, we verify that the element is not null and is of the type desired. If the token is valid, we can `poll()` and cast safely. Next, we `peek()` at the third token. Based on its type, we delegate to the correct method to finish the processing. If we find an unexpected `Token` type, we throw an `Exception`.

Before looking at those calculation methods, let's look at `validateToken()`:

```
private void validateToken(final Token token,
  final Class<? extends Token> expected) {
    if (token == null || !
      token.getClass().isAssignableFrom(expected)) {
        throw new DateCalcException(String.format(
          "Invalid format: Expected %s, found %s",
          expected, token != null ?
          token.getClass().getSimpleName() : "null"));
      }
  }
```

There's nothing too terribly exciting here, but eagle-eyed readers might notice that we're returning the class name of our token, and, by doing so, we're leaking the name of a non-exported class to the end user. That's probably not ideal, but we'll leave fixing that as an exercise for the reader.

The method to perform date math looks like this:

```
private DateCalculatorResult performDateMath(
  final DateToken startDateToken,
  final OperatorToken operatorToken,
  final Queue<Token> tokens) {
    LocalDate result = startDateToken.getValue();
    int negate = operatorToken.isAddition() ? 1 : -1;

    while (!tokens.isEmpty()) {
      validateToken(tokens.peek(), IntegerToken.class);
      int amount = ((IntegerToken) tokens.poll()).getValue() *
        negate;
      validateToken(tokens.peek(), UnitOfMeasureToken.class);
      result = result.plus(amount,
      ((UnitOfMeasureToken) tokens.poll()).getValue());
    }

    return new DateCalculatorResult(result);
}
```

Since we already have our starting and operator tokens, we pass those in, as well as the Queue so that we can process the remaining tokens. Our first step is to determine if the operator is a plus or a minus, assigning a positive 1 or a -1 to negate as appropriate. We do this so we can use a single method, LocalDate.plus(). If the operator is a minus, we add a negative number and get the same result as subtracting the original number.

Finally, we loop through the remaining tokens, verifying each one before we process it. We get the IntegerToken; grab its value; multiply it by our negative modifier, negate; then add that value to the LocalDate using the UnitOfMeasureToken to tell what **kind** of value we're adding.

Calculating the difference between dates is pretty straightforward, as we see here:

```
private DateCalculatorResult getDateDiff(
    final DateToken startDateToken, final Token thirdToken) {
  LocalDate one = startDateToken.getValue();
  LocalDate two = ((DateToken) thirdToken).getValue();
  return (one.isBefore(two)) ? new
    DateCalculatorResult(Period.between(one, two)) : new
      DateCalculatorResult(Period.between(two, one));
}
```

We extract the `LocalDate` from our two `DateToken` variables, then call `Period.between()`, which returns a `Period` that indicates the elapsed amount of time between the two dates. We do check to see which date comes first so that we return a positive `Period` to the user as a convenience, since most people don't typically think in terms of negative periods.

The time-based methods are largely identical. The big difference is the time difference method:

```
private DateCalculatorResult getTimeDiff(
    final OperatorToken operatorToken,
    final TimeToken startTimeToken,
    final Token thirdToken) throws DateCalcException {
  LocalTime startTime = startTimeToken.getValue();
  LocalTime endTime = ((TimeToken) thirdToken).getValue();
  return new DateCalculatorResult(
    Duration.between(startTime, endTime).abs());
}
```

The notable difference here is the use of `Duration.between()`. It looks identical to `Period.between()`, but the `Duration` class offers a method that `Period` does not: `abs()`. This method lets us return the absolute value of `Period`, so we can pass our `LocalTime` variable to `between()` in any order we want.

One final note before we leave this--we are wrapping our results in a `DateCalculatorResult` instance. Since the various operations return several different, unrelated types, this allows us to return a single type from our `calculate()` method. It will be up to the calling code to extract the appropriate value. We'll do that in our command-line interface, which we'll look at in the next section.

A brief interlude on testing

Before we move on, we need to visit a topic we've not discussed yet, that being testing. Anyone who has been in the industry for a while has likely heard the term **Test-Driven Development** (or **TDD** for short). It's an approach to software development that posits that the first thing that should be written is a test, which will fail (since there's no code to run), then the code should be written that makes the test **green**, a reference to the green indicator given in IDEs and other tools to indicate that the test has passed. This process repeats as many times as necessary to build the final system, always making changes in small increments, and always starting with a test. A myriad of books have been written on the topic, which is both hotly debated and oftentimes heavily nuanced. The exact way the approach is implemented, if at all, almost always comes in flavors.

Clearly, in our work here, we haven't followed the TDD principle strictly, but that doesn't mean we haven't tested. While TDD purists are likely to quibble, my general approach tends to be a bit looser on the testing side until my API starts to solidify some. How long this takes depends on how familiar I am with the technologies being used. If I'm very familiar with them, I might sketch out a quick interface, then scaffold a test based on that as a means of testing the API itself, then iterate over that. For new libraries, I might write a very broad test to help drive the investigation of the new library, using the test framework as a means for bootstrapping a runtime environment in which I can experiment. Regardless, at the end of the development effort, the new system should be **fully** tested (with the exact definition of **fully** being another hotly debated concept), which is what I have striven for here. A full treatise on testing and test-driven development is beyond our scope here, though.

When it comes to testing in Java, you have a **lot** of options. However, the two most common ones are TestNG and JUnit, with JUnit probably being the most popular. Which one should you pick? That depends. If you are working with an existing code-base, you should probably use whatever is already in use, unless you have a good reason to do otherwise. For example, the library could be old and no longer supported, it could be demonstrably insufficient for your needs, or you've been given an express directive to update/replace the existing system. If any of those conditions, or others similar to these, are true, we circle back to the question--*Which should I choose?* Again, that depends. JUnit is extremely popular and common, so using it might make sense in order to lower the barrier of entry into a project. However, TestNG has what some feel to be a much better, cleaner API. For example, TestNG does not require the use of static methods for certain test setup methods. It also aims to be much more than just a unit testing framework, providing tools for unit, functional, end-to-end, and integration testing. For our tests here, we will be using TestNG.

To get started with TestNG, we need to add it to our project. To do that, we will add a test dependency to the Maven POM file as follows:

```
<properties>
  <testng.version>6.9.9</testng.version>
</properties>
<dependencies>
  <dependency>
    <groupId>org.testng</groupId>
    <artifactId>testng</artifactId>
    <version>${testng.version}</version>
    <scope>test</scope>
  </dependency>
</dependencies>
```

Writing the tests is very simple. With the defaults of the TestNG Maven plugin, the class simply needs to be in `src/test/java` and end with the `Test` string. Each test method needs to be annotated with `@Test`.

There are a number of tests in the library module, so let's start with some of the very basic ones that test the regular expressions used by the tokens to identify and extract the relevant parts of the expression. For example, consider the following piece of code:

```
public class RegexTest {
  @Test
  public void dateTokenRegex() {
    testPattern(DateToken.REGEX, "2016-01-01");
    testPattern(DateToken.REGEX, "today");
  }
  private void testPattern(String pattern, String text) {
    testPattern(pattern, text, false);
  }

  private void testPattern(String pattern, String text,
    boolean exact) {
      Pattern p = Pattern.compile("(" + pattern + ")");
      final Matcher matcher = p.matcher(text);

      Assert.assertTrue(matcher.find());
      if (exact) {
        Assert.assertEquals(matcher.group(), text);
      }
  }
```

This is a very basic test of the `DateToken` regular expression. The test delegates to the `testPattern()` method, passing the regular expression to test, and a string to test it with. Our functionality is tested by following these steps:

1. Compiling the `Pattern`.
2. Creating a `Matcher`.
3. Calling the `matcher.find()` method.

With that, the logic of the system under test is exercised. What remains is to verify that it worked as expected. We do that with our call to `Assert.assertTrue()`. We assert that `matcher.find()` returns `true`. If the regex is correct, we should get a `true` response. If the regex is not correct, we'll get a `false` response. In the latter case, `assertTrue()` will throw an `Exception` and the test will fail.

This test is certainly very basic. It could--should--be more robust. It should test a greater variety of strings. It should include some strings known to be bad to make sure we're not getting incorrect results in our tests. There are probably a myriad of other enhancements that could be made. The point here, though, is to show a simple test to demonstrate how to set up a TestNG-based environment. Before moving on, let's look at a couple more examples.

Here's a test to check for failure (a **negative test**):

```
@Test
public void invalidStringsShouldFail() {
  try {
    parser.parse("2016/12/25 this is nonsense");
    Assert.fail("A DateCalcException should have been
      thrown (Unable to identify token)");
  } catch (DateCalcException dce) {
  }
}
```

In this test, we expect the call to `parse()` to fail, with a `DateCalcException`. Should the call **not** fail, we have a call to `Assert.fail()` that will force the test to fail with the message provided. If the `Exception` is thrown, it's swallowed silently and the test finishes successfully.

Swallowing the `Exception` is one approach, but you can also tell TestNG to expect an `Exception` to be thrown, as we've done here via the `expectedExceptions` attribute:

```
@Test(expectedExceptions = {DateCalcException.class})
public void shouldRejectBadTimes() {
  parser.parse("22:89");
}
```

Again, we're passing a bad string to the parser. However, this time, we're telling TestNG to expect the exception via the annotation--`@Test(expectedExceptions = {DateCalcException.class})`.

Much more could be written on testing in general and TestNG in particular. A thorough treatment of both topics is beyond our scope, but if you are not familiar with either topic, you would be well served to find one of the many great resources available and study them thoroughly.

For now, let's turn our attention to the command-line interface.

Building the command-line interface

In the last chapter, we built a command-line tool using the Crest library from Tomitribe, and it worked out pretty well, so we will return to the library in building this command line as well.

To enable Crest in our project, we must do two things. First, we have to configure our POM file as follows:

```
<dependency>
  <groupId>org.tomitribe</groupId>
  <artifactId>tomitribe-crest</artifactId>
  <version>0.8</version>
</dependency>
```

We must also update our module definition in `src/main/java/module-info.java` as follows:

```
module datecalc.cli {
  requires datecalc.lib;
  requires tomitribe.crest;
  requires tomitribe.crest.api;
  exports com.steeplesoft.datecalc.cli;
}
```

We can now define our CLI class like this:

```
public class DateCalc {
  @Command
  public void dateCalc(String... args) {
    final String expression = String.join(" ", args);
    final DateCalculator dc = new DateCalculator();
    final DateCalculatorResult dcr = dc.calculate(expression);
```

Unlike in the last chapter, this command line will be extremely simple, as the only input we need is the expression to evaluate. With the preceding method signature, we tell Crest to pass all of the command-line arguments as the `args` value, which we then join back together via `String.join()` into `expression`. Next, we create our calculator and calculate the result.

We now need to interrogate our `DateCalcResult` to determine the nature of the expression. Consider the following piece of code as an example:

```
String result = "";
if (dcr.getDate().isPresent()) {
  result = dcr.getDate().get().toString();
} else if (dcr.getTime().isPresent()) {
  result = dcr.getTime().get().toString();
} else if (dcr.getDuration().isPresent()) {
  result = processDuration(dcr.getDuration().get());
} else if (dcr.getPeriod().isPresent()) {
  result = processPeriod(dcr.getPeriod().get());
}
System.out.println(String.format("'%s' equals '%s'",
  expression, result));
```

The `LocalDate` and `LocalTime` responses are pretty straightforward--we can simply call the `toString()` method on them, as the defaults are, for our purposes here, perfectly acceptable. Duration and periods are a bit more complicated. Both provide a number of methods to extract the details. We will hide those details in separate methods:

```
private String processDuration(Duration d) {
  long hours = d.toHoursPart();
  long minutes = d.toMinutesPart();
  long seconds = d.toSecondsPart();
  String result = "";
  if (hours > 0) {
    result += hours + " hours, ";
  }
  result += minutes + " minutes, ";
  if (seconds > 0) {
    result += seconds + " seconds";
```

```
    }

    return result;
  }
```

The method itself is pretty simple--we extract the various parts from `Duration`, then build the string based on whether or not the part returns values.

The date-related method, `processPeriod()`, is similar:

```
private String processPeriod(Period p) {
  long years = p.getYears();
  long months = p.getMonths();
  long days = p.getDays();
  String result = "";

  if (years > 0) {
    result += years + " years, ";
  }
  if (months > 0) {
    result += months + " months, ";
  }
  if (days > 0) {
    result += days + " days";
  }
  return result;
}
```

Each of these methods returns the result as a string, which we then write to standard out. And that's it. It's not a terribly complicated command-line utility, but the purpose of the exercise here is found mostly in the library.

Summary

Our date calculator is now complete. The utility itself is not too terribly complex, although, it did serve as expected, which has to be a vehicle for experimenting with Java 8's Date/Time API. In addition to the new date/time API, we scratched the surface of regular expressions, a very powerful and complex tool to parse strings. We also revisited the command-line utility library from the last chapter, and dipped our toes in the waters of unit testing and test-driven development.

In the next chapter, we'll get a bit more ambitious and step into the world of social media, building an app to help us aggregate some of our favorite services into a single application.

5
Sunago - A Social Media Aggregator

For our next project, we'll try something a bit more ambitious; we'll build a desktop application that aggregates data from various social media networks and displays it in one seamless interaction. We're also going to try something new, and we're going to give this project a name, something that might be a bit more appealing than the dry, albeit accurate, `description-turned-name` that we've used to date. This application, then, we'll call Sunago, which is the phonetic spelling of the (Koine) Greek word συνάγω, which means **I gather together**, **collect**, **assemble**.

Building the app will cover several different topics, some familiar, some new. That list includes the following:

- JavaFX
- Internationalization and localization
- **Service Provider Interfaces** (**SPI**)
- REST API consumption
- `ClassLoader` manipulation
- Lambdas, lambdas, and more lambdas

As usual, those are the just the highlights with a number of interesting items sprinkled throughout.

Getting started

As with every application, before we get started, we need to think about what we want the application to do. That is, what are the functional requirements? At a high level, the description tells us what we want to achieve in broad terms, but, more specifically, we want the user to be able to do the following:

- Connect to several different social media networks
- Determine, on a network-by-network basis, which group of data (users, lists, and more) to retrieve
- See list of items from each network in a consolidated display
- Be able to determine from which network an item came
- Click on an item and have it loaded in the user's default browser

In addition to this list of things the application **should** do, the things it **shouldn't** do include the following:

- Respond/reply to items
- Comment on items
- Manage friends/following lists

These features would be great additions to the application, but they don't offer much that would be architecturally interesting beyond the basic application detailed previously, so, to keep things simple--and moving along--we'll limit the scope to the given basic set of requirements.

So where to start on the application? As in the previous chapters, we're going to make this a desktop application, so let's start there, with a JavaFX application. I'm going to tip my hand a little bit here to make things easier later on: this will be a multi-module project, so we first need to create the parent project. In NetBeans, click on **File | New Project...**, and select the Maven category, as seen in the following screenshot:

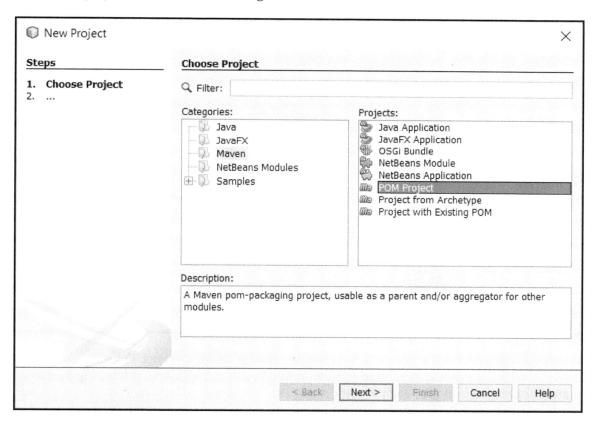

Click on the **Next** button, and fill in the project details, as shown next:

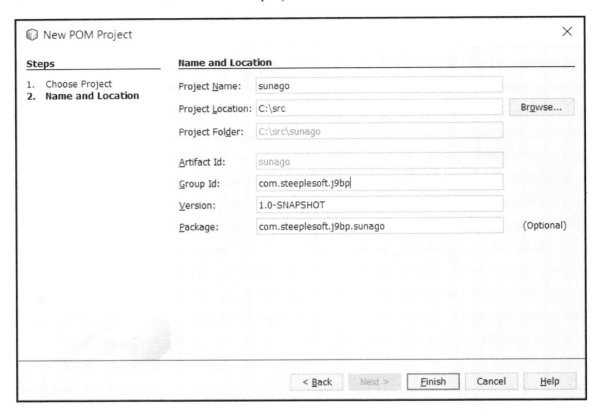

When you click on **Finish**, you will be presented with an empty project. Once we add modules to this project, differentiating them might become difficult, so something I do as a matter of practice is to give each module a distinct, "namespaced" name. That is to say, each module has its own name, of course, but I prefix that with the name of the project. For example, since this is the base POM of the project, I call it `Master`. To reflect that, I modify the generated POM to look something like this:

```xml
<?xml version="1.0" encoding="UTF-8"?>
<project xmlns="http://maven.apache.org/POM/4.0.0"
    xmlns:xsi="http://www.w3.org/2001/XMLSchema-instance"
    xsi:schemaLocation="http://maven.apache.org/POM/4.0.0
    http://maven.apache.org/xsd/maven-4.0.0.xsd">
    <modelVersion>4.0.0</modelVersion>
    <groupId>com.steeplesoft.sunago</groupId>
    <artifactId>master</artifactId>
    <version>1.0-SNAPSHOT</version>
```

```
      <name>Sunago - Master</name>
      <packaging>pom</packaging>
</project>
```

There's really not much to this yet. The advantage that a parent POM like this gives us is that we can build all the projects with one command if we so desire, and we can move any shared configuration to this shared parent POM to reduce duplication. What we need to add now, though, is a module, which NetBeans helps us do, as seen in this screenshot:

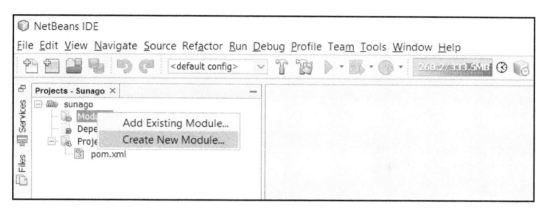

After clicking on **Create New Module...**, you will be presented with the familiar **New Project** window, from which you'll want to select **Maven | JavaFX Application**, and click on **Next**. In the **New Java Application** screen, enter app for the project name, and click on **Finish** (all of the other defaults are acceptable as-is).

Again, we want to give this module a meaningful name, so let's modify the generated pom.xml as follows:

```
<?xml version="1.0" encoding="UTF-8"?>
<project xmlns="http://maven.apache.org/POM/4.0.0"
  xmlns:xsi="http://www.w3.org/2001/XMLSchema-instance"
  xsi:schemaLocation="http://maven.apache.org/POM/4.0.0
  http://maven.apache.org/xsd/maven-4.0.0.xsd">
  <modelVersion>4.0.0</modelVersion>
  <parent>
    <groupId>com.steeplesoft.sunago</groupId>
    <artifactId>master</artifactId>
    <version>1.0-SNAPSHOT</version>
  </parent>
  <artifactId>sunago</artifactId>
  <name>Sunago - App</name>
  <packaging>jar</packaging>
</project>
```

When NetBeans creates the project, it will generate several artifacts for us--two classes, `FXMLController` and `MainApp`, as well as the resources, `fxml/Scene.xml` and `styles/Styles.css`. While this may be stating the obvious, artifacts should have names that clearly communicate their purpose, so let's rename these.

The class `FxmlContoller` should be renamed to `SunagoController`. Perhaps the quickest and easiest way to do this is to open the class by double-clicking on it in **Project View**, then, in the source editor, click on the name of the class in the class declaration, and press *Ctrl* + *R*. The **Rename Class** dialog should appear, in which you need to enter the new name, and press *Enter*. This will rename the class and the file for you. Now repeat that process for `MainApp`, renaming it to `Sunago`.

We also want to rename the generated FXML file, `Scene.xml`, to `sunago.fxml`. To do that, right-click on the file in **Project View** and select **Rename...** from the context menu. Enter the new name (without the extension) in the **Rename** dialog, and press *Enter*. While we're at it, let's also rename `Styles.css` to `styles.css` so that the case is consistent. It's a minor thing, but consistency in the code can help produce confidence in you in whoever might take over your code in the future.

Unfortunately, renaming these files doesn't adjust the references to them in the Java sources, so we need to edit `Sunago.java` to point to these new names, which is done as follows:

```
@Override
public void start(Stage stage) throws Exception {
  Parent root = fxmlLoader.load(
    getClass().getResource("/fxml/sunago.fxml"));

    Scene scene = new Scene(root);
    scene.getStylesheets().add("/styles/styles.css");

    stage.setTitle("Sunago, your social media aggregator");
    stage.setScene(scene);
    stage.show();
}
```

Note also that we changed the title to something more appropriate.

Setting up the user interface

If we wanted to, we could now run our application. It would be very boring, but it would run. Let's try to fix the boring part.

The default FXML created is just an **AnchorPane** with two children, a **Button** and a **Label**. We don't need any of those, so let's get rid of them. Our main user interface will be pretty simple--basically, just a vertical stack of components--so we can use a **VBox** as our root component. Perhaps, the easiest way to change the root component from the **AnchorPane** that's there to a **VBox** is to use Scene Builder to wrap that component in a **VBox**, and then delete the **AnchorPane**:

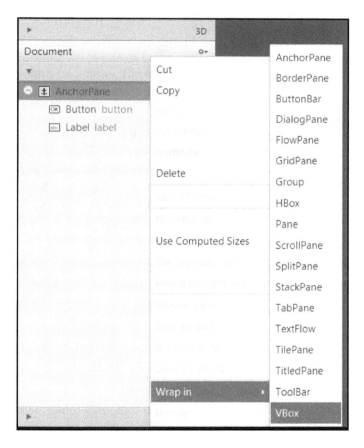

To do that, open the FXML file in Scene Builder by double-clicking on the file (assuming you've configured NetBeans correctly so that it knows where to find Scene Builder. If not, refer back to `Chapter 1`, *Introduction*). In Scene Builder, right-click on **AnchorPane** in the **Document** section of the accordion on the left, select **Wrap in**, and then **VBox**, as shown in the preceding screenshot. Scene Builder will then modify the FXML file, making **AnchorPane** a child of **VBox** as expected. Once that's done, you can right-click on **AnchorPane**, and click on **Delete** to remove it and its children. This leaves us with an empty user interface that's more boring than it was when we began. We can fix that now by adding a couple of controls--a **MenuBar** and a **ListView**. We do that by clicking on each component in the **Controls** section of the accordion and dragging them to **VBox**. If you drop the components on **VBox**, they will be appended to its list of children. Make sure that **MenuBar** comes before **ListView**, or you'll have a very strange user interface.

Let's configure these components a bit now before we return to the code. Selecting **VBox** from the **Document** section on the left, we then need to select the **Layout** section in the accordion on the right. For **Min Width** and **Min Height**, enter `640` and `480` respectively. This will make the window's default size larger and more user-friendly.

For **MenuBar**, we need to expand its entry under **Document**, then expand each of its **Menu** children, which should reveal one **MenuItem** per **Menu**. Click on the first **Menu**, then, on the right, set `Text` to `_File`, and check **Mnemonic Parsing**. This will allow the user to press *Alt + F* to activate (or show) this menu. Next, click on its `MenuItem` child, setting `Text` to `_Exit`, and check **Mnemonic Parsing.** (If the text for a `Menu`, `MenuItem`, `Button`, and more has an underscore in it, make sure that **Mnemonic Parsing** is checked. For brevity's sake, I won't flag this explicitly again.) Open the **Code** section, and set the **On Action** value to `closeApplication`.

The second `Menu` should have its **Text** value set to `_Edit`. Its `MenuItem` should be labeled `_Settings`, and have an **On Action** value of `showPreferences`. Finally, the third `Menu` should be labeled `_Help`, and its `MenuItem` labeled `About` with an **On Action** of `showAbout`.

Next, we want to give `ListView` an ID, so select that on the left, make sure the **Code** section is expanded on the right, and enter `entriesListView` for **fx:id**.

The last edit we need to make is to set the controller. We do that in the accordion on the left, in the **Controller** section at the very bottom. Expand that, and make sure that the **Controller class** value matches the Java class and package we just created in NetBeans, then save the file.

Setting up the controller

Back in NetBeans, we need to fix up our controller to reflect the changes we just made in our FXML. In `SunagoController`, we need to add the `entriesListView` property as follows:

```
@FXML
private ListView<SocialMediaItem> entriesListView;
```

Notice that the parameterized type is `SocialMediaItem`. That's a custom model we'll create in just a few moments. Before we tackle that, though, we need to finish wiring together our user interface. We defined three `onAction` handlers in the FXML. The corresponding code is as follows:

```
@FXML
public void closeApplication(ActionEvent event) {
  Platform.exit();
}
```

Closing the application is as simple as calling the `exit` method on the `Platform` class. Showing the "about" box is also fairly simple, as we see in the `showAbout` method:

```
@FXML
public void showAbout(ActionEvent event) {
  Alert alert = new Alert(Alert.AlertType.INFORMATION);
  alert.setTitle("About...");
  alert.setHeaderText("Sunago (συνάγω)");
  alert.setContentText("(c) Copyright 2016");
  alert.showAndWait();
}
```

Using the built-in `Alert` class, we construct an instance, and set the values appropriate for an About screen, then display it modally via `showAndWait()`.

The preferences window is a much more complicated piece of logic, so we wrap that up in a new controller class, and call its `showAndWait()` method.

```
@FXML
public void showPreferences(ActionEvent event) {
  PreferencesController.showAndWait();
}
```

Writing the model class

Before we look at that, though, there are a few more items in the main controller that we need to take care of. The first is the model class mentioned earlier, `SocialMediaItem`. As you can probably imagine, the structure of the data returned from a social network can be quite complex, and certainly, varied. The data requirements for a tweet, for example, are likely to be quite different from those for an Instagram post. What we'd like to be able to do, then, is to hide those complexities and differences behind a simple, reusable interface. In the real world, such a simple abstraction is not always possible, but, for our purposes here, we have such an interface in `SocialMediaItem`, as you can see in this piece of code:

```
public interface SocialMediaItem {
    String getProvider();
    String getTitle();
    String getBody();
    String getUrl();
    String getImage();
    Date getTimestamp();
}
```

One of the problems with abstractions is that, to make them reusable, you, occasionally, have to structure them in such a way that they expose properties that may not be used by every implementation. It's not obvious yet, but that is certainly the case here. It's a scenario that some consider to be unacceptable, and they may have a point, but it's really a question of trade-offs. Our options include a slightly bloated interface or a complex system in which each network support module (which we'll get to shortly) provides its own renderer, and the application has to interrogate each module, looking for the renderer that can handle each item while drawing `ListView`. There are likely others, of course, but faced with (at least) those two, for the sake of simplicity and performance, we'll take the first option. When faced with similar situations while designing your own systems, though, you'll need to evaluate the various requirements of your project, and make an appropriate choice. For our needs here, the simple approach is more than adequate.

At any rate, each social media network module will implement that interface to wrap its data. This will give a common interface for the application to consume without needing to know exactly where it came from. We do, though, now need to tell the `ListView` how to draw a cell containing a `SocialMediaItem`. We can do that with this line of code in the `initialize()` method of our controller, as follows:

```
entriesListView.setCellFactory(listView ->
    new SocialMediaItemViewCell());
```

Obviously, that's a lambda. For the curious, the pre-lambda version of the preceding method would look like this:

```
entriesListView.setCellFactory(
  new Callback<ListView<SocialMediaItem>,
  ListCell<SocialMediaItem>>() {
    @Override
    public ListCell<SocialMediaItem> call(
      ListView<SocialMediaItem> param) {
        return new SocialMediaItemViewCell();
      }
});
```

Finishing up the controller

Before we look at `SocialMediaItemViewCell`, there are two more controller items. The first is the list that holds the `ListView` data. Remember that `ListView` operates from an `ObservableList`. This lets us make changes to the data in the list, and have it automatically reflected in the user interface. To create that list, we'll use a JavaFX helper method when we define the class property as follows:

```
private final ObservableList<SocialMediaItem> entriesList =
  FXCollections.observableArrayList();
```

Then we need to connect that `List` to our `ListView`. Back in `intialize()`, we have the following:

```
entriesListView.setItems(entriesList);
```

To finish off the rendering of `SocialMediaItem` interfaces, let's define `SocialMediaItemViewCell` like this:

```
public class SocialMediaItemViewCell extends
  ListCell<SocialMediaItem> {
  @Override
  public void updateItem(SocialMediaItem item, boolean empty) {
    super.updateItem(item, empty);
    if (item != null) {
      setGraphic(buildItemCell(item));
      this.setOnMouseClicked(me -> SunagoUtil
        .openUrlInDefaultApplication(item.getUrl()));
    } else {
      setGraphic(null);
    }
  }
}
```

```java
private Node buildItemCell(SocialMediaItem item) {
  HBox hbox = new HBox();
  InputStream resource = item.getClass()
    .getResourceAsStream("icon.png");
  if (resource != null) {
    ImageView sourceImage = new ImageView();
    sourceImage.setFitHeight(18);
    sourceImage.setPreserveRatio(true);
    sourceImage.setSmooth(true);
    sourceImage.setCache(true);
    sourceImage.setImage(new Image(resource));
    hbox.getChildren().add(sourceImage);
  }

  if (item.getImage() != null) {
    HBox picture = new HBox();
    picture.setPadding(new Insets(0,10,0,0));
    ImageView imageView = new ImageView(item.getImage());
    imageView.setPreserveRatio(true);
    imageView.setFitWidth(150);
    picture.getChildren().add(imageView);
    hbox.getChildren().add(picture);
  }

  Label label = new Label(item.getBody());
  label.setFont(Font.font(null, 20));
  label.setWrapText(true);
  hbox.getChildren().add(label);

  return hbox;
  }

}
```

There's a fair amount happening here, but `updateItem()` is our first point of interest. This is the method that is called every time the row is updated on the screen. Notice that we check to see if `item` is null. We do that because `ListView` calls this method not for every item in its `List`, but for every row in `ListView` that's visible, whether there's data for it or not. That means that, if `List` has five items but `ListView` is tall enough to show ten rows, this method will be called ten times, with the last five calls being made with a null `item`. In those cases, we call `setGraphic(null)` to clear out any item that may have been previously rendered.

If `item` is not null, though, we need to build the `Node` to display the item, which is done in `buildItemCell()`. For each item, we want to render three items--the social media network icon (so users can tell at a glance where the item is from), any image embedded in the item, and, finally, any text/caption from the item. To help arrange that, we start with an `HBox`.

Next, we try to find an icon for the network. If we had a formal contract written up, we would include language in it that would stipulate that the module include a file called `icon.png`, which is in the same package as the module's `SocialMediaItem` implementation. Using the `ClassLoader` for the implementation, then, we try to get an `InputStream` for the resource. We check for null, just to make sure the image was actually found; if so, we create an `ImageView`, set some properties, then wrap the resource in an `Image`, hand that to `ImageView`, then add `ImageView` to `HBox`.

Adding an image for the item

If the item has an image, we handle it in the same way that we did with the network icon image. This time, though, we actually wrap the `ImageView` in another `HBox` before adding it to the outer `HBox`. We do that so that we can add padding around the image (via `picture.setPadding(new Insets())` to give this image some space between it and the network icon.

Finally, we create a `Label` to hold the item's body. We set the font size of the text to `20` points via `label.setFont(Font.font(null, 20))`, and add it to our `HBox`, which we then return to the caller, `updateItem()`.

Any time you have a `ListView`, you are likely going to want a custom `ListCell` implementation like we have here. In some cases, calling `toString()` on the `List` contents might be appropriate, but that's not always the case, and you certainly can't have a complex `ListCell` structure like we have here without implementing `ListCell` yourself. If you're planning on doing much JavaFX development, you would be well advised to get comfortable with this technique.

Building the preferences user interface

We're finally **finished** with the main controller, and we can turn our attention to the next big piece, PreferencesController. Our preferences dialog will be, as is usually expected, a modal dialog. It will offer a tabbed interface with one tab for general settings, then a tab for each supported social network. We start that work by adding a new FXML file and controller to our project, and NetBeans has a great wizard for that. Right-click on the desired package, and click on **New | Other**. From the **Categories** list, select JavaFX, and then, from the **File Types** lists, select Empty FXML as shown in the following screenshot:

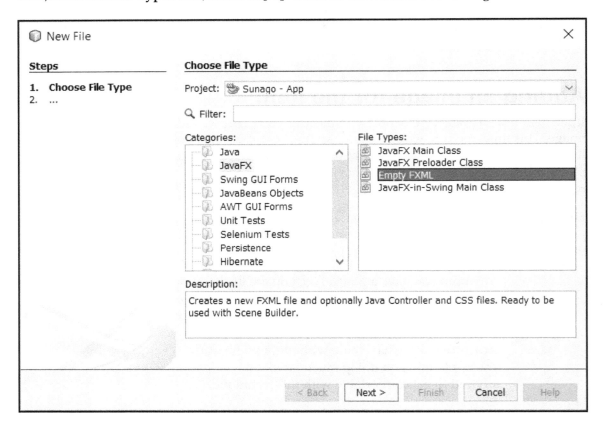

After clicking on **Next**, you should see the **FXML Name and Location** step. This will allow us to specify the name of our new file and the package in which it is created, as seen in this screenshot:

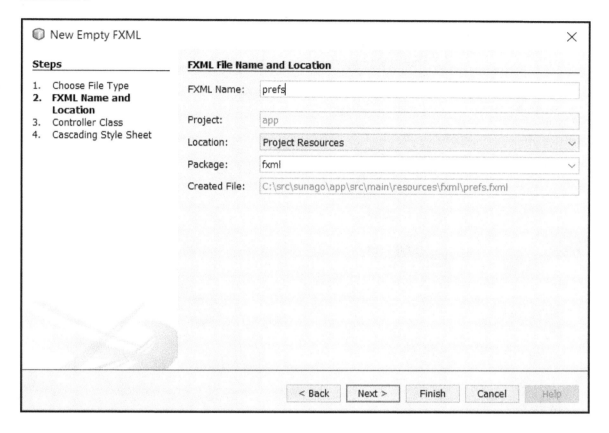

Clicking on **Next** brings us to the **Controller Class** step. Here we can either create a new controller class, or attach our file to an existing one. Since this is a new dialog/window for our app, we need to create a new controller as follows:

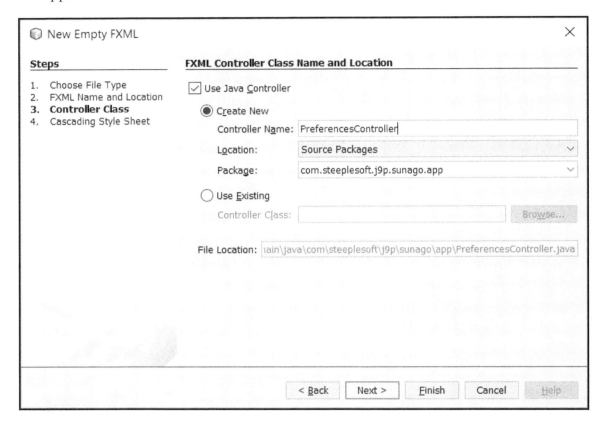

Check the **Use Java Controller** checkbox, enter `PreferencesController` for the name, and select the desired package. We could click on **Next**, which would take us to the **Cascading Style Sheet** step, but we're not interested in specifying that for this controller, so we end the wizard by clicking on **Finish**, which will take us to the source of our newly created controller class.

Let's start by laying out the user interface. Double-click on the new `prefs.fxml` file to open it in Scene Builder. Like our last FXML file, the default root element is **AnchorPane**. For this window, we'd like to use a **BorderPane**, so we use the same technique that we did last time to replace **AnchorPane**--right-click on the component, and click on **Wrap in | BorderPane**. The **AnchorPane** is now nested in **BorderPane**, so we right-click on it again and select **Delete**.

To build the user interface, we now drag a **TabPane** control from the accordion on the left, and drop it in the **CENTER** area of **BorderPane**. This will add a **TabPane** with two tabs to our user interface. We only want one right now, so delete the second one. We want to give our tab a meaningful label. We can do that by double-clicking on the tab in the preview window (or selecting the **Text** property in the **Properties** section of the **Inspector**) and typing General. Finally, expand the Inspector's **Code** section, and enter tabPane for **fx:id**.

Now we need to provide a means by which the user can close the window, and either save or discard changes. We implement that by dragging a **ButtonBar** component to our border pane's **BOTTOM** area. That will add a **ButtonBar** with one button, but we need two, so we drag another button on to the **ButtonBar**. The nice thing about this control is that it will handle button placement and padding for us, so, when we drop the new button, it's automatically added in the proper place on the right. (This behavior can be overridden, but it works exactly how we want it to, so we can just accept the defaults.)

For each Button, we need to set three properties--text, fx:id, and onAction. The first property is in the **Properties** section of the inspector, and the last two in the **Code** section. The values for the first button are Save, savePrefs, and savePreferences. For the second button, the values are Cancel, cancel, and closeDialog. Select the **Layout** section for the ButtonBar in the inspector, and set the right padding to 10 to make sure Button is not pressed against the edge of the window.

Finally, we'll add our only preference at this point. We want to allow the user to specify the maximum number of items to retrieve from each social media network for a given request. We do that for those scenarios where the application hasn't been used in a while (or ever). In those cases, we don't want to try to download, for example, thousands of tweets. To add support for this, we add two controls, Label and TextField.

Getting the position of the **Label** control right is pretty simple, as it's the first component. Scene Builder will provide red guidelines to help you position the component exactly where you want it, as shown in this screenshot:

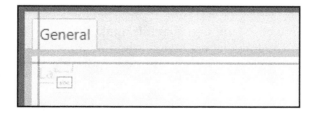

Making sure that `TextField` is lined up with the label can be trickier. By default, when you drop a component on **TabPane**, Scene Builder will add an **AnchorPane** to hold the new components. An **HBox** might be a better choice, but we'll go ahead and use **AnchorPane** to demonstrate this feature of Scene Builder. If you drag a **TextField** onto **TabPane** and try to position it, you should see more red lines show up. Positioned just right, you should see a red line running through the middle of the **Label** and the `TextField`, indicating that the two components are vertically aligned. This is what we want, so make sure there is a small space between `TextField` and the label and drop it.

We need to give **Label** some meaningful text, so double-click on it in the preview window, and enter `Number of items to retrieve`. We also need to give `TextField` an ID so that we can interact with it, so click on the component, expand the **Code** section in the Inspector, and set **fx:id** to `itemCount`.

Our user interface, while basic, is now as complete as we can make it here, so save the file, close Scene Builder, and return to NetBeans.

Saving user preferences

To allow our newly-defined user interface to be wired into our controller, we need to create instance variables to match the controls with the `fx:id` attributes set, so, we add these to `PreferencesController` as follows:

```
@FXML
protected Button savePrefs;
@FXML
protected Button cancel;
@FXML
protected TabPane tabPane;
```

In the `initialize()` method, we need to add support for loading the saved value for our `itemCount` field, so we need to talk a little bit about preferences.

Java, being the general-purpose language that it is, makes it possible to write any preference storing strategy that you can image. Fortunately, though, it also offers a couple of different standard APIs that allow you to do so in a more easily portable manner, those being `Preferences` and `Properties`.

The `java.util.Properties` class has been in the JDK since version 1.0, and while its basic, no-frills API might make that obvious, it's still a very useful abstraction. At its heart, `Properties` is a `Hashtable` implementation to which methods have been added for loading its data from input streams and readers, and writing its data to output streams and writers (in addition to a handful of other related methods). All the properties are treated as `String` values with `String` keys. Since `Properties` is a `Hashtable`, you can still use `put()` and `putAll()` to store non-string data, but that will result in `ClassCastException` should you call `store()`, so, it's probably best to avoid doing that.

The `java.util.prefs.Preferences` class was added in Java 1.4, and it's a much more modern API. Whereas with properties we have to handle persistence separately, preferences handle that for us opaquely--we don't need to worry about how or when it's written. In fact, the call to set a preference may return immediately, while the actual persistence may not occur for quite some time. The contract of the `Preferences` API guarantees that preferences will be persisted even if the JVM shuts down, assuming it's a normal, ordered shutdown (by definition, there's not much that can be done if the JVM process suddenly dies).

Additionally, the user also need not worry about how preferences are saved. The actual backing store is an implementation-specific detail. It could be a flat file, an OS-specific registry, a database or some sort of directory server. For the curious, the actual implementation is chosen by using the class name, if specified, in the `java.util.prefs.PreferencesFactory` system property. If that's not defined, the system will look for the file `META-INF/services/java.util.prefs.PreferencesFactory` (a mechanism known as SPI, which we will look at in depth later), and use the first class defined there. Finally, failing that, the implementation for the underlying platform is loaded and used.

So which to choose? Either will work as well as the other, but you have to decide if you want control of where the information is stored (`Properties`) or ease of implementation (`Preferences`). To a certain degree, portability might also be a concern. For example, if you have Java code running in some sort of a mobile or embedded device, you might not have permissions to write to the filesystem, and you might not have a filesystem at all. To show how similar the two implementations might be, though, we'll implement both.

To put my cards on the table a little bit, I would like for as much of this code as possible to be reusable in an Android environment. To help facilitate that, we'll create a very simple interface as follows:

```
public interface SunagoPreferences {
   String getPreference(String key);
   String getPreference(String key, String defaultValue);
   Integer getPreference(String key, Integer defaultValue);
   void putPreference(String key, String value);
   void putPreference(String key, Integer value);
}
```

We're only dealing with strings and integers, as the needs of the application are pretty basic. With the interface defined, how do we get a reference to an implementation? For that, we'll use a technique we've already seen mentioned briefly--the Service Provider Interface (SPI).

Plugins and extensions with the Service Provider Interface

We've already seen SPI mentioned before when we looked at the `Preferences` class, and how the implementation is selected and loaded, but what exactly is it? The Service Provider Interface is a somewhat generic term for an interface that a third party can implement (or a class, abstract or not, that can be extended) to provide extra functionality, replace existing components, and more.

In a nutshell, the author of the target system (for example, the JDK itself in our previous example) defines and publishes an interface. Ideally, this system would provide a default implementation, but that's not necessary in all cases. Any interested third party could then implement this interface, register it, and the target system could then load and use it. One of the advantages of this approach is that the target system can be extended easily, with no coupling to the third party. That is to say, while the third party knows about the target system via the interface, the target system has no knowledge at all of the third party. It's merely operating off the interface it defined.

How are these third-party plugins registered with the target system? The third-party developer would create a text file using a specific file in a specific directory. The file has the same name as the interface being implemented. For the `Preferences` class example, one would be implementing the `java.util.prefs.PreferencesFactory` interface, so that would be the name of the file, which would be in the `META-INF/services` directory in the root of the libraries classpath. In a Maven-based project, the file would be found in `src/main/resources/META-INF/services`. The file contains just the name of the class implementing the interface. It's also possible to have more than one class listed in the services file, each on a new line. It's up to the consuming system, though, as to whether or not each of those might be used.

So what does all of this look like for us? As noted earlier, we're going to take a rare opportunity to show multiple implementations for our `Preferences` support. Both classes are small enough that we can show the uses of both `Properties` and `Preferences`, and use SPI to pick one to use.

Let's start with the `Properties`-based implementation:

```
public class SunagoProperties implements SunagoPreferences {
  private Properties props = new Properties();
  private final String FILE = System.getProperty("user.home")
    + File.separator + ".sunago.properties";

  public SunagoProperties() {
    try (InputStream input = new FileInputStream(FILE)) {
      props.load(input);
    } catch (IOException ex) {
    }
  }
}
```

In the preceding code, we start by implementing our `SunagoPreferences` interface. We then create an instance of the `Properties` class, and we also define a constant for the file name and location, which we put--in a system-independent manner--in the user's home directory.

Resource handling with try-with-resources

The constructor shows something interesting that we haven't talked about--try-with-resources. Prior to Java 8, you might have written something like this:

```
public SunagoProperties(int a) {
  InputStream input = null;
  try {
```

```
            input = new FileInputStream(FILE);
            props.load(input);
        } catch (IOException ex) {
            // do something
        } finally {
            if (input != null) {
                try {
                    input.close();
                } catch (IOException ex1) {
                    Logger.getLogger(SunagoProperties.class.getName())
                        .log(Level.SEVERE, null, ex1);
                }
            }
        }
    }
```

This preceding, incredibly verbose code declares an `InputStream` outside the try block, then does some work with it in the `try` block. In the `finally` block, we try to close the `InputStream`, but we first have to check to see if it's null. If, say, the file doesn't exist (as it won't be the first time this class is created), an `Exception` will be thrown, and `input` will be null. If it's not null, we can call `close()` on it, but that might throw `IOException`, so we have to wrap that in a `try/catch` block as well.

Java 8 introduced the try-with-resources construct that makes this much smaller. If an object is an instance of `AutoCloseable`, then it can be defined **inside** the `try` declaration, and it will be closed automatically when the `try` block scope terminates regardless of whether or not an `Exception` was thrown. That allows us to take what would normally be fourteen lines of code, and express the exact same functionality in four with much less noise.

Aside from `AutoCloseable`, note that we load any existing values in the file into our `Properties` instance via `Properties.load(InputStream)`.

Moving on, what we see next are pretty straightforward getters and setters:

```
        @Override
        public String getPreference(String key) {
            return props.getProperty(key);
        }

        @Override
        public String getPreference(String key, String defaultValue) {
            String value = props.getProperty(key);
            return (value == null) ? defaultValue : value;
        }

        @Override
```

```
public Integer getPreference(String key, Integer defaultValue) {
  String value = props.getProperty(key);
  return (value == null) ? defaultValue :
    Integer.parseInt(value);
}

@Override
public void putPreference(String key, String value) {
  props.put(key, value);
  store();
}

@Override
public void putPreference(String key, Integer value) {
  if (value != null) {
    putPreference(key, value.toString());
  }
}
```

The final method is the one that writes our preferences back out, which is as follows:

```
private void store() {
  try (OutputStream output = new FileOutputStream(FILE)) {
    props.store(output, null);
  } catch (IOException e) { }
}
```

This last method looks a lot like our constructor, but we create an OutputStream, and call Properties.store(OutputStream) to write our values out to a file. Note that we call this method from every put method to make sure, insofar as possible, that the user preferences are faithfully persisted to disk.

What would a Preferences-based implementation look like? Not much different.

```
public class SunagoPreferencesImpl implements SunagoPreferences {
  private final Preferences prefs = Preferences.userRoot()
    .node(SunagoPreferencesImpl.class.getPackage()
    .getName());
  @Override
  public String getPreference(String key) {
    return prefs.get(key, null);
  }
  @Override
  public String getPreference(String key, String defaultValue) {
    return prefs.get(key, defaultValue);
  }

  @Override
```

```
    public Integer getPreference(String key,Integer defaultValue){
      return prefs.getInt(key, defaultValue);
    }
    @Override
    public void putPreference(String key, String value) {
      prefs.put(key, value);
    }
    @Override
    public void putPreference(String key, Integer value) {
      prefs.putInt(key, value);
    }
  }
```

Two things to note. First, we don't need to handle persistence, as `Preferences` does that for us. Second, the instantiation of the `Preferences` instance needs some attention. Clearly, I think, we want these preferences to be scoped to the user, so we start with `Preferences.userRoot()` to get the root preference node. Then we ask for the node in which we want to store our preferences, which we have chosen to name after the package of our class.

Where does that put things? On Linux, the file might look something like `~/.java/.userPrefs/_!':!bw"t!#4!cw"0!'`!~@"w!'w!~@"z!'8!~g"0!#4!ag!5!')` `!c!!u!(:!d@"u!'%!~w"v!#4!}@"w!(!=/prefs.xml` (yes, that's a directory name). On Windows, those preferences are saved in the Windows Registry under the key `HKEY_CURRENT_USER\SOFTWARE\JavaSoft\Prefs\com.steeplesoft.sunago.app`. Unless you want to interact directly with these files, though, their exact location and format are merely implementation details. Sometimes, though, it's a good thing to know.

We have two implementations, so how do we pick which one to use? In the file (including the source root for clarity) `src/main/resources/META-INF/service/com.steeplesoft.sunago.api.SunagoPreferences`, we can put one of these two lines:

```
com.steeplesoft.sunago.app.SunagoPreferencesImpl
com.steeplesoft.sunago.app.SunagoProperties
```

You can list both, but only the first will be chosen, which we'll see now. To make things simple, we've wrapped this up in a utility method as follows:

```
private static SunagoPreferences preferences;
public static synchronized
    SunagoPreferences getSunagoPreferences() {
  if (preferences == null) {
    ServiceLoader<SunagoPreferences> spLoader =
      ServiceLoader.load(SunagoPreferences.class);
    Iterator<SunagoPreferences> iterator =
```

```
        spLoader.iterator();
      preferences = iterator.hasNext() ? iterator.next() : null;
    }
    return preferences;
}
```

In what may be a bit of an overkill for our purposes here, we've implemented a singleton by declaring the instance of the `SunagoPreferences` interface as a private static, and made it available via a synchronized method, which checks for `null`, and creates the instance if needed.

While that's interesting, don't let it distract you from the meat of the method. We use the `ServiceLoader.load()` method to ask the system for any implementations of the `SunagoPreferences` interface. It's worth noting again, just to be clear, that it won't pick up **any** implementation in the system, but **only** those listed in the services file we described earlier. Using the `ServiceLoader<SunagoPreferences>` instance, we grab an iterator, and if it has an entry (`iterator.hasNext()`), we return that instance (`iterator.next()`). If it does not, we return `null`. There is a chance here for a `NullPointerException` since we are returning `null`, but we're also providing an implementation, so we avoid that risk. However, in your own code, you need to either ensure you have an implementation as we've done here, or to make sure that the consuming code is `null`-ready.

Adding a network - Twitter

So far, we have a pretty basic application, which can save and load its preferences, but let's get down to what we're here for and start connecting to social networks. What we hope to develop is a framework that makes it easy to add support for different social networks. Technically, as we'll soon see, the **network** need not even be social as the only thing that will imply a specific type of source is the name of the classes and interfaces involved. However, we will, in fact, focus on social networks, and we'll use a couple of different ones to show some variety. To that end, we'll start with Twitter, the massively popular microblogging platform, and Instagram, the increasingly photo-focused network that is now part of Facebook.

Speaking of Facebook, why are we not demonstrating integration with that social network? Two reasons--One, it's not significantly different from Twitter, so there would not be much that was new to cover; two, most importantly, the permissions that Facebook offers make it virtually impossible to integrate with it in a way that would be of interest here. For example, the permission to read a user's home timeline (or wall) is only granted to applications targeted at those platforms where Facebook is not currently available, and not at all to desktop applications, which is our target here.

As noted previously, we'd like to expose a way to add more networks without having to change the core application, so we need to develop an API. What we'll cover here is that API in a more or less **finished** state (is any software every truly finished?). However, while you will see a reasonably complete API, a word of caution--attempts to create an abstraction that start with that abstraction--that is, writing the abstraction from scratch--rarely end well. It is usually best to write a specific implementation to get a better understanding of the details required, then extract an abstraction. What you will see here is the end result of that process, so that process will not be covered here in any depth.

Registering as a Twitter developer

To create an application that integrates with Twitter, we need to create a Twitter developer account, and then create a Twitter application. To create the account, we need to visit `https://dev.twitter.com`, and click on the **Join** button. Once you've created your developer account, you can click the **My Apps** link to go to `https://apps.twitter.com`. Here, we need to click on the **Create New App** button, which will get us a form that looks a bit like this:

Create an application

Application Details

Name *

<Your Unique Application Name>

Description *

<A description of the application>

Website *

<Your website>

Callback URL

<Not required or necessary for desktop app>|

Developer Agreement

☐ Yes, I have read and agree to the Twitter Developer Agreement.

Create your Twitter application

While the application we're developing is called *Sunago*, you won't be able to use that name, as it's already taken; you'll have to create a unique name of your own, assuming you're planning to run the application yourself. Once you've created the application, you'll be taken to the **Application Management** page for your new app. From this page, you can manage your app's permissions and keys, and, if needed, you can delete your app.

One thing to note on this page, as we'll need this soon, is where to find your application's **Consumer Key** and **Secret**. These are long, alphanumeric strings that your application will use to authenticate with Twitter's services. To interact with Twitter on behalf of a user--our ultimate goal--requires a different set of tokens, which we'll fetch shortly. Your **Consumer Key** and **Secret**--especially, **Consumer Secret**--should be kept, well, secret. If this combination is ever revealed publicly, other users will be able to masquerade as your app, potentially causing you serious headaches if they abuse the service. For that reason, you won't see the key/secret combination I generated anywhere in this book or the source code, which is why you will need to generate your own.

Armed now with our **Consumer Key** and **Secret**, we need to decide how to talk to Twitter. Twitter offers a public REST API, which they document on their site. If we were so inclined, we could pick an HTTP client of some sort, and start making calls. In the interests of simplicity and clarity, though, not to mention robustness, fault tolerance, and so on, we might be better served using a higher-level library of some sort. As luck would have it, there is a such a library, Twitter4J, which will make our integration much simpler and cleaner (for the curious, Twitter4J has over 200 Java classes. While we won't need all of the functionality represented there and exposed via the REST API, it should give you an idea of the scope of the effort required to write a reasonable wrapper for Twitter's REST interface).

As mentioned earlier, we want to be able to add networks to Sunago without having to change the core application, so we will write our Twitter integration in a separate Maven module. This will require that some of the code we've already written for Sunago be extracted into yet another module. Both our Twitter module and the main application module will then add a dependency on this new module. Since we'll have multiple modules at play here, we'll be sure to indicate to which module each class belongs. When we're finished, our project dependency graph will look like this:

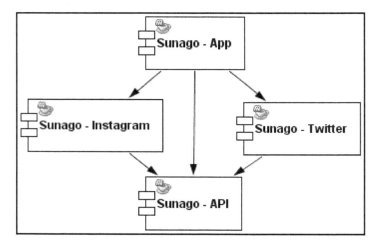

Technically, the only reason we show a dependency between the Application module and the Instagram and Twitter modules is because we're building them as part of the same project. A third-party developer, as we'll see, could easily develop an independent module, add it to the application's runtime classpath, and see the change in the application, all without this build-level dependency. Hopefully, though, this graph helps explain how the modules are related.

Adding Twitter preferences to Sunago

Let's start by adding Twitter to our preferences screen. Before we can do any integration, we need to be able to configure the application, or, more accurately, the Twitter module, so that it can connect as a specific user. To enable that, we'll add a new interface to the API module as follows:

```
public abstract class SocialMediaPreferencesController {
  public abstract Tab getTab();
  public abstract void savePreferences();
}
```

This interface will give Sunago two hooks into the module--one giving the module a chance to draw its own preferences user interface, and one to allow it to save those preferences. We can then implement that in our module. Before we do so, though, let's see how the application will find these implementations so that they can be used. For that, we will again turn to SPI. In Sunago's `PreferencesController` interface, we add this code:

```
private List<SocialMediaPreferencesController> smPrefs =
  new ArrayList<>();
@Override
public void initialize(URL url, ResourceBundle rb) {
  itemCount.setText(SunagoUtil.getSunagoPreferences()
    .getPreference(SunagoPrefsKeys.ITEM_COUNT.getKey(), "50"));
  final ServiceLoader<SocialMediaPreferencesController>
  smPrefsLoader = ServiceLoader.load(
    SocialMediaPreferencesController.class);
  smPrefsLoader.forEach(smp -> smPrefs.add(smp));
  smPrefs.forEach(smp -> tabPane.getTabs().add(smp.getTab()));
}
```

We have an instance variable to hold a list of any `SocialMediaPreferencesController` instances we find. Next, in `initialize()`, we call the now familiar `ServiceLoader.load()` method to find any implementations, which we then add to the `List` that we created previously. Once we have our list of controllers, we call `getTab()` on each of them, adding the returned `Tab` instance to the `PreferencesController` interface's `tabPane`.

With the loading part clarified, let's now take a look at the Twitter preferences user interface implementation. We start by implementing the controller that will back this part of the user interface as follows:

```
public class TwitterPreferencesController
  extends SocialMediaPreferencesController {
    private final TwitterClient twitter;
```

```
    private Tab tab;

    public TwitterPreferencesController() {
      twitter = new TwitterClient();
    }

    @Override
    public Tab getTab() {
      if (tab == null) {
        tab = new Tab("Twitter");
        tab.setContent(getNode());
      }

      return tab;
    }
}
```

We'll take a look at `TwitterClient` in a moment, but, first, a note on `getTab()`. Notice that we create the `Tab` instance, which we need to return, but we delegate the creation of its contents to the `getNode()` method. `Tab.setContent()` allows us to completely replace the contents of the tab with a single call, something we'll make use of next. The `getNode()` method looks like this:

```
    private Node getNode() {
      return twitter.isAuthenticated() ? buildConfigurationUI() :
        buildConnectUI();
    }
```

If the user has already authenticated, then we want to present some configuration options. If not, then we need to offer a means to connect to Twitter.

```
    private Node buildConnectUI() {
      HBox box = new HBox();
      box.setPadding(new Insets(10));
      Button button = new Button(MessageBundle.getInstance()
        .getString("connect"));
      button.setOnAction(event -> connectToTwitter());

      box.getChildren().add(button);

      return box;
    }
```

In this simple user interface, we create an HBox primarily so we can add some padding. Without the new Insets(10) instance we pass to setPadding(), our button would be pressed right up against the top and left edges of the window, which is not visually appealing. Next, we create the Button, and set the onAction handler (ignore that constructor parameter for now).

The interesting part is hidden away in connectToTwitter, as shown in this code:

```
private void connectToTwitter() {
  try {
    RequestToken requestToken =
      twitter.getOAuthRequestToken();
    LoginController.showAndWait(
      requestToken.getAuthorizationURL(),
        e -> ((String) e.executeScript(
          "document.documentElement.outerHTML"))
            .contains("You've granted access to"),
          e -> {
            final String html =
              "<kbd aria-labelledby=\"code-desc\"><code>";
              String body = (String) e.executeScript(
                "document.documentElement.outerHTML");
              final int start = body.indexOf(html) +
                html.length();
              String code = body.substring(start, start+7);
              saveTwitterAuthentication(requestToken, code);
              showConfigurationUI();
          });
  } catch (TwitterException ex) {
    Logger.getLogger(getClass().getName())
      .log(Level.SEVERE, null, ex);
  }
}
```

OAuth and logging on to Twitter

We'll take a detour into `LoginController` in just a moment, but first, let's make sure we understand what's going on here. To log on to Twitter on behalf of a user, we need to generate an OAuth request token from which we get an authorization URL. The details of which are hidden nicely behind the Twitter4J API, but it is, basically, the OAuth authorization URL listed on the **Application Management** page with a request token passed as a query string. As we'll see, this URL is opened in a `WebView`, which prompts the user to authenticate against Twitter, and then authorize the application (or decline to):

If the user successfully authenticates and authorizes the application, the `WebView` is redirected to a success page, which displays a numeric code that we need to capture to finish gathering the authentication/authorization credentials needed. The success page might look like this:

For those not familiar with OAuth, what this allows us to do is to authenticate as the user, now and at any arbitrary moment in the future, without needing to store the user's actual password. The end result of this handshake between our application and Twitter is a token and token secret, which we'll pass to Twitter for authentication. As long as this token is valid--the user can invalidate it at any time via Twitter's web interface--we can connect and act as that user. Should the key ever be compromised, the user can revoke the key, affecting only the intended app and anyone attempting to use the stolen key.

`LoginController`, which is part of the API module, handles all of the boilerplate code for us, as seen in this code:

```
public class LoginController implements Initializable {
  @FXML
  private WebView webView;
  private Predicate<WebEngine> loginSuccessTest;
  private Consumer<WebEngine> handler;

  public static void showAndWait(String url,
    Predicate<WebEngine> loginSuccessTest,
    Consumer<WebEngine> handler) {
      try {
        fxmlLoader loader = new fxmlLoader(LoginController
          .class.getResource("/fxml/login.fxml"));

        Stage stage = new Stage();
        stage.setScene(new Scene(loader.load()));
        LoginController controller =
            loader.<LoginController>getController();
        controller.setUrl(url);
        controller.setLoginSuccessTest(loginSuccessTest);
        controller.setHandler(handler);

        stage.setTitle("Login...");
        stage.initModality(Modality.APPLICATION_MODAL);

        stage.showAndWait();
      } catch (IOException ex) {
        throw new RuntimeException(ex);
      }
  }
}
```

This preceding code is a basic FXML-backed JavaFX controller, but we do have a static helper method to handle the details of creating, configuring, and showing an instance. We load the scene using FXML, get the controller (which is an instance of the enclosing class), set the `loginSuccessTest` and `handler` properties, and then show the dialog.

Do `loginSuccessTest` and `handler` look odd? They are instances of the Java 8 functional interfaces `Predicate<T>` and `Consumer<T>`. `Predicate` is a functional interface that takes a type, `WebEngine` in our case, and returns a `boolean`. It is designed to check for a certain condition given a variable of the specified type. In this instance, we call `WebEngine.executeScript().contains()` to extract a piece of the document, and see if it contains a certain piece of text indicating that we've been redirected to the login success page.

`Consumer<T>` is a functional interface (or, in our case, a lambda) that takes a single parameter of the specified type, and returns void. Our handler is a `Consumer`, which is called once our `Predicate` returns true. The lambda extracts the code from the HTML page, calls `saveTwitterAuthentication()` to finish authenticating the user, then `showConfigurationUI()` to change the user interface so that the user can configure Twitter-related settings.

The method `saveTwitterAuthentication()` is very straightforward, and is given as follows:

```
private void saveTwitterAuthentication(RequestToken requestToken,
  String code) {
    if (!code.isEmpty()) {
      try {
        AccessToken accessToken = twitter
          .getAcccessToken(requestToken, code);
        prefs.putPreference(TwitterPrefsKeys.TOKEN.getKey(),
          accessToken.getToken());
        prefs.putPreference(TwitterPrefsKeys.TOKEN_SECRET.getKey(),
          accessToken.getTokenSecret());
      } catch (TwitterException ex) {
        Logger.getLogger(TwitterPreferencesController
          .class.getName()).log(Level.SEVERE, null, ex);
      }
    }
  }
```

The method `twitter.getAccessToken()` takes our request token and the code we extracted from the web page, and sends an HTTP POST to a Twitter REST endpoint, which generates the token secret we need. When that request returns, we store the token and token secret to our `Preferences` store (again, oblivious to where and how).

The method `showConfigurationUI()` and the related method should also be familiar.

```
private void showConfigurationUI() {
  getTab().setContent(buildConfigurationUI());
}
private Node buildConfigurationUI() {
  VBox box = new VBox();
  box.setPadding(new Insets(10));

  CheckBox cb = new CheckBox(MessageBundle.getInstance()
    .getString("homeTimelineCB"));
  cb.selectedProperty().addListener(
    (ObservableValue<? extends Boolean> ov,
      Boolean oldVal, Boolean newVal) -> {
        showHomeTimeline = newVal;
      });

  Label label = new Label(MessageBundle.getInstance()
    .getString("userListLabel") + ":");

  ListView<SelectableItem<UserList>> lv = new ListView<>();
  lv.setItems(itemList);
  lv.setCellFactory(CheckBoxListCell.forListView(
    item -> item.getSelected()));
  VBox.setVgrow(lv, Priority.ALWAYS);

  box.getChildren().addAll(cb, label, lv);
  showTwitterListSelection();

  return box;
}
```

One new item in this preceding method is the listener we add to the `selectedProperty` of the `CheckBox`. Any time the selected value changes, our listener is called, which sets the value of the `showHomeTimeline` boolean.

The `ListView` also needs special attention. Notice the parameterized type, `SelectableItem<UserList>`. What is that? That's an abstract class we've created to wrap items for use in `CheckBoxListCell`, which you can see in the call to `setCellFactory()`. That class looks like this:

```
public abstract class SelectableItem<T> {
  private final SimpleBooleanProperty selected =
    new SimpleBooleanProperty(false);
  private final T item;
  public SelectableItem(T item) {
    this.item = item;
  }
  public T getItem() {
    return item;
  }
  public SimpleBooleanProperty getSelected() {
    return selected;
  }
}
```

This class, which lives in the API module, is a simple wrapper around an arbitrary type that adds a `SimpleBooleanProperty`. We see how this property is manipulated when the cell factory is set up--`lv.setCellFactory(CheckBoxListCell .forListView(item -> item.getSelected()))`. We expose `SimpleBooleanProperty` via the `getSelected()` method, which the `CheckBoxListCell` uses to set and read the state of each line.

Our final user interface-related method is this:

```
private void showTwitterListSelection() {
  List<SelectableItem<UserList>> selectable =
    twitter.getLists().stream()
      .map(u -> new SelectableUserList(u))
      .collect(Collectors.toList());
  List<Long> selectedListIds = twitter.getSelectedLists(prefs);
  selectable.forEach(s -> s.getSelected()
    .set(selectedListIds.contains(s.getItem().getId())));
  itemList.clear();
  itemList.addAll(selectable);
}
```

Using the same `SelectableItem` class, we request from Twitter all of the lists the user might have created, which we wrap in `SelectableUserList`, a `SelectableItem` child that overrides the `toString()` method to provide user-friendly text in `ListView`. We load any checked lists from preferences, set their respective booleans/checkboxes, and update our `ObservableList` and, thus, the user interface.

The final method we need to implement to satisfy the `SocialMediaPreferencesController` contract is `savePreferences()`, which is as follows:

```
public void savePreferences() {
  prefs.putPreference(TwitterPrefsKeys.HOME_TIMELINE.getKey(),
   Boolean.toString(showHomeTimeline));
  List<String> selectedLists = itemList.stream()
   .filter(s -> s != null)
   .filter(s -> s.getSelected().get())
   .map(s -> Long.toString(s.getItem().getId()))
   .collect(Collectors.toList());
  prefs.putPreference(TwitterPrefsKeys.SELECTED_LISTS.getKey(),
   String.join(",", selectedLists));
}
```

This is a mostly straightforward saving of the user's options to preferences, but the list handling is worth pointing out. Rather than manually iterating over each item in the list, we can use a stream and apply a couple of `filter()` operations to strip out entries that are of no interest to us, `map()` each `SelectableUserList` that makes it through to `Long` (which is the list's ID), then collect them in a `List<String>`. We join that `List` using `String.join()`, and write it out to our preferences.

Adding a model for Twitter

There are still a couple of other interfaces that we need to implement to finish our Twitter support. The first, and simpler, one is `SocialMediaItem`:

```
public interface SocialMediaItem {
  String getProvider();
  String getTitle();
  String getBody();
  String getUrl();
  String getImage();
  Date getTimestamp();
}
```

This preceding interface provides us with a nice abstraction over the various types of data that a social network might return without being too heavily burdened with fields that aren't used by most (or many, at least) networks. The Twitter implementation of this `Tweet` class is as follows:

```
public class Tweet implements SocialMediaItem {
  private final Status status;
  private final String url;
  private final String body;

  public Tweet(Status status) {
    this.status = status;
    body = String.format("@%s: %s (%s)",
      status.getUser().getScreenName(),
      status.getText(), status.getCreatedAt().toString());
    url = String.format("https://twitter.com/%s/status/%d",
      status.getUser().getScreenName(), status.getId());
  }
```

Taking the Twitter4J class `Status`, we extract information of interest to us, and store it in instance variables (whose getters are not shown, as they're just simple getters). For the `getImage()` method, we make a reasonable effort to extract any image from the tweet, as follows:

```
public String getImage() {
  MediaEntity[] mediaEntities = status.getMediaEntities();
  if (mediaEntities.length > 0) {
    return mediaEntities[0].getMediaURLHttps();
  } else {
    Status retweetedStatus = status.getRetweetedStatus();
    if (retweetedStatus != null) {
      if (retweetedStatus.getMediaEntities().length > 0) {
        return retweetedStatus.getMediaEntities()[0]
          .getMediaURLHttps();
      }
    }
  }
  return null;
}
```

Implementing a Twitter client

The second interface is `SocialMediaClient`. This interface serves not only as an abstraction that Sunago can use to interact with an arbitrary social network integration, but also as a guideline for interested developers to show them the minimum requirements for the integration. It looks like this:

```
public interface SocialMediaClient {
  void authenticateUser(String token, String tokenSecret);
  String getAuthorizationUrl();
  List<? Extends SocialMediaItem> getItems();
  boolean isAuthenticated();
}
```

For Twitter support, this preceding interface is implemented by the class `TwitterClient`. Most of the class is pretty basic, so we won't reproduce that here (you can peruse it in the source repository if you'd like details), but one implementation detail might be worth spending some time over. That method is `processList()`, which is as follows:

```
private List<Tweet> processList(long listId) {
  List<Tweet> tweets = new ArrayList<>();

  try {
    final AtomicLong sinceId = new AtomicLong(
      getSinceId(listId));
    final Paging paging = new Paging(1,
      prefs.getPreference(SunagoPrefsKeys.
      ITEM_COUNT.getKey(), 50), sinceId.get());
    List<Status> statuses = (listId == HOMETIMELINE) ?
      twitter.getHomeTimeline(paging) :
       twitter.getUserListStatuses(listId, paging);
    statuses.forEach(s -> {
      if (s.getId() > sinceId.get()) {
        sinceId.set(s.getId());
      }
      tweets.add(new Tweet(s));
    });
    saveSinceId(listId, sinceId.get());
  } catch (TwitterException ex) {
    Logger.getLogger(TwitterClient.class.getName())
      .log(Level.SEVERE, null, ex);
  }
  return tweets;
}
```

There are several things going on in this last method. First, we want to limit how many tweets we actually retrieve. If this is the first time the app is used, or the first time that it's used in a long time, there could be a significant number of tweets. Retrieving all of them would be quite expensive in terms of network usage, memory and, perhaps, processing time. We implement that limit using the `Paging` object from Twitter4J.

We also don't want to retrieve tweets we already have, so, for each list, we keep a `sinceId`, which we can pass to the Twitter API. It will use this to find up to the specified number of tweets whose ID is greater than `sinceId`.

Wrapping all of this up in the `Paging` object, we call either `twitter.getHomeTimeline()` if the list ID is `-1` (an internal ID we've used to identify the home timeline) or `twitter.getUserListStatus()` for a user-defined list. For each `Status` returned, we update `sinceId` (which we've modeled using an `AtomicLong`, as any method variable used inside a lambda must be final or effectively final), and add the tweet to our `List`. Before exiting, we store `sinceId` for the list in our in-memory store, and then return the tweets for the Twitter list.

A brief look at internationalization and localization

While somewhat basic, our integration with Twitter is now complete, as it fulfills our functional requirements for the network. However, there is one more piece of code that we need to take a quick look at. Earlier, in some of the code samples, you might have noticed code that looks like this:
`MessageBundle.getInstance().getString("homeTimelineCB")`. What is that, and what does it do?

The `MessageBundle` class is a small wrapper around the internationalization and localization facilities (also known as i18n and l10n, where the numbers represent the number of letters dropped from the words to make the abbreviation) provided by the JDK. The code for this class is as follows:

```
public class MessageBundle {
  ResourceBundle messages =
    ResourceBundle.getBundle("Messages", Locale.getDefault());

  private MessageBundle() {
  }

  public final String getString(String key) {
```

```
      return messages.getString(key);
    }
    private static class LazyHolder {
      private static final MessageBundle INSTANCE =
        new MessageBundle();
    }

    public static MessageBundle getInstance() {
      return LazyHolder.INSTANCE;
    }
  }
```

There are two main items of interest here. We'll start at the end of the class with the `getInstance()` method. This is an example of what is known as the **initialize on demand holder (IODH)** pattern. There is a single, static instance of the class `MessageBundle` in the JVM. It is not initialized, however, until the `getInstance()` method is called. This is accomplished by taking advantage of how the JVM loads and initializes statics. As soon as a class is referenced in any way, it is loaded into `ClassLoader`, at which point any statics on the class will be initialized. The private static class `LazyHolder` is **not** initialized until the JVM is sure that something needs to access it. Once we call `getInstance()`, which references `LazyHolder.INSTANCE`, the class is initialized and the singleton instance created.

 It should be noted that are ways around the singleton nature we're trying to implement (for example, via reflection), but our use case here does not warrant any worries over such an attack.

The actual functionality is implemented in the first line of the class, which is as follows

```
      ResourceBundle messages =
        ResourceBundle.getBundle("Messages", Locale.getDefault());
```

The `ResourceBundle` files, in the words of the Javadoc, *contain locale-specific objects*. Usually, this means Strings, as it does in our case. The `getBundle()` method will attempt to find and load a bundle with the name given for the specified locale. In our case, we're looking for a bundle named `Messages`. Technically, we're looking for a bundle in a family of bundles with the shared base name `Messages`. The system will use the `Locale` specified to find the correct file. This resolution will follow the same lookup logic that `Locale` uses, so the `getBundle()` method will return the bundle with the most specific matching name available.

Let's say we're running this application on my computer. I live in the United States, so my system's default locale is `en_US`. Following the rules of the `Locale` lookup, then, `getBundle()` will try to locate files in this order:

1. `Messages_en_US.properties`.
2. `Messages_en.properties`.
3. `Messages.properties`.

The system will go from the most specific file to the least until it finds the key requested. If it's not found in any file, `MissingResourceException` is thrown. Each file consists of key/value pairs. Our `Messages.properties` file looks like this:

```
homeTimelineCB=Include the home timeline
userListLabel=User lists to include
connect=Connect
twitter=Twitter
```

It is just a simple mapping of keys to localized text. We could have `Messages_es.properties` with this line:

```
userListLabel=Listas de usuarios para incluir
```

If that were the only entry in the file, that one label in the file would be in Spanish, with everything else being in the default from `Message.properties`, which, in our case, is English.

Making our JAR file fat

With that, our implementation is now complete. Before this can be used in the way we intend, though, we need to make a build change. If you recall the discussion of the requirements at the beginning of the chapter, we want to build a system that easily allows third-party developers to write modules that will add support for arbitrary social networks without the need to modify the core application. To deliver that functionality, these developers would need to offer a JAR that Sunago users could drop in a folder. When the application is started, the new functionality is now available.

That leaves us, then, with the task of bundling all of the required code. As the project stands now, a single JAR is created, which holds just our classes. That's not entirely sufficient, though, as we depend on the Twitter4J jar. Other modules could have even more dependencies. Requiring users to drop in, say, half a dozen or more jars is probably asking a bit much. Fortunately, Maven has a mechanism that will allow us to avoid that problem altogether: the shade plugin.

By configuring this plugin in our build, we can generate a single jar that holds our classes and resources, plus those of every dependency declared in the project. This is often called a **fat jar**, and is as follows:

```
<build>
  <plugins>
    <plugin>
      <artifactId>maven-shade-plugin</artifactId>
        <version>${plugin.shade}</version>
          <executions>
            <execution>
              <phase>package</phase>
                <goals>
                  <goal>shade</goal>
                </goals>
            </execution>
          </executions>
    </plugin>
  </plugins>
</build>
```

This is an official Maven plugin, so we can omit `groupId`, and we've defined a property, `plugin.shade`, somewhere up the POM's inheritance tree. When the package phase is run, the shade goal of this plugin will execute and build our fat jar.

```
$ ll target/*.jar
total 348
-rwx------+ 1 jason None  19803 Nov 20 19:22 original-twitter-1.0-
SNAPSHOT.jar
-rwx------+ 1 jason None 325249 Nov 20 19:22 twitter-1.0-
SNAPSHOT.jar
```

The original jar, which is considerably smaller, is renamed to `original-twitter-1.0-SNAPSHOT.jar`, and the fat jar receives the configured final name. It is this fat jar that is installed in the local maven repository, or deployed to an artifact manager, such as Artifactory.

There is a small bug, though. Our twitter module depends on the API module so that it can see the interfaces and classes exposed by the application. Currently, even those are included in the fat jar, which we don't want, as that can cause some `ClassLoader` issues down the road in some situations. To prevent that, we mark that dependency as `provided`, as shown next:

```
<dependency>
  <groupId>${project.groupId}</groupId>
  <artifactId>api</artifactId>
  <version>${project.version}</version>
  <scope>provided</scope>
</dependency>
```

If we issue a `mvn clean install` now, we'll have a nice fat jar with only the classes we need to bundle, and one that's ready for distribution.

To make things as simple as possible, we're just going to declare a dependency on this jar in Sunago's app module, as follows:

```
<dependencies>
  <dependency>
    <groupId>${project.groupId}</groupId>
    <artifactId>api</artifactId>
    <version>${project.version}</version>
  </dependency>
  <dependency>
    <groupId>${project.groupId}</groupId>
    <artifactId>twitter</artifactId>
    <version>${project.version}</version>
  </dependency>
</dependencies>
```

If we run Sunago now, we'll see Twitter added to our settings screen, and, once connected and configured, we'll see tweets showing up on the main screen. We'll also notice that the main screen is a little plain, and, more importantly, doesn't provide any way of refreshing the contents, so let's fix that.

Adding a refresh button

In the **Projects** window, find `sunago.fxml`, right-click on it, and select `Edit`. We'll make this user interface change by hand, only for the sake of experience. Scroll down until you find the closing `Menubar` tag (`</Menubar>`). On the line right after that, insert these lines:

```
<ToolBar >
  <items>
    <Button fx:id="refreshButton" />
    <Button fx:id="settingsButton" />
  </items>
</ToolBar>
```

In `SunagoController`, we need to add the instance variables as follows:

```
@FXML
private Button refreshButton;
@FXML
private Button settingsButton;
```

Then, in `initialize()`, we need to set them up like this:

```
refreshButton.setGraphic(getButtonImage("/images/reload.png"));
refreshButton.setOnAction(ae -> loadItemsFromNetworks());
refreshButton.setTooltip(new Tooltip("Refresh"));

settingsButton.setGraphic(getButtonImage("/images/settings.png"));
settingsButton.setOnAction(ae -> showPreferences(ae));
settingsButton.setTooltip(new Tooltip("Settings"));
```

Notice that we're doing a bit more than setting up an action handler. The first thing we do is call `setGraphic()`. Remember from our discussion of the Twitter preference tab, calling `setGraphic()` will replace the child nodes with the `Node` that you specify. In these two cases, that `Node` is an `ImageView`, and comes from the `getButtonImage()` method.

```
private ImageView getButtonImage(String path) {
  ImageView imageView = new ImageView(
    new Image(getClass().getResourceAsStream(path)));
  imageView.setFitHeight(32);
  imageView.setPreserveRatio(true);
  return imageView;
}
```

After we set the action handler, we also set a tooltip. This will give our graphical buttons a textual description when the user hovers over the button with the mouse, as seen in this screenshot:

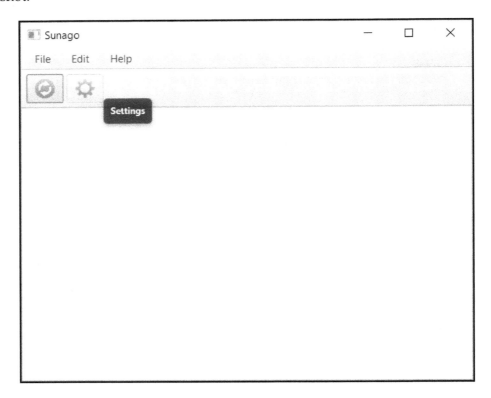

The action handler for the refresh button is worth looking at, and is given as follows:

```
private void loadItemsFromNetworks() {
  List<SocialMediaItem> items = new ArrayList<>();
  clientLoader.forEach(smc -> {
    if (smc.isAuthenticated()) {
        items.addAll(smc.getItems());
    }
  });

  items.sort((o1, o2) ->
    o2.getTimestamp().compareTo(o1.getTimestamp()));
  entriesList.addAll(0, items);
}
```

This is the same method that we call from `initialize()`. Using the Service Provider Interface that we discussed earlier, we iterate over each `SocialMediaClient` available in the system. If the client has authenticated against its network, we call the `getItems()` method, and add whatever it may return to a local variable, `items`. Once we've queried all of the networks configured in the system, we then sort our list. This will cause the entries of the various networks to be intermingled, as they're sorted by their timestamps in descending chronological order. This sorted list is then added to our `ObservableList` at the head, or the zeroth element, to cause them to appear at the top of the list in the user interface.

Adding another network - Instagram

So that we can see another type of integration, as well as to demonstrate how the interfaces we've defined make adding new networks relatively quick and easy, let's add one more network to Sunago--Instagram. While Instagram is owned by Facebook, at the time of this writing, its APIs are much more permissive than the social-media giant's, so we'll be able to add an interesting integration relatively easily.

Much like with Twitter, we have a choice to make about how our interactions with the Instragram API will be handled. Just like Twitter, Instagram offers a public REST API that is secured using OAuth. Also, just like Twitter, though, manually implementing a client to consume those APIs is not an attractive proposition due to the level of effort required. Again, unless there's a compelling reason to write your own client library, I would suggest that using some sort of client wrapper should be the preferred route if one is available. Fortunately, there is--jInstagram.

Registering as an Instagram developer

Before starting to write our client, we need to register a new Instagram client with the service. We do that by first creating, if needed, an Instagram developer account at `https://www.instagram.com/developer`. Once we have an account, we need to register our application either by clicking the **Register Your Application** button on the page, or by visiting `https://www.instagram.com/developer/clients/manage/` directly. From here, we need to click on **Register a New Client**, which will present this form:

Register new Client ID

Details   Security

Application Name:

*Do not use **Instagram, IG, insta** or **gram** in your app name. Make sure to adhere to the API Terms of Use and Brand Guidelines .*

Description:

Company Name:

Website URL:

Valid redirect URIs:

Press Enter to confirm.

The redirect_uri specifies where we redirect users after they have chosen whether or not to authenticate your application.

Privacy Policy URL:

Contact email:

An email that Instagram can use to get in touch with you. Please specify a valid email address to be notified of important information about your app.

Register   Cancel

Once you've registered your new client, you can click on the **Manage** button on the resulting web page to get your client ID and secret. Hold on to those, as you'll need them in a moment.

Next, we'll start the actual client by creating a new module just like we did for the Twitter module. This one, though, we'll call `Sunago - Instagram` and the `artifactIdinstagram`. We'll also go ahead and add the jInstagram dependency as follows:

```
<artifactId>instagram</artifactId>
<name>Sunago - Instagram</name>
<packaging>jar</packaging>
<dependencies>
  <dependency>
    <groupId>${project.groupId}</groupId>
    <artifactId>api</artifactId>
    <version>${project.version}</version>
    <scope>provided</scope>
  </dependency>
  <dependency>
    <groupId>com.sachinhandiekar</groupId>
    <artifactId>jInstagram</artifactId>
    <version>1.1.8</version>
  </dependency>
</dependencies>
```

Note that we have the Sunago `api` dependency added as well already, scoped as provided. We also need to add the Shade plugin configuration, which looks just like it does in the Twitter module, so it's not shown here.

Implementing the Instagram client

With our new module created, we need to create three specific items to fulfill the contract provided by the Sunago API module. We need `SocialMediaPreferencesController`, `SocialMediaClient`, and `SocialMediaItem`.

Our `SocialMediaPreferencesController` instance is `InstagramPreferencesController`. It has the same `getTab()` method required by the interface, which is as follows:

```
public Tab getTab() {
  if (tab == null) {
    tab = new Tab();
    tab.setText("Instagram");
```

```
      tab.setContent(getNode());
    }

    return tab;
  }

  private Node getNode() {
    Node node = instagram.isAuthenticated()
      ? buildConfigurationUI() : buildConnectUI();
    return node;
  }
```

To save time and space, for this example, we've left the Instagram implementation much more basic than the one we created for Twitter, so the user interface definition does not hold much of interest. However, the authentication handling is interesting, as, while it has the same OAuth flow that Twitter uses, the data is returned in a manner that is much more easily consumed. The connect button calls this method:

```
  private static final String CODE_QUERY_PARAM = "code=";
  private void showConnectWindow() {
    LoginController.showAndWait(instagram.getAuthorizationUrl(),
      e -> e.getLocation().contains(CODE_QUERY_PARAM),
      e -> {
        saveInstagramToken(e.getLocation());
        showInstagramConfig();
      });
  }
```

This uses the `LoginController` that we saw with Twitter, but our `Predicate` and `Consumer` are much more concise. The page to which the user is redirected has the code in the URL as a query parameter, so there's no need to scrape the HTML. We can just pull it straight from the URL as follows:

```
  private void saveInstagramToken(String location) {
    int index = location.indexOf(CODE_QUERY_PARAM);
    String code = location.substring(index +
      CODE_QUERY_PARAM.length());
    Token accessToken = instagram.
      verifyCodeAndGetAccessToken(code);
    instagram.authenticateUser(accessToken.getToken(),
      accessToken.getSecret());
  }
```

Once we have the code, we use an API on our `instagram` object to get the access token, which we then use to authenticate the user. So what does the `instagram` object look like? Like `TwitterClient`, `InstagramClient` is a `SocialMediaClient` that wraps the jInstagram API.

```
public final class InstagramClient implements
SocialMediaClient {

    private final InstagramService service;
    private Instagram instagram;
```

The jInstagram API has two objects that we need to use. `InstagramService` encapsulates the OAuth logic. We get an instance of it using a builder as follows:

```
service = new InstagramAuthService()
 .apiKey(apiKey)
 .apiSecret(apiSecret)
 .callback("http://blogs.steeplesoft.com")
 .scope("basic public_content relationships follower_list")
 .build();
```

As discussed earlier, to run the application locally, you'll need to provide your own API key and secret pair. The only use we have for the callback URL is to provide Instagram with a place to redirect our client to. Once it does that, we pull the code from the query parameters as we saw previously. Finally, we have to provide a list of scopes, which is what Instagram calls permissions, roughly. This list will allow us to get a list of the accounts that the authenticated user follows, which we'll use to get images:

```
@Override
public List<? extends SocialMediaItem> getItems() {
  List<Photo> items = new ArrayList<>();
  try {
    UserFeed follows = instagram.getUserFollowList("self");
    follows.getUserList().forEach(u ->
      items.addAll(processMediaForUser(u)));
  } catch (InstagramException ex) {
    Logger.getLogger(InstagramClient.class.getName())
      .log(Level.SEVERE, null, ex);
  }

  return items;
}
```

If you read the jInstagram documentation, you'll be tempted to use the method `instagram.getUserFeeds()`, and if you do, you'll get what I got--a `404` error page. Instagram has done some work on their API that jInstagram has not yet reflected. What we need to do, then, is implement our own wrapper for that, which jInstagram makes fairly simple. Here, we get a list of the people that the user follows. For each user, we call `processMediaForUser()` to fetch and store any pending images.

```
private List<Photo> processMediaForUser(UserFeedData u) {
  List<Photo> userMedia = new ArrayList<>();
  try {
    final String id = u.getId();
    instagram.getRecentMediaFeed(id,
      prefs.getPreference(SunagoPrefsKeys.ITEM_COUNT
        .getKey(), 50),
      getSinceForUser(id), null, null, null).getData()
        .forEach(m -> userMedia.add(new Photo(m)));
    if (!userMedia.isEmpty()) {
      setSinceForUser(id, userMedia.get(0).getId());
    }
  } catch (InstagramException ex) {
    Logger.getLogger(InstagramClient.class.getName())
      .log(Level.SEVERE, null, ex);
  }
  return userMedia;
}
```

Using the same **since ID** and max count approach we used for the Twitter client, we request any recent media for the user. Each returned item is wrapped (via the lambda) in a `Photo` instance, which is our `SocialMediaItem` child for Instagram. Once we have our list, if it is not empty, we grab the first `Photo`, which we know is the oldest, because that's how the Instagram API returns its data, and we get the ID, which we store as the since ID for the next time this method is called. Finally, we return the `List` so that it can be added to the main `Photo` list given earlier.

Loading our plugins in Sunago

With that, our new integration is done. To see it in action, we add the dependency to Sunago's POM as follows:

```
<dependency>
  <groupId>${project.groupId}</groupId>
  <artifactId>instagram</artifactId>
  <version>${project.version}</version>
</dependency>
```

We then run the application.

Clearly, adding a dependency for each new integration is not an ideal solution, if for no other reason than that the user won't be running the application from an IDE or with Maven. What we need, then, is a way for the application to find any modules (or plugins, if you prefer that term) at runtime on the user's machine. The simplest solution would be to launch the application via a shell script like this:

```
#!/bin/bash
JARS=sunago-1.0-SNAPSHOT.jar
SEP=:
for JAR in `ls ~/.sunago/*.jar` ; do
  JARS="$JARS$SEP$JAR"
done

java -cp $JARS com.steeplesoft.sunago.app.Sunago
```

This preceding shell script creates a classpath using the main Sunago jar, plus any JARs found in `~/.sunago`, and then runs the application. This is simple and effective, but does require per-operating system versions. Fortunately, that just means this shell script for Mac and Linux, plus a batch file for Windows. That's not hard to do or difficult to maintain, but it does require that you have access to those operating systems to test and verify your scripts.

Another option is to make use of classloaders. As simple as it may seem to say it out loud, a `ClassLoader` is simply an object that is responsible for loading classes (and other resources). There are several classloaders at work in any given JVM, all arranged in a hierarchical fashion, starting with the bootstrap `ClassLoader`, then the platform `ClassLoader`, and, finally, the system--or application--`ClassLoader`. It is possible that a given application or runtime environment, such as a **Java Enterprise Edition (Java EE)** application server, might add one or more `ClassLoader` instances as children of the application `ClassLoader`. These added `ClassLoader` instances may themselves be hierarchical or they may be **siblings**. Either way, they are almost certainly children of the application `ClassLoader`.

A full treatment of classloaders and all that they entail is well beyond the scope of this book, but suffice it to say that we can create a new `ClassLoader` to allow the application to find the classes and resources in our **plugin** jars. To do this, we need to add a few methods--three to be exact--to our application class, Sunago. We'll start with the constructor:

```
public Sunago() throws Exception {
  super();
  updateClassLoader();
}
```

Typically (though not always), when a JavaFX application starts, the `public static void main` method is run, which calls the `launch()` static method on the `Application` class, which we subclass. According to the Javadoc for `javafx.application.Application`, the JavaFX runtime performs the following steps when starting an application:

1. Constructs an instance of the specified `Application` class.
2. Calls the `init()` method.
3. Calls the `start(javafx.stage.Stage)` method.
4. Waits for the application to finish, which happens when any of the following occur:
    1. The application calls `Platform.exit()`.
    2. The last window has been closed, and the `implicitExit` attribute on platform is true.
5. Calls the `stop()` method.

We want to perform our `ClassLoader` work at step 1, in the constructor of our `Application`, to make sure that everything that follows has an up-to-date `ClassLoader`. That work is done in the second method that we need to add, which is this:

```
private void updateClassLoader() {
  final File[] jars = getFiles();
  if (jars != null) {
    URL[] urls = new URL[jars.length];
    int index = 0;
    for (File jar : jars) {
      try {
        urls[index] = jar.toURI().toURL();
        index++;
      } catch (MalformedURLException ex) {
          Logger.getLogger(Sunago.class.getName())
            .log(Level.SEVERE, null, ex);
      }
    }
    Thread.currentThread().setContextClassLoader(
      URLClassLoader.newInstance(urls));
  }
}
```

We start by getting a list of the jar files (we'll see that code in a moment), then, if the array is non-null, we need to build an array of URLs, so, we iterate over the `File` array, and call `.toURI().toURL()` to do so. Once we have our URL array we create a new `ClassLoader` (`URLClassLoader.newInstance(urls)`), then set the `ClassLoader` for the current Thread via `Thread.currentThread().setContextClassLoader()`.

This is our final additional method `getFiles()`:

```
private File[] getFiles() {
    String pluginDir = System.getProperty("user.home")
    + "/.sunago";
    return new File(pluginDir).listFiles(file -> file.isFile() &&
    file.getName().toLowerCase().endsWith(".jar"));
}
```

This last method simply scans the files in $HOME/.sunago, looking for a file that ends with .jar. A list of zero or more jar files is returned to our calling code for inclusion in the new `ClassLoader`, and our work is done.

So there you have two ways of adding plugin jars to the runtime dynamically. Each has its strengths and weaknesses. The first requires multi-platform development and maintenance, while the second is a bit riskier, as classloaders can be tricky. I have tested the second approach on Windows and Linux and Java 8 and 9 with no errors detected. Which approach you use will, of course, depend on your unique environment and requirements, but you have at least two options with which to start your evaluation.

Summary

With all of that said, our application is complete. Of course, hardly any software is truly complete, and there's much more that could be done to Sunago. Twitter support could be expanded to include direct messages. The Instagram module needs some configuration options added. While the capabilities exposed via the Facebook API are limiting, some sort of meaningful Facebook integration could be added. Sunago itself could be modified to, say, add support for in-application viewing of social media content (as opposed to shelling out to the host operating system's default browser). There are a handful of minor user experience bugs that could be addressed. And the list can go on and on. What we do have, though, is a moderately complex, networked application, that demonstrates a number of features and capabilities of the Java platform. We've built an extensible, internationalized JavaFX application that demonstrates the use of the Service Provider Interface and `ClassLoader` magic, and offers many more examples of lambdas, stream operations, and functional interfaces.

In the next chapter, we're going to build on the ideas presented here, and build an Android port of Sunago so that we can take our social media aggregation on-the-go with us.

6
Sunago - An Android Port

In the last chapter, we built Sunago, a social media aggregation application. In that chapter, we learned that Sunago is a JavaFX-based application that can pull posts, tweets, photos, and so on from a variety of social media networks and display them in one place. The application certainly provided a number of interesting architectural and technical examples, but the application itself could be more practical--we tend to interact with social networks from mobile devices such as phones and tablets, so a mobile version would be much more useful. In this chapter, then, we'll write an Android port, reusing as much of the code as possible.

Android applications, while built in Java, look quite a bit different than, say, a desktop application. While we can't cover every aspect of Android development, we'll cover enough in this chapter to get you started, including the following:

- Setting up an Android development environment
- Gradle builds
- Android views
- Android state management
- Android services
- Application packaging and deployment

Like the other chapters, there will be too many small items to call out each of them, but we'll do our best to highlight the new ones as they're introduced.

Getting started

The first step is to get the Android development environment set up. As with *regular* Java development, an IDE isn't strictly necessary, but it sure helps, so we'll install Android Studio, which is an IDE based on IntelliJ IDEA. If you already have IDEA installed, you can just install the Android plugin and have everything you need. For our purposes here, though, we'll assume you don't have either installed.

1. To download Android Studio, go to
   `https://developer.android.com/studio/index.html`, and download the package appropriate for your operating system. When you start **Android Studio** for the first time, you should see following screen:

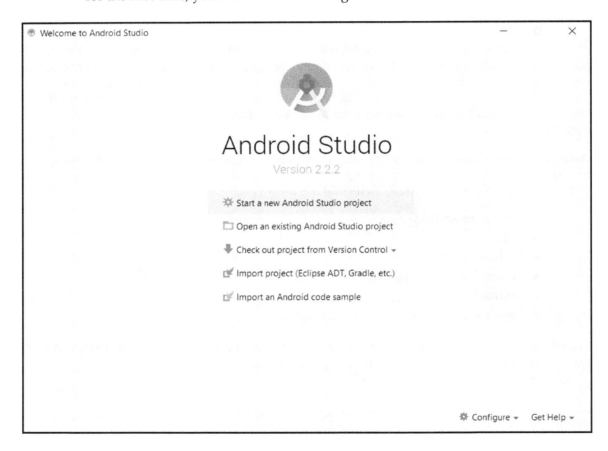

2. Before we start a new project, let's configure the Android SDKs that are available. Click on the **Configure** menu in the bottom-right corner, then click on **SDK Manager** to get this screen:

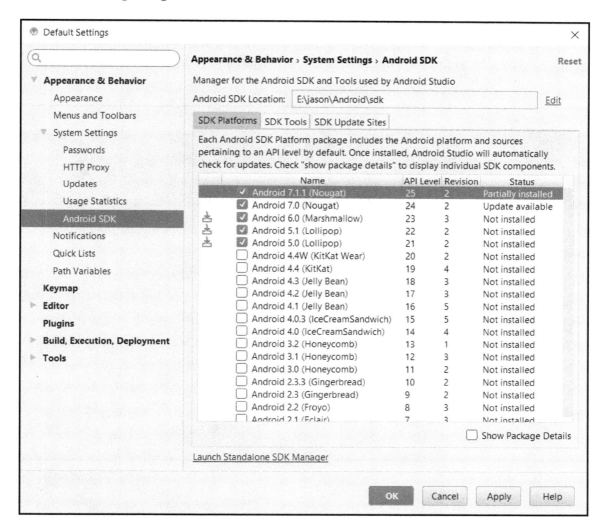

Which SDKs you select will vary depending on your needs. You may need to support older devices as far back as, say, Android 5.0, or maybe you just want to support the very latest with Android 7.0 or 7.1.1.

3. Once you know what need, select the appropriate SDKs (or do as I've done in the preceding screenshot and select everything from 5.0 and forward), then click on **OK**. You will need to read and accept the license before continuing.

4. Once you've done that, Android Studio will begin downloading the selected SDKs and any dependencies. This process can take a while, so be patient.

5. When the SDK installation completes, click on the **Finish** button, which will take you take to the Welcome screen. Click on **Start a new Android Studio** project to get the following screen:

6. Nothing exciting here--we need to specify the **Application name**, **Company domain**, and **Project location** of our app:

7. Next, though, we need to specify the form factor for our app. Our options are Phone and Tablet, Wear, TV, Android Auto, and Glass. As seen in this preceding screenshot, all we're interested in for this application is **Phone and Tablet**.

8. On the next window, we need to select a type for the main `Activity` for the application. In an Android application, what we might refer to as a *screen* (or maybe *page*, if you're coming from a web application background) is known as an `Activity`. Not every `Activity` is a screen, though.

From the Android developer documentation (`https://developer.android.com/reference/android/app/Activity.html`), we learn the following:

> *[a]n activity is a single, focused thing that the user can do. Almost all activities interact with the user, so the Activity class takes care of creating a window for you...*

For our purposes, it's probably acceptable to equate the two, but do so loosely, and always with this caveat in mind. The wizard gives us many options, as seen in this screenshot:

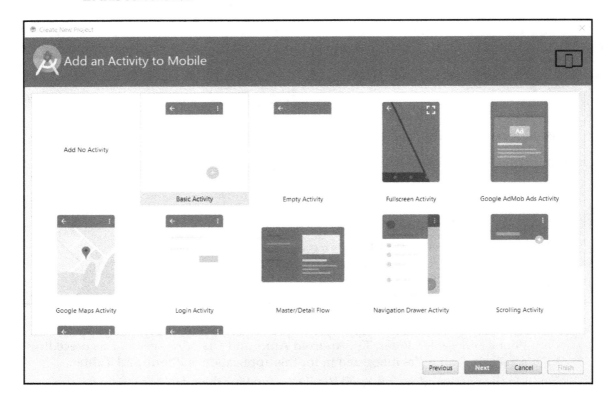

9. As you can see, there are several options: **Basic**, **Empty**, **Fullscreen**, **Google AdMobs Ads**, **Google Maps**, **Login**, and so on. Which to choose depends, again, on what your requirements are for the application. Our bare minimum requirements, in terms of user interface, are that it tells the user the name of the app, shows the list of social media items, and provides a menu for changing the application settings. From the preceding list, then, the **Basic Activity** is the closest match, so we select that, and click on **Next**:

10. The defaults in the preceding screen are mostly acceptable (notice that **Activity Name** was changed), but before we click on **Finish**, there are a few final words. When building an Android application of any size, you are going to have a lot of layouts, menus, activities, and so on. I have found it helpful to name these artifacts as you see here--the layout for an `Activity` is named `activity_` plus the `Activity` name; menus are `menu_` plus the activity name, or, for shared menus, a meaningful summary of its contents. Each artifact type is prefixed by its type. This general pattern will help you quickly navigate to the source file as the number of files grows, as the arrangement of these files is very flat and shallow.

11. Finally, notice the **Use a Fragment** checkbox. *A Fragment is a piece of an application's user interface or behavior that can be placed in an Activity.* It is, effectively, a way for you, as the developer, to decompose the user interface definition into multiple pieces (or Fragments, thus, the name) that can be composed into a whole in an Activity in different ways depending on the current context of the application. For example, a Fragment-based user interface might have two screens for certain operations on a phone, but might combine those into one Activity for the larger screen on a tablet. It's a bit more complicated than that, of course, but I include that brief and incomplete description simply to give some explanation of the checkbox. We will not be using Fragments in our application, so we leave that unchecked, and click on **Finish**.

After processing for some time, Android Studio now creates a basic application for us. Before we start coding the application, let's run it to see what that process looks like. We can run the app in a few ways--we can click on **Run | Run 'app'**; click on the green play button in the middle of the toolbar, or press *Shift + F10*. All three will bring up the same **Select Deployment Target** window, as follows:

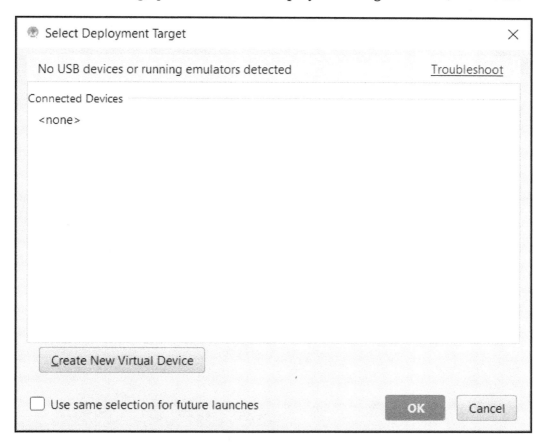

Since we just installed Android Studio, we don't have any emulators created, so we need to do that now. To create the emulators, follow these steps:

1. Clicking on the **Create New Virtual Device** button gets us this screen:

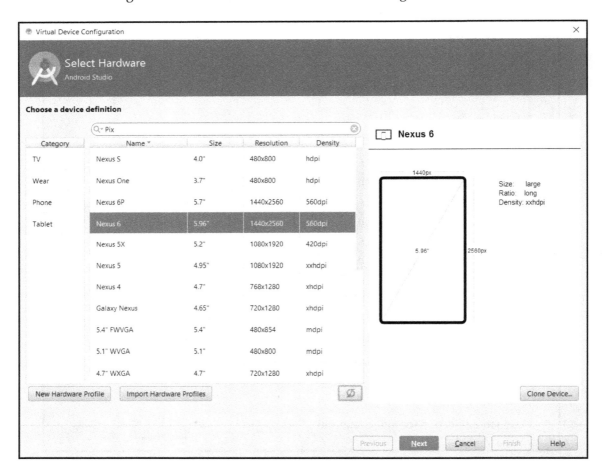

2. Let's start with a reasonably modern Android phone--select the **Nexus 6** profile, and click on **Next**:

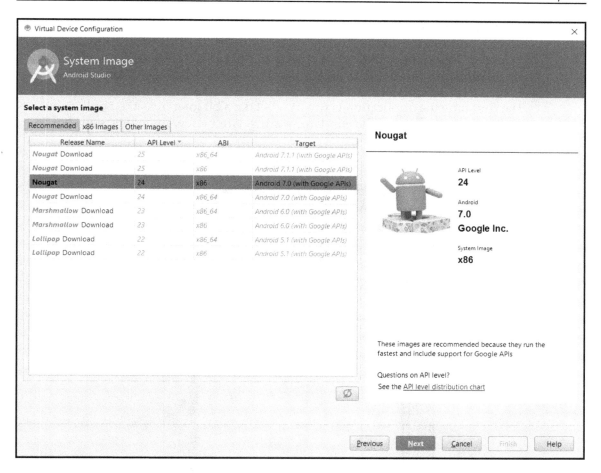

In the preceding screen, your options will vary based on which SDKs you've installed. Which SDK you choose, again, depends on your target audience, application needs, and so on. As enjoyable as it always is to use the latest and greatest, we don't strictly need any APIs from, say, **Nougat**. Choosing Android 7.x would restrict the availability of Sunago to those on very new phones, and do so for no good reason. We will, then, target **Lollipop** (**Android 5.0**), which strikes a good balance between supporting as many users as possible and providing access to newer Android features.

3. Click the **Download** link if necessary for the **x86_64** ABI, select that release, click on **Next**, and then click on **Finish** on the **Verify Configuration** screen.

4. With an emulator created, we can now select it in the **Select Deployment Target** screen, and run the application by clicking on **OK**. If you want to skip the selection screen the next time you run the application, you can check the **Use same selection for future launches** checkbox before clicking on **OK**.

The first time the application is run, it will take a bit longer, as the application is built and packaged and the emulator started. After a few moments, you should see the following screen:

It's nothing special, but it shows that everything is working as expected. Now, we're ready to start the real work in porting Sunago.

Building the user interface

Put simply, Android user interfaces are based on Activities, which use layout files to describe the structure of the user interface. There's more to it, of course, but this simple definition should be sufficient for our work on Sunago. Let's start, then, by looking at our Activity, MainActivity, which is as follows:

```java
public class MainActivity extends AppCompatActivity {
    @Override
    protected void onCreate(Bundle savedInstanceState) {
        super.onCreate(savedInstanceState);
        setContentView(R.layout.activity_main);
        Toolbar toolbar = (Toolbar) findViewById(R.id.toolbar);
        setSupportActionBar(toolbar);

        FloatingActionButton fab =
            (FloatingActionButton) findViewById(R.id.fab);
        fab.setOnClickListener(new View.OnClickListener() {
            @Override
            public void onClick(View view) {
                Snackbar.make(view,
                        "Replace with your own action",
                        Snackbar.LENGTH_LONG)
                    .setAction("Action", null).show();
            }
        });
    }

    @Override
    public boolean onCreateOptionsMenu(Menu menu) {
        getMenuInflater().inflate(R.menu.menu_main, menu);
        return true;
    }
    @Override
    public boolean onOptionsItemSelected(MenuItem item) {
        int id = item.getItemId();

        if (id == R.id.action_settings) {
            return true;
        }

        return super.onOptionsItemSelected(item);
    }
}
```

This last bit of code is the class exactly as it was generated by Android Studio. It's very basic, but it has most of what you need to create an `Activity`. Note that the class extends `AppCompatActivity`. While Google has been very active in pushing the Android platform, they have also worked tirelessly to make sure that older devices aren't left behind any sooner than they have to be. To achieve that, Google has backported many new features in "compat" (or compatibility) packages, which means many of the newer APIs will actually run on older versions of Android. The changes, though, since they are in separate packages, won't break any existing functionality--they must be explicitly opted for, which is what we're doing here. While we're not planning on supporting older versions of Android, such as KitKat, it is still suggested that your `Activity` classes extend the compatibility classes, like this one, as there is a significant number of features built in to these classes that we would otherwise have to implement ourselves. Let's walk through this class to get a sense of what all is going on in the following steps:

1. The first method is `onCreate()`, which is an `Activity` life cycle method (we'll talk more about Activity life cycle in a moment). When the system creates the `Activity` class, this method is called. It is here that we initialize the user interface, setting values, connection controls to data sources, and so on. Note that the method takes a **Bundle**. This is how Android passes in the Activity state so that it may be restored.

   In the `setContentView(R.layout.activity_main)` method, we tell the system what layout we want to use for this `Activity`. Once we've set the content `View` for `Activity`, we can then start acquiring references to various elements. Notice that we first look for the `Toolbar` defined in the view, `findViewById(R.id.toolbar)`, then we tell Android to use that as our action bar via `setSupportActionBar()`. This is an example of a functionality that is implemented for us via the `compat` class. If we extended, say, `Activity` directly, we would be required to do much more work to make the action bar work. As it is, we call one setter and we're done.

2. Next, we look up another user interface element, the `FloatingActionButton`. In the preceding screenshot, this is the button in the lower-right corner with the email icon. We will actually be removing this, but, since Android Studio generated it, we can learn what we can from it before it is removed. Once we have a reference to it, we can attach listeners. In this case, we're adding an `on` `Click` listener by creating an anonymous inner class of type `View.OnClickListener`. This works, but we've just spent the last five chapters getting rid of those.

3. The Android build system now natively supports using Java 8, so we can modify the `onClick` listener registration to look like this:

```
fab.setOnClickListener(view -> Snackbar.make(view,
    "Replace with your own action",
        Snackbar.LENGTH_LONG)
    .setAction("Action", null).show());
```

When the user taps the button, the Snackbar appears. According to the Google documentation, *Snackbars provide brief feedback about an operation through a message at the bottom of the screen*. And that's exactly what we get--a message telling us to replace the `onClick` result with our own action. As stated earlier, though, we don't need the floating button, so we'll remove this method and, later, the view definition from the layout.

4. The next method in the class is `onCreateOptionsMenu()`. This method is called when the options menu is first opened to populate the list of items. We use `MenuInflater` to inflate the menu definition file, and add what it defined there to `Menu` that the system passes in. This method is called only once, though, so if you need a menu that changes, you should override `onPrepareOptionsMenu(Menu)`.

5. The final method, `onOptionsItemSelected()`, is called when the user taps an options menu item. The specific `MenuItem` selected is passed in. We get its ID, and call the method appropriate for the menu item.

That's a basic `Activity`, but what does a layout look like? Here are the contents of `activity_main.xml`:

```xml
<?xml version="1.0" encoding="utf-8"?>
<android.support.design.widget.CoordinatorLayout
  xmlns:android="http://schemas.android.com/apk/res/android"
  xmlns:app="http://schemas.android.com/apk/res-auto"
  xmlns:tools="http://schemas.android.com/tools"
  android:layout_width="match_parent"
  android:layout_height="match_parent"
  android:fitsSystemWindows="true"
  tools:context="com.steeplesoft.sunago.MainActivity">

  <android.support.design.widget.AppBarLayout
    android:layout_width="match_parent"
    android:layout_height="wrap_content"
    android:theme="@style/AppTheme.AppBarOverlay">

  <android.support.v7.widget.Toolbar
```

```
      android:id="@+id/toolbar"
      android:layout_width="match_parent"
      android:layout_height="?attr/actionBarSize"
      android:background="?attr/colorPrimary"
      app:popupTheme="@style/AppTheme.PopupOverlay" />

  </android.support.design.widget.AppBarLayout>

  <include layout="@layout/content_main" />

  <android.support.design.widget.FloatingActionButton
      android:id="@+id/fab"
      android:layout_width="wrap_content"
      android:layout_height="wrap_content"
      android:layout_gravity="bottom|end"
      android:layout_margin="@dimen/fab_margin"
      app:srcCompat="@android:drawable/ic_dialog_email" />

  </android.support.design.widget.CoordinatorLayout>
```

That's a fair bit of XML, so let's walk through the major items of interest quickly, as follows:

1. The root element is `CoordinatorLayout`. Its Java document describes it as a super-powered `FrameLayout`. One of its intended purposes is as *a top-level application decor or chrome layout*, which is exactly what we're using it for here. Layouts such as `CoordinatorLayout` are roughly analogous to JavaFX's containers. Different layouts (or `ViewGroup`) provide a variety of capabilities such as laying out elements with exact X/Y coordinates (`AbsoluteLayout`), in a grid (`GridLayout`), relative to each other (`RelativeLayout`), and so on.

2. In addition to providing our top-level container, the element defines a number of required XML namespaces. It also sets the height and width for the control. There are three possible values for this field--`match_parent` (in earlier versions of the SDK, this was called `fill_parent` should you ever come across that), which means that the control should match the value of its parent, `wrap_content`, which means the control should be just big enough for its contents; or an exact number.

3. The next element is `AppBarLayout`, which is a `ViewGroup` that implements a number of the material designs app bar concepts. **Material design** is the latest **visual language** being developed and supported by Google. It provides a modern, consistent look and feel across Android apps. Its usage is encouraged by Google, and fortunately, the new `Activity` wizard has set us up to use it out of the box. The layout's width is set to `match_parent` so that it fills the screen, and the width is set to `wrap_content` so that's it's just big enough to show its content, which is a single `Toolbar`.

4. Skipping the `include` element for a moment, the last element in the view is `FloatingActionButton`. Our only interest here is noting that the widget exists, should the need for one arise in other projects. As we did in the `Activity` class though, we need to remove this widget.

5. Finally, there's the `include` element. This does what you would think it should-- the specified file is included in the layout definition as if its contents were hard coded into the file. This allows us to keep our layout files small, reuse user interface element definitions (which is especially helpful for complex scenarios), and so on.

The included file, `content_main.xml`, looks like this:

```xml
<RelativeLayout
  xmlns:android="http://schemas.android.com/apk/res/android"
  xmlns:app="http://schemas.android.com/apk/res-auto"
  xmlns:tools="http://schemas.android.com/tools"
  android:id="@+id/content_main"
  android:layout_width="match_parent"
  android:layout_height="match_parent"
  android:paddingBottom="@dimen/activity_vertical_margin"
  android:paddingLeft="@dimen/activity_horizontal_margin"
  android:paddingRight="@dimen/activity_horizontal_margin"
  android:paddingTop="@dimen/activity_vertical_margin"
  app:layout_behavior="@string/appbar_scrolling_view_behavior"
  tools:context="com.steeplesoft.sunago.MainActivity"
  tools:showIn="@layout/activity_main">

  <TextView
    android:layout_width="wrap_content"
    android:layout_height="wrap_content"
    android:text="Hello World!" />
</RelativeLayout>
```

This preceding view uses `RelativeLayout` to wrap its only child, a `TextView`. Note that we can set the padding of a control. This controls how much space is *inside* the control around its children. Think of it like packing a box--inside the box, you may have a fragile ceramic antique, so you pad the box to protect it. You can also set the margin of a control, which is the space *outside* the control, akin to the personal space around us we are so often fond of.

The `TextView`, though, isn't helpful, so we'll remove that, and add what we really need, which is a `ListView`, as follows:

```
<ListView
    android:id="@+id/listView"
    android:layout_width="match_parent"
    android:layout_height="match_parent"
    android:layout_alignParentTop="true"
    android:layout_alignParentStart="true"/>
```

`ListView` is a control that shows items in a vertically scrolling list. In terms of user experience, this works pretty much like the `ListView` we looked at in JavaFX. How it works, though, is quite different. To see how, we need to make some adjustments to activity's `onCreate()` method as follows:

```
protected void onCreate(Bundle savedInstanceState) {
    super.onCreate(savedInstanceState);
    setContentView(R.layout.activity_main);

    if (!isNetworkAvailable()) {
        showErrorDialog(
            "A valid internet connection can't be established");
    } else {
        Toolbar toolbar = (Toolbar) findViewById(R.id.toolbar);
        setSupportActionBar(toolbar);
        findPlugins();

        adapter = new SunagoCursorAdapter(this, null, 0);
        final ListView listView = (ListView)
            findViewById(R.id.listView);
        listView.setAdapter(adapter);
        listView.setOnItemClickListener(
                new AdapterView.OnItemClickListener() {
            @Override
            public void onItemClick(AdapterView<?> adapterView,
                    View view, int position, long id) {
                Cursor c = (Cursor)
                    adapterView.getItemAtPosition(position);
                String url = c.getString(c.getColumnIndex(
```

```
                    SunagoContentProvider.URL));
                Intent intent = new Intent(Intent.ACTION_VIEW,
                    Uri.parse(url));
                startActivity(intent);
            }
        });

        getLoaderManager().initLoader(0, null, this);
    }
}
```

There are several things going on here, which sets us up nicely for discussing data access in Android. Before we get to that in detail, though, a quick overview is in order:

1. We check to make sure that the device has a working network connection via `isNetworkAvailable()`, which we'll look at later in this chapter.

2. If the connection is available, we configure the user interface, starting with setting the toolbar.

3. Next, we create an instance of `SunagoCursorAdapter`, which we'll discuss in detail later. For now, though, just note that an `Adapter` is how the `ListView` is connected to the data source, and they can be backed by things as varied as an SQL datasource or an `Array`.

4. We pass the adapter to `ListView`, thus completing this connection via `ListView.setAdapter()`. Much like JavaFX's `Observable` model property, we'll be able to use this to update the user interface without direct interaction any time the data changes.

5. Next, we set up an `onClick` listener for the items in the list. We'll use this to display the item the user taps (or clicks) on in an external browser. In a nutshell, given the `position` parameter, we get the item at that position, a `Cursor`, extract the URL of the item, then display the page at that URL using the device's default browser via an `Intent` (which we'll discuss in detail later).

6. Finally, completing our data binding, we initialize the `LoaderManager` that will handle loading and updating the `Adapter` in an asynchronous manner.

One last bit of code to look at before diving into data access--`isNetworkAvailable()`-- is as follows:

```
public boolean isNetworkAvailable() {
  boolean connected = false;
  ConnectivityManager cm = (ConnectivityManager)
    getSystemService(Context.CONNECTIVITY_SERVICE);
  for (Network network : cm.getAllNetworks()) {
    NetworkInfo networkInfo = cm.getNetworkInfo(network);
```

```
          if (networkInfo.isConnected() == true) {
              connected = true;
              break;
          }
      }
    return connected;
  }

  private void showErrorDialog(String message) {
      AlertDialog alertDialog = new AlertDialog.Builder(this)
        .create();
      alertDialog.setTitle("Error!");
      alertDialog.setMessage(message);
      alertDialog.setIcon(android.R.drawable.alert_dark_frame);
      alertDialog.setButton(DialogInterface.BUTTON_POSITIVE,
      "OK", new DialogInterface.OnClickListener() {
        @Override
        public void onClick(DialogInterface dialog, int which) {
          MainActivity.this.finish();
        }
      });

      alertDialog.show();
  }
```

In the preceding code, we start by getting a reference to the system service, ConnectivityManager, then we loop through each Network known to the system. For each Network, we get a reference to its NetworkInfo and call isConnected(). If we find one connected network, we return true, otherwise, we return false. In the calling code, if our return value is false, we show an error dialog, the method for which is shown here as well. This is a standard Android dialog. We have, however, added an onClick listener to the **OK** button, which closes the application. Using this, we tell the user that a network connection is needed, then close the app when the user taps on **OK**. It is debatable, of course, if this behavior is desirable, but the process for determining a device's network state is interesting enough, so I've included it here.

Let's turn our attention now to how data access is often done in Android apps-- CursorAdapters.

Android data access

With any platform, there are multiple ways to access data, from built-in facilities to homegrown APIs. Android is no different, so while you can write your own way to load data from some arbitrary data source, unless you have very particular requirements, there is often no need, as Android has a system built in--the `ContentProvider`.

The Android documentation will tell you that a *content provider manages access to a central repository of data*, and that it offers a consistent, *standard interface to data that also handles inter-process communication and secure data access*. If you intend to expose your application's data to external sources (either for read or write), `ContentProvider` is a great way to go. However, if you don't intend to expose your data, you are more than welcome to write the needed CRUD methods yourself, manually issuing various SQL statements. In our case, we'll use a `ContentProvider`, as we have an interest in allowing third-party developers access to the data.

To create a `ContentProvider`, we need to create a new class that extends `ContentProvider` as follows:

```
public class SunagoContentProvider extends ContentProvider {
```

We also need to register the provider in `AndroidManfest.xml`, which we'll do like this:

```
<provider android:name=".data.SunagoContentProvider
  android:authorities="com.steeplesoft.sunago.SunagoProvider" />
```

Interaction with `ContentProvider` is never done directly. The client code will specify the URL of the data to be manipulated, and the Android system will direct the request to the appropriate provider. To make sure our `ContentProvider` functions as expected, then, we need to register the provider's authority, which we've already seen in the previous XML. In our provider, we'll create some static fields to help us manage the parts of our authority and the related URLs in a DRY manner.

```
private static final String PROVIDER_NAME =
  "com.steeplesoft.sunago.SunagoProvider";
private static final String CONTENT_URL =
  "content://" + PROVIDER_NAME + "/items";
public static final Uri CONTENT_URI = Uri.parse(CONTENT_URL);
```

The first two fields in the preceding bit of code are private, as they're not needed outside the class. We define them as separate fields here, though, for clarity's sake. The third field, CONTENT_URI, is public, as we'll be referencing that field elsewhere in our app. Third-party consumers won't have access to the field, obviously, but will need to know its value, content://com.steeplesoft.sunago.SunagoProvider/items, which we would document somewhere for add-on developers. The first part of the URL, the protocol field, tells Android that we're looking for a ContentProvider. The next section is the authority, which uniquely identifies a particular ContentProvider, and the final field specifies the type of data, or model, that we're interested in. For Sunago, we have a single data type, items.

Next, we need to specify the URIs we want to support. We only have two--one for the items collection, and one for a particular item. Please, refer to following code snippet:

```
private static final UriMatcher URI_MATCHER =
  new UriMatcher(UriMatcher.NO_MATCH);
private static final int ITEM = 1;
private static final int ITEM_ID = 2;
static {
  URI_MATCHER.addURI(PROVIDER_NAME, "items", ITEM);
  URI_MATCHER.addURI(PROVIDER_NAME, "items/#", ITEM_ID);
}
```

In the last code, we start by creating a UriMatcher. Note that we pass UriMatcher.NO_MATCH to the constructor. It's not immediately clear what this value is for, but this is the value that will be returned if the user passes in a URI that doesn't match any of those registered. Finally, we register each URI with a unique int identifier.

Next, like many Android classes, we need specify an onCreate lifecycle hook as follows:

```
public boolean onCreate() {
  openHelper = new SunagoOpenHelper(getContext(), DBNAME,
    null, 1);
  return true;
}
```

SunagoOpenHelper is a child of SQLiteOpenHelper, which manages the creation and/or update of the underlying SQLite database. The class itself is pretty simple, and is given as follows:

```
public class SunagoOpenHelper extends SQLiteOpenHelper {
  public SunagoOpenHelper(Context context, String name,
      SQLiteDatabase.CursorFactory factory, int version) {
    super(context, name, factory, version);
  }
```

```
@Override
public void onCreate(SQLiteDatabase db) {
  db.execSQL(SQL_CREATE_MAIN);
}

@Override
public void onUpgrade(SQLiteDatabase db, int oldVersion,
  int newVersion) {
}
}
```

I've not shown the table creation DDL, as it's a pretty simple table creation, but this class is all you need to create and maintain your database. If you have multiple tables, you would issue multiple creates in `onCreate`. When the application updates, `onUpgrade()` is called to allow you to modify the schema if needed.

Back in our `ContentProvider`, we need to implement two methods, one to read data, and one to insert (given the nature of the app, we're not interested in deletes or updates right now). For reading data, we override `query()` as follows:

```
public Cursor query(Uri uri, String[] projection,
  String selection, String[] selectionArgs,
  String sortOrder) {
    switch (URI_MATCHER.match(uri)) {
      case 2:
        selection = selection + "_ID = " +
          uri.getLastPathSegment();
          break;
    }
    SQLiteDatabase db = openHelper.getReadableDatabase();
    Cursor cursor = db.query("items", projection, selection,
      selectionArgs, null, null, sortOrder);
    cursor.setNotificationUri(
      getContext().getContentResolver(), uri);
    return cursor;
}
```

This last code is where our URIs and their `int` identifiers come in. Using `UriMatcher`, we check the `Uri` passed in by the caller. Given that our provider is simple, the only one we need to do anything special for is #2, which is the query for a specific item. In that case, we extract the ID passed in as the last path segment, and add it to the selection criteria specified by the caller.

Once we have the query configured as requested, we get a readable SQLiteDatabase from our openHelper, and query it using the values passed by the caller. This is one of the areas where the ContentProvider contract comes in handy--we don't need to write any SELECT statements manually.

Before returning the cursor, we need to do something to it, as follows:

```
cursor.setNotificationUri(getContext().getContentResolver(), uri);
```

With this preceding call, we tell the system that we want the cursor notified when the data is updated. Since we're using a Loader, this will allow us to update the user interface automatically when data is inserted.

For inserting data, we override insert() as follows:

```
public Uri insert(Uri uri, ContentValues values) {
  SQLiteDatabase db = openHelper.getWritableDatabase();
  long rowID = db.insert("items", "", values);

  if (rowID > 0) {
    Uri newUri = ContentUris.withAppendedId(CONTENT_URI,
        rowID);
    getContext().getContentResolver().notifyChange(newUri,
        null);
    return newUri;
  }

  throw new SQLException("Failed to add a record into " + uri);
}
```

Using openHelper, this time, we get a writable instance of the database, on which we call insert(). The insert method returns the ID of the row just inserted. If we get a non-zero ID, we generate a URI for the row, which we'll eventually return. Before we do so, however, we notify the content resolver of the change in the data, which triggers our auto-reload in the user interface.

We have one more step to finish our data loading code, though. If you look back on MainActivity.onCreate(), you'll see this line:

```
getLoaderManager().initLoader(0, null, this);
```

This last line tells the system that we want to initialize a `Loader` and that the `Loader` is `this` or `MainActivity`. In our definition of `MainActivity`, we've specified that it implements the `LoaderManager.LoaderCallbacks<Cursor>` interface. This requires us to implement a few methods as follows:

```
public Loader<Cursor> onCreateLoader(int i, Bundle bundle) {
  CursorLoader cl = new CursorLoader(this,
    SunagoContentProvider.CONTENT_URI,
    ITEM_PROJECTION, null, null,
      SunagoContentProvider.TIMESTAMP + " DESC");
  return cl;
}

public void onLoadFinished(Loader<Cursor> loader, Cursor cursor) {
  adapter.swapCursor(cursor);
}

public void onLoaderReset(Loader<Cursor> loader) {
  adapter.swapCursor(null);
}
```

In `onCreateLoader()`, we specify both what to load and where to load it. We pass in the URI of the `ContentProvider` we just created, we specify the fields we're interested in via the `ITEM_PROJECTION` variable (which is a `String[]`, and not shown here), and, finally, the sort order (which we've specified as the timestamp of the items in descending order so that we get the newest items on top). The method `onLoadFinished()` is where the auto-reload happens. Once a new `Cursor` is created for the updated data, we swap it in for the `Cursor` that `Adapter` is currently using. While you can write your own persistence code, this highlights why using the platform facilities, whenever possible, can be a wise choice.

There is one large item left to look at with regard to data handling--`SunagoCursorAdapter`. Looking again at the Android Javadocs, we learn that *an* `Adapter` *object acts as a bridge between an* `AdapterView` *and the underlying data for that view*, and that `CursorAdapter` *exposes data from a* `Cursor` *to a* `ListView` *widget*. Often--if not in the majority of cases--a particular `ListView` will require a custom `CursorAdapter` to allow the underlying data to be rendered correctly. Sunago is no exception. To create our `Adapter`, then, we create a new class as follows:

```
public class SunagoCursorAdapter extends CursorAdapter {
  public SunagoCursorAdapter(Context context, Cursor c,
  int flags) {
    super(context, c, flags);
}
```

This is pretty standard fare. The truly interesting parts come in the view creation, which is one of the reasons for being for a `CursorAdapter`. When the `Adapter` needs to create a new view to hold the data pointed to by the cursor, it calls the following method. This is where we specify what the view should look like with the call to `LayoutInflater.inflate()`:

```
public View newView(Context context, Cursor cursor,
    ViewGroup viewGroup) {
  View view = LayoutInflater.from(context).inflate(
  R.layout.social_media_item, viewGroup, false);
  ViewHolder viewHolder = new ViewHolder();
  viewHolder.text = (TextView)
  view.findViewById(R.id.textView);
  viewHolder.image = (ImageView) view.findViewById(
  R.id.imageView);

  WindowManager wm = (WindowManager) Sunago.getAppContext()
    .getSystemService(Context.WINDOW_SERVICE);
  Point size = new Point();
  wm.getDefaultDisplay().getSize(size);
  viewHolder.image.getLayoutParams().width =
    (int) Math.round(size.x * 0.33);

  view.setTag(viewHolder);
  return view;
}
```

We'll look at our layout definition in a moment, but first, let's take a look at `ViewHolder`:

```
private static class ViewHolder {
  public TextView text;
  public ImageView image;
}
```

Finding views by ID can be an expensive operation, so a very common pattern is this `ViewHolder` approach. After the view is inflated, we immediately look up the fields we're interested in, and store those references in a `ViewHolder` instance, which is then stored as the tag on the `View`. Since views are recycled by the `ListView` class (meaning, they're reused as needed as you scroll through the data), this expensive `findViewById()` is called once and cached per `View` rather than once per item in the underlying data. For large datasets (and complex views), this can be a substantial performance boost.

In this method, we also set the size of the `ImageView` class. Android doesn't support setting the width of a view to a percentage via the XML markup (given next), so we do that manually here as we create the `View`. We get the `WindowManager` system service from which we get the default display's size. We multiply the display's width by 0.33, which will restrict the image, if any, to 1/3 of the display's width, and set the `ImageView`'s width to that.

So, what does the view look like for each row?

```
<LinearLayout
  xmlns:android="http://schemas.android.com/apk/res/android"
  xmlns:app="http://schemas.android.com/apk/res-auto"
  xmlns:tools="http://schemas.android.com/tools"
  android:layout_width="match_parent"
  android:layout_height="match_parent"
  android:orientation="horizontal">

  <ImageView
    android:id="@+id/imageView"
    android:layout_width="wrap_content"
    android:layout_height="wrap_content"
    android:layout_marginEnd="5dip"
    android:layout_gravity="top"
    android:adjustViewBounds="true"/>

  <TextView
    android:layout_width="match_parent"
    android:layout_height="wrap_content"
    android:id="@+id/textView"
    android:scrollHorizontally="false"
    android:textSize="18sp" />
</LinearLayout>
```

As the `ViewHolder` hinted, our view consists of an `ImageView` and a `TextView`, presented horizontally, thanks to the enclosing `LinearLayout`.

While `CursorAdapter` calls `newView()` to create a `View`, it calls `bindView()` to--if you can imagine--bind the `View` to a specific row in the `Cursor`. This is where `View` recycling comes into play. The `Adapter` has a number of `View` instances cached, and passes one to this method as needed. Our method looks like this:

```
public void bindView(View view, Context context, Cursor cursor) {
  final ViewHolder viewHolder = (ViewHolder) view.getTag();
  String image = cursor.getString(INDEX_IMAGE);
  if (image != null) {
    new DownloadImageTask(viewHolder.image).execute(image);
```

```
  } else {
    viewHolder.image.setImageBitmap(null);
    viewHolder.image.setVisibility(View.GONE);
  }
  viewHolder.body.setText(cursor.getString(INDEX_BODY));
}
```

We start by getting the `ViewHolder` instance. As discussed previously, we'll use the widget references stored here to update the user interface. Next, we pull the image URL from the cursor. It's up to each `SocialMediaItem` to decide how this field is populated, but it might be a tweeted image or a photo in an Instagram post. If the item has one, we need to download it so that it can be displayed. Since this requires a network operation, and we're running on the user interface thread, we hand that work off to `DownloadImageTask`. If there is no image for this item, we need to set the bitmap for the image to `null` (otherwise, the image that was there the last time this view instance was used would be displayed again). That frees up some memory, which is always good, but we also set the `ImageView` class' visibility to `GONE`, which hides it from the user interface. You might be tempted to use `INVISIBLE`, but that only makes it invisible **while preserving its space in the user interface**. The end result of that would be a big blank square, which is not what we want. Finally, we set the text of the `TextView` body to the text specified for the item.

The image downloading is handled off-thread by an `AsyncTask`, which is as follows:

```
private static class DownloadImageTask extends
    AsyncTask<String, Void, Bitmap> {
  private ImageView imageView;

  public DownloadImageTask(ImageView imageView) {
    this.imageView = imageView;
  }
```

Android will create a background `Thread` on which to run this task. The main entry point for our logic is `doInBackground()`. Please refer the following snippet:

```
protected Bitmap doInBackground(String... urls) {
  Bitmap image = null;
  try (InputStream in = new URL(urls[0]).openStream()) {
    image = BitmapFactory.decodeStream(in);
  } catch (java.io.IOException e) {
    Log.e("Error", e.getMessage());
  }
  return image;
}
```

This is not the most robust download code imaginable (for example, redirect status codes are happily ignored), but it's certainly usable. Using Java 7's `try-with-resources`, we create a `URL` instance on which we call `openStream()`. Assuming no `Exception` is thrown in either of those operations, we call `BitmapFactory.decodeStream()` to convert the incoming bytes into a `Bitmap`, which is what the method is expected to return.

So, what happens to the `Bitmap` once we return it? We process that in `onPostExecute()` like this:

```
protected void onPostExecute(Bitmap result) {
    imageView.setImageBitmap(result);
    imageView.setVisibility(View.VISIBLE);
    imageView.getParent().requestLayout();
}
```

In this last method, we update `ImageView` with our now downloaded `Bitmap`, makes it `VISIBLE`, then request that the view update itself on the screen.

So far, we've built an app that's capable of displaying `SocialMediaItem` instances, but we have nothing for it to show. We'll fix that now with a look at Android Services.

Android services

For the desktop version of Sunago, we defined an API that would allow third-party developers (or ourselves) to add support for an arbitrary social network to Sunago. That was a great goal for the desktop, and it's a great goal for mobile. Fortunately, Android provides us with a mechanism that can be used to do just that: Services. *A Service is an application component representing either an application's desire to perform a longer-running operation while not interacting with the user or to supply functionality for other applications to use.* While services were designed for more than extensibility, we can leverage this facility to that end.

While there are a number of ways to implement and interact with services, we are going to bind the services to our `Activity` so that their life cycle is tied to that of our `Activity`, and we'll send messages to them asynchronously. We'll start by defining our class as follows:

```
public class TwitterService extends IntentService {
  public TwitterService() {
    super("TwitterService");
  }

  @Override
  protected void onHandleIntent(Intent intent) {
}
```

Technically, these are the only methods required to create a service. Clearly, it doesn't do much, but we'll fix that in just a moment. Before we do that, we need to declare our new `Service` to Android which is done in `AndroidManifest.xml`, as follows:

```
<service android:name=".twitter.TwitterService"
 android:exported="false">
  <intent-filter>
    <action
      android:name="com.steeplesoft.sunago.intent.plugin" />
    <category
      android:name="android.intent.category.DEFAULT" />
  </intent-filter>
</service>
```

Notice that, in addition to the service declaration, we also specify an `IntentFilter` via the `intent-filter` element. We'll use that in `MainActivity` later to find and bind our services. While we're looking at our service, though, let's look at this side of the binding process. We'll need to implement these two lifecycle methods:

```
public IBinder onBind(Intent intent) {
  receiver = new TwitterServiceReceiver();
  registerReceiver(receiver,
    new IntentFilter("sunago.service"));
  return null;
}

public boolean onUnbind(Intent intent) {
  unregisterReceiver(receiver);
  return super.onUnbind(intent);
}
```

These preceding methods are called when the service is bound and unbound, which give us an opportunity to register our receiver, which may lead to the question: What's that? Android provides an **Interprocess Communication (IPC)**, but it is somewhat limited in that the payload size can not exceed 1 MB. Though our payload is only text, we can (and certainly will, based on my testing) exceed that. Our approach, then, will be to use asynchronous communication, via a receiver, and have the service persist the data via our ContentProvider.

To create a receiver, we extend android.content.BroadcastReceiver as follows:

```
private class TwitterServiceReceiver extends BroadcastReceiver {
    @Override
    public void onReceive(Context context, Intent intent) {
        if ("REFRESH".equals(intent.getStringExtra("message"))) {
            if (SunagoUtil.getPreferences().getBoolean(
                getString(R.string.twitter_authd), false)) {
                new TwitterUpdatesAsyncTask().execute();
            }
        }
    }
}
```

Our message scheme is very simple--Sunago sends the message REFRESH, and the service performs its work, which we have wrapped up in TwitterUpdatesAsyncTask. In onBind(), we register the receiver with a specific IntentFilter that specifies the Intent broadcasts that we're interested in. In onUnbind(), we unregister our receiver as the service is released.

The rest of our service is in our AsyncTask, which is given as follows:

```
private class TwitterUpdatesAsyncTask extends
AsyncTask<Void, Void, List<ContentValues>> {
    @Override
    protected List<ContentValues> doInBackground(Void... voids) {
        List<ContentValues> values = new ArrayList<>();
        for (SocialMediaItem item :
                TwitterClient.instance().getItems()) {
            ContentValues cv = new ContentValues();
            cv.put(SunagoContentProvider.BODY, item.getBody());
            cv.put(SunagoContentProvider.URL, item.getUrl());
            cv.put(SunagoContentProvider.IMAGE, item.getImage());
            cv.put(SunagoContentProvider.PROVIDER,
                item.getProvider());
            cv.put(SunagoContentProvider.TITLE, item.getTitle());
            cv.put(SunagoContentProvider.TIMESTAMP,
                item.getTimestamp().getTime());
```

```
            values.add(cv);
        }
        return values;
    }

    @Override
    protected void onPostExecute(List<ContentValues> values) {
      Log.i(MainActivity.LOG_TAG, "Inserting " + values.size() +
        " tweets.");
      getContentResolver()
        .bulkInsert(SunagoContentProvider.CONTENT_URI,
          values.toArray(new ContentValues[0]));
    }
}
```

We need to make sure that the network operation isn't performed on the user interface thread, so we perform the work in `AsyncTask`. We don't need any parameters passed into the task, so we set the `Params` and `Progress` types to `Void`. We are, though, interested in the `Result` type, which is `List<ContentValue>`, which we see reflected in both the type declaration and the return type of `execute()`. In `onPostExecute()`, we then issue a bulk insert on `ContentProvider` to save the data. In this way, we can make the newly-retrieved data available to the application without running afoul the 1 MB limit with `IBinder`.

With our service defined, we need now to look at how to find and bind the services. Looking back at `MainActivity`, we'll finally look at a method we've already seen mentioned, `findPlugins()`:

```
private void findPlugins() {
 Intent baseIntent = new Intent(PLUGIN_ACTION);
 baseIntent.setFlags(Intent.FLAG_DEBUG_LOG_RESOLUTION);
 List<ResolveInfo> list = getPackageManager()
        .queryIntentServices(baseIntent,
        PackageManager.GET_RESOLVED_FILTER);
 for (ResolveInfo rinfo : list) {
    ServiceInfo sinfo = rinfo.serviceInfo;
    if (sinfo != null) {
        plugins.add(new
            ComponentName(sinfo.packageName, sinfo.name));
    }
  }
}
```

To find the plugins we're interested in, we create an `Intent` with a specific action. In this case, that action is `com.steeplesoft.sunago.intent.plugin`, which we've already seen in the service definition in `AndroidManifest.xml`. Using this `Intent`, we query `PackageManager` for all `IntentServices` matching Intent. Next, we iterate over the list of `ResolveInfo` instances, getting the `ServiceInfo` instances, and create and store a `ComponentName` representing the plugin.

The actual binding of the services is done in the following `bindPlugins()` method, which we call from the `onStart()` method to make sure the binding occurs at the appropriate time in activity's lifecycle:

```
private void bindPluginServices() {
  for (ComponentName plugin : plugins) {
    Intent intent = new Intent();
    intent.setComponent(plugin);
    PluginServiceConnection conn =
        new PluginServiceConnection();
    pluginServiceConnections.add(conn);
    bindService(intent, conn, Context.BIND_AUTO_CREATE);
  }
}
```

For each plugin found, we create an `Intent` using the `ComponentName` we created earlier. Each service binding will need a `ServiceConnection` object. For that, we created `PluginServiceConnection`, which implements the interface. Its methods are empty, so we'll not look at that class here. With our `ServiceConnection` instance, we can now bind the service with a call to `bindService()`.

Finally, to clean up as the application is closing, we need to unbind our services. From `onStop()`, we call this method:

```
private void releasePluginServices() {
  for (PluginServiceConnection conn :
        pluginServiceConnections) {
    unbindService(conn);
  }
  pluginServiceConnections.clear();
}
```

Here, we simply loop through our `ServiceConnection` plugins, passing each to `unbindService()`, which will allow Android to garbage collect any services we may have started.

So far, we've defined a service, looked it up, and bound it. But how do we interact with it? We'll go the simple route, and add an option menu item. To do that, we modify `res/menu/main_menu.xml` as follows:

```
<menu xmlns:android="http://schemas.android.com/apk/res/android"
  xmlns:app="http://schemas.android.com/apk/res-auto"
  xmlns:tools="http://schemas.android.com/tools">
  <item android:id="@+id/action_settings"
    android:orderInCategory="100"
    android:
    app:showAsAction="never" />
 <item android:id="@+id/action_refresh"
    android:orderInCategory="100"
    android:
    app:showAsAction="never" />
</menu>
```

To respond to the menu item being selected, we need to revisit `onOptionsItemSelected()` here:

```
@Override
public boolean onOptionsItemSelected(MenuItem item) {
  switch (item.getItemId()) {
    case R.id.action_settings:
       showPreferencesActivity();
       return true;
    case R.id.action_refresh:
       sendRefreshMessage();
       break;
  }

  return super.onOptionsItemSelected(item);
}
```

In the `switch` block of the preceding code, we add a `case` label for `R.id.action_refresh`, which matches the ID of our newly added menu item in which we call the method `sendRefreshMessage()`:

```
private void sendRefreshMessage() {
  sendMessage("REFRESH");
}

private void sendMessage(String message) {
  Intent intent = new Intent("sunago.service");
  intent.putExtra("message", message);
  sendBroadcast(intent);
}
```

The first method is pretty straightforward. In fact, it might not even be necessary, given its simplicity, but it does add semantic clarity to the consuming code, so I think it's a good method to add.

The interesting part, however, is the method `sendMessage()`. We start by creating an `Intent` that specifies our action, `sunago.service`. This is an arbitrary string that we define, and then document for any third-party consumers. This will help our services filter out messages that are of no interest, which is exactly what we did in `TwitterService.onBind()` with the call to `registerReceiver(receiver, new IntentFilter("sunago.service"))`. We then add the message that our app wants to send (`REFRESH`, in this case) as an extra on `Intent`, which we then broadcast via `sendBroadcast()`. From here, Android will handle delivering the message to our service, which is already running (since we've bound it to our `Activity`) and listening (as we registered a `BroadcastReceiver`).

Android tabs and fragments

We've looked at quite a bit, but there is still a fair bit we haven't seen, such as the implementation for `TwitterClient`, as well as any details on the integration of networks, such as Instagram, which we saw in the last chapter. For the most part, `TwitterClient` is identical to what we saw in Chapter 5, *Sunago - A Social Media Aggregator*. The only major difference is in the use of the stream APIs. Some APIs are only available in certain Android versions, specifically, version 24, also known as Nougat. Since we're targeting Lollipop (SDK version 21), we are unable to use them. That aside, the internal logic and API usage are identical. You can see the details in the source repository. Before we finish, though, we need to take a look at the Twitter preferences screen, as there are some interesting items there.

We'll start with a tab layout activity, as follows:

```java
public class PreferencesActivity extends AppCompatActivity {
    private SectionsPagerAdapter sectionsPagerAdapter;
    private ViewPager viewPager;

    @Override
    protected void onCreate(Bundle savedInstanceState) {
        super.onCreate(savedInstanceState);
        setContentView(R.layout.activity_preferences);

        setSupportActionBar((Toolbar) findViewById(R.id.toolbar));
        sectionsPagerAdapter =
        new SectionsPagerAdapter(getSupportFragmentManager());
```

```
            viewPager = (ViewPager) findViewById(R.id.container);
            viewPager.setAdapter(sectionsPagerAdapter);

            TabLayout tabLayout = (TabLayout) findViewById(R.id.tabs);
            tabLayout.setupWithViewPager(viewPager);
    }
```

For making a tabbed interface, we need two things--FragmentPagerAdapter and ViewPager. The ViewPager is a user-interface element that actually shows the tabs. Think of it as ListView for tabs. The FragmentPagerAdapter, then, is like CursorAdapter for the tabs. Instead of an SQL-backed data source, though, FragmentPagerAdapter is an adapter that represents pages as Fragments. In this method, we create an instance of our SectionsPagerAdapter, and set it as the adapter on our ViewPager. We also associate the ViewPager element with the TabLayout.

SectionsPagerAdapter is a simple class, and is written as follows:

```
        public class SectionsPagerAdapter extends FragmentPagerAdapter {
          public SectionsPagerAdapter(FragmentManager fm) {
            super(fm);
        }

        @Override
        public Fragment getItem(int position) {
            switch (position) {
                case 0 :
                    return new TwitterPreferencesFragment();
                case 1 :
                    return new InstagramPreferencesFragment();
                default:
                    throw new RuntimeException("Invalid position");
            }
        }

        @Override
        public int getCount() {
            return 2;
        }

        @Override
        public CharSequence getPageTitle(int position) {
            switch (position) {
                case 0:
                    return "Twitter";
                case 1:
                    return "Instagram";
            }
```

```
          return null;
    }
  }
```

The method `getCount()` tells the system how many tabs we support, the title for each tab that is returned by `getPageTitle()`, and the `Fragment` representing the selected tab is returned from `getItem()`. In this example, we create a `Fragment` instance as needed. Note, we hint at Instagram support here, but its implementation looks strikingly similar to the Twitter implementation, so we won't go into detail on that here.

`TwitterPreferencesFragment` looks as follows:

```
public class TwitterPreferencesFragment extends Fragment {
  @Override
   public View onCreateView(LayoutInflater inflater,
   ViewGroup container, Bundle savedInstanceState) {
   return inflater.inflate(
    R.layout.fragment_twitter_preferences,
    container, false);
  }

  @Override
  public void onStart() {
    super.onStart();
    updateUI();
  }
```

Fragments have a slightly different lifecycle than an `Activity`. Here, we inflate the view in `onCreateView()`, then we update the user interface with the current state from `onStart()`. What does the view look like? That's determined by `R.layout.fragment_twitter_preferences`.

```
<LinearLayout
  xmlns:android="http://schemas.android.com/apk/res/android"
  xmlns:tools="http://schemas.android.com/tools"
  android:layout_width="match_parent"
  android:layout_height="match_parent"
  android:paddingBottom="@dimen/activity_vertical_margin"
  android:paddingLeft="@dimen/activity_horizontal_margin"
  android:paddingRight="@dimen/activity_horizontal_margin"
  android:paddingTop="@dimen/activity_vertical_margin"
  android:orientation="vertical">

<Button
  android:text="Login"
  android:layout_width="wrap_content"
  android:layout_height="wrap_content"
```

```
        android:id="@+id/connectButton" />

    <LinearLayout
      android:orientation="vertical"
      android:layout_width="match_parent"
      android:layout_height="match_parent"
      android:id="@+id/twitterPrefsLayout">

    <CheckBox
      android:text="Include the home timeline"
      android:layout_width="match_parent"
      android:layout_height="wrap_content"
      android:id="@+id/showHomeTimeline" />

    <TextView
      android:text="User lists to include"
      android:layout_width="match_parent"
      android:layout_height="wrap_content"
      android:id="@+id/textView2" />

    <ListView
      android:layout_width="match_parent"
      android:layout_height="match_parent"
      android:id="@+id/userListsListView" />
    </LinearLayout>
  </LinearLayout>
```

In a nutshell, as you can see in the preceding code, we have a button for logging in and out, and a `ListView` for allowing the user to select which Twitter lists from which to load data.

Given the frequent use of the network for interacting with Twitter plus Android's aversion to network access on the user interface thread, the code here gets a little complicated. We can see the start of that in `updateUI()`, as follows:

```
private void updateUI() {
  getActivity().runOnUiThread(new Runnable() {
    @Override
    public void run() {
      final Button button = (Button)
      getView().findViewById(R.id.connectButton);
      final View prefsLayout =
      getView().findViewById(R.id.twitterPrefsLayout);
      if (!SunagoUtil.getPreferences().getBoolean(
      getString(R.string.twitter_authd), false)) {
        prefsLayout.setVisibility(View.GONE);
        button.setOnClickListener(
          new View.OnClickListener() {
          @Override
```

```
public void onClick(View view) {
 new TwitterAuthenticateTask().execute();
}
});
} else {
  button.setText(getString(R.string.logout));
  button.setOnClickListener(
  new View.OnClickListener() {
    @Override
    public void onClick(View view) {
      final SharedPreferences.Editor editor =
      SunagoUtil.getPreferences().edit();
      editor.remove(getString(
      R.string.twitter_oauth_token));
      editor.remove(getString(
      R.string.twitter_oauth_secret));
      editor.putBoolean(getString(
      R.string.twitter_authd), false);
      editor.commit();
      button.setText(getString(R.string.login));
      button.setOnClickListener(
      new LoginClickListener());
    }
  });

  prefsLayout.setVisibility(View.VISIBLE);
  populateUserList();
  }
 }
});
}
```

The first thing that should stand out in the last code is that first line. Since we're updating the user interface, we have to make sure this code runs on the user interface thread. To make that happen, we wrap our logic in a Runnable, and pass that to the method runOnUiThread(). In Runnable, we check to see if the user is logged in or not. If not, we set the prefsLayout section's visibility to GONE, set the Button's text to Login, and set its onClick listener to a View.OnClickListener method that executes TwitterAuthenticateTask.

If the user is not logged in, we do the opposite--make prefsLayout visible, set the Button text to Logout, set the onClick to an anonymous View.OnClickListener class that removes the authentication-related preferences, and recursively call updateUI() to make sure the interface is updated to reflect the logout.

`TwitterAuthenticateTask` is another `AsyncTask` that handles authenticating with Twitter. To authenticate, we have to get a Twitter request token, which requires network access, so this must be done off of the user interface thread, thus, `AsyncTask`. Please refer to the following code snippet:

```
private class TwitterAuthenticateTask extends
    AsyncTask<String, String, RequestToken> {
  @Override
  protected void onPostExecute(RequestToken requestToken) {
    super.onPostExecute(requestToken);

    Intent intent = new Intent(getContext(),
      WebLoginActivity.class);
    intent.putExtra("url",
      requestToken.getAuthenticationURL());
    intent.putExtra("queryParam", "oauth_verifier");
    startActivityForResult(intent, LOGIN_REQUEST);
  }

  @Override
  protected RequestToken doInBackground(String... strings) {
    try {
      return TwitterClient.instance().getRequestToken();
    } catch (TwitterException e) {
      throw new RuntimeException(e);
    }
  }
}
```

Once we have the `RequestToken`, we show the `WebLoginActivity` from which the user will enter the credentials for the service. We'll look at that in the next code.

When that activity returns, we need to check the results and respond appropriately.

```
public void onActivityResult(int requestCode, int resultCode,
Intent data) {
  super.onActivityResult(requestCode, resultCode, data);
  if (requestCode == LOGIN_REQUEST) {
    if (resultCode == Activity.RESULT_OK) {
      new TwitterLoginAsyncTask()
          .execute(data.getStringExtra("oauth_verifier"));
    }
  }
}
```

When we started `WebLoginActivity`, we specified that we wanted to get a result, and we specified an identifier, `LOGIN_REQUEST`, which is set to 1, to uniquely identify which `Activity` was returning the result. If `requestCode` is `LOGIN_REQUEST`, and the result code is `Activity.RESULT_OK` (see `WebLoginActivity` given next), then we have a successful response, and we need to finish the login process, for which we'll use another `AsyncTask`.

```
private class TwitterLoginAsyncTask
extends AsyncTask<String, String, AccessToken> {
  @Override
  protected AccessToken doInBackground(String... codes) {
    AccessToken accessToken = null;
    if (codes != null && codes.length > 0) {
        String code = codes[0];
        TwitterClient twitterClient =
          TwitterClient.instance();
        try {
          accessToken = twitterClient.getAcccessToken(
            twitterClient.getRequestToken(), code);
        } catch (TwitterException e) {
          e.printStackTrace();
        }
        twitterClient.authenticateUser(accessToken.getToken(),
          accessToken.getTokenSecret());
    }

    return accessToken;
  }

  @Override
  protected void onPostExecute(AccessToken accessToken) {
    if (accessToken != null) {
      SharedPreferences.Editor preferences =
        SunagoUtil.getPreferences().edit();
      preferences.putString(getString(
          R.string.twitter_oauth_token),
        accessToken.getToken());
      preferences.putString(getString(
          R.string.twitter_oauth_secret),
        accessToken.getTokenSecret());
      preferences.putBoolean(getString(
          R.string.twitter_authd), true);
        preferences.commit();
      updateUI();
    }
  }
}
```

In `doInBackground()`, we perform the network operation. When we have a result, the `AccessToken`, we use that to authenticate our `TwitterClient` instance, then we return the token. In `onPostExecute()`, we save the `AccessToken` details to `SharedPreferences`. Technically, all of this could have been done in `doInBackground()`, but I find it helpful, especially when learning something new, not to cut corners. Once you're comfortable with how all of this works, you are, of course, free to cut corners when and where you feel comfortable doing so.

We have one last piece to look over, `WebLoginActivity`. Functionally, it is identical to `LoginActivity`--it presents a web view which displays the login page for the given network. When the login succeeds, the needed information is returned to the calling code. This being Android rather than JavaFX, the mechanics are, of course, a little different.

```
public class WebLoginActivity extends AppCompatActivity {
  @Override
  protected void onCreate(Bundle savedInstanceState) {
    super.onCreate(savedInstanceState);
    setContentView(R.layout.activity_web_view);
    setTitle("Login");
    Toolbar toolbar = (Toolbar) findViewById(R.id.toolbar);
    setSupportActionBar(toolbar);
    Intent intent = getIntent();
    final String url = intent.getStringExtra("url");
    final String queryParam =
        intent.getStringExtra("queryParam");
    WebView webView = (WebView)findViewById(R.id.webView);
    final WebViewClient client =
        new LoginWebViewClient(queryParam);
    webView.setWebViewClient(client);
    webView.loadUrl(url);
  }
```

Most of this preceding code looks very much like the other `Activity` classes we've written. We do some basic user interface set up, then, getting a reference to the `Intent`, we extract the two parameters of interest--the URL of the login page, and the query parameter that indicates a successful login.

To participate in the page loading life cycle, we extend `WebViewClient` (which we then attach to `WebView` in `Activity`, as seen previously). This is done as follows:

```
private class LoginWebViewClient extends WebViewClient {
  private String queryParam;

  public LoginWebViewClient(String queryParam) {
    this.queryParam = queryParam;
```

```
        }

        @Override
        public void onPageStarted(WebView view, String url,
                Bitmap favicon) {
            final Uri uri = Uri.parse(url);
            final String value = uri.getQueryParameter(queryParam);
            if (value != null) {
                Intent resultIntent = new Intent();
                for (String name : uri.getQueryParameterNames()) {
                    resultIntent.putExtra(name,
                        uri.getQueryParameter(name));
                }
                setResult(Activity.RESULT_OK, resultIntent);
                finish();
            }
            super.onPageStarted(view, url, favicon);
        }
    }
```

While `WebViewClient` offers a myriad of life cycle events, we're only concerned with one right now, `onPageStarted()`, which is fired, as expected, when the page starts to load. By hooking in here, we can look at the URL before the related network activity begins. We can examine the desired URL to see if the query parameter of interest is present. If it is, we create a new `Intent` to pass data back to the caller, copy all of the query parameters to it, set the `Activity` result to RESULT_OK, and finish the `Activity`. If you look back at `onActivityResult()`, you should see now from where `resultCode` comes.

Summary

With that, our application is complete. It's not a perfect application, but it is a complete Android application, which demonstrates a number of features you might need in your own app including `Activities`, services, database creation, content providers, messaging, and asynchronous processing. Clearly, there are parts of the application where the error handling could be more robust, or the design generalized a bit more to be more readily reusable. Doing so in this context, however, would obscure the basics of the application too much. Making these changes, then, will make a great exercise for the reader.

In the next chapter, we'll take a look at a completely different type of application. We'll build a small utility to handle what can be a serious problem--too much email. This application will allow us to describe a set of rules that will delete or move emails. It's a simple concept, but it will allow us to work with JSON APIs and the `JavaMail` package. You'll learn a bit and end up with a useful little utility as well.

7
Email and Spam Management with MailFilter

In computer science, we have a number of **laws**, the most famous of which is, perhaps, Moore's Law, which addresses the rate at which the computer processing power increases. Another law, although not as well known, and certainly not as serious, is one known as **Zawinski's Law**. Jamie Zawinski, best known for his role at Netscape and Mozilla, once noted that "Every program attempts to expand until it can read mail. Those programs which cannot so expand are replaced by ones which can." While Zawinski's Law hasn't been quite as accurate as Moore's Law, there does seem to be a ring of truth to it, doesn't there?

In the spirit of Zawinski's Law, even if not quite the letter, we will turn our attention to email in this chapter and see if we can address something that plagues us all: email clutter. Ranging from spam to mailing list postings, those messages just keep coming, and they keep piling up.

I have several email accounts. As the head--and head geek--of my household, I'm often tasked with managing, whether they realize it or not, our digital assets, and while one little piece of spam might seem like nothing, over time, it can become a real problem. At a certain point, it almost seems too daunting to handle.

In this chapter, we'll take this very real, if perhaps somewhat overstated problem, and try to address it. That will give us the perfect excuse to use the standard Java email API, appropriately called JavaMail.

In this chapter, we'll cover the following topics:

- The JavaMail API
- Email protocols

- Some more JavaFX work (of course)
- Creating job schedules in Java with Quartz
- Installing OS-specific services written in Java

It may be that you have your email inboxes well under control, in which case, congratulations! However, despite how tidy or overwhelming your mail client may be, we should have fun in this chapter while exploring the small but capable JavaMail API and the wonderful world of electronic mail.

Getting started

Before we get too far into the application, let's stop and take a quick look at what is involved in email. For being such a ubiquitous tool, it seems that it's a fairly opaque topic for most people, even the technically minded who might be inclined to read a book such as this. If we're going to work with it, it will be extremely helpful to understand it, even if just a bit. If you are not interested in the details of the protocols themselves, then feel free to skip ahead to the next section.

A brief look at the history of email protocols

Like many great computing concepts, **email--electronic mail--**was first introduced in the 1960s, though it looked much different then. A thorough history of email, while certainly a great technical curiosity, is beyond the scope of our purposes here, but I think it would be helpful to take a look at a few of the email protocols still relevant today, those being SMTP for sending mail, and POP3 and IMAP for (from your email client's perspective) receiving mail. (Technically, the email is received by the server via SMTP as that is the on-the-wire protocol used by **Mail Transfer Agents** (**MTAs**), to transfer mail from one server to another. We non-MTA authors never think of it in those terms, so we need not be overly concerned by that distinction).

We'll start with sending an email, as our focus in this chapter will be more on folder management. **SMTP** (**Simple Mail Transport Protocol**), created in 1982 and last updated in 1998, is the dominant protocol to send an email. Typically, in the days of SSL and TLS-secured connections, clients connected to the SMTP server via port 587. The conversation between the server and a client, often referred to as a dialog, may look like this (as taken from the SMTP RFC at `https://tools.ietf.org/html/rfc5321`):

```
S: 220 foo.com Simple Mail Transfer Service Ready
C: EHLO bar.com
```

```
S: 250-foo.com greets bar.com
S: 250-8BITMIME
S: 250-SIZE
S: 250-DSN
S: 250 HELP
C: MAIL FROM:<Smith@bar.com>
S: 250 OK
C: RCPT TO:<Jones@foo.com>
S: 250 OK
C: RCPT TO:<Green@foo.com>
S: 550 No such user here
C: RCPT TO:<Brown@foo.com>
S: 250 OK
C: DATA
S: 354 Start mail input; end with <CRLF>.<CRLF>
C: Blah blah blah...
C: ...etc. etc. etc.
C: .
S: 250 OK
C: QUIT
S: 221 foo.com Service closing transmission channel
```

In this simple example, the client shakes hands with the server, then says who the email is from and who it's going to. Note that the email addresses are listed twice, but it is only these first instances (MAIL FROM and RCPT TO, the latter of which is repeated for each recipient) that matter. The second set is simply for the formatting and display of the email. That peculiarity noted, the actual email comes after the DATA line, which should be fairly self-explanatory. The lone period on a line marks the end of the message, at which point, the server confirms receipt of the message, and we sign off by saying QUIT. This example looks very simple, and it is, but things get much more complicated when the message has an attachment, such as an image or office document, or if the email is formatted in HTML.

While SMTP is used to send mail, the POP3 protocol is used to retrieve it. POP, or Post Office Protocol, was first introduced in 1984. The bulk of the current standard, POP3, was introduced in 1988 with an update released in 1996. POP3 servers are meant to receive or download mail by a client such as Mozilla Thunderbird. If the server allows, the client can make an unsecured connection on port 110, with secure connections typically being made on port 995.

POP3 at one point was the dominant protocol by which users downloaded their mail. It was quick and efficient, and, for a while, our only option. Folder management was something that had to be done on the client side, as POP3 sees the mailbox as one big store, with no notion of folders (POP4 was intended to add some notion of folders, among other things, but there has not been any progress on the proposed RFC for several years). The POP3 (RC 1939, found at `https://tools.ietf.org/html/rfc1939`) gives this example dialog:

```
S: <wait for connection on TCP port 110>
C: <open connection>
S:    +OK POP3 server ready <1896.697170952@dbc.mtview.ca.us>
C:    APOP mrose c4c9334bac560ecc979e58001b3e22fb
S:    +OK mrose's maildrop has 2 messages (320 octets)
C:    STAT
S:    +OK 2 320
C:    LIST
S:    +OK 2 messages (320 octets)
S:    1 120
S:    2 200
S:    .
C:    RETR 1
S:    +OK 120 octets
S:    <the POP3 server sends message 1>
S:    .
C:    DELE 1
S:    +OK message 1 deleted
C:    RETR 2
S:    +OK 200 octets
S:    <the POP3 server sends message 2>
S:    .
C:    DELE 2
S:    +OK message 2 deleted
C:    QUIT
S:    +OK dewey POP3 server signing off (maildrop empty)
C: <close connection>
S: <wait for next connection>
```

Note that the client sends a RETR command to retrieve the message, followed by a DELE command to remove it from the server. This seems to be the standard/default configuration for most POP3 clients.

Although, many clients can be configured to leave the mail on the server either for a certain number of days, or forever, possibly deleting the message from the server when it is deleted locally. If you've ever managed your mail this way, you've seen firsthand how this can complicate email management.

For example, back in the days before laptops, imagine you have one desktop computer at the office and one at the house. You'd like to be able to read your email in both locations, so you set up your POP3 client on both machines. You spend your work day reading, deleting, and maybe sorting email. When you get home, those, say, 40 messages you managed at work are now sitting in your inbox, in big bold letters to indicate an unread message. You now have to repeat your email management tasks at home if you have any hope of keeping the two clients in similar states. It was tedious and error prone, and that led us to the creation of IMAP.

IMAP or **Internet Access Message Protocol**, was created in 1986, with one of its design goals being permitting the complete management of a mailbox, folders, and all, by multiple clients. It has seen several revisions over the years, with IMAP 4 revision 1 being the current standard. Clients connect to an IMAP server on port 143 for unsecured connections, and 993 for SSL to TLS-based connections.

IMAP, since it offers much more robust functionality than POP, is a more complicated protocol. From the RFC (https://tools.ietf.org/html/rfc3501), we can look at the following sample dialog:

```
S:      * OK IMAP4rev1 Service Ready
C:      a001 login mrc secret
S:      a001 OK LOGIN completed
C:      a002 select inbox
S:      * 18 EXISTS
S:      * FLAGS (\Answered \Flagged \Deleted \Seen \Draft)
S:      * 2 RECENT
S:      * OK [UNSEEN 17] Message 17 is the first unseen message
S:      * OK [UIDVALIDITY 3857529045] UIDs valid
S:      a002 OK [READ-WRITE] SELECT completed
C:      a003 fetch 12 full
S:      * 12 FETCH (FLAGS (\Seen) INTERNALDATE
        "17-Jul-1996 02:44:25 -0700"
    RFC822.SIZE 4286 ENVELOPE ("Wed,
        17 Jul 1996 02:23:25 -0700 (PDT)"
    "IMAP4rev1 WG mtg summary and minutes"
    (("Terry Gray" NIL "gray" "cac.washington.edu"))
    (("Terry Gray" NIL "gray" "cac.washington.edu"))
    (("Terry Gray" NIL "gray" "cac.washington.edu"))
    ((NIL NIL "imap" "cac.washington.edu"))
    ((NIL NIL "minutes" "CNRI.Reston.VA.US")
    ("John Klensin" NIL "KLENSIN" "MIT.EDU")) NIL NIL
    "<B27397-0100000@cac.washington.edu>")
        BODY ("TEXT" "PLAIN" ("CHARSET" "US-ASCII") NIL NIL "7BIT" 3028
        92))
S:      a003 OK FETCH completed
C:      a004 fetch 12 body[header]
```

```
S:    * 12 FETCH (BODY[HEADER] {342}
S:    Date: Wed, 17 Jul 1996 02:23:25 -0700 (PDT)
S:    From: Terry Gray <gray@cac.washington.edu>
S:    Subject: IMAP4rev1 WG mtg summary and minutes
S:    To: imap@cac.washington.edu
S:    cc: minutes@CNRI.Reston.VA.US, John Klensin <KLENSIN@MIT.EDU>
S:    Message-Id: <B27397-0100000@cac.washington.edu>
S:    MIME-Version: 1.0
S:    Content-Type: TEXT/PLAIN; CHARSET=US-ASCII
S:
S:    )
S:    a004 OK FETCH completed
C:    a005 store 12 +flags \deleted
S:    * 12 FETCH (FLAGS (\Seen \Deleted))
S:    a005 OK +FLAGS completed
C:    a006 logout
S:    * BYE IMAP4rev1 server terminating connection
S:    a006 OK LOGOUT completed
```

As you can see, there's much more detail there than in our example POP3 dialog. This should also highlight why we're using an API like JavaMail rather than opening a socket and talking directly to the server ourselves. Speaking of JavaMail, let's turn our attention to this standard API and see what it can do for us.

JavaMail, the Standard Java API for Email

The JavaMail API is a set of abstractions that provide a protocol and platform-independent way of working with email. While it is a required part of **Java Enterprise Edition (Java EE)**, it is an add-on library for Java SE, meaning you'll have to download it separately, which we'll handle via our POM file.

Our primary interest with this chapter's application is message management, but we'll take a bit of time to look at sending email using the API, so you'll have something to work with should you ever find yourself needing to do so.

To start sending mails, we need to get a JavaMail `Session`. To do that, we'll need to set up some properties as follows:

```
Properties props = new Properties();
props.put("mail.smtps.host", "smtp.gmail.com");
props.put("mail.smtps.auth", "true");
props.put("mail.smtps.port", "465");
props.put("mail.smtps.ssl.trust", "*");
```

We'll send email through Gmail's server, and we'll use SMTP over SSL. With this `Properties` instance, we can create our `Session` instance as follows:

```
Session session = Session.getInstance(props,
   new javax.mail.Authenticator() {
   @Override
   protected PasswordAuthentication getPasswordAuthentication() {
     return new PasswordAuthentication(userName, password);
   }
});
```

To log in to the server, we need to specify credentials, which we do via the anonymous `PasswordAuthentication` instance. Once we have our `Session` instance, we need to create a `Transport` as follows:

```
transport = session.getTransport("smtps");
   transport.connect();
```

Note that for the protocol parameter, we specify `smtps`, which tells the JavaMail implementation that we want SMTP over SSL/TLS. We're now ready to build our message using the following block of code:

```
MimeMessage message = new MimeMessage(session);
message.setFrom("jason@steeplesoft.com");
message.setRecipients(Message.RecipientType.TO,
   "jason@steeplesoft.com");
message.setSubject("JavaMail Example");
```

An email message is modeled using the `MimeMessage` class, so we create an instance of that using our `Session` instance. We set the from and to addresses, as well as the subject. To make things more interesting, we'll attach a file using a `MimeBodyPart`, as we see here:

```
MimeBodyPart text = new MimeBodyPart();
text.setText("This is some sample text");

MimeBodyPart attachment = new MimeBodyPart();
attachment.attachFile("src/test/resources/rules.json");

Multipart multipart = new MimeMultipart();
multipart.addBodyPart(text);
multipart.addBodyPart(attachment);
message.setContent(multipart);
```

Our message will have two parts, modeled using `MimeBodyPart`, one is the body of the message, which is simple text, and the other is an attachment. In this case, we're simply attaching a data file from our tests, which we'll see later. Once we've defined the parts, we combine them using `MimeMultipart`, then set it as the content on our message, which we can now using the `transport.sendMessage()` method:

```
transport.sendMessage(message, new Address[] {
  new InternetAddress("jason@steeplesoft.com") });
  if (transport != null) {
    transport.close();
  }
```

Within just a few seconds, you should see the following email show up in your inbox:

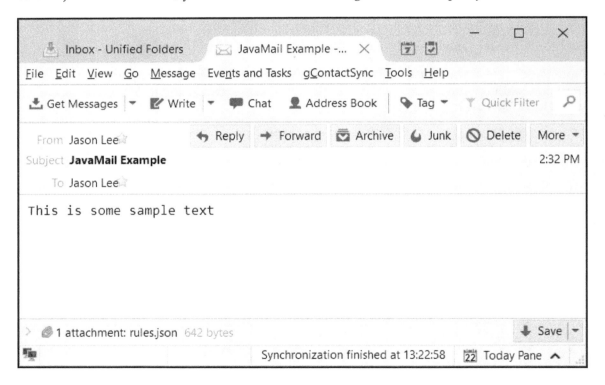

If you want to send an HTML email with a text alternative, you can do this using the following code:

```
MimeBodyPart text = new MimeBodyPart();
text.setContent("This is some sample text", "text/plain");
MimeBodyPart html = new MimeBodyPart();
html.setContent("<strong>This</strong> is some <em>sample</em>
```

```
    <span style=\"color: red\">text</span>", "text/html");
Multipart multipart = new MimeMultipart("alternative");
multipart.addBodyPart(text);
multipart.addBodyPart(html);
message.setContent(multipart);
transport.sendMessage(message, new Address[]{
    new InternetAddress("jason@example.com")});
```

Note that we set the content on each `MimeBodyPart`, specifying the mime type, and when we create the `Multipart`, we pass alternative as the `subtype` parameter. Failure to do so will result in an email that shows both parts, one after the other, which is certainly not what we want. If we've written our application correctly, we should see something like the following in our email client:

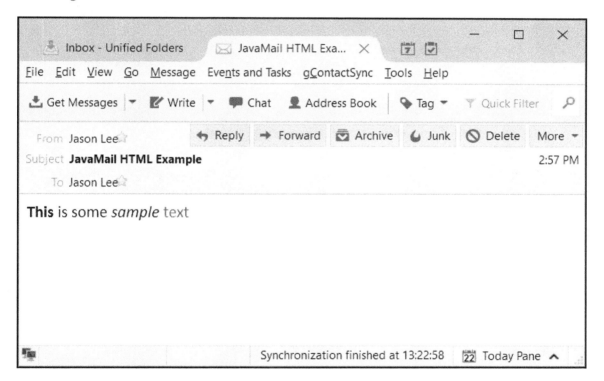

You can't see the red text, of course, in black and white print, but you can see the bold and italicized text, which means the HTML version was shown, rather than the text version. Mission accomplished!

Sending emails is pretty fun, but we're here to learn about folder and message management, so let's turn our attention to that, and we'll start by setting up our project.

Building the CLI

This project, like the others, will be a multi-module Maven project. We'll have one module for all of the core code, and we'll have another for the GUI we'll write to help manage the rules.

To create the project, we'll do something a little different this time. Rather than creating the project using NetBeans, we'll create it from the command line using Maven archetypes, which can be thought of roughly as project templates, so you can see how it's done that way:

```
$ mvn archetype:generate \ -DarchetypeGroupId=
  org.codehaus.mojo.archetypes \ -DarchetypeArtifactId=pom-root -
  DarchetypeVersion=RELEASE
  ...
Define value for property 'groupId': com.steeplesoft.mailfilter
Define value for property 'artifactId': mailfilter-master
Define value for property 'version': 1.0-SNAPSHOT
Define value for property 'package': com.steeplesoft.mailfilter
```

Once Maven has finished processing, change directory into the new project's directory, `mailfilter-master`. From here, we can create the first of our projects, the CLI:

```
$ mvn archetype:generate \ -DarchetypeGroupId=
  org.apache.maven.archetypes \ -DarchetypeArtifactId=
  maven-archetype-quickstart \ -DarchetypeVersion=RELEASE
Define value for property 'groupId': com.steeplesoft.mailfilter
Define value for property 'artifactId': mailfilter-cli
Define value for property 'version': 1.0-SNAPSHOT
Define value for property 'package': com.steeplesoft.mailfilter
```

This will create a new project under `mailfilter-master` called `mailfilter-cli`. We can now open `mailfilter-cli` in NetBeans and get to work.

The first thing we need to do is spec out how we want this tool to work. At a high level, we want to be able to specify an arbitrary number of rules for an account. These rules will allow us to move or delete emails based on certain criteria, such as the sender or the email's age. To keep things simple, we'll scope all of the rules to a specific account, and limit the operations to move and delete.

Let's start by taking a look at what the account may look like:

```
public class Account {
  @NotBlank(message="A value must be specified for serverName")
  private String serverName;
  @NotNull(message = "A value must be specified for serverPort")
  @Min(value = 0L, message = "The value must be positive")
  private Integer serverPort = 0;
  private boolean useSsl = true;
  @NotBlank(message = "A value must be specified for userName")
  private String userName;
  @NotBlank(message = "A value must be specified for password")
  private String password;
  private List<Rule> rules;
```

This is basically a very simple **POJO (Plain Old Java Object)** with six properties: serverName, serverPort, useSsl, userName, password, and rules. What are those annotations, though? Those come from a library called Bean Validation that provides some annotations and supporting code that allows us to express, declaratively, constraints on the values , which the variable can hold. Here are the annotations we're using, and what they mean:

- @NotBlank: This tells the system that the value can't be null, nor can it be an empty string (effectively, string != null && !string.trim().equals(""))
- @NotNull: This tells the system that the value can't be null
- @Min: This describes a minimum valid value

There are, of course, many, many others, and the system defines a means for you to define your own, so it's a very simple, yet very powerful framework to validate input, which brings up an important point: these constraints are only validated when the Bean Validation framework is asked to do so. We could easily build up a large collection of these Account instances with every field holding invalid data, and the JVM would be perfectly happy with that. The only way to apply the Bean Validation constraints is to ask it to check the instances we provide it with. In a nutshell, it's the API and not the JVM that enforces these constraints. That may seem obvious, but, sometimes, it pays to be explicit.

Before we go any further, we need to add Bean Validation to our project. We'll use the reference implementation: Hibernate Validator. We'll also need the Expression Language API and an implementation in our project. We get all of those by adding the following dependencies to pom.xml:

```
<dependency>
  <groupId>org.hibernate</groupId>
```

```
      <artifactId>hibernate-validator</artifactId>
      <version>5.3.4.Final</version>
   </dependency>
   <dependency>
      <groupId>javax.el</groupId>
      <artifactId>javax.el-api</artifactId>
      <version>2.2.4</version>
   </dependency>
   <dependency>
      <groupId>org.glassfish.web</groupId>
      <artifactId>javax.el</artifactId>
      <version>2.2.4</version>
   </dependency>
```

Getting back to our model, there are some getters and setters, of course, but those are not very interesting. What is interesting, though, is the implementation of equals() and hashCode(). Josh Bloch, in his seminal work, Effective Java, says this:

Always override hashCode *when you override* equals.

The main point of his assertion is that failure to do so violates the equals() contract, which states that equals objects must have equals hashes, which can result in incorrect and/or unpredictable behavior if your class is used in any hash-based collection, such as HashMap. Bloch then lists some rules to create a good hashCode implementation, as well as a good equals implementation, but here's my advice: let the IDE do the work for you, which is what we've done in the following code block for equals():

```java
public boolean equals(Object obj) {
  if (this == obj) {
    return true;
  }
  if (obj == null) {
    return false;
  }
  if (getClass() != obj.getClass()) {
    return false;
  }
  final Account other = (Account) obj;
  if (this.useSsl != other.useSsl) {
    return false;
  }
  if (!Objects.equals(this.serverName, other.serverName)) {
    return false;
  }
  if (!Objects.equals(this.userName, other.userName)) {
    return false;
  }
```

```
  if (!Objects.equals(this.password, other.password)) {
    return false;
  }
  if (!Objects.equals(this.serverPort, other.serverPort)) {
    return false;
  }
  if (!Objects.equals(this.rules, other.rules)) {
      return false;
  }
  return true;
}
```

We have done the same for `hashCode()` here:

```
public int hashCode() {
  int hash = 5;
  hash = 59 * hash + Objects.hashCode(this.serverName);
  hash = 59 * hash + Objects.hashCode(this.serverPort);
  hash = 59 * hash + (this.useSsl ? 1 : 0);
  hash = 59 * hash + Objects.hashCode(this.userName);
  hash = 59 * hash + Objects.hashCode(this.password);
  hash = 59 * hash + Objects.hashCode(this.rules);
  return hash;
}
```

Note that every method tested in `equals()` is also used in `hashCode()`. It's absolutely vital that your implementations follow this rule, or you'll end up with methods that don't really work as they should. It's possible that your IDE can help with this as you are generating the methods, but you must make sure that you are indeed using the same list of fields, and certainly, should you ever modify one of the methods, the other method must be updated accordingly.

We now have `Account`, so what does `Rule` look like? Let's take a look at the following piece of code:

```
@ValidRule
public class Rule {
  @NotNull
  private RuleType type = RuleType.MOVE;
  @NotBlank(message = "Rules must specify a source folder.")
  private String sourceFolder = "INBOX";
  private String destFolder;
  private Set<String> fields = new HashSet<>();
  private String matchingText;
  @Min(value = 1L, message = "The age must be greater than 0.")
  private Integer olderThan;
```

The validation on this class is two-fold. First, we can see the same field-level constraints we saw on `Account`: `type` cannot be null, `sourceFolder` cannot be blank, and `olderThan` must be at least 1. While you may not recognize it for what it is, we also have a class-level constraint in `@ValidRule`.

Field-level constraints can see only the field to which they have been applied. This means that if the valid values for a field are dependent on the value of some other field, these types of constraints are not appropriate. Class-level rules, though, allow us to look at the whole object when doing validation, so we can look to see what the value of one field is when validating another. This also means a bit more code for us, so we'll start with the following annotation:

```
@Target({ElementType.TYPE, ElementType.ANNOTATION_TYPE})
@Retention(RetentionPolicy.RUNTIME)
@Constraint(validatedBy = ValidRuleValidator.class)
@Documented
public @interface ValidRule {
  String message() default "Validation errors";
  Class<?>[] groups() default {};
  Class<? extends Payload>[] payload() default {};
}
```

In case you've never seen the source for an annotation before, this is a fairly typical example. Rather than declaring the type of the object to be `class` or `interface`, we used `@interface`, a subtle but important difference. The fields of the annotation are also a bit different, as there are no visibility modifiers, and the types cannot be primitives. Note the use of the `default` keyword.

The annotation itself also has annotations, which are as follows:

- `@Target`: This restricts the types of elements this annotation can be applied to; in this case, types and other annotations.
- `@Retention`: This instructs the compiler whether or not it should write the annotation to the class file, and making it available at runtime.
- `@Constraint`: This is a Bean Validation annotation that identifies our annotation as a new constraint type. The value of this annotation tells the system what `ConstraintValidator` processes the validation logic for this constraint.
- `@Documented`: This indicates that the presence of this annotation on any type should be considered a part of that type's public API.

Our `ConstraintValidator` implementation to handle this new constraint is a bit more complicated. We declared the class like this:

```
public class ValidRuleValidator implements
    ConstraintValidator<ValidRule, Object> {
```

Bean Validation provides a parameterized interface for constraint validation that takes the type of the constraint and the object type to which the logic in the validator applies. This allows you to write different validators of a given constraint for different object types. In our case, we could specify `Rule` rather than `Object`. If we were to do that, any time something other than `Rule` is annotated with `@ValidRule` and the instance is validated, the calling code will see an exception thrown. What we've done instead, as you will see, is validate the annotated type, specifically adding a constraint violation if needed.

The interface requires that we implement this method as well, but we have no work to be done here, so it has an empty method body, as shown here:

```
@Override
public void initialize(ValidRule constraintAnnotation) {
}
```

The interesting method is called `isValid()`. It's a bit long, so let's step through it piece by piece:

```
public boolean isValid(Object value,
    ConstraintValidatorContext ctx) {
    if (value == null) {
        return true;
    }
```

The first step is to make sure `value` is not null. We have two choices: return `true` if it's null, indicating there's no problem, or return `false`, indicating that there is a problem. Our choice depends on how we want the application to behave. Reasonable arguments can be made for either approach, but it seems that it would make sense for a null `Rule` to be considered invalid, so let's change the body of that for it to look like this:

```
ctx.disableDefaultConstraintViolation();
ctx.buildConstraintViolationWithTemplate(
    "Null values are not considered valid Rules")
    .addConstraintViolation();
return false;
```

We build `ConstraintViolation` using the specified message, add that to `ConstraintValidatorContext`, `ctx`, and return false to indicate a failure.

Next, we want to make sure we're dealing with an instance of `Rule`:

```
if (!(value instanceof Rule)) {
  ctx.disableDefaultConstraintViolation();
  ctx.buildConstraintViolationWithTemplate(
    "Constraint valid only on instances of Rule.")
  .addConstraintViolation();
  return false;
}
```

Once we're sure we have a non-null instance of `Rule`, we can get to the heart of our validation logic:

```
boolean valid = true;
Rule rule = (Rule) value;
if (rule.getType() == RuleType.MOVE) {
  valid &= validateNotBlank(ctx, rule, rule.getDestFolder(),
  "A destination folder must be specified.");
}
```

We'd like to be able to gather all of the violations, so we create a `boolean` variable to hold the current state, then we cast the value as `Rule` to make dealing with the instance a bit more natural. In our first test, we make sure that, if the type of `Rule` is `RuleType. MOVE`, it has a destination folder specified. We do so using this private method:

```
private boolean validateNotBlank(ConstraintValidatorContext ctx,
  String value, String message) {
  if (isBlank(value)) {
    ctx.disableDefaultConstraintViolation();
    ctx.buildConstraintViolationWithTemplate(message)
    .addConstraintViolation();
    return false;
  }
  return true;
}
```

If `value` is blank, we add `ConstraintViolation`, as we've already seen, using the specified message, and return `false`. If it is not blank, we return `true`. This value is then ANDed with `valid` to update the current state of the `Rule` validation.

The `isBlank()` method is very simple:

```
private boolean isBlank(String value) {
  return (value == null || (value.trim().isEmpty()));
}
```

This is a very common check, and is actually logically identical to the validator behind Bean Validation's @NotBlank.

Our next two tests are related. The logic is this: the rule must specify either text to match, or a maximum age in days. The test for that looks like this:

```
if (!isBlank(rule.getMatchingText())) {
  valid &= validateFields(ctx, rule);
} else if (rule.getOlderThan() == null) {
  ctx.disableDefaultConstraintViolation();
  ctx.buildConstraintViolationWithTemplate(
    "Either matchingText or olderThan must be specified.")
  .addConstraintViolation();
  valid = false;
}
```

If Rule specifies matchingText, then we validate that fields has been set properly. If neither matchingText nor olderThan were set, then we add ConstraintViolation with a message to that effect and set valid to false. Our fields validation looks like this:

```
private boolean validateFields(ConstraintValidatorContext ctx, Rule rule) {
  if (rule.getFields() == null || rule.getFields().isEmpty()) {
    ctx.disableDefaultConstraintViolation();
    ctx.buildConstraintViolationWithTemplate(
      "Rules which specify a matching text must specify the field(s)
        to match on.")
    .addConstraintViolation();
    return false;
  }
  return true;
}
```

We make sure that fields is neither null nor empty. We do not do any validation here on the actual contents of the field Set, though we certainly could.

We have now written, possibly, our very first custom validation. Your reaction is likely something like, "Wow! That's a lot of code for a 'simple' validation", and you're right. Before you throw the baby out with the bath water, think about this: the value of Bean Validation is that you can take potentially complex validation logic and hide it behind a very small annotation. You can then reuse this logic wherever you want simply by placing your constraint annotation in the appropriate places. The logic is expressed in one place, maintained in one place, but used in many, all very neatly and concisely.

So, yes, that's a good deal of code, but you only have to write it once, and the consumers of the constraints never need to see it. There's not really much extra work over and above what you'd normally write, but it's up to you to decide if this extra bit of work is worth the time.

Now that we've taken a quick look at custom Bean Validation constraints, let's return to our data model. The final piece to show is the `RuleType` enum:

```
public enum RuleType {
  DELETE, MOVE;
  public static RuleType getRuleType(String type) {
    switch(type.toLowerCase()) {
      case "delete" : return DELETE;
      case "move" : return MOVE;
      default : throw new IllegalArgumentException(
        "Invalid rule type specified: " + type);
    }
  }
}
```

This is a basic Java `enum` with two possible values, `DELETE` and `MOVE`, but we've also added a helper method to return the appropriate `RuleType` instance for a given String representation. This will help us when we're unmarshaling a `Rule` from JSON, for example.

With our data model defined, we're ready to start writing the code for the utility itself. While the Maven module is called `mailfilter-cli`, we will not concern ourselves here with a robust command-line interface, like we saw in previous chapters. Instead, we'll provide a very basic interaction with the command line, leaving an OS service, which we'll look at later, as the preferred means of usage.

It is at this point that we will begin using the JavaMail API, so we need to make sure we have our project set up correctly, so we add the following lines of code to `pom.xml`:

```
<dependency>
  <groupId>com.sun.mail</groupId>
  <artifactId>javax.mail</artifactId>
  <version>1.5.6</version>
</dependency>
```

In our IDE, we create a new class, `MailFilter`, and create the familiar `public static void main` method as follows:

```
public static void main(String... args) {
  try {
    final MailFilter mailFilter =
      new MailFilter(args.length > 0 ? args[1] : null);
```

```
      mailFilter.run();
      System.out.println("\tDeleted count: "
        + mailFilter.getDeleted());
      System.out.println("\tMove count:      "
        + mailFilter.getMoved());
    } catch (Exception e) {
      System.err.println(e.getLocalizedMessage());
    }
  }
}
```

NetBeans supports a number of code templates. The template of interest here is `psvm`, which will create a `public static void main` method. To use it, make sure you are on an empty line inside the class definition (to avoid odd formatting issues), then type `psvm` and press tab. NetBeans creates the method for you and places the cursor on the first line of the empty method, ready for you to start coding. You can find dozens of other helpful code templates by navigating to **Tools | Options | Editor | Code Templates**. You can even define your own.

In our `main()` method, we create an instance of `MainFilter`, passing in any rule definition file that may have been specified on the command line, and calling `run()`:

```
public void run() {
  try {
    AccountService service = new AccountService(fileName);

    for (Account account : service.getAccounts()) {
      AccountProcessor processor =
        new AccountProcessor(account);
      processor.process();
      deleted += processor.getDeleteCount();
      moved += processor.getMoveCount();
    }
  } catch (MessagingException ex) {
    Logger.getLogger(MailFilter.class.getName())
    .log(Level.SEVERE, null, ex);
  }
}
```

We start by creating an instance of `AccountService`, which wraps up the details of reading and writing the `Rules` file. For each account in the specified file, we create `AccountProcessor`, which encapsulates the rule processing logic.

The `AccountService` instance may not sound very exciting, but there are some pretty interesting technical bits hidden away behind that public interface. We see where the Bean Validation constraints are actually checked, and we also see the use of the Jackson JSON library to read and write the `Rules` file. Before we can start using Jackson, we need to add it to our project, which we do by adding this `pom.xml`:

```xml
<dependency>
  <groupId>com.fasterxml.jackson.core</groupId>
  <artifactId>jackson-databind</artifactId>
  <version>2.8.5</version>
</dependency>
```

You should, as always, make sure that you are on the latest version of the library.

This is not a big class to start with, but only three methods are of any interest here. We'll start with the most basic one, which is as follows:

```java
private File getRulesFile(final String fileName) {
    final File file = new File(fileName != null ? fileName
        : System.getProperty("user.home") + File.separatorChar
        + ".mailfilter" + File.separatorChar + "rules.json");
    if (!file.exists()) {
      throw new IllegalArgumentException(
        "The rules file does not exist: " + rulesFile);
    }
    return file;
}
```

The only reason I include this here is that reading a file from the user's home directory is something I find myself doing fairly frequently, and you might too. This example shows you how to do just that, attempting to find the rule file at `~/.mailfilter/rules.json` if the user does not specify a file explicitly. Generated or specified, if the rule file can't be found, we throw an exception.

Perhaps the most interesting method is the `getAccounts()` method. We'll step through this one slowly:

```java
public List<Account> getAccounts() {
  final Validator validator = Validation
    .buildDefaultValidatorFactory().getValidator();
  final ObjectMapper mapper = new ObjectMapper()
    .configure(DeserializationFeature.
    ACCEPT_SINGLE_VALUE_AS_ARRAY, true);
  List<Account> accounts = null;
```

These three statements are setting up some objects required to process the accounts. The first is `Validator`, which is the Bean Validation class that is our entry point to apply and check the constraints we've described on our data models. The next, `ObjectMapper`, is a Jackson class that will map a JSON data structure onto our Java data model. We need to specify `ACCEPT_SINGLE_VALUE_AS_ARRAY` to make sure that Jackson properly handles any lists in our model. Finally, we create `List` to hold our `Account` instances.

Reading the rules file into memory and getting that as instances of our data model is extremely easy with Jackson:

```
accounts = mapper.readValue(rulesFile,
  new TypeReference<List<Account>>() {});
```

Since the property names in our Java classes match the keys used in our JSON file, `ObjectMapper` can easily read the data from the JSON file and build our in-memory model with just this one line. Note the `TypeReference` instance. We want Jackson to return a `List<Account>` instance, but due to some design decisions in the JVM, direct access to parameterized types at runtime is not possible. The `TypeReference` class, however, helps capture this information, which Jackson then uses in creating the data model. If we passed `List.class`, we would get a type cast failure at runtime.

Now that we have our `Account` instances, we're ready to start validation:

```
accounts.forEach((account) -> {
  final Set<ConstraintViolation<Account>> violations =
    validator.validate(account);
  if (violations.size() > 0) {
    System.out.println(
      "The rule file has validation errors:");
    violations.forEach(a -> System.out.println("  \"" + a));
    throw new RuntimeException("Rule validation errors");
  }
  account.getRules().sort((o1, o2) ->
    o1.getType().compareTo(o2.getType()));
});
```

Using `List.forEach()`, we iterate over each account in `List` (the null check was not shown here). For each `Account`, we call `validator.validate()`, which is when the constraints are actually validated. Up to this point, they were just annotations stored in the class, with the JVM happily carrying them along, but not doing anything else with them. Bean Validation, as we discussed earlier, is the enforcer of the constraints described by the annotations, and here we see that manual API call.

When the call to the `validator` returns, we need to see if there were any `ConstraintViolations`. If there were, we fairly naively print a message to standard out detailing each of the failures. If the rule has multiple violations, thanks to how we wrote our validator, we'll see them all at once, so the user can fix them without having to attempt to process the rules multiple times. Printing these to the console is not necessarily the best approach, as we can't process them programmatically, but it is sufficient for our needs at the moment.

Where Bean Validation really shines is in frameworks that integrate it on your behalf. For example, JAX-RS, the standard Java API to build REST resources, offers this type of integration. We see a usage of the functionality in this sample REST resource method:

```
@GET
public Response getSomething (
@QueryParam("foo") @NotNull Integer bar) {
```

When a request is routed to this method, JAX-RS ensures that the query parameter `foo` is converted, if possible, to an `Integer`, and that it is not `null`, so in your code, you can assume that you have a valid `Integer` reference.

The final method we want to look at in this class is `saveAccounts()`, which, as crazy as it may sound, saves the `Account` instances to the rules file specified:

```
public void saveAccounts(List<Account> accounts) {
  try {
    final ObjectMapper mapper =
      new ObjectMapper().configure(DeserializationFeature.
      ACCEPT_SINGLE_VALUE_AS_ARRAY, true);
    mapper.writeValue(rulesFile, accounts);
  } catch (IOException ex) {
    // ...
  }
}
```

Much like reading the file, writing to it is extremely simple, so long as your Java classes and your JSON structures match. If you do have differing names (for example, the Java class may have the `accountName` property, while the JSON file uses `account_name`), Jackson offers some annotations that can be applied to the POJO to explain how to map the fields correctly. You can find complete details for those on Jackson's website (https://github.com/FasterXML/jackson).

With our `Account` instances loaded into memory and validated for correctness, we now need to process them. The entry point is the `process()` method:

```
public void process() throws MessagingException {
  try {
    getImapSession();

    for (Map.Entry<String, List<Rule>> entry :
      getRulesByFolder(account.getRules()).entrySet()) {
      processFolder(entry.getKey(), entry.getValue());
    }
  } catch (Exception e) {
    throw new RuntimeException(e);
  } finally {
    closeFolders();
    if (store != null) {
      store.close();
    }
  }
}
```

The three lines to pay attention to are the calls to `getImapSession()`, `getRulesByFolder()`, and `processFolder()`, which we'll look at in detail now:

```
private void getImapSession()
  throws MessagingException, NoSuchProviderException {
  Properties props = new Properties();
  props.put("mail.imap.ssl.trust", "*");
  props.put("mail.imaps.ssl.trust", "*");
  props.setProperty("mail.imap.starttls.enable",
    Boolean.toString(account.isUseSsl()));
  Session session = Session.getInstance(props, null);
  store = session.getStore(account.isUseSsl() ?
    "imaps" : "imap");
  store.connect(account.getServerName(), account.getUserName(),
    account.getPassword());
}
```

To get an IMAP `Session`, as we saw earlier in this chapter, we create a `Properties` instance and set a few important properties. We get a `Store` reference using the protocol specified by the user in the rule file: `imap` for non-SSL-based connections and `imaps` for SSL-based connections.

Once we have our session, we then iterate over our rules, grouping them by source folder:

```
private Map<String, List<Rule>> getRulesByFolder(List<Rule> rules) {
  return rules.stream().collect(
    Collectors.groupingBy(r -> r.getSourceFolder(),
    Collectors.toList()));
}
```

We can now process the folder as follows:

```
private void processFolder(String folder, List<Rule> rules)
  throws MessagingException {
  Arrays.stream(getFolder(folder, Folder.READ_WRITE)
    .getMessages()).forEach(message ->
    rules.stream().filter(rule ->
    rule.getSearchTerm().match(message))
    .forEach(rule -> {
      switch (rule.getType()) {
        case MOVE:
          moveMessage(message, getFolder(
            rule.getDestFolder(),
            Folder.READ_WRITE));
        break;
        case DELETE:
          deleteMessage(message);
        break;
      }
  }));
}
```

Using `Stream`, we iterate over each message in the source folder, filtering for only those that match `SearchTerm`, but what is that, and where did it come from?

There are a couple of extra items on the `Rule` class that we haven't looked at yet:

```
private SearchTerm term;
@JsonIgnore
public SearchTerm getSearchTerm() {
  if (term == null) {
    if (matchingText != null) {
      List<SearchTerm> terms = fields.stream()
      .map(f -> createFieldSearchTerm(f))
      .collect(Collectors.toList());
      term = new OrTerm(terms.toArray(new SearchTerm[0]));
    } else if (olderThan != null) {
      LocalDateTime day = LocalDateTime.now()
      .minusDays(olderThan);
      term = new SentDateTerm(ComparisonTerm.LE,
```

```
           Date.from(day.toLocalDate().atStartOfDay()
           .atZone(ZoneId.systemDefault()).toInstant())));
      }
    }
    return term;
  }
```

We add a private field to cache `SearchTerm` so we don't have to create it more than once. It's a minor optimization, but we want to avoid unnecessary performance hits from recreating `SearchTerm` for every message on a large folder. If the rule has a `matchingText` set, we create a `List<SearchTerm>` based on the fields specified. Once we have that list, we wrap it in `OrTerm`, which will instruct JavaMail to match the message if *any* of the specified fields match the text.

If `olderThan` is set, then we create `SentDateTerm` to match any messages that were sent at least `olderThan` days ago. We save the `SearchTerm` reference in our private instance variable then return it.

Notice that the method has the `@JsonIgnore` annotation. We use this to make sure that Jackson doesn't try to marshall the value returned by this getter to the JSON file.

For the curious, `createFieldSearchTerm()` looks like this:

```
  private SearchTerm createFieldSearchTerm(String f) {
    switch (f.toLowerCase()) {
      case "from":
        return new FromStringTerm(matchingText);
      case "cc":
        return new RecipientStringTerm(
          Message.RecipientType.CC, matchingText);
      case "to":
        return new RecipientStringTerm(
          Message.RecipientType.TO, matchingText);
      case "body":
        return new BodyTerm(matchingText);
      case "subject":
        return new SubjectTerm(matchingText);
      default:
          return null;
    }
  }
```

So, how are the messages actually moved or deleted? There is, of course, a JavaMail API for that, whose usage might look something like this:

```
private static final Flags FLAGS_DELETED =
  new Flags(Flags.Flag.DELETED);
private void deleteMessage(Message toDelete) {
  if (toDelete != null) {
    try {
      final Folder source = toDelete.getFolder();
      source.setFlags(new Message[]{toDelete},
        FLAGS_DELETED, true);
      deleteCount++;
    } catch (MessagingException ex) {
      throw new RuntimeException(ex);
    }
  }
}
```

We do a quick null check, then we get a reference to the messages `Folder`. With that, we instruct JavaMail to set a flag, `FLAGS_DELETED`, on the messages in the folder. The JavaMail API more often than not works on arrays of `Message` (`Message[]`), so we need to wrap `Message` in an array as we pass it to `setFlags()`. As we finish up, we increment our deleted message counter so we can print our report when we're finished.

Moving a `Message` is very similar:

```
private void moveMessage(Message toMove, Folder dest) {
  if (toMove != null) {
    try {
      final Folder source = toMove.getFolder();
      final Message[] messages = new Message[]{toMove};
      source.setFlags(messages, FLAGS_DELETED, true);
      source.copyMessages(messages, dest);
      moveCount++;
    } catch (MessagingException ex) {
      throw new RuntimeException(ex);
    }
  }
}
```

The bulk of this method looks just like `deleteMessage()`, but there is a subtle difference. JavaMail doesn't have a `moveMessages()` API. What we have to do instead is call `copyMessages()` to create a copy of the message in the destination folder, then delete the message from the source folder. We increment the moved counter and return.

The final two methods of interest deal with folders. First, we need to get the folder, which we do here:

```
final private Map<String, Folder> folders = new HashMap<>();
private Folder getFolder(String folderName, int mode) {
  Folder source = null;
  try {
    if (folders.containsKey(folderName)) {
      source = folders.get(folderName);
    } else {
      source = store.getFolder(folderName);
      if (source == null || !source.exists()) {
        throw new IllegalArgumentException(
          "Invalid folder: " + folderName);
      }
      folders.put(folderName, source);
    }
    if (!source.isOpen()) {
      source.open(mode);
    }
  } catch (MessagingException ex) {
    //...
  }
  return source;
}
```

For performance reasons, we cache each `Folder` instance in `Map`, keyed by the folder name. If we find `Folder` in `Map`, we use that. If we do not, then we ask the IMAP `Store` for a reference to the desired `Folder`, and cache it in `Map`. Finally, we make sure `Folder` is open, or our move and delete commands will throw `Exception`.

We also need to make sure we close the `Folder` when we're finished:

```
private void closeFolders() {
  folders.values().stream()
  .filter(f -> f.isOpen())
  .forEachOrdered(f -> {
    try {
      f.close(true);
    } catch (MessagingException e) {
    }
  });
}
```

We filter our stream of `Folder` for only those that are open, then call `folder.close()`, swallowing any failure that might occur. At this point in the processing, there's not much that can be done.

Our mail filter is now technically complete, but it's not as usable as it could be. We need some way to run this on a schedule, and being able to view and edit the rules in a GUI would be really nice, so we'll build both of those. Since it doesn't make sense to schedule something if we have nothing to run, we'll start with the GUI.

Building the GUI

Since we want to make this as easy to use as possible, we'll now build a GUI to help manage these rules. To create the project, we'll use the same Maven archetype we used in creating the CLI:

```
$ mvn archetype:generate \ -DarchetypeGroupId=org.apache.maven.archetypes \
-DarchetypeArtifactId=maven-archetype-quickstart \ -
DarchetypeVersion=RELEASE
Define value for property 'groupId': com.steeplesoft.mailfilter
Define value for property 'artifactId': mailfilter-gui
Define value for property 'version':  1.0-SNAPSHOT
Define value for property 'package':  com.steeplesoft.mailfilter.gui
```

Once the POM has been created, we need to edit it a bit. We need to set the parent by adding this element to `pom.xml`:

```
<parent>
  <groupId>com.steeplesoft.j9bp.mailfilter</groupId>
  <artifactId>mailfilter-master</artifactId>
  <version>1.0-SNAPSHOT</version>
</parent>
```

We will also add a dependency on the CLI module as follows:

```
<dependencies>
  <dependency>
    <groupId>${project.groupId}</groupId>
    <artifactId>mailfilter-cli</artifactId>
    <version>${project.version}</version>
  </dependency>
</dependencies>
```

Since we're not depending on NetBeans to generate the JavaFX project for us, we'll also need to create a few basic artifacts by hand. Let's start with the application's entry point:

```
public class MailFilter extends Application {
  @Override
  public void start(Stage stage) throws Exception {
    Parent root = FXMLLoader.load(getClass()
    .getResource("/fxml/mailfilter.fxml"));
    Scene scene = new Scene(root);
    stage.setTitle("MailFilter");
    stage.setScene(scene);
    stage.show();
  }

  public static void main(String[] args) {
    launch(args);
  }
}
```

This is a very typical JavaFX main class, so we'll skip right to the FXML file. For now, we'll just create a stub using the following piece of code:

```
<?xml version="1.0" encoding="UTF-8"?>
<?import java.lang.*?>
<?import java.util.*?>
<?import javafx.scene.*?>
<?import javafx.scene.control.*?>
<?import javafx.scene.layout.*?>

<AnchorPane id="AnchorPane" prefHeight="200" prefWidth="320"
  xmlns:fx="http://javafx.com/fxml"
  fx:controller=
    "com.steeplesoft.mailfilter.gui.Controller">
  <children>
    <Button layoutX="126" layoutY="90" text="Click Me!"
      fx:id="button" />
    <Label layoutX="126" layoutY="120" minHeight="16"
      minWidth="69" fx:id="label" />
  </children>
</AnchorPane>
```

And finally, we create the controller:

```
public class Controller implements Initializable {
  @Override
  public void initialize(URL url, ResourceBundle rb) {
  }
}
```

This gives us a working JavaFX application that starts and runs, but doesn't do much else. In previous chapters, we've walked through building a JavaFX application in painstaking detail, so we won't do that again here, but there are some interesting challenges in this one that are worth taking a look at.

To give you a sense of what we're working toward, here's a screenshot of the final user interface:

On the left, we have `ListView` to display the `Account` configured in our rules file. Below `ListView`, we have a few controls to edit the currently selected `Account`. On the right, we have `TableView` to display the `Rule`, and a similar area below it for editing a `Rule`.

When the user clicks on `Account` or `Rule`, we want the form area below to be populated with the relevant information. As the user modifies the data, `Account/Rule` as well as `ListView/TableView` should be updated.

Ordinarily, this is one of the areas in which JavaFX really shines, that of property binding. We've already seen a small part of that with `ObservableList`: we can add an item to `List`, and it is automatically added to the UI component to which it has been bound. The situation we find ourselves in now is a little different though, in that our model is a POJO, one that doesn't use any JavaFX APIs, so we don't get that functionality quite so easily. Let's look at what it will take to wire these things together.

First, let's look at the `Account` list. We have `ObservableList`:

```
private final ObservableList<Account> accounts =
    FXCollections.observableArrayList();
```

We add our accounts to this `ObservableList` as follows:

```
private void configureAccountsListView() {
  accountService = new AccountService();
  accounts.addAll(accountService.getAccounts());
```

Then, we bind `List` and `ListView`, as follows:

```
accountsListView.setItems(accounts);
```

Here is where things change a little bit. To encapsulate our POJO binding setup, we'll create a new class called `AccountProperty`, which we'll look at shortly. Although, let's first add the following code snippet to handle the `ListView` clicks:

```
accountProperty = new AccountProperty();
accountsListView.setOnMouseClicked(e -> {
  final Account account = accountsListView.getSelectionModel()
  .getSelectedItem();
  if (account != null) {
    accountProperty.set(account);
  }
});
```

When the user clicks on `ListView`, we set `Account` on the `AccountProperty` instance. Before we leave this method and look at `AccountProperty`, we need to set up one last item:

```
final ChangeListener<String> accountChangeListener =
  (observable, oldValue, newValue) ->
  accountsListView.refresh();
serverName.textProperty().addListener(accountChangeListener);
userName.textProperty().addListener(accountChangeListener);
```

We define `ChangeListener`, which simply calls `accountsListView.refresh()`, which instructs `ListView` to redraw itself. We'll want it to do this when the model itself is updated, a change that `ObservableList` doesn't bubble up to `ListView`. The next two lines add `Listener` to `serverName` and `userNameTextField`. These two controls edit the properties by the same name on `Account`, and are the only two used to generate the display String for `ListView`, which we don't show here.

`AccountProperty` is a custom JavaFX property, so we extend `ObjectPropertyBase` as follows:

```
private class AccountProperty extends ObjectPropertyBase<Account> {
```

This offers part of the binding solution, but the heavy lifting is handled by a class from the excellent JFXtras project, `BeanPathAdapter`:

```
private final BeanPathAdapter<Account> pathAdapter;
```

The JFXtras library is not, as of the writing of this book, Java 9 compatible. All we need from the library is this one class, so I have copied the source of class from the JFXtras repository into this project for the time being. Once JFXtras runs under Java 9, we can remove this copy.

The documentation describes this class as an "adapter that takes a POJO bean and internally and recursively binds/unbinds its fields to other `Property` components". This is an extremely powerful class that we can't cover in its entirety here, so we'll just jump to our particular usage, which is as follows:

```
public AccountProperty() {
    pathAdapter = new BeanPathAdapter<>(new Account());
    pathAdapter.bindBidirectional("serverName",
        serverName.textProperty());
    pathAdapter.bindBidirectional("serverPort",
        serverPort.textProperty());
    pathAdapter.bindBidirectional("useSsl",
        useSsl.selectedProperty(), Boolean.class);
```

```
pathAdapter.bindBidirectional("userName",
    userName.textProperty());
pathAdapter.bindBidirectional("password",
    password.textProperty());
addListener((observable, oldValue, newValue) -> {
    rules.setAll(newValue.getRules());
});
}
```

BeanPathAdapter allows us to bind a JavaFX Property to a property on a POJO, which could be nested to an arbitrary depth and referenced using a dot-separated path notation. In our case, the properties are top-level properties on the Account object, so the path is short and simple. After we've bound our controls to the properties, we add a Listener to update the ObservableList rules with Rule for the current account.

The set() method that is called in the preceding code when the Account selection changes in ListView is very straightforward:

```
@Override
public void set(Account newValue) {
  pathAdapter.setBean(newValue);
  super.set(newValue);
}
```

With these pieces in place, the Account object is updated as we type in the various controls, and the ListView label is updated as the serverName and/or userName fields are edited.

Now we need to do the same for the TableView that will display each Rule the user has configured. The setup is almost identical:

```
private void configureRuleFields() {
    ruleProperty = new RuleProperty();
    fields.getCheckModel().getCheckedItems().addListener(
      new RuleFieldChangeListener());
    final ChangeListener<Object> ruleChangeListener =
        (observable, oldValue, newValue) ->
            rulesTableView.refresh();
    sourceFolder.textProperty()
      .addListener(ruleChangeListener);
    destFolder.textProperty().addListener(ruleChangeListener);
    matchingText.textProperty()
        .addListener(ruleChangeListener);
    age.textProperty().addListener(ruleChangeListener);
    type.getSelectionModel().selectedIndexProperty()
        .addListener(ruleChangeListener);
}
```

Here, we see the same basic structure: instantiate `RuleProperty`, create `ChangeListener` to request that `TableView` refresh itself, and add that listener to the relevant form fields.

`RuleProperty` is also similar to `AccountProperty`:

```
private class RuleProperty extends ObjectPropertyBase<Rule> {
  private final BeanPathAdapter<Rule> pathAdapter;

  public RuleProperty() {
    pathAdapter = new BeanPathAdapter<>(new Rule());
    pathAdapter.bindBidirectional("sourceFolder",
      sourceFolder.textProperty());
    pathAdapter.bindBidirectional("destFolder",
      destFolder.textProperty());
    pathAdapter.bindBidirectional("olderThan",
      age.textProperty());
    pathAdapter.bindBidirectional("matchingText",
      matchingText.textProperty());
    pathAdapter.bindBidirectional("type",
      type.valueProperty(), String.class);
    addListener((observable, oldValue, newValue) -> {
      isSelectingNewRule = true;
      type.getSelectionModel().select(type.getItems()
      .indexOf(newValue.getType().name()));

      IndexedCheckModel checkModel = fields.getCheckModel();
      checkModel.clearChecks();
      newValue.getFields().forEach((field) -> {
        checkModel.check(checkModel.getItemIndex(field));
      });
      isSelectingNewRule = false;
    });
  }
```

The biggest difference here is `Listener` that is created. Given the use of `CheckListView`, a custom control from the great ControlsFX project, it's worth noting the logic: we get `IndexedCheckModel`, which we clear, then we iterate over each field, finding its index in `CheckModel` and checking it.

We control updating the value of the fields set on `Rule` via `RuleFieldChangeListener`:

```
private class RuleFieldChangeListener implements ListChangeListener {
  @Override
  public void onChanged(ListChangeListener.Change c) {
    if (!isSelectingNewRule && c.next()) {
      final Rule bean = ruleProperty.getBean();
      bean.getFields().removeAll(c.getRemoved());
```

```
          bean.getFields().addAll(c.getAddedSubList());
        }
      }
    }
```

`ListChangeListener` tells us what was removed and what was added, so we processed those accordingly.

There are several other moving parts to the GUI, but we've seen them in one for another in previous chapters, so we'll not cover them here. If you're curious about these details, you can find them in this book's source code repository. Let's turn our attention to the final part of our project: the OS-specific service.

Building the service

One of the stated goals of this project is to be able to define rules to manage and filter email, and to have it run more or less all the time, not just when the email client is running. (There is, of course, not much we can do about the machine running this being turned off, so we can't promise constant coverage). To fulfill this part of the promise, we'll need a few extra parts. We already have the part of the system that does the actual work, but we also need a way to run that part on a schedule, and we also need a part that will start the scheduled job.

For the scheduling aspect, we have many options, but we'll use a library called Quartz. The Quartz Job Scheduling Library is an open source library that can be used in Java SE as well as Java EE applications. It provides a clean and simple API that is perfect for use here. To add Quartz to our project, we need to do this to `pom.xml`:

```
<dependency>
  <groupId>org.quartz-scheduler</groupId>
  <artifactId>quartz</artifactId>
  <version>2.2.3</version>
</dependency>
```

How simple is the API? Here's our `Job` definition:

```
public class MailFilterJob implements Job {
  @Override
  public void execute(JobExecutionContext jec)
    throws JobExecutionException {
    MailFilter filter = new MailFilter();
    filter.run();
  }
}
```

We extend `org.quartz.Job` overriding `execute()`, in which we simply instantiate `MailFilter` and call `run()`. That's really all there is to it. With our job defined, we just need to schedule it, which we'll do in `MailFilterService`:

```
public class MailFilterService {
  public static void main(String[] args) {
    try {
      final Scheduler scheduler =
        StdSchedulerFactory.getDefaultScheduler();
      scheduler.start();

      final JobDetail job =
        JobBuilder.newJob(MailFilterJob.class).build();
      final Trigger trigger = TriggerBuilder.newTrigger()
      .startNow()
      .withSchedule(
        SimpleScheduleBuilder.simpleSchedule()
        .withIntervalInMinutes(15)
        .repeatForever())
      .build();
      scheduler.scheduleJob(job, trigger);
    } catch (SchedulerException ex) {
      Logger.getLogger(MailFilterService.class.getName())
      .log(Level.SEVERE, null, ex);
    }
  }
}
```

We begin by getting a reference to the default `Scheduler` and starting it. Next, we create a new job using `JobBuilder`, then build `Trigger` using `TriggerBuilder`. We tell `Trigger` to start executing now, but note that it won't start until it is actually built and assigned to `Scheduler`. Once that happens, `Job` will execute immediately. Finally, we define `Schedule` for `Trigger` using the `SimpleScheduleBuilder` helper class, specifying a fifteen minute interval, which will run forever. We want this to run until the computer is shut down or the service is stopped.

If we run/debug `MailFilterService` now, we can watch `MailFilter` run. If you do this, and you're not extremely patient, I would suggest that you lower the interval to something more reasonable.

This leaves us with one final piece: the OS integration. In a nutshell, what we want to be able to do is run `MailFilterService` when the operating system boots up. Ideally, we'd prefer not to have ad hoc scripts cobble together to make this happen. Fortunately, we are again presented with a number of options.

We will be using the excellent Java Service Wrapper library from Tanuki Software (details of which can be found at `https://wrapper.tanukisoftware.com`). While we can manually build the service artifacts, we'd much rather let our build do the work for us, and, of course, there's a Maven plugin, called `appassembler-maven-plugin`, to do just that. To integrate them both into our project, we need to modify the `build` section of our POM by adding the following code snippet:

```
<build>
  <plugins>
    <plugin>
      <groupId>org.codehaus.mojo</groupId>
      <artifactId>appassembler-maven-plugin</artifactId>
      <version>2.0.0</version>
```

The transitive dependencies of this plugin will pull in everything we need for the Java Service Wrapper, so all we need to do is configure our usage .We start by adding an execution, telling Maven to run the `generate-daemons` goal when packaging the project:

```
<executions>
  <execution>
    <id>generate-jsw-scripts</id>
    <phase>package</phase>
    <goals>
      <goal>generate-daemons</goal>
    </goals>
```

Next we need to configure the plugin, which we do with the `configuration` element:

```
<configuration>
  <repositoryLayout>flat</repositoryLayout>
```

The `repositoryLayout` option tells the plugin to build a **lib** style repository, as opposed to the Maven 2 style layout, which is a number of nested directories. This is largely a style concern, at least for our purposes here, but I find it helpful to be able to scan the generated directory and see what is included at a glance.

Next, we need to define the **daemons** (another term for OS service that comes from the Unix world and which stands for **Disk And Execution Monitor**) as follows:

```
<daemons>
  <daemon>
    <id>mailfilter-service</id>
    <wrapperMainClass>
      org.tanukisoftware.wrapper.WrapperSimpleApp
    </wrapperMainClass>
    <mainClass>
```

```
      com.steeplesoft.mailfilter.service.MailFilterService
    </mainClass>
    <commandLineArguments>
      <commandLineArgument>start</commandLineArgument>
    </commandLineArguments>
```

The Java Service Wrapper is a very flexible system, providing a number of ways to wrap your Java project. Our needs are simple, so we instruct it to use `WrapperSimpleApp` and point it to the main class, `MailFilterService`.

The plugin supports a couple of other service wrapper methods, but we're interested in the Java Service Wrapper, so we specify that here, with the `platform` element:

```
    <platforms>
      <platform>jsw</platform>
    </platforms>
```

Finally, we need to configure the generator, telling it which OS to support:

```
    <generatorConfigurations>
      <generatorConfiguration>
        <generator>jsw</generator>
        <includes>
          <include>linux-x86-64</include>
          <include>macosx-universal-64</include>
          <include>windows-x86-64</include>
        </includes>
      </generatorConfiguration>
    </generatorConfigurations>
  </daemon>
</daemons>
```

Each of those OS definitions offers a 32-bit option that you can add if needed, but, for the sake of brevity, I've omitted them here.

When we build the app now, either via `mvn package` or `mvn install`, this plugin will generate a wrapper for our service, complete with binaries appropriate for the configured operating systems. The nice thing is that it will build wrappers for each OS, regardless of what OS the build is actually run under. For example, here's the output of building this on a Windows machine (note the Linux and Mac binaries):

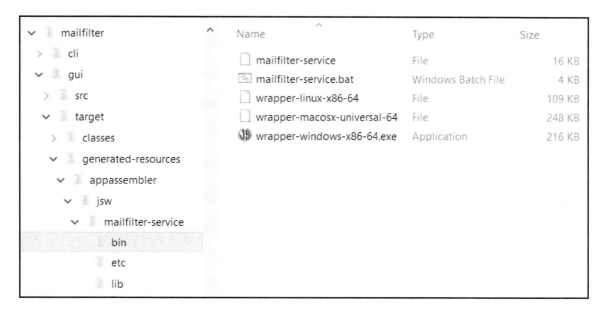

The wrapper is capable of much, much more, so if you're interested, you can read all the details on Tanuki Software's website.

Summary

Just like that, once again, our application is **finished**. We've covered quite a bit in this chapter. We started by learning a little bit about the history and technical details of several email protocols (SMTP, POP3, and IMAP4), then learned how to interact with services based on those using the JavaMail API. In the process of doing so, we discovered the Jackson JSON Parser and used it to marshal and unmarshal POJOs to and from the disk. We used the ControlsFX class, `BeanPathAdapter`, to bind non-JavaFX-aware POJOs to JavaFX controls, and the Quartz Job Scheduling Library to execute code on a schedule. Finally, we wrapped up our application using the Java Service Wrapper to create installation artifacts.

We're left with what I hope is an application that is both interesting and helpful. There are several ways to improve on it, of course, if you feel so motivated. The account/rule data structure could be extended to allow defining global rules that are shared across accounts. The GUI could support viewing email in the folders on the account and generating rules based on live data. The build could be extended to create an installer for the application. You can probably think of many more. Always feel free to check out the code and hack away. If you come up with something interesting, be sure to share it, as I'd love to see what you've done.

With another project wrapped up (no pun intended), we're ready to turn our attention to another. In the next chapter, we'll spend our entire time in a GUI and build a photo management system. This will give us the opportunity to look at some of JDK's imaging handling capabilities, including the newly added TIFF support, a feature that should make image aficionados quite happy. Turn the page and let's get started!

8
Photo Management with PhotoBeans

So far, we've written libraries. We've written command-line utilities. We've also written GUIs using JavaFX. In this chapter, we're going to try something completely different. We're going to build a photo management system, which, of course, needs to be a graphical application, but we're going to take a different approach. Rather than using pure JavaFX and building everything from the ground up, we'll use an existing application framework. That framework is the NetBeans **Rich Client Platform** (**RCP**), a mature, stable, and powerful framework, that powers not just the NetBeans IDE we've been using, but countless applications in a myriad of industries from oil and gas to air and space.

In this chapter, we'll cover the following topics:

- How to bootstrap a NetBeans RCP project
- How to integrate JavaFX with the NetBeans RCP
- The fundamentals of an RCP application such as Nodes, Actions, Lookups, Services, and TopComponents

Without further ado then, let's jump right in.

Getting started

Probably the question at or near the top of your list is, **Why would I want to use NetBeans RCP?**. Before we get into the details of the application, let's address this very fair question, and try to understand why we're building it the way we are.

One of the first things you'll notice when you start looking into the NetBeans platform is the strong notion of modularity. With the Java Module System being such a prominent feature of Java 9, this may seem like a minor detail, but NetBeans exposes this concept to us at the application level, making plugins incredibly simple, as well as allowing us to update the application on a piecemeal basis.

The RCP also provides a robust, well-tested framework for handling windows, menus, actions, nodes, services, and so on. If we were to build this application from scratch, as we've done in the previous chapters using **plain** JavaFX, we would have to manually define areas on the screen, then handle window placement by hand. With the RCP, we have a rich windowing specification already defined, which we can easily use. It offers features such as maximizing/minimizing windows, sliding, detaching, and docking windows, and so on.

The RCP also provides a strong notion of **nodes**, an encapsulation of domain-specific data in a user interface concept, which is most often seen as entries in a tree view on the left side of an application, as well as actions that can be associated with these nodes (or menu items) to act on the data they represent. Again, all of this can be done in JavaFX (or Swing), but you would have to code all of these features yourself. In fact, there are a number of open source frameworks that offer to do just that, such as Canoo's Dolphin Platform (http://www.dolphin-platform.io), though none have had the years of production hardening and testing that the NetBeans RCP has had, so we'll keep our focus here.

Bootstrapping the project

How you create a NetBeans RCP project will have a very fundamental impact on how the rest of the project will be approached. By default, NetBeans uses Ant as the build system for all RCP apps. Almost all of the online documentation from the NetBeans project, and blog entries from the NetBeans evangelists, often reflect this preference as well. We've been using Maven for every other project, and we're not going to change that here. Fortunately, NetBeans does allow us to create an RCP project with Maven, which is what we'll do.

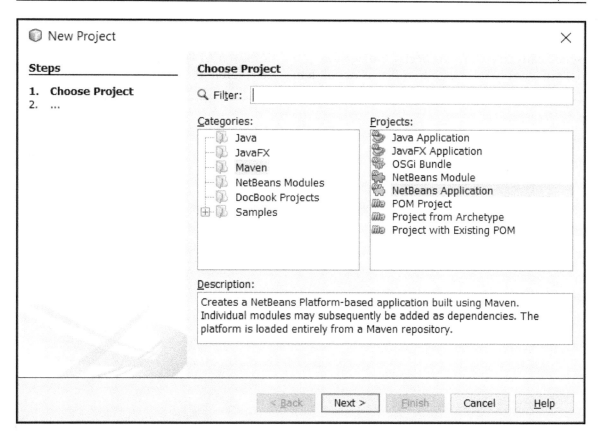

In the **New Project** window, we select **Maven**, then **NetBeans Application**. On the next screen, we configure the project as usual, specifying the project name, photobeans, project location, package, and so on.

When we click on **Next**, we'll be presented with the **Module Options** step of the **New Project** wizard. In this step, we configure some basic aspects of the RCP application. Specifically, we need to specify the version of the NetBeans APIs we'll use, and whether or not we want to use OSGi bundles as dependencies, as seen in the following screenshot:

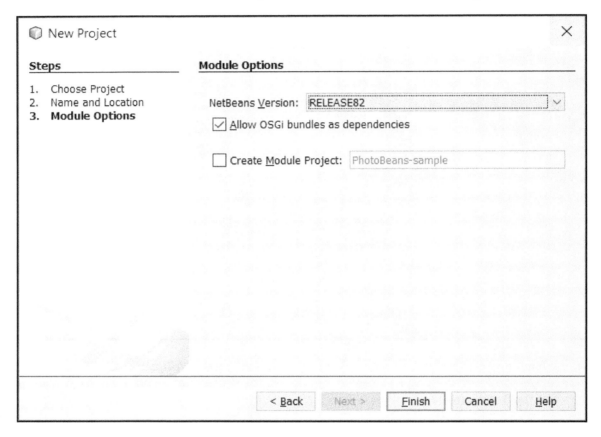

At the time of writing, the latest platform version is **RELEASE82**. By the time Java 9 ships, it is reasonable to expect that NetBeans 9.0, and, therefore **RELEASE90**, will be available. We want the latest version available, but note that, depending on the release schedule of the NetBeans project, it may very well *not* be 9.0. For the **Allow OSGi bundles as dependencies** option we can safely accept the default, though changing it won't cause us any issues, and we can easily change the value later should the need arise.

Once the project is created, we should see three new entries in the projects window: `PhotoBeans-parent`, `PhotoBeans-app`, and `PhotoBeans-branding`. The `-parent` project has no real deliverables. Like the `master` projects from other chapters, this serves merely to organize related modules, coordinate dependencies, and so on.

Branding your application

The `-branding` module is where we can define, as you may have already guessed, the details of the application's branding. You can access these branding properties by right-clicking on the branding module, and selecting `Branding...` near the bottom of the content menu. Upon doing so, you will be prompted with a screen like this one:

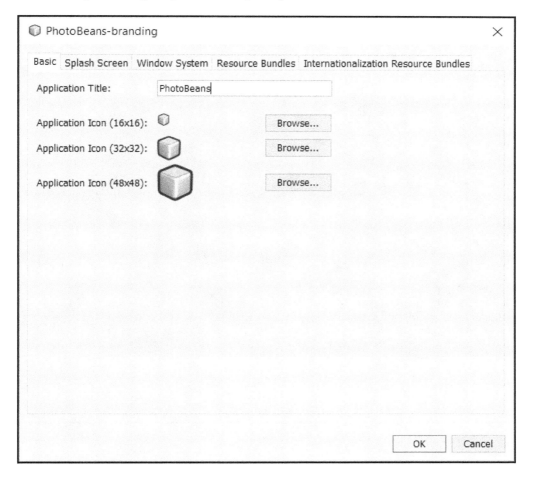

In this preceding tab, you can set or change the name of the application, as well as specify the application icon.

In the **Splash Screen** tab, you can configure, most importantly, the image that is displayed on the splash screen as the application loads. You can also enable or disable the progress bar, and set the colors, font sizes, and positions of the progress bar and startup messages:

The only other tab that is of interest to us at the moment is the **Window System** tab. In this tab, we can configure a number of features such as window drag and drop, window sliding, closing, and so on:

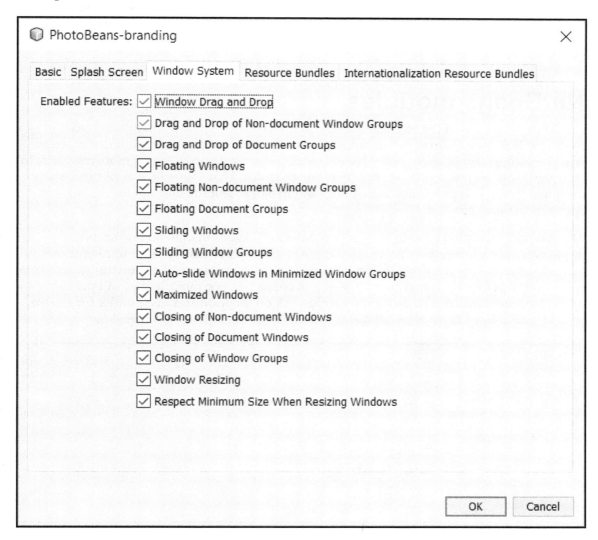

More likely than not, the defaults are acceptable for our purposes here. However, in your own NetBeans RCP application, this screen may be much more important.

Our main interest is the `-app` module. This module is the one that will define all of the application's dependencies, and will be its entry point. Unlike the JavaFX applications we've seen in previous chapters, though, we don't need to define a `public static void main` method, as NetBeans handles that for us. In fact, the `-app` module doesn't have any Java classes in it at all, yet the app can run right out-of-the-box, though it doesn't do much. We'll fix that now.

NetBeans modules

One of the strengths of the NetBeans platform is its modularity. If you've ever used the NetBeans IDE itself (before, say, reading this book), you've seen this modularity in action when working with plugins: every NetBeans plugin is made up of one or more modules. In fact, NetBeans itself is composed of numerous modules. That's how RCP applications are designed to work. It promotes decoupling, and makes extending and upgrading the application much simpler.

The generally accepted pattern is to, say, put the API classes in one module and the implementations in another. This makes the API classes reusable by other implementers, can help enforce low coupling by hiding private classes, and so on. To keep things simple as we learn the platform, though, we are going to create just one module that will provide all of the core functionality. To do that, we right-click on the **Modules** node under the parent project, and select **Create New Module...**: as shown in the following screenshot:

Once selected, you will be shown the **New Project** window. Here, you will need to select the **Maven** category, and the **NetBeans Module** project type, as follows:

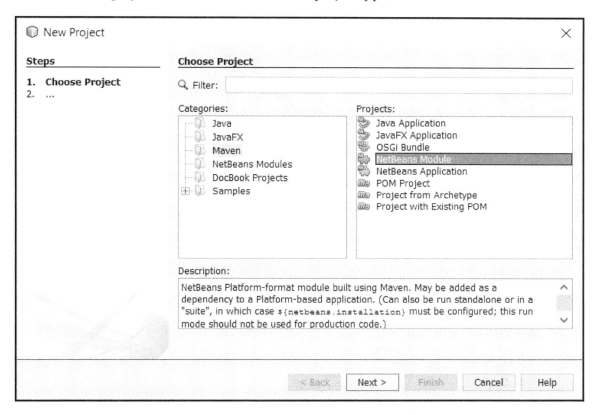

Clicking on **Next** will get you the **Name** and **Location** step we've seen several times already in this book. On this pane, we'll name the module main, set the package to com.steeplesoft.photobeans.main, and accept the defaults for the other fields. On the next pane, **Module Options**, we will make sure that the **NetBeans Version** is the same as was selected earlier, and click on **Finish**.

TopComponent - the class for tabs and windows

We now have a module that is mostly empty. NetBeans created a few artifacts for us, but we need not concern ourselves with those, as the build will manage those for us. What we do need to do, though, is create our first GUI element, which will be something that NetBeans calls a TopComponent. From the NetBeans Javadoc, found at `http://bits.netbeans.org/8.2/javadoc/`, we find this definition:

> *Embeddable visual component to be displayed in NetBeans. This is the basic unit of display--windows should not be created directly, but rather use this class. A top component may correspond to a single window, but may also be a tab (e.g.) in a window. It may be docked or undocked, have selected nodes, supply actions, etc.*

As we'll see, this class is the main component of a NetBeans RCP application. It will hold and control various related user interface elements. It is, to put it another way, at the top of a component hierarchy in the user interface. To create TopComponent, we can use the NetBeans wizard by right-clicking on our now empty package in the **Project Explorer** tree, and selecting **New** | **Window**. If **Window** is not an option, select **Other** | **Module Development** | **Window**.

You should now see the following **Basic Settings** window:

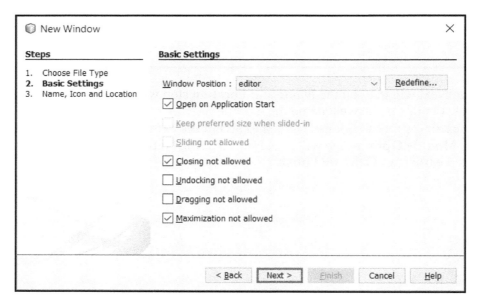

We have a number of options in the preceding window. What we're creating is a window that will show a list of photos, so some reasonable settings would be to select the following:

- **Open on Application Start**
- **Closing not allowed**
- **Maximization not allowed**

These options seem pretty straightforward, but what is **Window Position**? Another of the benefits of using the NetBeans RCP as opposed to writing everything from scratch is that the platform provides a number of predefined concepts and facilities so that we don't need to worry about them. One such concern is window positioning and placement. The NetBeans user interface specification (which can be found on the NetBeans site at `https://ui.netbeans.org/docs/ui/ws/ws_spec-netbeans_ide.html`) defines the following areas:

- **Explorer:** This is used for all windows that provide access to user objects, usually in tree browsers
- **Output:** This is used for the Output window and VCS Output window by default
- **Debugger:** This is used for all the debugger windows and other supporting windows that require a horizontal layout
- **Palette:** This is used for the component palette window
- **Inspector:** This is used for the component inspector window
- **Properties:** This is used for the properties window
- **Documents:** This is used for all the document windows

The documentation also provides this helpful illustration:

Explorer	Documents		Palette
			Inspector
			Properties
Output		Debugger	

The specification page has a great deal of additional information, but this should be enough for now to get you going. We would like our photo list to be on the left side of the application window, so we select editor for the window position. Clicking on **Next**, we configure the name and icon for the component. Strictly speaking, we don't need to specify an icon for TopComponent, so we can just enter `PhotoList` for **Class Name Prefix:**, and click on **Finish**:

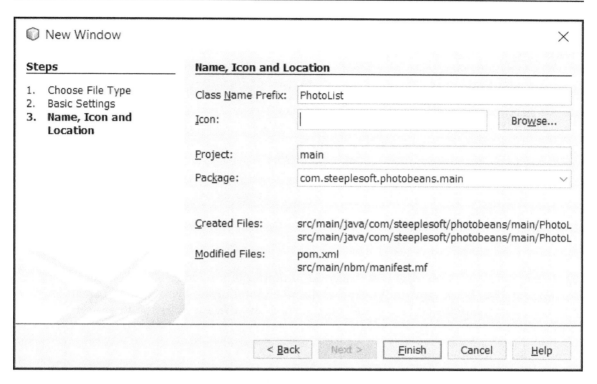

When you click on **Finish** here, NetBeans will create a couple of files for you, though only one will show up in the **Project Explorer** tree, that being `PhotoListTopComponent.java`. There is also a file called `PhotoListTopComponent.form` that you need to know about, though you will never edit it directly. NetBeans provides a very nice **WYSIWYG (what you see is what you get)** editor for building your user interface. The user interface definition is stored in the `.form` file, which is simply an XML file. As you make changes, NetBeans modifies this file for you, and generates the equivalent Java code in a method called `initComponents()`. You'll also notice that NetBeans will not allow you to modify the method. You can, of course, use another editor to do so, but any changes you make that way will be lost if you make changes in the GUI editor, so it's best just to leave the method alone. What does the rest of TopComponent look like?

```
@ConvertAsProperties(
    dtd = "-//com.steeplesoft.photobeans.main//PhotoList//EN",
    autostore = false
)
@TopComponent.Description(
    preferredID = "PhotoListTopComponent",
    //iconBase="SET/PATH/TO/ICON/HERE",
    persistenceType = TopComponent.PERSISTENCE_ALWAYS
```

```
)
@TopComponent.Registration(mode = "editor",
 openAtStartup = true)
@ActionID(category = "Window", id =
  "com.steeplesoft.photobeans.main.PhotoListTopComponent")
@ActionReference(path = "Menu/Window" /*, position = 333 */)
@TopComponent.OpenActionRegistration(
   displayName = "#CTL_PhotoListAction",
   preferredID = "PhotoListTopComponent"
)
@Messages({
   "CTL_PhotoListAction=PhotoList",
   "CTL_PhotoListTopComponent=PhotoList Window",
   "HINT_PhotoListTopComponent=This is a PhotoList window"
})
public final class PhotoListTopComponent
 extends TopComponent {
```

That's a lot of annotations, but is also a good reminder of how much the NetBeans platform is doing for you. During the build process, these annotations are processed to create the metadata that the platform will use at runtime to configure and wire together your application.

Some of the highlights are as follows:

```
@TopComponent.Registration(mode = "editor",
  openAtStartup = true)
```

This registers our `TopComponent`, and reflects our choices of where to put it and when to open it.

We also have some internationalization and localization work being done for us, as shown next:

```
@ActionID(category = "Window", id =
  "com.steeplesoft.photobeans.main.PhotoListTopComponent")
@ActionReference(path = "Menu/Window" /*, position = 333 */)
@TopComponent.OpenActionRegistration(
   displayName = "#CTL_PhotoListAction",
   preferredID = "PhotoListTopComponent"
)
@Messages({
   "CTL_PhotoListAction=PhotoList",
   "CTL_PhotoListTopComponent=PhotoList Window",
   "HINT_PhotoListTopComponent=This is a PhotoList window"
})
```

Without getting too far into the details and risking confusing things, the first three annotations register an open Action, and expose an item in the `Window` menu of our application. The last annotation, `@Messages`, is used to define the localization keys and strings. When this class is compiled, a class called `Bundle` is created in the same package, which defines methods using the specified keys to return the localized string. For example, for `CTL_PhotoListAction`, we get the following:

```
static String CTL_PhotoListAction() {
  return org.openide.util.NbBundle.getMessage(Bundle.class,
    "CTL_PhotoListAction");
}
```

This preceding code looks up the key in the standard Java `.properties` file for a localized message. These key/value pairs are merged with any entries found in the `Bundle.properties` file that the NetBeans wizard generated for us.

The following constructor of our `TopComponent` is also of interest:

```
public PhotoListTopComponent() {
  initComponents();
  setName(Bundle.CTL_PhotoListTopComponent());
  setToolTipText(Bundle.HINT_PhotoListTopComponent());
  putClientProperty(TopComponent.PROP_CLOSING_DISABLED,
    Boolean.TRUE);
  putClientProperty(TopComponent.PROP_MAXIMIZATION_DISABLED,
    Boolean.TRUE);
}
```

In the preceding constructor, we can see how the component's name and tool tip are set, as well as where our window-related options are set.

If we run our application now, we won't see any changes. What we need to do, then, is add a dependency on the `main` module to the application. We do that by right-clicking on the **Dependencies** node of the app module, as shown in this screenshot:

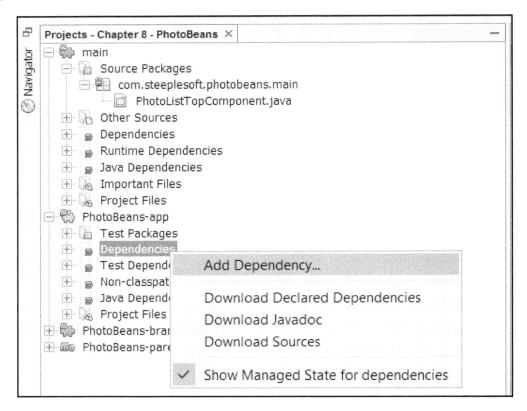

You should now see the **Add Dependency** window. Select the **Open Projects** tab, then select `main` as shown in this screenshot:

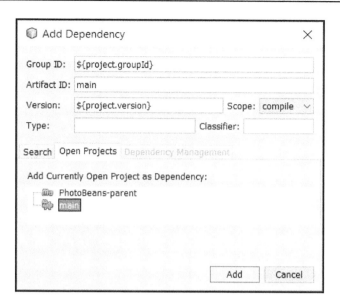

Once we've added the dependency, we need to build both modules, first `main` and then `app`, and then we'll be ready to run PhotoBeans for the first time:

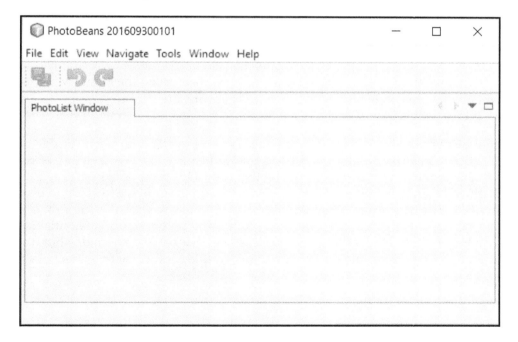

Notice the odd date in the window title in the preceding screen? That's the build date of the NetBeans platform, and it's not very pretty in our app, so, let's fix that. We have two options. The first is to use the Branding user interface we looked at earlier. The other is to edit the file directly. To keep things interesting, and to help understand where things are on the disk, we'll use this second approach.

In the branding module, under **Other Sources | nbm-branding,** you should find the `modules/org-netbeans-core-windows.jar/org/netbeans/core/windows/view/ui/Bundle.properties` file. In this file, you should see these lines:

```
CTL_MainWindow_Title=PhotoBeans {0}
CTL_MainWindow_Title_No_Project=PhotoBeans {0}
```

All we need to do is remove the {0} portions, rebuild this module and the app, and our title bar is much prettier. While that looks better, what about our TopComponent? To fix that, we need to learn a few new concepts.

Nodes, a NetBeans presentation object

You've already heard the term Node. I've used it several times to describe what and where to click. Officially, a Node represents one element in a hierarchy of objects (beans). It provides all the methods that are needed for communication between an explorer view and the bean. In the explorer section of our application, we want to represent a list of photos to the user. We'll represent each photo, as well as the year and month in which it was taken, as a Node. To display these Nodes, we'll use a NetBeans class called the `BeanTreeView`, which will display this node hierarchy as a tree. There are a few more concepts to learn, but let's start with what we have first.

We'll begin by defining our Nodes, which will serve as a sort of wrapper or bridge between our application's business domain model and the NetBeans APIs. We have not, of course, defined such a model, so we need to settle on that now. Our basic data item is a photograph, a file on disk that holds an image. In the application, we're going to display these photos in a nested tree structure, grouping the photos by year, then month. If you expand a year node, you'll see a list of month Nodes, and if you expand a month Node, you'll see a list of photo Nodes. It's a very basic, somewhat naive data model, but it's both, effective enough to demonstrate the concepts, and simple enough that we don't obscure the concepts.

As with all hierarchies, we need a root node, so we'll start with that:

```
public class RootNode extends AbstractNode
```

The base class of all nodes is, technically, Node, but extending that class puts much more of a burden on us, so we use the NetBeans-provided `AbstractNode`, which implements a fair amount of the basic behavior of the node for us with reasonable defaults.

Next, we define some constructors as follows:

```
public RootNode() {
    this(new InstanceContent());
}

protected RootNode(InstanceContent ic) {
    super(Children.create(new YearChildFactory(), true),
      new AbstractLookup(ic));
    setDisplayName(Bundle.LBL_RootNode());
    setShortDescription(Bundle.HINT_RootNode());

    instanceContent = ic;
}
```

Note that we have two constructors, one `public` and one `protected`. The reason for that is that we want to create and capture an instance of `InstanceContent`, which can be used by us, the creators of this class' Lookup, to control what is actually in the lookup. Since we need to pass `Lookup` to our class' parent constructor, we have this two-step approach to object instantiation.

Lookup, a NetBeans fundamental

What's a Lookup? It is a **general registry permitting clients to find instances of services (implementation of a given interface)**. To put it another way, it is a mechanism by which we can publish various artifacts, and other parts of the system can look up these artifacts by a key (either a `Class` or a `Lookup.Template`, which we'll not discuss here), with no coupling between the modules.

This is often used, as we'll see, to look up the implementations of a service interface. Do you recall earlier when I mentioned that often we see APIs defined in one module and implementations in another? This is where that comes in especially handy. Suppose you're developing an API to retrieve photos from an online service (which would be a great feature for this application!). You plan to deliver an implementation for one service, say Google Photos, but want to enable a third-party developer to provide an implementation for, say, Flickr. If you put the required API interfaces, classes, and so on in one module, and your Google Photos implementation in another, the third-party developer can depend on your API module alone, and avoid the weight of your implementation module. The Flickr module would declare an implementation of the photo service API, and we could load both that and our own Google Photos implementation via a request to the Lookup. In a nutshell, the system allows for decoupling the API definition, implementation, and instance acquisition in a very clean, simple API.

That's Lookup, but what is `InstanceContent`? The Lookup API only exposes methods for getting items. There is no mechanism for adding items to the Lookup, which makes sense as the Lookup instance is used by unknown third parties, and we don't want them changing the contents of our Lookup randomly. We, however, may actually want to change those contents, and we do that via `InstanceContent`, which exposes the methods we need to add or remove items. We'll see a demonstration of this concept later in the application.

Writing our own nodes

The preceding section covered those two classes, but what is `YearChildFactory`? The class `RootNode` defines for the system the root node of what will become our tree. Each node, though, if it has children, is responsible for loading and building those child Nodes, which is done through this `ChildFactory` class. Our instance looks like this:

```
public class YearChildFactory extends ChildFactory<String> {
  private final PhotoManager photoManager;
  private static final Logger LOGGER =
    Logger.getLogger(YearChildFactory.class.getName());
  public YearChildFactory() {
    this.photoManager =
      Lookup.getDefault().lookup(PhotoManager.class);
    if (photoManager == null) {
      LOGGER.log(Level.SEVERE,
      "Cannot get PhotoManager object");
      LifecycleManager.getDefault().exit();
    }
  }
```

```
@Override
protected boolean createKeys(List<String> list) {
  list.addAll(photoManager.getYears());
  return true;
}

@Override
protected Node createNodeForKey(String key) {
  return new YearNode(Integer.parseInt(key));
}
}
```

We are creating a `ChildFactory` interface that will return nodes that operate on Strings. If you have a more complex data model, one that uses, for example, POJOs, you would specify that class as the parameterized type.

In our constructor, we see an example of finding a service implementation via the Lookup, which is this:

```
this.photoManager=Lookup.getDefault().lookup(
  PhotoManager.class);
```

We'll look at defining services later, but, for now, all you need to understand is that we're asking the global Lookup (which is, unlike the Lookup we created previously, not tied to a particular class) for an instance of the `PhotoManager` interface. Perhaps naively, we assume there is only one instance of this interface, but since we're not exporting the interface, we are safe in our assumption. We do, though, check to make sure there is at least one, exiting the application if there is not.

The next two methods are how the factory is used to create the child Nodes. The first method, `createKeys(List<String> list)`, is called by the system to generate a list of keys for the child nodes. In our implementation, we ask the `PhotoManager` interface for a list of years (which, as we'll see, is a simple query of the database to get a list of the years for which we have photos in the system). The platform then takes these keys, and passes them, one at a time, to `createNodeForKey(String key)` to create the actual node. Here, we create an instance of `YearNode` to represent the year.

YearNode, like RootNode, extends AbstractNode.

```
public class YearNode extends AbstractNode {
  public YearNode(int year) {
    super(Children.create(new MonthNodeFactory(year), true),
     Lookups.singleton(year));
    setName("" + year);
    setDisplayName("" + year);
  }
}
```

The preceding is clearly a simpler node, but the basics are the same--we create ChildFactory to create our children, and we create a Lookup, which, in this case, holds a single value, the year that the Node represents.

MonthNodeFactory looks almost exactly like YearNodeFactory with the exception that it loads months for the given year, so we'll not show the source here. It also creates MonthNode instances for each month in the list. Like YearNode, MonthNode is pretty simple, as you can see in the following code snippet:

```
public class MonthNode extends AbstractNode {
  public MonthNode(int year, int month) {
    super(Children.create(
      new PhotoNodeFactory(year, month), true),
      Lookups.singleton(month));
    String display = month + " - " +
     Month.values()[month-1].getDisplayName(
        TextStyle.FULL, Locale.getDefault());
    setName(display);
    setDisplayName(display);
  }
}
```

We do a bit more work to give the Node a meaningful name and display name, but it's pretty much the same. Note also that we have yet another ChildFactory that will generate, as the name implies, the PhotoNodes we'll need as children. The factory itself has nothing new of interest, but PhotoNode does, so let's take a look at that:

```
public class PhotoNode extends AbstractNode {
  public PhotoNode(String photo) {
    this(photo, new InstanceContent());
  }

  private PhotoNode(String photo, InstanceContent ic) {
    super(Children.LEAF, new AbstractLookup(ic));
    final String name = new File(photo).getName();
    setName(name);
```

```
    setDisplayName(name);

    ic.add((OpenCookie) () -> {
      TopComponent tc = findTopComponent(photo);
      if (tc == null) {
        tc = new PhotoViewerTopComponent(photo);
        tc.open();
      }
      tc.requestActive();
    });
}
```

Here we again see the dual constructor approach, though, in this case, we do make use of `InstanceContent`. Note that the first parameter to `super()` is `Children.LEAF`, indicating that this Node does not have any children. We also pass the now familiar `new AbstractLookup(ic)`.

After setting the name and display name, we add a lambda to our `InstanceContent` object. The non-lambda version of this would look like this:

```
ic.add(new OpenCookie() {
  @Override
  public void open() {
  }
});
```

What is `OpenCookie`? It's a child of the marker interface `Node.Cookie`, and a cookie is **a design pattern used to add behaviors to existing data objects and nodes, or to separate implementation from the main object**. Using this cookie, we can neatly abstract away the signaling that something can be opened as well as how to open it.

In this case, when the system tries to open the photo represented by the node, it will call our definition of `OpenCookie.open()`, which will attempt to find an open instance of the photo. Whether it finds an existing one or needs to create a new one, it instructs the system to make it active (or give it focus).

Note that the open photo is represented by another TopComponent. To find it, we have this method:

```
private TopComponent findTopComponent(String photo) {
  Set<TopComponent> openTopComponents =
    WindowManager.getDefault().getRegistry().getOpened();
  for (TopComponent tc : openTopComponents) {
    if (photo.equals(tc.getLookup().lookup(String.class))) {
      return tc;
    }
```

```
        }
        return null;
    }
```

We ask the Lookup of `WindowManager` for all the opened TopComponents, then iterate through each, comparing `String photo`, which is the full path of the image, with any `String` stored in the Lookup of TopComponent. If there's a match, we return that TopComponent. This lookup by `String` is somewhat naive though, and could, in more complex applications, result in unexpected matches. We're likely safe enough in this application, but you'll need to make sure in your own application that the matching criteria are strict and unique enough to avoid false hits.

Performing Actions

We'll look at `PhotoViewerTopComponent` in a moment, but there are a few more items we need to look at before moving on to that.

`PhotoNode` overrides two additional methods, which are as follows:

```
        @Override
        public Action[] getActions(boolean context) {
            return new Action[]{SystemAction.get(OpenAction.class)};
        }

        @Override
        public Action getPreferredAction() {
            return SystemAction.get(OpenAction.class);
        }
```

Unsurprisingly, the `getActions()` method returns an array of Actions for this Node. Actions are an abstraction (from Swing, not NetBeans) that allow us to add items to menus, and provide a means for a user to interact with the system. Each entry you see in the main menu or a context menu is backed by an Action. In our case, we're associating the NetBeans-defined `OpenAction` with our node, which will, when clicked, look for an `OpenCookie` instance in the Node's lookup and call `OpenCookie.open()`, which we defined previously.

We also override `getPreferredAction()`, which lets us define the behavior for when a Node is double-clicked. The combination of these two methods makes it possible for the user to right-click a Node and select `Open`, or double-click a Node, with the end result being that the TopComponent for that Node is opened.

Services - exposing decoupled functionality

Before looking at the definition of our `TopComponent`, let's look at `PhotoManager`, and learn a bit about its services. The `PhotoManager` interface itself is pretty simple:

```
public interface PhotoManager extends Lookup.Provider {
  void scanSourceDirs();
  List<String> getYears();
  List<String> getMonths(int year);
  List<String> getPhotos(int year, int month);
}
```

There is little of interest in the preceding code beyond the `extends Lookup.Provider` portion. Adding this here, we can force implementations to implement the lone method on that interface, as we'll need that later. The interesting part comes from the implementation, which is as follows:

```
@ServiceProvider(service = PhotoManager.class)
public class PhotoManagerImpl implements PhotoManager {
```

That is all it takes to register a service with the platform. The annotation specifies the metadata needed, and the build takes care of the rest. Let's take a look at the rest of the implementation:

```
public PhotoManagerImpl() throws ClassNotFoundException {
  setupDatabase();

  Preferences prefs =
    NbPreferences.forModule(PhotoManager.class);
  setSourceDirs(prefs.get("sourceDirs", ""));
  prefs.addPreferenceChangeListener(evt -> {
    if (evt.getKey().equals("sourceDirs")) {
      setSourceDirs(evt.getNewValue());
      scanSourceDirs();
    }
  });

  instanceContent = new InstanceContent();
  lookup = new AbstractLookup(instanceContent);
  scanSourceDirs();
}
```

In this preceding, very simple, implementation, we're going to use SQLite to store information about the photos we find. The service will provide the code to scan the configured source directories, store information about the photos found, and expose methods for retrieving those pieces of that information that vary in specificity.

To start with, we need to make sure that the database is properly set up if this is the first time the application is run. We could include a prebuilt database, but creating it on the user's machine adds a bit of resilience for those situations where the database is accidentally deleted.

```
private void setupDatabase() {
  try {
    connection = DriverManager.getConnection(JDBC_URL);
    if (!doesTableExist()) {
      createTable();
    }
  } catch (SQLException ex) {
    Exceptions.printStackTrace(ex);
  }
}

private boolean doesTableExist() {
  try (Statement stmt = connection.createStatement()) {
    ResultSet rs = stmt.executeQuery("select 1 from images");
    rs.close();
    return true;
  } catch (SQLException e) {
    return false;
  }
}

private void createTable() {
  try (Statement stmt = connection.createStatement()) {
    stmt.execute(
      "CREATE TABLE images (imageSource VARCHAR2(4096), "
      + " year int, month int, image VARCHAR2(4096));");
    stmt.execute(
      "CREATE UNIQUE INDEX uniq_img ON images(image);");
  } catch (SQLException e) {
    Exceptions.printStackTrace(e);
  }
}
```

Next, we ask for a reference to the NetBeans preferences for the module `PhotoManager`. We'll look at managing preferences later in the chapter where we'll delve into this API in more detail, but, for now, we'll say only that we are going to ask the system for the `sourceDirs` preference, which we'll then use to configure our scanning code.

We also create `PreferenceChangeListener` to capture when the user changes the preferences. In this listener, we verify that the preference we care about, `sourceDirs`, was changed, and, if it was, we store the new value in our `PhotoManager` instance, and initiate a directory scan.

Finally, we create `InstanceContent`, create and store a Lookup, and start a directory scan to make sure the application is up-to-date with the state of the photos on disk.

The `getYears()`, `getMonths()`, and `getPhotos()` methods are largely the same, differing only, of course, in the type of data they're working with, so we'll let `getYears()` serve as an explanation of all three:

```
@Override
public List<String> getYears() {
  List<String> years = new ArrayList<>();
  try (Statement yearStmt = connection.createStatement();
  ResultSet rs = yearStmt.executeQuery(
    "SELECT DISTINCT year FROM images ORDER BY year")) {
      while (rs.next()) {
        years.add(rs.getString(1));
      }
    } catch (SQLException ex) {
      Exceptions.printStackTrace(ex);
    }
  return years;
}
```

If you are familiar with JDBC, this should not be surprising. We use Java 7's `try-with-resources` syntax to declare and instantiate both our `Statement` and our `ResultSet` objects. For those not familiar with this construct, it allows us to declare certain types of resource, and not have to worry about closing them as the system automatically closes them for us once the scope of the `try` terminates. The major restriction to be aware of with this, however, is that the class must implement `AutoCloseable`; a `Closeable` will not work. The other two `get*` methods are logically similar, so they are not shown here.

The last major piece of functionality here is the scanning of source directories, which is coordinated by the `scanSourceDirs()` method, given as follows:

```
private final ExecutorService executorService =
  Executors.newFixedThreadPool(5);
public final void scanSourceDirs() {
  RequestProcessor.getDefault().execute(() -> {
    List<Future<List<Photo>>> futures = new ArrayList<>();
    sourceDirs.stream()
      .map(d -> new SourceDirScanner(d))
```

```
      .forEach(sds ->
      futures.add((Future<List<Photo>>)
      executorService.submit(sds)));
    futures.forEach(f -> {
      try {
        final List<Photo> list = f.get();
        processPhotos(list);
      } catch (InterruptedException|ExecutionException ex) {
        Exceptions.printStackTrace(ex);
      }
    });
    instanceContent.add(new ReloadCookie());
  });
}
```

To speed the process up a bit, we create Future for each configured source directory, which we pass to our ExecutorService. We have it configured at a maximum of five threads in the pool, which is largely arbitrary. A more sophisticated approach might make this configurable, or perhaps, auto-tuned, but this should be sufficient for our purposes here.

Once the Futures are created, we iterate over the list, requesting each result. If the number of source directories exceeds the size of our thread pool, the excess Futures will wait until a Thread becomes available, at which point the ExecutorService will pick one to run. Once they're all done, the calls to .get() will no longer block, and the application can continue. Note that we're not blocking the user interface to allow this to work, as we pass the bulk of this method as a lambda to RequestProcessor.getDefault().execute() to request that this run off the user interface thread.

When the list of photos has been built and returned, we process those photos with this method:

```
private void processPhotos(List<Photo> photos) {
  photos.stream()
    .filter(p -> !isImageRecorded(p))
    .forEach(p -> insertImage(p));
}
```

The isImageRecorded() method checks to see if the image path is already in the database, returning true if it is. We filter() the stream based on the result of this test, so forEach() only operates on previously unknown images, which are then inserted into the database via insertImage(). Those two methods look like this:

```
private boolean isImageRecorded(Photo photo) {
  boolean there = false;
  try (PreparedStatement imageExistStatement =
    connection.prepareStatement(
```

```
       "SELECT 1 FROM images WHERE image = ?")) {
         imageExistStatement.setString(1, photo.getImage());
         final ResultSet rs = imageExistStatement.executeQuery();
         there = rs.next();
         close(rs);
       } catch (SQLException ex) {
         Exceptions.printStackTrace(ex);
       }
     return there;
   }

   private void insertImage(Photo photo) {
     try (PreparedStatement insertStatement =
      connection.prepareStatement(
        "INSERT INTO images (imageSource, year, month, image)
        VALUES (?, ?, ?, ?);")) {
          insertStatement.setString(1, photo.getSourceDir());
          insertStatement.setInt(2, photo.getYear());
          insertStatement.setInt(3, photo.getMonth());
          insertStatement.setString(4, photo.getImage());
          insertStatement.executeUpdate();
     } catch (SQLException ex) {
       Exceptions.printStackTrace(ex);
     }
   }
```

We are using `PreparedStatement`, as it is, generally, unwise to create SQL statements via concatenation, which can, and often does, lead to SQL injection attacks, so we can't use `try-with-resources` fully in the first method, requiring us to close the `ResultSet` manually.

PhotoViewerTopComponent

We can now find images, but we still can't tell the system where to look. Before turning our attention to handling preferences with the NetBeans platform, though, we have one more TopComponent to look at--`PhotoViewerTopComponent`.

If you think back to our discussion of the areas provided by the NetBeans window system, when we view an image, we want the image to be loaded in the Editor area. To create a TopComponent for that, we instruct NetBeans to create a new Window by right-clicking on the desired package, and selecting **New** | **Window**:

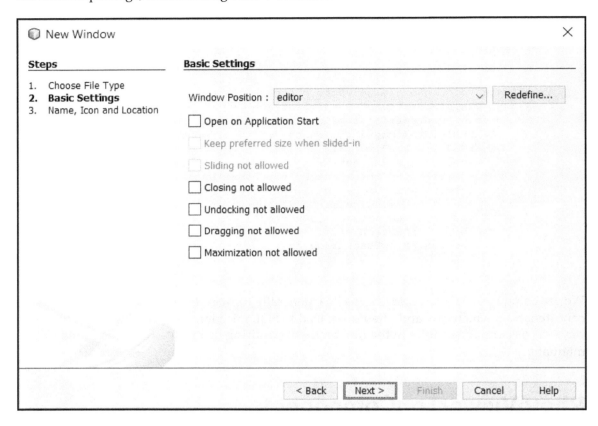

In the next pane, we specify a class name prefix for our new TopComponent--PhotoViewer as seen in the following screenshot:

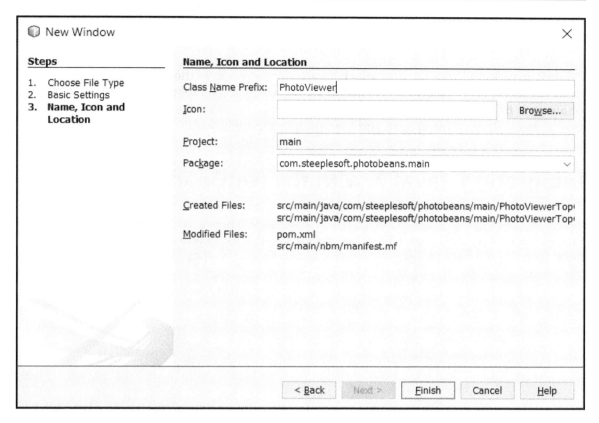

NetBeans will now create the files `PhotoViewerTopComponent.java` and
`PhotoViewerTopComponent.form` just as was discussed earlier. For this TopComponent,
though, we need to make a couple of changes. When we open the `Window`, we need to
specify an image for it to load, so we need to provide a constructor that takes the path to the
image. However, TopComponents must have a no-argument constructor, so we leave it but
have it call our new constructor with an empty image path.

```java
public PhotoViewerTopComponent() {
  this("");
}

public PhotoViewerTopComponent(String photo) {
  initComponents();
  this.photo = photo;
  File file = new File(photo);
  setName(file.getName());
  setToolTipText(photo);
  associateLookup(Lookups.singleton(photo));
```

```
        setLayout(new BorderLayout());
        init();
    }
```

While it may seem like a lot, the steps here are simple: we save the photo path in an instance variable, we create a `File` instance from it to get the file name more easily, add the photo path to TopComponent's Lookup (which is how we find the TopComponent for a given photo), change the layout, and then initialize the window.

Integrating JavaFX with the NetBeans RCP

The `init()` method is interesting, though, in that we're going to do something slightly different; we're going to use JavaFX to view the image. There's no reason we couldn't use Swing like we are in our other TopComponent, but this gives us a good opportunity to demonstrate both how to integrate JavaFX and Swing, as well as JavaFX and the NetBeans platform.

```
private JFXPanel fxPanel;
private void init() {
    fxPanel = new JFXPanel();
    add(fxPanel, BorderLayout.CENTER);
    Platform.setImplicitExit(false);
    Platform.runLater(this::createScene);
}
```

`JFXPanel` is a Swing component that is used to embed JavaFX into Swing. Our Window's layout is `BorderLayout`, so we add our `JFXPanel` to it in the `CENTER` area, and let it expand to fill the `Window`. Any complex layout of the JavaFX components will be handled by yet another container inside our `JFXPanel`. Our user interface, though, is fairly simple. As with our earlier JavaFX systems, we define our user interface via FXML as follows:

```
<BorderPane fx:id="borderPane" prefHeight="480.0"
  prefWidth="600.0"
  xmlns="http://javafx.com/javafx/8.0.111"
  xmlns:fx="http://javafx.com/fxml/1"
  fx:controller=
    "com.steeplesoft.photobeans.main.PhotoViewerController">
  <center>
    <ScrollPane fx:id="scrollPane">
      <content>
        <Group>
          <children>
            <ImageView fx:id="imageView"
              preserveRatio="true" />
```

```
        </children>
      </Group>
    </content>
  </ScrollPane>
 </center>
</BorderPane>
```

Since FXML needs a root element, we specify a `BorderLayout`, which, as discussed, gives us a `BorderLayout` in a `JFXPanel` in a `BorderLayout`. That may sound really odd, but that's how embedding JavaFX works. Note also that we still specify a controller. In that controller, our `initialize()` method looks like this:

```
@FXML
private BorderPane borderPane;
@FXML
private ScrollPane scrollPane;
public void initialize(URL location,
 ResourceBundle resources) {
    imageView.fitWidthProperty()
     .bind(borderPane.widthProperty());
    imageView.fitHeightProperty()
     .bind(borderPane.heightProperty());
}
```

In this last method, all we're doing is binding the width and height properties to those of the border pane. We've also set `preserveRatio` to `True` in the FXML, so the image won't be distorted. This will be important as we rotate the image next.

We haven't seen the code for rotation, so let's look at that now. We'll start by adding a button as follows:

```
<top>
  <ButtonBar prefHeight="40.0" prefWidth="200.0"
    BorderPane.alignment="CENTER">
    <buttons>
      <SplitMenuButton mnemonicParsing="false"
        text="Rotate">
        <items>
          <MenuItem onAction="#rotateLeft"
            text="Left 90°" />
          <MenuItem onAction="#rotateRight"
            text="Right 90°" />
        </items>
      </SplitMenuButton>
    </buttons>
  </ButtonBar>
</top>
```

To the `top` section of `BorderPane`, we add `ButtonBar`, to which we add a single `SplitMenuButton`. That gives us a button like the one to the right. In its non-focused state, it looks like a normal button. When the user clicks on the arrow, the menu, as seen here, is presented to the user, offering the ability to rotate the image in the directions listed:

We've tied those MenuItems to the appropriate methods in the controller in our FXML definition:

```
@FXML
public void rotateLeft(ActionEvent event) {
    imageView.setRotate(imageView.getRotate() - 90);
}
@FXML
public void rotateRight(ActionEvent event) {
    imageView.setRotate(imageView.getRotate() + 90);
}
```

Using the APIs provided by the JavaFX `ImageView`, we set the image rotation.

We can find images, view them, and rotate them, but we still can't tell the system where to look for those images. It's time to fix that.

NetBeans preferences and the Options panel

The key to managing preferences is two-fold: `NbPreferences` and the **Options** panel. `NbPreferences` is the means by which preferences are stored and loaded, and the options panel is the means by which the user is presented with a user interface for editing those preferences. We'll start by looking at how to add an **Options** panel, which will lead naturally to the `NbPreferences` discussion. Next is the NetBeans Options window:

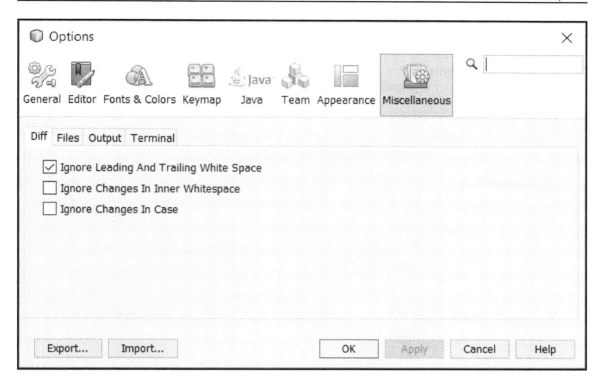

In the preceding window, we can see the two types of **Options** panel--primary and secondary. A primary **Options** panel is represented by icons across the top: **General, Editor, Fonts & Colors**, and so on. A secondary **Options** panel is a tab like we see in the middle section: **Diff, Files, Output**, and **Terminal**. When adding an **Options** panel, you must choose either primary or secondary. We'd like to add a new primary panel, as it will separate our preferences from the rest of the panels visually as well as giving us an opportunity to create both types of panel.

Adding a primary panel

To create a primary **Options** panel, right-click on the desired package or the project node, and click on **New** | **Options Panel**. If **Options Panel** is not visible, select **New** | **Other** | **Module Development** | **Options Panel**. Next, select **Create Primary Panel**:

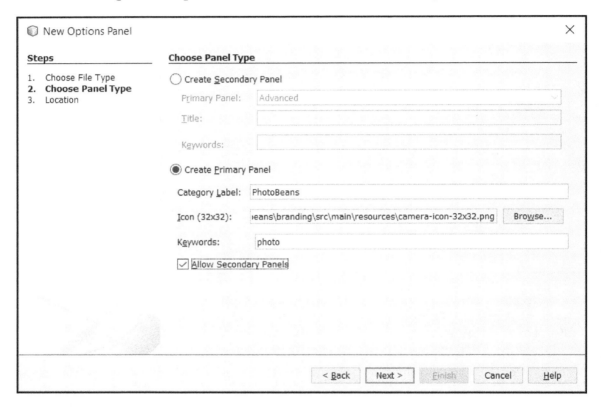

We must specify a label, which is the text we'll see under the icon. We must also select an icon. The system will let you select something other than a 32x32 image, but if it's not the right size, it will look strange in the user interface; so, choose carefully. The system will also require you to enter keywords, which will be used if the user applies a filter to the Options window. Finally, select **Allow Secondary Panels**. The primary panel doesn't have any real content and serves only to display secondary panels, which we'll create shortly.

When you click on **Next**, you will be asked for the class prefix and package:

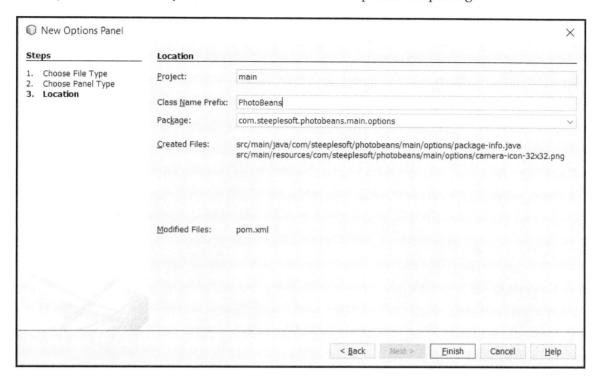

When you click on **Finish**, NetBeans will create this single file, `package-info.java`:

```
@OptionsPanelController.ContainerRegistration(id = "PhotoBeans",
  categoryName = "#OptionsCategory_Name_PhotoBeans",
  iconBase = "com/steeplesoft/photobeans/main/options/
  camera-icon-32x32.png",
  keywords = "#OptionsCategory_Keywords_PhotoBeans",
  keywordsCategory = "PhotoBeans")
@NbBundle.Messages(value = {
  "OptionsCategory_Name_PhotoBeans=PhotoBeans",
  "OptionsCategory_Keywords_PhotoBeans=photo"})
package com.steeplesoft.photobeans.main.options;

import org.netbeans.spi.options.OptionsPanelController;
import org.openide.util.NbBundle;
```

Adding a secondary panel

With the primary panel defined, we're ready to create the secondary panel, which will do our work. We right-click on the package again, and select **New** | **Options Panel**, this time selecting **Create Secondary Panel**:

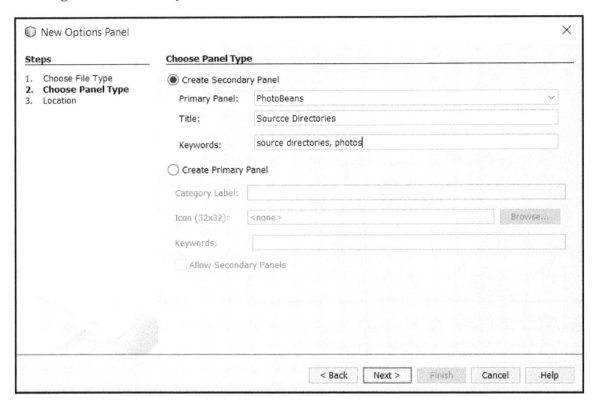

Since we've defined our own primary panel, we can select that as our parent, and we set the title and keywords as we did before. Click on **Next**, select and/or verify the class prefix and package, then click on **Finish**. This will create three artifacts--
`SourceDirectoriesOptionPanelController.java`, `SourceDirectoriesPanel.java`, and `SourceDirectoriesPanel.form`, and NetBeans will present you with the GUI editor for your panel.

We want to add four elements to our panel--a label, a list view, and two buttons. We add those by dragging them from the palette on the right, and arranging them in the form as shown next:

To make working with these user interface elements more meaningful, we need to set the variable names. We also need to set the text of the user interface so that each element is meaningful for the user. We can do both by right-clicking on each element, as shown in this screenshot:

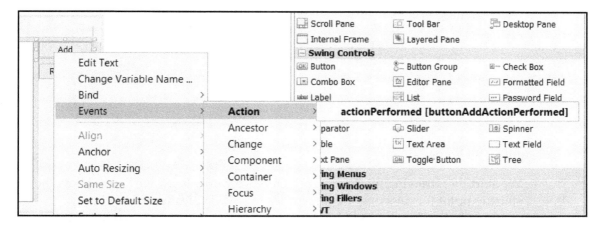

In the preceding screen, we can see the three items of interest--**Edit Text, Change Variable Name...,** and **Events | Action | actionPeformed [buttonAddActionPerformed]**. For our buttons, we need to use all three, so we set the text to Add (or Remove), change the variable name to buttonAdd/buttonRemove, and select actionPerformed. Back in our Java source, we see a method created for us, which we need to fill out:

```java
private void buttonAddActionPerformed(ActionEvent evt) {
    String lastDir = NbPreferences
        .forModule(PhotoManager.class).get("lastDir", null);
    JFileChooser chooser = new JFileChooser();
    if (lastDir != null) {
      chooser.setCurrentDirectory(
        new java.io.File(lastDir));
    }
    chooser.setDialogTitle("Add Source Directory");
    chooser.setFileSelectionMode(
      JFileChooser.DIRECTORIES_ONLY);
    chooser.setAcceptAllFileFilterUsed(false);
    if (chooser.showOpenDialog(null) ==
      JFileChooser.APPROVE_OPTION) {
        try {
          String dir = chooser.getSelectedFile()
          .getCanonicalPath();
          ensureModel().addElement(dir);
          NbPreferences.forModule(PhotoManager.class)
          .put("lastDir", dir);
        } catch (IOException ex) {
          Exceptions.printStackTrace(ex);
        }
      } else {
        System.out.println("No Selection ");
      }
}
```

We have quite a bit going on here:

1. We start by retrieving the lastDir preference value. If set, we'll use this as the starting point for selecting the directories to add. Typically, at least in my experience, the directories of interest are, usually, pretty close to one another in the filesystem, so we use this preference to save the user some clicks.

2. Next we create JFileChooser, which is the Swing class that will allow us to choose the directory.

3. If lastDir is not null, we pass it to setCurrentDirectory().

4. We set the title of the dialog to something meaningful.

5. We specify that the dialog should only let us choose directories.

6. Finally, we disable the **Select All file filter** option.

7. We call `chooser.showOpenDialog()` to present the dialog to the user, and wait for it close.

8. If the return code from the dialog is `APPROVE_OPTION`, we need to add the chosen directory to our model.

9. We get the canonical path for the selected file.

10. We call `ensureModel()`, which we'll look at in a moment, to get the model for our `ListView`, then add this new path to it.

11. Finally, we store the chosen path as `lastDir` in our preferences to set the starting directory as discussed earlier.

12. The action for the **Remove** button is much simpler, and is as follows:

```
private void buttonRemoveActionPerformed(ActionEvent evt) {
    List<Integer> indexes = IntStream.of(
      sourceList.getSelectedIndices())
      .boxed().collect(Collectors.toList());
    Collections.sort(indexes);
    Collections.reverse(indexes);
    indexes.forEach(i -> ensureModel().remove(i));
}
```

When we are removing items from the model, we remove them by the item index. However, when we remove an item, the index numbers for anything after that change. What we do here, then, is create a List of the selected indices, sort it to make sure it's in the right order (which is possibly excessive here, but it's a relatively inexpensive operation, and makes the next operation safer), then we reverse the order of the List. With our indices now in descending order, we can iterate over the List, removing each index from our model.

We've used `ensureModel()` a couple of times now, so let's see what that looks like:

```
private DefaultListModel<String> ensureModel() {
    if (model == null) {
      model = new DefaultListModel<>();
      sourceList.setModel(model);
    }
    return model;
}
```

It's important that we treat the model as `DefaultListModel` rather than the `ListModel` type that `ListView` expects, as the latter does not expose any methods for mutating the contents of the model, whereas the former does. By dealing with `DefaultListModel`, we can add and remove items as needed, as we've done here.

Loading and saving preferences

There are two more methods we need to look at in this class, the ones that load and store the options represented in the panel. We'll start with `load()`, which is as follows:

```
protected void load() {
  String dirs = NbPreferences
    .forModule(PhotoManager.class).get("sourceDirs", "");
  if (dirs != null && !dirs.isEmpty()) {
    ensureModel();
    model.clear();
    Set<String> set = new HashSet<>(
      Arrays.asList(dirs.split(";")));
    set.forEach(i -> model.addElement(i));
  }
}
```

`NbPreferences` does not support storing a list of strings, so, as we'll see below, we store the list of source directories as a semicolon-delimited list of strings. Here, we load the value of `sourceDirs`, and, if not null, we split on the semicolon, and add each entry to our `DefaultListModel`.

Saving the source directories is also fairly straightforward:

```
protected void store() {
  Set<String> dirs = new HashSet<>();
  ensureModel();
  for (int i = 0; i < model.getSize(); i++) {
    final String dir = model.getElementAt(i);
    if (dir != null && !dir.isEmpty()) {
      dirs.add(dir);
    }
  }
  if (!dirs.isEmpty()) {
    NbPreferences.forModule(PhotoManager.class)
      .put("sourceDirs", String.join(";", dirs));
  } else {
    NbPreferences.forModule(PhotoManager.class)
      .remove("sourceDirs");
  }
}
```

We iterate over `ListModel`, adding each directory to a local `HashSet` instance, which helps us remove any duplicate directories. If `Set` is not empty, we use `String.join()` to create our delimited list, and `put()` it into our preferences store. If it is empty, we remove the preference entry from the store to clear out any old data that may have been persisted earlier.

Reacting to changes in preferences

Now that we can persist changes, we need to make the application react to the changes. Fortunately, the NetBeans RCP provides a neat, decoupled way to handle that. We need not explicitly call a method from our code here. We can attach a listener at the point in the system where we're interested in the change. We've already seen this code back in `PhotoManagerImpl`:

```
prefs.addPreferenceChangeListener(evt -> {
  if (evt.getKey().equals("sourceDirs")) {
    setSourceDirs(evt.getNewValue());
    scanSourceDirs();
  }
});
```

When we save any preference for the `PhotoManager` module, this listener is called. We simply check to make sure it's for a key that we're interested in, and act accordingly, which, as we've seen, involves restarting the source directory scanning process.

Once new data has been loaded, how do we make the user interface reflect that change? Do we have to update the user interface manually? Again, thanks to the RCP, the answer is no. We've seen the first half at the end of `scanSourceDirs()`, which is this:

```
instanceContent.add(new ReloadCookie());
```

NetBeans has a number of cookie classes for indicating that certain actions should take place. While we don't share the class hierarchy (due to the unfortunate dependency on the Nodes API), we do share the same nomenclature with the hope of stealing, so to speak, a bit of the familiarity. So what does `ReloadCookie` look like? There's not much to it; it is given like this:

```
public class ReloadCookie {
}
```

In our case, we just have an empty class. We don't intend for this to be used elsewhere, so we don't need to encode any functionality in the class. We will just be using this as an indicator, as we see in the constructor of `RootNode`, which is as follows:

```
reloadResult = photoManager.getLookup().lookup(
    new Lookup.Template(ReloadCookie.class));
reloadResult.addLookupListener(event -> setChildren(
    Children.create(new YearChildFactory(), true)));
```

`Lookup.Template` is used to define the pattern by which the system can filter our `Lookup` requests. Using our template, we create a `Lookup.Result` object, `reloadResult`, and add a listener to it via a lambda. The lambda creates a new set of children using `Children.create()` and the `YearChildFactory` we looked at earlier, and passes those to `setChildren()` to update the user interface.

That may seem like a fair bit of code just to update the user interface when a preference is changed, but the decoupling is certainly worth it. Imagine a more complicated application or a dependent module tree. Using this listener approach, we need not expose methods, or even classes, to the outside world, allowing our internal code to be modified without breaking client code. That is, in short, one of the primary reasons for decoupled code.

Summary

Once again, we've come to the end of another application. You learned how to bootstrap a Maven-based NetBeans Rich Client Platform application. You learned about RCP modules, and how to include those modules in our application build. You also learned the basics of the NetBeans RCP Node API, how to create our own nodes, and how to nest child nodes. We explained how to use the NetBeans Preferences API, including creating new Options panels for editing preferences, how to load and store them, and how to react to changes in preferences.

One final word on the NetBeans RCP--While we have built a respectable application here, we have in no way pushed the limits of the RCP. I have attempted to cover just enough of the platform to get you going, but you will almost certainly need to learn more if you are to continue using the platform. While the official documentation is helpful, the go-to source for comprehensive coverage is *NetBeans Platform for Beginners* by Jason Wexbridge and Walter Nyland (`https://leanpub.com/nbp4beginners`). It's a great book, and I highly recommend it.

In the next chapter, we're going to dip our toes into the waters of client/server programming, and implement our own note-taking application. It won't be as robust and full-featured as the competitors already in the market, but we'll make good headway in that direction and, hopefully, learn a lot along the way.

9
Taking Notes with Monumentum

For our eighth project, we will again do something new--we'll build a web app. Whereas all of our other projects have been command lines, GUIs, or some combination thereof, this project will be a single module consisting of a REST API and a JavaScript frontend, all built with an eye toward the current microservice trend.

To build the application, you'll learn about the following topics:

- Some of the Java options to build microservice applications
- Payara Micro and `microprofile.io`
- Java API for RESTful Web Services
- Document data stores and MongoDB
- OAuth authentication (against Google, specifically)
- **JSON Web Tokens (JWT)**

As you can see, this will be, in many ways, a much different type of project than what we've looked at to this point.

Getting started

Most of us have likely used some sort of note-taking application such as EverNote, OneNote, or Google Keep. They're an extremely handy way of jotting down notes and thoughts, and having them available from just about every environment imaginable-- desktop, mobile, and web. In this chapter, we'll build a fairly basic clone of these industry giants in order to exercise a number of concepts. We will call this app Monumentum, which is Latin for a reminder or memorial, an apt name for this type of application.

Before we get into those, let's take some time to list the requirements for our application:

- Be able to create notes
- Be able to list notes
- Be able to edit notes
- Be able to delete notes
- Note bodies must be capable of storing/displaying rich text
- Be able to create a user account
- Must be able to log into the application using OAuth2 credentials against an existing system

Our non-functional requirements are fairly modest:

- Must have a RESTful API
- Must have an HTML 5/JavaScript frontend
- Must have a flexible, scalable data store
- Must be easily deployable on resource-constrained systems

Of course, this list of non-functional requirements was chosen in part because they reflect real-world requirements, but they also set us up very nicely to discuss some of the technologies I'd like to cover in this chapter. To cut to the chase, we'll create a web application that provides both a REST-based API and a JavaScript client. It will be backed by a document data store, and built using one of the many microservice libraries/frameworks available to the JVM.

So what does this stack look like? Let's take a quick survey of our options before we settle on a particular choice. Let's start with a look at the microservice frameworks.

Microservice frameworks on the JVM

While I am reluctant to spend a great deal of time on what a microservice is given that most people are familiar with the topic at this point, I think it would be a remiss not to give at least a brief description in case you are not familiar with the idea. With that said, here is a nice, concise definition of microservice from SmartBear, a provider of software quality tools perhaps best known for their stewardship of the Swagger API and related libraries:

> *Essentially, microservice architecture is a method of developing software applications as a suite of independently deployable, small, modular services in which each service runs a unique process and communicates through a well-defined, lightweight mechanism to serve a business goal.*

To put it another way, rather than the older, more established approach of bundling several related systems in one web application and deploying it to a large application server, such as GlassFish/Payara Server, Wildfly, WebLogic Server, or WebSphere, each of these systems would instead be run separately in their own JVM process. The benefits of this approach include easier, piecemeal upgrades, increased stability through process isolation, smaller resource requirements, greater machine utilization, and so on. The concept itself is not necessarily new, but it has certainly gained popularity in recent years, and continues to grow at a rapid pace.

So what do our options look like on the JVM? We have several, including, in no particular order, the following:

- **Eclipse Vert.x**: This is officially *a tool-kit for building reactive applications on the JVM*. It provides an event-driven application framework that lends itself well to writing microservices. Vert.x can be used in a number of languages, including Java, Javascript, Kotlin, Ceylon, Scala, Groovy, and Ruby. More information can be found at http://vertx.io/.

- **Spring Boot**: This is a library to build stand alone Spring applications. Spring Boot applications have full access to the entire Spring ecosystem, and can be run using a single fat/uber JAR. Spring Boot lives at https://projects.spring.io/spring-boot/.

- **Java EE MicroProfile**: This is a community and vendor-led effort to create a new profile for Java EE, specifically tailored to microservices. At the time of writing, the profile includes **Java API for RESTful Web Services (JAX-RS)**, CDI, and JSON-P, and is sponsored by several companies including Tomitribe, Payara, Red Hat, Hazelcast, IBM, and Fujitsu, and user groups such as London Java Community and SouJava. The MicroProfile home page is http://microprofile.io/.

- **Lagom**: This fairly new framework is a reactive microservices framework from Lightbend, the company behind Scala. It is described as an opinionated microservice framework, and is built using two of Lightbend's more famous libraries--Akka and Play. Lagom applications can be written either in Java or Scala. More details can be found at
  `https://www.lightbend.com/platform/development/lagom-framework`.
- **Dropwizard**: This is a Java framework to develop ops-friendly, high-performance, RESTful web services. It is a framework that offers Jetty for HTTP, Jersey for REST services, and Jackson for JSON. It also provides support for other libraries such as Guava, Hibernate Validator, Freemarker, and others. You can find Dropwizard at `http://www.dropwizard.io/`.

There are a few other options, but it should be clear that, as JVM developers, we have a myriad of choices, which is almost always good. Since we can only build using one, I have chosen to use the MicroProfile. Specifically, we'll base our application on Payara Micro, Payara's implementation, which is based on the GlassFish sources (plus Payara's bug fixes, enhancements, and so on).

By choosing the MicroProfile and Payara Micro, we choose, implicitly, JAX-RS as the basis for our REST services. We are free, of course, to use whatever we want, but deviating from what the framework offers lessens the value of the framework itself.

That leaves us with our choice of data store. One option we've already seen is the relational database. It is a tried and true choice that powers a wide swath of the industry. They are, however, not without their limitations and problems. While databases themselves can be complicated in terms of classifications and functionality, perhaps the most popular alternatives to relational databases are NoSQL databases. While these have existed for half a century, the idea had not gained any significant market traction until sometime in the last decade or so with the advent of **Web 2.0**.

While the term **NoSQL** is very broad, most examples of this type of database tend to be key-value, document, or graph data stores, each offering distinct performance and behavior characteristics. A full treatment of each type of NoSQL database and its various implementations is beyond the scope of this book, so, in the interest of time and space, we'll just get straight to our selection--MongoDB. Its scalability and flexibility, especially in regard to document schemas, meshes well with our target use case.

Finally, on the client side, we have a myriad of options again. Among the most popular are ReactJS from Facebook and Angular from Google. There is a variety of other frameworks, including older options such as Knockout and Backbone, as well as newer ones such as Vue.js. It is this latter option that we'll use. Not only is it a very powerful and flexible option, it also presents the least amount of friction getting started. Since this book is focused on Java, I felt it prudent to select an option that will require the least amount of setup while meeting our needs.

Creating the application

To use Payara Micro, we create a Java web application like we normally would. In NetBeans, we will select **File** | **New Project** | **Maven** | **Web Application** and click on **Next**. For the project name, enter `monumentum`, select the appropriate **Project Location**, and fix up the **Group ID** and **Package** as desired:

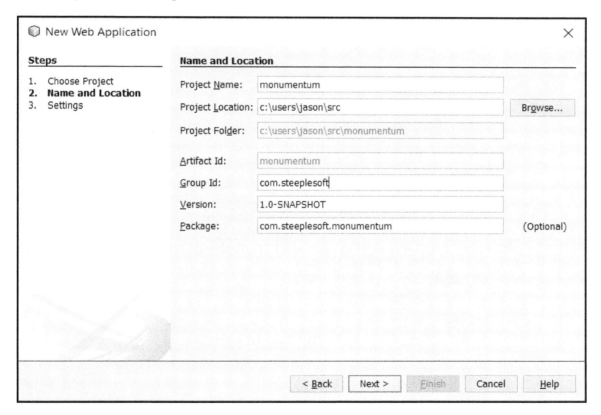

The next window will ask us to choose a server, which we can leave blank, and a Java EE version, which we want to set to **Java EE 7 Web**:

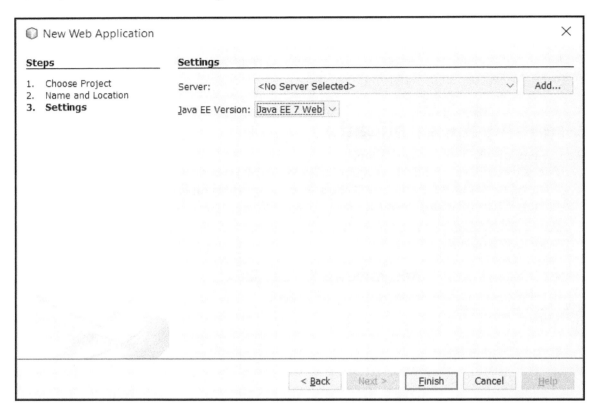

After a few moments, we should have our project created and ready to go. Since we created a Java EE 7 web application, NetBeans has already added the Java EE API dependency to the project. Before we jump into coding, let's add Payara Micro to the build to get that part ready. To do that, we need to add a plugin to the build. That will look something like this (though we've only shown the highlights here):

```
<plugin>
  <groupId>org.codehaus.mojo</groupId>
  <artifactId>exec-maven-plugin</artifactId>
  <version>1.5.0</version>
  <dependencies>
    <dependency>
      <groupId>fish.payara.extras</groupId>
      <artifactId>payara-microprofile</artifactId>
      <version>1.0</version>
```

```
    </dependency>
  </dependencies>
```

This sets up the Maven exec plugin, which is used to execute either an external application or, as we'll do here, a Java application:

```
<executions>
  <execution>
    <id>payara-uber-jar</id>
    <phase>package</phase>
    <goals>
      <goal>java</goal>
    </goals>
```

Here, we're associating the execution of this plugin with Maven's package phase. This means that when we run Maven to build our project, the plugin's java goal will be run as Maven starts to package the project, allowing us to alter exactly what gets packaged in the JAR:

```
<configuration>
  <mainClass>
    fish.payara.micro.PayaraMicro
  </mainClass>
  <arguments>
    <argument>--deploy</argument>
    <argument>
      ${basedir}/target/${warfile.name}.war
    </argument>
    <argument>--outputUberJar</argument>
    <argument>
      ${basedir}/target/${project.artifactId}.jar
    </argument>
  </arguments>
</configuration>
```

This last section configures the plugin. It will run the `PayaraMicro` class, passing the `--deploy <path> --outputUberJar ...` command. Effectively, we're telling Payara Micro how to run our application, but, rather than executing the package right now, we want it to create an uber JAR that will run the application later.

Typically, when you build your project, you get a jar file that contains only the classes and resources that are directly included in your project. Any external dependencies are left as something that the execution environment has to provide. With an uber JAR, all of the dependencies are included in our project's jar as well, which is then configured in such a way that the execution environment can find them as needed.

The problem with the setup is that, left as is, when we build, we'll get an uber JAR, but we won't have any easy way to run the application from NetBeans. To fix that, we need a slightly different plugin configuration. Specifically, it needs these lines:

```
<argument>--deploy</argument>
<argument>
  ${basedir}/target/${project.artifactId}-${project.version}
</argument>
```

These replace the preceding `deploy` and `outputUberJar` options. To help speed up our builds, we also don't want the uber JAR created until we ask for it, so we can separate these two plugin configurations into two separate profiles, as follows:

```
<profiles>
  <profile>
    <id>exploded-war</id>
    <!-- ... -->
  </profile>
  <profile>
    <id>uber</id>
    <!-- ... -->
  </profile>
</profiles>
```

When we're ready to build the deployment artifact, we activate the uber profile when we execute Maven, and we'll get our executable jar:

$ mvn -Puber install

The `exploded-war` profile is the configuration that we'll use from the IDE, which runs Payara Micro, pointing it at the exploded war in our build directory. To instruct NetBeans to use that, we need to modify a couple of action configurations. To do that, right-click on the project in NetBeans and select **Properties** from the bottom of the context menu. Under **Actions**, find **Run Project** and select it, then enter `exploded-war` under **Activate Profiles**:

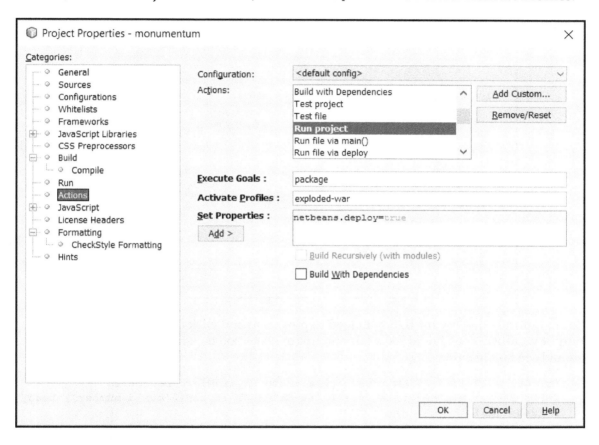

If we run the application now, NetBeans will complain because we haven't selected a server. While this is a web application and those have typically needed a server, we're using Payara Micro, so we don't need an application server defined. Fortunately, NetBeans will let us tell it that, as demonstrated in the following screenshot:

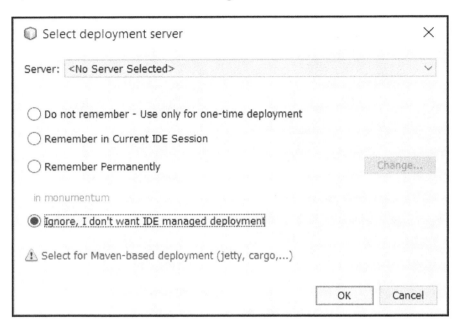

Select **Ignore, I don't want IDE managed deployment** and click on **OK**, then watch the output window. You should see a fair amount of text scroll by, and after a few seconds, you should see text like this:

```
Apr 05, 2017 1:18:59 AM fish.payara.micro.PayaraMicro bootStrap
INFO: Payara MicroProfile  4.1.1.164-SNAPSHOT (build ${build.number}) ready
in 9496 (ms)
```

Once you see that, we're ready to test our application, such as it is at this point. In your browser, open http://localhost:8080/monumentum-1.0-SNAPSHOT/index.html and you should see a large and exciting *Hello World!* message on the page. If you see this, you have successfully bootstrapped a Payara Micro project. Take a moment to congratulate yourself, and then we'll make the application do something useful.

Creating REST Services

This being basically a Java EE application, albeit one that it is packaged and deployed a bit differently, everything you may have learned about writing Java EE applications most likely still applies. Of course, you may not have ever written such an application, so we'll walk through the steps.

REST applications in Java EE are written using JAX-RS, and our starting point for JAX-RS is an `Application`. The `Application` is a deployment-agnostic means for declaring root-level resources to the runtime. How the runtime finds the `Application` is, of course, dependent on the runtime itself. For a MicroProfile application like ours, we'll be running in a Servlet 3.0 environment, so we need not do anything special, as Servlet 3.0 supports a descriptor-less deployment option. The runtime will scan for a class of type `Application` that is annotated with `@ApplicationPath` and uses that to configure the JAX-RS application, as shown here:

```
@ApplicationPath("/api")
  public class Monumentum extends javax.ws.rs.core.Application {
  @Override
  public Set<Class<?>> getClasses() {
    Set<Class<?>> s = new HashSet<>();
    return s;
  }
}
```

With the `@ApplicationPath` annotation, we specify the root URL of our application's REST endpoints, which is, of course, relative to the web application's root context itself. `Application` has three methods we can override, but we're only interested in the one listed here: `getClasses()`. We'll provide more details on this method shortly, but, for now, keep in mind that this is how we will describe to JAX-RS what our top-level resources are.

Monumentum will have a very simple API, with the primary endpoint being that to interact with notes. To create that endpoint, we create a simple Java class and mark it up with the appropriate JAX-RS annotations:

```
@Path("/notes")
@RequestScoped
@Produces(MediaType.APPLICATION_JSON)
public class NoteResource {
}
```

With this class, we're describing an endpoint that will live at /api/notes and will produce JSON results. JAX-RS supports, for example, XML, but most REST developers are accustomed to JSON and are expecting nothing else, so we need not support anything other than JSON. The needs of your application may vary, of course, so you can adjust the list of supported media types as needed.

While this will compile and run, and JAX-RS will attempt to handle requests to our endpoint, we haven't actually defined it yet. To do that, we need to add some methods to our endpoint that will define the inputs and outputs of the endpoint, as well as the HTTP verb/method we'll use. Let's start with the notes collection endpoint:

```
@GET
public Response getAll() {
  List<Note> notes = new ArrayList<>();
  return Response.ok(
    new GenericEntity<List<Note>>(notes) {}).build();
}
```

We now have an endpoint that answers GET requests at /api/notes and returns a List of Note instances. There is some debate among REST developers on the proper return from methods like these. There are some who prefer to return the actual type the client will see, for example List<Note> in our case, as it makes it clear to developers reading the source, or documentation generated from it. Others prefer, as we've done here, to return a JAX-RS Response object, as that gives greater control over the response, including HTTP headers, status code, and more. I tend to prefer this second approach as we've done here. You, of course, are free to use either approach.

One last thing to note here is the way in which we build the response body:

```
new GenericEntity<List<Note>>(notes) {}
```

Typically, at runtime, the parameterized type of the List is lost due to type erasure. Using a GenericEntity like this allows us to capture the parameterized type, allowing the runtime to marshal the data. Using this allows us to avoid writing our own MessageBodyWriter. Less code is almost always a good thing.

If we run our application now, we'll get the following response, albeit a very boring one:

```
$ curl http://localhost:8080/monumentum-1.0-SNAPSHOT/api/notes/
[]
```

That's both satisfying, and it's not, but it does demonstrate that we're on the right track. Clearly, we want that endpoint to return data, but we have no way of adding a note, so let's fix that now.

Creating a new entity via REST is accomplished by POSTing a new entity to its collection. That method looks like this:

```
@POST
public Response createNote(Note note) {
  Document doc = note.toDocument();
  collection.insertOne(doc);
  final String id = doc.get("_id",
    ObjectId.class).toHexString();

  return Response.created(uriInfo.getRequestUriBuilder()
    .path(id).build())
  .build();
}
```

The `@POST` annotation indicates the use of the HTTP POST verb. The method takes a `Note` instance, and returns a `Response` as we saw in the preceding code. Notice that we don't deal with JSON directly. By specifying a `Note` in the method signature, we can take advantage of one of JAX-RS's great features--POJO mapping. We've already seen a hint of it in the previous code with `GenericEntity`. JAX-RS will attempt to unmarshal--that is, convert from a serialized form to a model object--the JSON request body. If the client sends a JSON object in the correct format, we get a usable `Note` instance. If the client sends an improperly built object, it gets a response. This feature allows us to deal solely with our domain objects and not worry about JSON encoding and decoding, which can save considerable time and energy.

Adding MongoDB

In the body of the method, we get our first glimpse of the integration with MongoDB. To make this compile, we need to add a dependency on the MongoDB Java Driver:

```
<dependency>
  <groupId>org.mongodb</groupId>
  <artifactId>mongodb-driver</artifactId>
  <version>3.4.2</version>
</dependency>
```

MongoDB deals with documents, so we need to convert our domain model to a `Document`, which we accomplish via a method on our model class. We haven't looked at the details of the `Note` class, so let's do that now:

```
public class Note {
  private String id;
  private String userId;
```

```
private String title;
private String body;
private LocalDateTime created = LocalDateTime.now();
private LocalDateTime modified = null;

// Getters, setters and some constructors not shown

public Note(final Document doc) {
  final LocalDateTimeAdapter adapter =
    new LocalDateTimeAdapter();
  userId = doc.getString("user_id");
  id = doc.get("_id", ObjectId.class).toHexString();
  title = doc.getString("title");
  body = doc.getString("body");
  created = adapter.unmarshal(doc.getString("created"));
  modified = adapter.unmarshal(doc.getString("modified"));
}

public Document toDocument() {
  final LocalDateTimeAdapter adapter =
    new LocalDateTimeAdapter();
  Document doc = new Document();
  if (id != null) {
    doc.append("_id", new ObjectId(getId()));
  }
  doc.append("user_id", getUserId())
    .append("title", getTitle())
    .append("body", getBody())
    .append("created",
      adapter.marshal(getCreated() != null
      ? getCreated() : LocalDateTime.now())))
    .append("modified",
      adapter.marshal(getModified())));
  return doc;
}
}
```

This is mostly just a normal POJO. We have added a constructor and an instance method to handle converting to and from MongoDB's Document type.

There are a couple of things to call out here. The first is how the ID of the MongoDB Document is handled. Every document stored in a MongoDB database gets _id assigned to it. In the Java API, this _id is represented as ObjectId. We don't want that detail exposed in our domain model, so we convert it to a String and back again.

We also need to do some special handling for our date fields. We've chosen to represent the `created` and `modified` properties as `LocalDateTime` instances since the new date/time API is superior to the old `java.util.Date`. Unfortunately, the MongoDB Java Driver does not yet support Java 8, so we need to handle the conversion ourselves. We'll store these dates as strings and convert them as needed. That conversion is handled via the `LocalDateTimeAdapter` class:

```
public class LocalDateTimeAdapter
    extends XmlAdapter<String, LocalDateTime> {
    private static final Pattern JS_DATE = Pattern.compile
      ("\\d{4}-\\d{2}-\\d{2}T\\d{2}:\\d{2}:\\d{2}\\.\\d+Z");
    private static final DateTimeFormatter DEFAULT_FORMAT =
      DateTimeFormatter.ISO_LOCAL_DATE_TIME;
    private static final DateTimeFormatter JS_FORMAT =
      DateTimeFormatter.ofPattern
      ("yyyy-MM-dd'T'HH:mm:ss.SSS'Z'");

    @Override
    public LocalDateTime unmarshal(String date) {
      if (date == null) {
        return null;
      }
      return LocalDateTime.parse(date,
        (JS_DATE.matcher(date).matches())
        ? JS_FORMAT : DEFAULT_FORMAT);
    }

    @Override
    public String marshal(LocalDateTime date) {
      return date != null ? DEFAULT_FORMAT.format(date) : null;
    }
}
```

This is probably a bit more complicated than you might expect, and that's because it's doing more than we've discussed so far. The usage we're looking at now, that from our model class, is not this class' primary purpose, but we'll get to that in a moment. That aside, the class' behavior is pretty straightforward--take a `String`, determine which of the two supported formats it represents, and convert it to a `LocalDateTime`. It also goes the other way.

This class' primary purpose is for JAX-RS' use. When we pass `Note` instances across the wire, `LocalDateTime` needs to be unmarshalled as well, and we can tell JAX-RS how to do this via an `XmlAdapter`.

With the class defined, we need to tell JAX-RS about it. We can do that in a couple of different ways. We could use an annotation on each property in our model like this:

```
@XmlJavaTypeAdapter(value = LocalDateTimeAdapter.class)
private LocalDateTime created = LocalDateTime.now();
```

While this works, it's a fairly large annotation, as far as these kinds of things go, and you have to put this on every `LocalDateTime` property. If you have several models with fields of this type, you will have to touch each property. Fortunately, there's a way to associate the type with the adapter once. We can do that in a special Java file called `package-info.java`. Most people have never heard of this file, and even fewer use it, but it is simply a place for package-level documentation and annotations. It is this latter use case that interests us. In the package for our model class, create `package-info.java` and put this in it:

```
@XmlJavaTypeAdapters({
  @XmlJavaTypeAdapter(type = LocalDateTime.class,
    value = LocalDateTimeAdapter.class)
})
package com.steeplesoft.monumentum.model;
```

We have the same annotation we saw in the preceding code, but it's wrapped in `@XmlJavaTypeAdapters`. The JVM allows only annotation of a given type on an element, so this wrapper allows us to work around that limitation. We also need to specify the type parameter on the `@XmlJavaTypeAdapter` annotation since it is no longer on the target property. With this in place, every `LocalDateTime` property will be handled correctly without any additional work.

That's quite a bit of setup, but we're still not quite ready. We have everything set up on the REST side. We now need to get the MongoDB classes in place. To connect to a MongoDB instance, we start with a `MongoClient`. From the `MongoClient`, we then acquire a reference to a `MongoDatabase` from which we get a `MongoCollection`:

```
private MongoCollection<Document> collection;
private MongoClient mongoClient;
private MongoDatabase database;

@PostConstruct
public void postConstruct() {
  String host = System.getProperty("mongo.host", "localhost");
  String port = System.getProperty("mongo.port", "27017");
  mongoClient = new MongoClient(host, Integer.parseInt(port));
  database = mongoClient.getDatabase("monumentum");
  collection = database.getCollection("note");
}
```

The @PostConstruct method runs on the bean after the constructor has run. In this method, we initialize our various MongoDB classes and store them in instance variables. With these classes ready, we can revisit, for example, getAll():

```
@GET
public Response getAll() {
  List<Note> notes = new ArrayList<>();
  try (MongoCursor<Document> cursor = collection.find()
  .iterator()) {
    while (cursor.hasNext()) {
      notes.add(new Note(cursor.next()));
    }
  }

  return Response.ok(
    new GenericEntity<List<Note>>(notes) {})
  .build();
}
```

We can now query the database for our notes, and with the implementation of createNote() shown in the preceding code, we can create the following notes:

```
$ curl -v -H "Content-Type: application/json" -X POST -d '{"title":"Command
line note", "body":"A note from the command line"}'
http://localhost:8080/monumentum-1.0-SNAPSHOT/api/notes/
*   Trying ::1...
* TCP_NODELAY set
* Connected to localhost (::1) port 8080 (#0)
> POST /monumentum-1.0-SNAPSHOT/api/notes/ HTTP/1.1
...
< HTTP/1.1 201 Created
...
$ curl http://localhost:8080/monumentum-1.0-SNAPSHOT/api/notes/ | jq .
[
  {
    "id": "58e5d0d79ccd032344f66c37",
    "userId": null,
    "title": "Command line note",
    "body": "A note from the command line",
    "created": "2017-04-06T00:23:34.87",
    "modified": null
  }
]
```

> For this to work on your machine, you'll need an instance of MongoDB running. You can download an installer appropriate for your operating system as well as find installation instructions on the MongoDB website (`https://docs.mongodb.com/manual/installation/`).

Before we move on to the other resource methods, let's take one last look at our MongoDB API instances. While instantiating the instances like we have works, it also puts a fair amount of work on the resource itself. Ideally, we should be able to move those concerns elsewhere and inject the instances. Hopefully, this sounds familiar to you, as this is exactly the type of concern that **dependency injection (DI)** or **inversion of control (IoC)** frameworks were created to solve.

Dependency injection with CDI

Java EE provides a framework such as CDI. With CDI, we can inject any container-controlled object into another with compile-time type safety. The problem, though, is the objects in question need to be container controlled, which our MongoDB API objects are not. Fortunately, CDI provides a means by which the container can create these instances, a facility known as producer methods. What might this look like? Let's start with the injection point, as that is the simplest piece:

```
@Inject
@Collection("notes")
private MongoCollection<Document> collection;
```

When the CDI container sees `@Inject`, it inspects the element the annotation is on to determine the type. It will then attempt to look up an instance that will satisfy the injection request. If there is more than one, the injection would typically fail. Although, we have used a qualifier annotation to help CDI determine what to inject. That annotation is defined like this:

```
@Qualifier
@Retention(RetentionPolicy.RUNTIME)
@Target({ElementType.METHOD, ElementType.FIELD,
  ElementType.PARAMETER, ElementType.TYPE})
public @interface Collection {
  @Nonbinding String value() default "unknown";
}
```

With this annotation, we can pass hints to the container that will help it select an instance for injection. As we've mentioned, `MongoCollection` is not container-managed, so we need to fix that, which we do via the following producer method:

```
@RequestScoped
public class Producers {
  @Produces
  @Collection
  public MongoCollection<Document>
    getCollection(InjectionPoint injectionPoint) {
      Collection mc = injectionPoint.getAnnotated()
      .getAnnotation(Collection.class);
    return getDatabase().getCollection(mc.value());
  }
}
```

The `@Produces` method tells CDI that this method will produce instances needed by the container. CDI determines the type of the injectable instance from the method signature. We also place the qualifier annotation on the method as an additional hint to the runtime as it tries to resolve our injection request.

In the method itself, we add `InjectionPoint` to the method signature. When CDI calls this method, it will provide an instance of this class, from which we can get information about each particular injection point as they are processed. From `InjectionPoint`, we get the `Collection` instance from which we can get the name of the MongoDB collection we're interested in. We are now ready to get the `MongoCollection` instance we saw earlier. The `MongoClient` and `MongoDatabase` instantiation is handled internally in the class and is not changed significantly from our earlier usage.

There is one small setup step for CDI. In order to avoid potentially expensive classpath scanning by the CDI container, we need to tell the system that we want the CDI turned on, so to speak. To do that, we need a `beans.xml` file, which can either be full of CDI configuration elements, or completely empty, which is what we'll do. For Java EE web applications, `beans.xml` needs to be in the `WEB-INF` directory, so we create the file in `src/main/webapp/WEB-INF`.

Make sure that the file is truly empty. If there's even a blank line, Weld, Payara's CDI implementation, will attempt to parse the file, giving you an XML parsing error.

Finish the notes resource

Before we can move on from the `Note` resource, we need to finish up a few operations, namely, read, update, and delete. Reading a single note is very straightforward:

```
@GET
@Path("{id}")
public Response getNote(@PathParam("id") String id) {
  Document doc = collection.find(buildQueryById(id)).first();
  if (doc == null) {
    return Response.status(Response.Status.NOT_FOUND).build();
  } else {
    return Response.ok(new Note(doc)).build();
  }
}
```

We've specified the use of the HTTP verb `GET` as we've already seen, but we have an additional annotation on this method, `@Path`. Using this annotation, we tell JAX-RS that this endpoint has additional path segments that the request needs to be matched against. In this case, we specify one additional segment, but we've wrapped it in curly braces. Without those braces, the match would be a literal match, that is to say, "Does this URL have the string 'id' on the end?" With the braces, though, we're telling JAX-RS that we want to match the additional segment, but its contents can be anything, and we want to capture that value and give it the name `id`. In our method signature, we instruct JAX-RS to inject the value via the `@PathParam` annotation, giving us access to the user-specified `Note` ID in our method.

To retrieve the note from MongoDB, we get our first real glimpse of how one queries MongoDB:

```
Document doc = collection.find(buildQueryById(id)).first();
```

In a nutshell, pass `BasicDBObject` to the `find()` method on `collection`, which returns a `FindIterable<?>` object, on which we call `first()` to get what should be the only element returned (assuming there is one, of course). The interesting bits here are hidden in `buildQueryById()`:

```
private BasicDBObject buildQueryById(String id) {
  BasicDBObject query =
    new BasicDBObject("_id", new ObjectId(id));
  return query;
}
```

Our query filter is defined using this BasicDBObject, which we initialize with a key and value. In this case, we want to filter by the _id field in the document, so we use that as a key, but note that we pass ObjectId as the value, and not just String. If we want to filter by more fields, we would append more key/value pairs to the BasicDBObject variable, which we will see later.

Once we've queried the collection and gotten the document the user requested, we convert it from Document to Note using the helper method on Note, and return it with a status code of 200 or OK.

Updating a document in the database is a bit more complicated, but not excessively so, as you can see here:

```
@PUT
@Path("{id}")
public Response updateNote(Note note) {
  note.setModified(LocalDateTime.now());
  UpdateResult result =
    collection.updateOne(buildQueryById(note.getId()),
    new Document("$set", note.toDocument()));
  if (result.getModifiedCount() == 0) {
    return Response.status(Response.Status.NOT_FOUND).build();
  } else {
    return Response.ok().build();
  }
}
```

The first thing to notice is the HTTP method--PUT. There is some debate on what verb to use for updates. Some, such as Dropbox and Facebook, say POST, while others, such as Google (depending on which API you look at), say PUT. I would contend that the choice is largely up to you. Just be consistent in your choice. We will be completely replacing the entity on the server with what the client passes in, so the operation is idempotent. By choosing PUT, we can signal this fact to the client, making the API a bit more self-describing for clients.

Inside the method, we start by setting the modified date to reflect the operation. Next, we call `Collection.updateOne()` to modify the document. The syntax is a little odd, but here's what's happening--we're querying the collection for the note we want to modify, then telling MongoDB to replace the loaded document with the new one we're providing. Finally, we query `UpdateResult` to see how many documents were updated. If none were, then the requested document doesn't exist, so we return `NOT_FOUND` (`404`). If it's non-zero, we return `OK` (`200`).

Finally, our delete method looks like this:

```
@DELETE
@Path("{id}")
public Response deleteNote(@PathParam("id") String id) {
    collection.deleteOne(buildQueryById(id));
    return Response.ok().build();
}
```

We tell MongoDB to filter the collection using the same query filter we've seen before, then delete one document, which should be all it finds, of course, given our filter, but `deleteOne()` is a sensible safeguard. We could do a check like we did above in `updateNote()` to see if something was actually deleted, but there's little point--whether the document was there at the start of the request or not, it's not there at the end and that's our goal, so there's little to be gained from returning an error response.

We can now create, read, update, and delete notes, but the eagle-eyed among you may have noticed that anyone can read every note in the system. For a multi-user system, that's not a good thing, so let's fix that.

Adding authentication

Authentication systems can easily get extremely complex. From homegrown systems, complete with custom user management screens, to sophisticated single sign-on solutions, we have a lot of options. One of the more popular options is OAuth2, and there are a number of options. For Monumentum, we'll implement sign in using Google. To do that, we need to create an application in Google's Developer Console, which can be found at `https://console.developers.google.com`.

Once you've logged in, click on the project dropdown at the top of page and click on **Create Project**, which should present this screen to you:

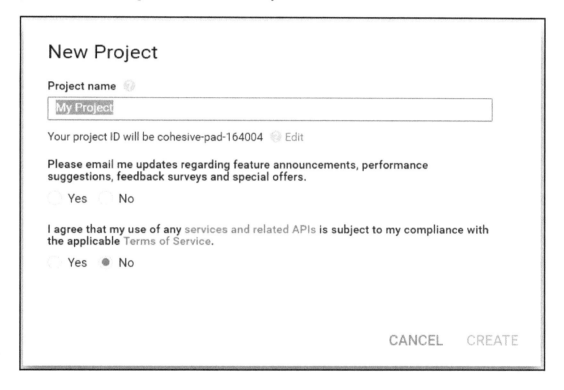

Provide **Project Name**, make your choices for the next two questions, then click on **CREATE**. Once the project has been created, you should be redirected to the Library page. Click on the **Credentials** link on the left, then click on **Create credentials** and select **OAuth Client ID**. If needed, fill out the **OAuth Consent** screen as directed. Select **Web Application** for **Application Type**, enter **Name**, and provide **Authorized redirect URIs** as shown in this screenshot:

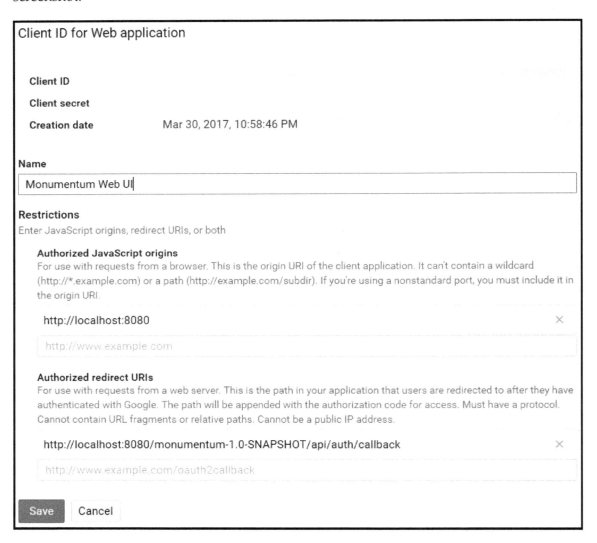

Before this is moved to production, we will need to add a production URI to this screen, but this configuration will work in development just fine. When you click on **Save**, you will be shown your new client ID and client secret. Make note of these:

With this data (note that these are not my actual ID and secret, so you'll have to generate your own), we are ready to start working on our authentication resource. We'll start by defining the resource as follows:

```
@Path("auth")
public class AuthenticationResource {
```

We need to register this in our `Application`, as follows:

```
@ApplicationPath("/api")
public class Monumentum extends javax.ws.rs.core.Application {
  @Override
  public Set<Class<?>> getClasses() {
    Set<Class<?>> s = new HashSet<>();
    s.add(NoteResource.class);
    s.add(AuthenticationResource.class);
    return s;
  }
}
```

To work with the Google OAuth provider, we'll need to declare a few instance variables and instantiate a few Google API classes:

```
private final String clientId;
private final String clientSecret;
private final GoogleAuthorizationCodeFlow flow;
private final HttpTransport HTTP_TRANSPORT =
  new NetHttpTransport();
private static final String USER_INFO_URL =
  "https://www.googleapis.com/oauth2/v1/userinfo";
private static final List<String> SCOPES = Arrays.asList(
  "https://www.googleapis.com/auth/userinfo.profile",
  "https://www.googleapis.com/auth/userinfo.email");
```

The variables `clientId` and `clientSecret` will hold the values that Google just gave us. The other two classes are necessary for the process we're about to walk through, and `SCOPES` holds the permissions we want from Google, which is just access to the user's profile and email. The class constructor finishes the setup of these items:

```
public AuthenticationResource() {
  clientId = System.getProperty("client_id");
  clientSecret = System.getProperty("client_secret");
  flow = new GoogleAuthorizationCodeFlow.Builder(HTTP_TRANSPORT,
    new JacksonFactory(), clientId, clientSecret,
    SCOPES).build();
}
```

The first part of the authentication flow is to create an authentication URL, which is done like this:

```
@Context
private UriInfo uriInfo;
@GET
@Path("url")
public String getAuthorizationUrl() {
  return flow.newAuthorizationUrl()
  .setRedirectUri(getCallbackUri()).build();
}
private String getCallbackUri()
  throws UriBuilderException, IllegalArgumentException {
  return uriInfo.getBaseUriBuilder().path("auth")
    .path("callback").build()
    .toASCIIString();
}
```

Using the JAX-RS class, `UriInfo`, we create a URI that points to another endpoint in our application, `/api/auth/callback`. We then pass that to `GoogleAuthorizationCodeFlow` to finish building our login URL. When the user clicks on the link, the browser will be directed to a login dialog from Google. Upon successful authentication, the user will be redirected to our callback URL, which is handled by this method:

```
@GET
@Path("callback")
public Response handleCallback(@QueryParam("code")
@NotNull String code) throws IOException {
  User user = getUserInfoJson(code);
  saveUserInformation(user);
  final String jwt = createToken(user.getEmail());
  return Response.seeOther(
    uriInfo.getBaseUriBuilder()
    .path("../loginsuccess.html")
    .queryParam("Bearer", jwt)
    .build())
  .build();
}
```

When Google redirects to our `callback` endpoint, it will provide a code that we can use to finish the authentication. We do that in the `getUserInfoJson()` method:

```
private User getUserInfoJson(final String authCode)
throws IOException {
  try {
    final GoogleTokenResponse response =
      flow.newTokenRequest(authCode)
      .setRedirectUri(getCallbackUri())
      .execute();
    final Credential credential =
      flow.createAndStoreCredential(response, null);
    final HttpRequest request =
      HTTP_TRANSPORT.createRequestFactory(credential)
      .buildGetRequest(new GenericUrl(USER_INFO_URL));
    request.getHeaders().setContentType("application/json");
    final JSONObject identity =
      new JSONObject(request.execute().parseAsString());
    return new User(
      identity.getString("id"),
      identity.getString("email"),
      identity.getString("name"),
      identity.getString("picture"));
  } catch (JSONException ex) {
    Logger.getLogger(AuthenticationResource.class.getName())
```

```
        .log(Level.SEVERE, null, ex);
        return null;
    }
}
```

Using the authentication code we just got from Google, we send another request to Google, this time to get the user information. When the request returns, we take the JSON object in the response body and use it to build a `User` object, which we return.

Back in our REST endpoint method, we call this method to save the user to the database, if needed:

```
private void saveUserInformation(User user) {
    Document doc = collection.find(
        new BasicDBObject("email", user.getEmail())).first();
    if (doc == null) {
        collection.insertOne(user.toDocument());
    }
}
```

Once we've gotten the user's information from Google, we no longer need the code as we do not need to interact with any other Google resources, so we do not persist it anywhere.

Finally, we want to return something to the client --some kind of token -- which can be used to prove the client's identity. To do that, we'll use a technology called a JSON Web Token, or JWT for short. JWT is *a JSON-based open standard (RFC 7519) for creating access tokens that assert some number of claims.* We'll create a JWT using the user's email address. We'll sign it with a key only the server uses, so we can safely pass it to the client, which will pass it back with each request. Since it must be encrypted/signed with the server key, untrustworthy clients will not be able to alter or forge the token successfully.

To create JWTs, we need to add the library to our project as follows:

```
<dependency>
    <groupId>io.jsonwebtoken</groupId>
    <artifactId>jjwt</artifactId>
    <version>0.7.0</version>
</dependency>
```

We can then write this method:

```
@Inject
private KeyGenerator keyGenerator;
private String createToken(String login) {
    String jwtToken = Jwts.builder()
    .setSubject(login)
    .setIssuer(uriInfo.getAbsolutePath().toString())
```

```
    .setIssuedAt (new Date ())
    .setExpiration (Date.from (
      LocalDateTime.now ().plusHours (12L)
    .atZone (ZoneId.systemDefault ()).toInstant ()))
    .signWith (SignatureAlgorithm.HS512,
      keyGenerator.getKey ())
    .compact ();
    return jwtToken;
  }
```

The subject of the token is the email address, our API's base address is the issuer, the expiration date and time is 12 hours in the future, and the token is signed by a key we generate with a new class, KeyGenerator. When we call compact (), a URL-safe String is generated, which we return to the caller. We can use the JWT debugger at http://jwt.io to look inside the token:

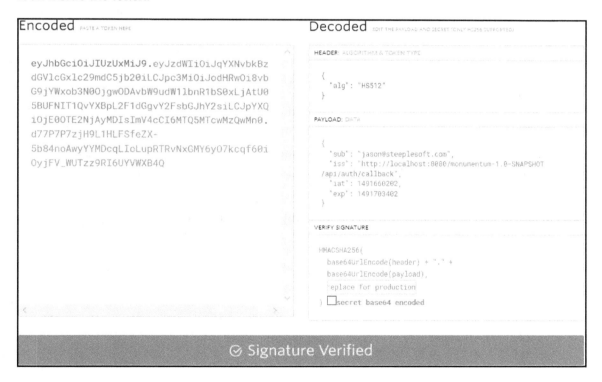

Clearly, the claims in the token are readable, so don't store anything sensitive in them. What makes this secure is the use of a secret key when signing the token, making it impossible, in theory, to change its contents without detection.

The `KeyGenerator` class used to give us our signing key looks like this:

```
@Singleton
public class KeyGenerator {
  private Key key;
  public Key getKey() {
    if (key == null) {
      String keyString = System.getProperty("signing.key",
        "replace for production");
      key = new SecretKeySpec(keyString.getBytes(), 0,
        keyString.getBytes().length, "DES");
    }
    return key;
  }
}
```

The class is annotated with `@Singleton`, so the container guarantees that one and only one instance of this bean will exist in the system. The `getKey()` method will use the system property `signing.key` as the key, allowing the user to specify a unique secret when starting the system. Of course, completely random keys are safer, but that adds some complexity should we ever try to scale this system out horizontally. We would need all instances to use the same signing key so that JWTs can be validated regardless of what server the client is directed to. A data grid solution, such as Hazelcast, would be an appropriate tool for those situations. As it is now, this is sufficient for our needs here.

Our authentication resource is now complete, but our system has not actually been secured yet. To do that, we need to tell JAX-RS how to authenticate requests, and we'll do that with a new annotation and `ContainerRequestFilter`.

If we were to install a request filter with no additional information, it would apply to every resource, including our authentication resource. That would mean we'd have to authenticate in order to authenticate. Clearly that doesn't make sense, so we need a way to discriminate between requests so that only requests for certain resources have this filter applied, and that means a new annotation:

```
@NameBinding
@Retention(RetentionPolicy.RUNTIME)
@Target({ElementType.TYPE, ElementType.METHOD})
public @interface Secure {
}
```

We've defined an annotation that is semantically meaningful. The `@NameBinding` annotation tells JAX-RS to apply the annotation only to certain resources, which are bound by name (as opposed to dynamically bound at runtime). With the annotation defined, we need to define the other side of things, the request filter:

```
@Provider
@Secure
@Priority(Priorities.AUTHENTICATION)
public class SecureFilter implements ContainerRequestFilter {
  @Inject
  private KeyGenerator keyGenerator;

  @Override
  public void filter(ContainerRequestContext requestContext)
   throws IOException {
    try {
      String authorizationHeader = requestContext
      .getHeaderString(HttpHeaders.AUTHORIZATION);
      String token = authorizationHeader
      .substring("Bearer".length()).trim();
      Jwts.parser()
      .setSigningKey(keyGenerator.getKey())
      .parseClaimsJws(token);
    } catch (Exception e) {
      requestContext.abortWith(Response.status
      (Response.Status.UNAUTHORIZED).build());
    }
  }
}
```

We start by defining a class that implements the `ContainerRequestFilter` interface. We have to annotate it with `@Provider` so that JAX-RS will recognize and load the class. We apply the `@Secure` annotation to associate the filter with the annotation. We'll apply this to the resource in a moment. Finally, we apply the `@Priority` annotation to instruct the system that this filter should be applied earlier in the request cycle.

Inside the filter, we inject the same `KeyGenerator` we looked at earlier. Since this is a singleton, we are guaranteed that the key used here and in the authentication method are the same. The only method on the interface is `filter()`, and in this method, we get the Authorization header from the request, extract the Bearer token, which is the JWT, and validate it using the JWT API. If we can decode and validate the token, then we know the user has successfully authenticated against the system. To tell the system about this new filter, we need to modify our JAX-RS `Application` as follows:

```
@ApplicationPath("/api")
public class Monumentum extends javax.ws.rs.core.Application {
```

```
@Override
public Set<Class<?>> getClasses() {
  Set<Class<?>> s = new HashSet<>();
  s.add(NoteResource.class);
  s.add(AuthenticationResource.class);
  s.add(SecureFilter.class);
  return s;
}
}
```

The system knows about the filter now, but before it will do anything, we need to apply it to the resources that we want to secure. We do that by applying the @Secure annotation to the appropriate resources. It can either be applied at class level, which means that every endpoint in the class will be secured, or at the resource method level, which means that only those particular endpoints will be secured. In our case, we want every Note endpoint secured, so put the following annotation on the class:

```
@Path("/notes")
@RequestScoped
@Produces(MediaType.APPLICATION_JSON)
@Secure
public class NoteResource {
```

Just a few more steps, and our application will be secured. We need to make some modifications to NoteResource so that it knows who is logged in, and so that notes are associated with the authenticated user. We will start by injecting User:

```
@Inject
private User user;
```

This is obviously not a container-managed class, so we need to write another Producer method. There's a small bit of work to do there, so we'll wrap that in its own class:

```
@RequestScoped
public class UserProducer {
  @Inject
  private KeyGenerator keyGenerator;
  @Inject
  HttpServletRequest req;
  @Inject
  @Collection("users")
  private MongoCollection<Document> users;
```

We define this as a request-scoped CDI bean, and inject our `KeyGenerator`, the `HttpServletRequest`, and our users collection. The actual work is done in the `Producer` method:

```
@Produces
public User getUser() {
  String authHeader = req.getHeader(HttpHeaders.AUTHORIZATION);
  if (authHeader != null && authHeader.contains("Bearer")) {
    String token = authHeader
    .substring("Bearer".length()).trim();
    Jws<Claims> parseClaimsJws = Jwts.parser()
    .setSigningKey(keyGenerator.getKey())
    .parseClaimsJws(token);
    return getUser(parseClaimsJws.getBody().getSubject());
  } else {
    return null;
  }
}
```

Using the Servlet request, we retrieve the `AUTHORIZATION` header. If it's present and contains the `Bearer` string, we can process the token. If that condition is not true, we return null. To process the token, we extract the token value from the header, and then have `Jwts` parse the claims for us, which returns an object of type `Jws<Claims>`. We build the user in the `getUser()` method as follows:

```
private User getUser(String email) {
  Document doc = users.find(
    new BasicDBObject("email", email)).first();
  if (doc != null) {
    return new User(doc);
  } else {
    return null;
  }
}
```

With the claims parsed, we can extract the subject and use it to query our `Users` collection, returning either the `User` if it is found, or `null` if not.

Back in our `NoteResource`, we need to modify our resource methods to be `User-aware`:

```
public Response getAll() {
  List<Note> notes = new ArrayList<>();
  try (MongoCursor<Document> cursor =
    collection.find(new BasicDBObject("user_id",
    user.getId())).iterator()) {
  // ...
  @POST
```

```
public Response createNote(Note note) {
  Document doc = note.toDocument();
  doc.append("user_id", user.getId());
  // ...
@PUT
@Path("{id}")
public Response updateNote(Note note) {
  note.setModified(LocalDateTime.now());
  note.setUser(user.getId());
  // ...
private BasicDBObject buildQueryById(String id) {
  BasicDBObject query =
  new BasicDBObject("_id", new ObjectId(id))
    .append("user_id", user.getId());
  return query;
}
```

We now have a complete and secured REST API. Other than a command-line tool like curl, we don't have any nice way to use it, so let's build a user interface.

Building the user interface

For a UI, we have a number of options. We've already looked at JavaFX and the NetBeans RCP in this book. While those are great options, we'll do something a little different for this app and build a web-based interface. Even here, we have many, many options: JSF, Spring MVC, Google Web Toolkit, Vaadin, and more. Oftentimes, in real-world applications, while we may have a Java backend, we may have a JavaScript frontend, so that's what we'll do here, and that's where your choices can get really dizzying.

The two biggest players in that market at the time of the writing of this book are React from Facebook and Angular from Google. There are several smaller contenders, such as React API-compatible Preact, VueJS, Backbone, Ember, and so on. Which you choose will have a significant impact on the application, everything from architecture to the more mundane things such as building the project itself, or you could let architecture drive the framework if there's a compelling need for a specific architecture. As always, your particular environment will vary and should drive that decision more than what you read in a book or online.

Since this is a Java book, and I'd like to avoid getting too far into the intimate details of JavaScript build systems and alternate **JavaScript VM** languages, transpiling, and so on, I've chosen to use Vue, as it is a fast, modern, and popular framework that meets our needs, yet still allows us to build a simple system without requiring complicated build configurations. If you have experience with, or a preference for, another framework, it should be fairly simple for you to build a comparable system using the framework of your choice.

 Note that I am *not* a JavaScript developer. The application we'll build in this part of the chapter should not be construed to be an example of best practices. It is merely an attempt to build a usable, albeit plain, JavaScript frontend to demonstrate a full stack application. Please consult the documentation for Vue or your framework of choice for details on how to build idiomatic applications with the tool.

Let's start with the index page. In the project explorer window in NetBeans, expand the **Other Sources** node, right-click on the **webapp** node, and select **New** | **Empty File**, giving it the name index.html. The bare minimum we need in the file at this point is the following:

```
<!DOCTYPE html>
  <html>
    <head>
      <title>Monumentum</title>
      <meta charset="UTF-8">
      <link rel="stylesheet" href="monumentum.css">
      <script src="https://unpkg.com/vue"></script>
    </head>
    <body>
      <div id="app">
        {{ message }}
      </div>
      <script type="text/javascript" src="index.js"></script>
    </body>
  </html>
```

This will display a blank page at the moment, but it does import the source for Vue, as well as the JavaScript for our client app, index.js, which we need to create:

```
var vm = new Vue({
  el: '#app',
  data: {
    message : 'Hello, World!'
  }
});
```

If we deploy those changes (HINT: If the app is already running, just press *F11* to tell NetBeans to build; that won't make any Java changes take effect, but it will copy these static resources to the output directory) and refresh the page in the browser, we should now see *Hello, World!* on the page.

Roughly put, what's happening is that we're creating a new `Vue` object, anchoring to the (`el`) element with the `app` ID. We're also defining some state for this component (`data`), which includes the single property, `message`. On the page, anywhere inside the element `app`, we can access the component's state using the Mustache syntax we see in the index page--`{{ message }}`. Let's expand our component a bit:

```
var vm = new Vue({
  el: '#app',
  store,
  computed: {
    isLoggedIn() {
      return this.$store.state.loggedIn;
    }
  },
  created: function () {
    NotesActions.fetchNotes();
  }
});
```

We've added three items here:

- We've introduced a global data store, aptly called `store`
- We've added a new property called `isLoggedIn`, which gets its value from a method call
- We've added a lifecycle method, `created`, which will load `Note` from the server when the component is created on the page

Our data store is based on Vuex, a state-management pattern + library for `Vue.js` applications. It serves as a centralized store for all the components in an application, with rules ensuring that the state can only be mutated in a predictable fashion. (`https://vuex.vuejs.org`). To add it to our application, we need to add the following line of code to our page:

```
<script src="https://unpkg.com/vuex"></script>
```

We then add a field called `store` to our component, which you can see in the preceding code. Most of the work so far takes place in the `NotesActions` object:

```
var NotesActions = {
  buildAuthHeader: function () {
    return new Headers({
      'Content-Type': 'application/json',
      'Authorization': 'Bearer ' +
      NotesActions.getCookie('Bearer')
    });
  },
  fetchNotes: function () {
    fetch('api/notes', {
      headers: this.buildAuthHeader()
    })
    .then(function (response) {
      store.state.loggedIn = response.status === 200;
      if (response.ok) {
        return response.json();
      }
    })
    .then(function (notes) {
      store.commit('setNotes', notes);
    });
  }
}
```

When the page loads, the application will immediately send a request to the backend for Notes, sending the bearer token, if there is one, in the `Authorization` header. When the response returns, we update the state of the `isLoggedIn` property in the store, and, if the request was successful, we update the list of `Notes` on the page. Note that we're using `fetch()`. That is the new, experimental API for sending XHR, or Ajax, requests in browsers. As of the writing of this book, it is supported in every major browser except Internet Explorer, so be careful using this in production apps if you can't dictate the client's browser.

We've seen the store used a few times, so let's take a look at it:

```
const store = new Vuex.Store({
  state: {
    notes: [],
    loggedIn: false,
    currentIndex: -1,
    currentNote: NotesActions.newNote()
  }
};
```

The store is of type `Vuex.Store`, and we specify the various state fields in its `state` property. Handled properly, any Vue component bound to one of these state fields is automatically updated for you. You don't need to track and manage state, manually reflecting changes on the page as the application state changes. Vue and Vuex handle that for you. Mostly. There are some situations, such as array mutation (or replacement), that require some special handling. Vuex offers **mutations** to help with that. For example, `NotesAction.fetchNotes()`, upon a successful request, we will make this call:

```
store.commit('setNotes', notes);
```

The preceding code tells the store to `commit` a mutation called `setNotes`, with `notes` as the payload. We define mutations like this:

```
mutations: {
  setNotes(state, notes) {
    state.notes = [];
    if (notes) {
      notes.forEach(i => {
        state.notes.push({
          id: i.id,
          title: i.title,
          body: i.body,
          created: new Date(i.created),
          modified: new Date(i.modified)
        });
      });
    }
  }
}
```

What we are passing into this mutation (you can probably think of this as a function or a method with a peculiar invocation syntax if that helps) is a JSON array (hopefully, we show no type checking here), so we start by clearing out the current list of notes, then iterating over this array, creating and storing new objects, and reformatting some of the data as we do so. Strictly using only this mutation to replace the set of notes, we can guarantee that the user interface is kept in sync with the changing state of the application, all for free.

So how are these notes displayed? To do that, we define a new Vue component and add it to the page, as follows:

```
<div id="app">
  <note-list v-bind:notes="notes" v-if="isLoggedIn"></note-list>
</div>
```

Here, we've referenced a new component called note-list. We've bound the template variable notes to the application variable of the same name, and specified that the component is only displayed if the user is logged. The actual component definition happens in JavaScript. Back in index.js, we have this:

```
Vue.component('note-list', {
  template: '#note-list-template',
  store,
  computed: {
    notes() {
      return this.$store.state.notes;
    },
    isLoggedIn() {
      return this.$store.state.loggedIn;
    }
  },
  methods: {
    loadNote: function (index) {
      this.$store.commit('noteClicked', index);
    },
    deleteNote: function (index) {
      if (confirm
        ("Are you sure want to delete this note?")) {
          NotesActions.deleteNote(index);
        }
    }
  }
});
```

This component is named note-list; its template is found in an element with the note-list-template ID; it has two computed values: notes and isLoggedIn; and it provides two methods. In a typical Vue application, we would have a number of files, all ultimately compiled together using something like Grunt or Gulp, and one of these files would be our component's template. Since we are trying to make this as simple as possible by avoiding the JS build processes, we have everything declared right on our page. In index.html, we can find the template for our component:

```
<script type="text/x-template" id="note-list-template">
  <div class="note-list">
    <h2>Notes:</h2>
    <ul>
      <div class="note-list"
        v-for="(note,index) in notes" :key="note.id">
      <span :
        v-on:click="loadNote(index,note);">
      {{ note.title }}
```

```
      </span>
      <a v-on:click="deleteNote(index, note);">
        <img src="images/x-225x225.png" height="20"
           width="20" alt="delete">
      </a>
    </div>
  </ul>
  <hr>
 </div>
</script>
```

Using a `script` tag with with the `text/x-template` type, we can add the template to the DOM without it rendering on the page. Inside this template, the interesting part is the `div` tag with the `note-list` class. We have the `v-` attribute on it, which means the Vue template processor will iterate over the `notes` list using this `div` as a template for displaying each `note` in the array.

Each note will be rendered using the `span` tag. Using the template markup `:title`, we are able to create a value for the title tag using our application state (we can't say because string interpolation was deprecated in Vue 2.0). The sole child of the `span` tag is the `{{ note.title }}` expression, which renders the title of the `note` list as a string. When the user clicks on the note title on the page, we want to react to that, so we bind the `onClick` handler to the DOM element via `v-on:click`. The function referenced here is the `loadNote()` function that we defined in the `methods` block of our component definition.

The `loadNote()` function calls a mutation we haven't looked at yet:

```
noteClicked(state, index) {
  state.currentIndex = index;
  state.currentNote = state.notes[index];
  bus.$emit('note-clicked', state.currentNote);
}
```

This mutation modifies the state to reflect the note that the user clicked on, then fires (or emits) an event called `note-clicked`. The event system is really quite simple. It is set up like this:

```
var bus = new Vue();
```

That's literally it. This is just a bare bones, globally scoped Vue component. We fire events by calling `bus.$emit()` method, and register event listeners by calling the `bus.$on()` method. We'll see what that looks like in the note form.

We will add the note form component to the page like we did the `note-list` component:

```
<div id="app">
  <note-list v-bind:notes="notes" v-if="isLoggedIn"></note-list>
  <note-form v-if="isLoggedIn"></note-form>
</div>
```

And, again, the component is defined in `index.js` as follows:

```
Vue.component('note-form', {
  template: '#note-form-template',
  store,
  data: function () {
    return {
      note: NotesActions.newNote()
    };
  },
  mounted: function () {
    var self = this;
    bus.$on('add-clicked', function () {
      self.$store.currentNote = NotesActions.newNote();
      self.clearForm();
    });
    bus.$on('note-clicked', function (note) {
      self.updateForm(note);
    });
    CKEDITOR.replace('notebody');
  }
});
```

The template is also in `index.html`, as shown here:

```
<script type="text/x-template" id="note-form-template">
  <div class="note-form">
    <h2>{{ note.title }}</h2>
    <form>
      <input id="noteid" type="hidden"
        v-model="note.id"></input>
      <input id="notedate" type="hidden"
        v-model="note.created"></input>
      <input id="notetitle" type="text" size="50"
        v-model="note.title"></input>
      <br/>
      <textarea id="notebody"
        style="width: 100%; height: 100%"
        v-model="note.body"></textarea>
      <br>
      <button type="button" v-on:click="save">Save</button>
```

```
    </form>
  </div>
</script>
```

This is mostly normal HTML form. The interesting bit is the v-model that ties the form element to the component's property. Changes made on the form are automatically reflected in the component, and changes made in the component (for example, via an event handler) are automatically reflected in the UI. We also attach an onClick handler via the now familiar v-on:click attribute.

Did you notice the reference to CKEDITOR in our component definition? We'll use the rich text editor CKEditor to provide a better experience. We could go to CKEditor and download the distribution bundle, but we have a better way--WebJars. The WebJars project takes popular client-side web libraries and packages them as JARs. This makes adding supported libraries to the project very simple:

```
<dependency>
  <groupId>org.webjars</groupId>
  <artifactId>ckeditor</artifactId>
  <version>4.6.2</version>
</dependency>
```

When we package the application, this binary jar is added to the web archive. However, if it's still archived, how do we access the resources? There are a number of options depending on the type of application you are building. We'll make use of Servlet 3's static resource handling (anything under META-INF/resources that's packaged in the web application's lib directory are automatically exposed). In index.html, we add CKEditor to the page with this simple line:

```
<script type="text/javascript"
  src="webjars/ckeditor/4.6.2/standard/ckeditor.js"></script>
```

CKEditor is now ready to use.

One last major piece on the frontend is enabling the user to log in. To do that, we'll create another component as follows:

```
<div id="app">
  <navbar></navbar>
  <note-list v-bind:notes="notes" v-if="isLoggedIn"></note-list>
  <note-form v-if="isLoggedIn"></note-form>
</div>
```

Then, we will add the following component definition:

```
Vue.component('navbar', {
  template: '#navbar-template',
  store,
  data: function () {
    return {
      authUrl: "#"
    };
  },
  methods: {
    getAuthUrl: function () {
      var self = this;
      fetch('api/auth/url')
      .then(function (response) {
        return response.text();
      })
      .then(function (url) {
        self.authUrl = url;
      });
    }
  },
  mounted: function () {
    this.getAuthUrl();
  }
});
```

And, finally, we will add the template as follows:

```
<script type="text/x-template" id="navbar-template">
  <div id="nav" style="grid-column: 1/span 2; grid-row: 1 / 1;">
    <a v-on:click="add" style="padding-right: 10px;">
      <img src="images/plus-225x225.png" height="20"
        width="20" alt="add">
    </a>
    <a v-on:click="logout" v-if="isLoggedIn">Logout</a>
    <a v-if="!isLoggedIn" :href="authUrl"
      style="text-decoration: none">Login</a>
  </div>
</script>
```

When this component is **mounted** (or attached to the element in the DOM), we call the
getAuthUrl() function that sends an Ajax request to the server for our Google login URL.
Once that's fetched, the login anchor tag is updated to refer to the URL.

There are a few more details in the JavaScript file we've not covered here explicitly, but interested parties can check out the source code in the repository and read through it for the remaining details. We do have a working JavaScript frontend for our note-taking app that supports listing, creating, updating, and deleting notes, as well as supporting multiple users. It's not a pretty application, but it works. Not bad for a Java guy!

Summary

Now we're back to the familiar refrain--our application is **finished**. What have we covered in the chapter? We've created a REST API using JAX-RS that doesn't require direct JSON manipulation. We've learned how to apply request filters to JAX-RS endpoints to restrict access to authenticated users, which we authenticate against their Google accounts using Google's OAuth2 workflow. We've packaged the application using Payara Micro, a great option to develop microservices, and we've integrated MongoDB into our application using the MongoDB Java API. Finally, we built a very basic JavaScript client using Vue.js to access our application.

There are a lot of new concepts and technologies interacting in this application, which makes it interesting from a technical perspective, but there's still more that could be done. The application could use a great deal of styling, and support for embedded images and videos would be nice, as would a mobile client. There is lots of room for improvements and enhancements with the app, but interested parties have a solid foundation to start from. Although, for us, it's time to turn to the next chapter and a new project, where we'll jump into the world of cloud computing with Functions as a Service.

10
Serverless Java

In recent years, the concept of microservices, which we've already looked at, has swept across the industry, quickly displacing the battle-tested application server with something smaller and leaner. Right on the heels of microservices comes a new concept--Functions as a Service, more commonly called **serverless**. In this chapter, you'll learn more about this new deployment model and build an application to demonstrate how to use it.

The application will be a simple notification system using the following technologies:

- Amazon Web Services
    - Amazon Lambda
    - Amazon **Identity and Access Management (IAM)**
    - Amazon **Simple Notification System (SNS)**
    - Amazon **Simple Email System (SES)**
    - Amazon DynamoDB
- JavaFX
- The options offered by cloud providers can be quite vast, and Amazon Web Services is no exception. In this chapter, we will attempt to use just enough of what AWS has to offer to help us build a compelling application as we wade into cloud-native application development.

Getting started

Before we get to our application, we should spend some time getting a better understanding of the term **Function as a Service (FaaS)**. The term itself is a continuation of the **blank** as a service trend we've seen for a few years now. There is a host of such terms and offerings, but the big three are **Infrastructure as a Service (IaaS)**, **Platform as a Service (PaaS)**, and **Software as a Service (SaaS)**. Oftentimes, these three build on each other as seen in the following diagram:

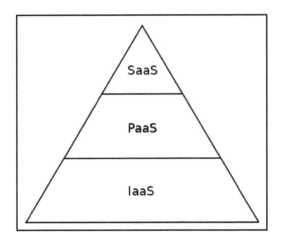

The lowest level of the cloud computing offerings, Infrastructure as a Service providers, offers infrastructure-related assets **in the cloud**. Typically, this can be as simple as file storage, but usually means virtual machines. By using an Infrastructure as a Service provider, clients need not worry about buying, maintaining, or replacing hardware, as that is handled by the provider. Clients are billed, instead, only on resources used.

Moving up the stack, Platform as a Service providers offer cloud-hosted application execution environments. This may include things such as an application server, a database server, a web server, and so on. The details of the physical environment are abstracted away, with customers specifying storage and RAM requirements. Some providers also allow the customer to choose the operating system, as this can have implications on the application stack, support tools, and more.

Software as a Service is a higher-level abstraction that doesn't focus on the hardware at all but, instead, offers hosted software that customers subscribe to, typically per user, and typically on a monthly or yearly basis. This is often seen in complicated business software, such as financial systems or human resource applications, but it is also seen with simpler systems, such as blogging software. The user simply subscribes and uses the software, leaving the installation and maintenance, including upgrades, to the provider. While this can reduce flexibility for the user (for example, it is often not possible to customize the software), it also reduces operational costs by pushing maintenance costs to the provider as well as guaranteeing, in most cases, access to the latest version of the software.

There are several other variations on this type of service, such as **Mobile Backend as a Service** (**MBaaS**) and **Database as a Service** (**DBaaS**). As the market continues to gain confidence in cloud computing, and as the internet speeds up while the prices go down, we are likely to see more and more of these types of systems developed, which brings us to our topic in this chapter.

Function as a Service, or **serverless** computing, is the deployment of a small piece of code, very literally a function, that can be called from other applications, usually via some sort of trigger. Use cases include things such as image conversion, log analysis, and, as we will build in this chapter, notification systems.

Despite what the name **serverless** implies, there is actually a server involved, which only stands to reason; however, you, as an application developer, need not think about the server too deeply. In fact, as we'll see in this chapter, the only thing we need to worry about is how much memory our function will need. Everything else about the server is completely handled by the Function as a Service provider--the operating system, storage, networking, even starting and stopping the virtual machine are all handled for us by the provider.

With that basic understanding of serverless, we need to pick a provider. As can be expected, there are a number of options--Amazon, Oracle, IBM, Red Hat, and more. Unfortunately, currently, there is no standardized means by which we can write a serverless system and deploy it to an arbitrary provider, so that means our solution will be necessarily tied to a specific provider, which will be **Amazon Web Services** (**AWS**), the dominant provider of cloud computing services. As mentioned in the introduction to this chapter, we use a number of AWS offerings, but the centerpiece will be AWS Lambda, Amazon's serverless computing offering.

Let's jump in.

Planning the application

The application we will build is a very simple **cloud notification** service. In a nutshell, our function will **listen** for messages, then forward those messages to email addresses and phone numbers registered in the system. While our system will be somewhat contrived and certainly very simple, hopefully the more practical use cases are clear:

- Our system reminds students and/or parents about upcoming events
- Parents are notified when children enter or leave certain geographic boundaries
- Systems administrators are notified of certain events as they occur

The possibilities are quite vast. For our purposes here, we'll develop not only the cloud-based system, but also a simple desktop application to simulate these types of scenarios. We'll start where the fun is: in the cloud.

Building your first function

The heart of Functions as a Service is, of course, the function. In Amazon Web Services, these are deployed using the service AWS Lambda. That's not the only AWS feature we'll use, as we've already mentioned. Once we have a function, we need a way to execute it. This is done via one or more triggers, and the function itself has tasks it needs to perform, so we'll demonstrate more service usage via API calls when we finally write the function.

It might be helpful at this point, given that our application is structured significantly differently than anything else we've looked at, to look at a system diagram:

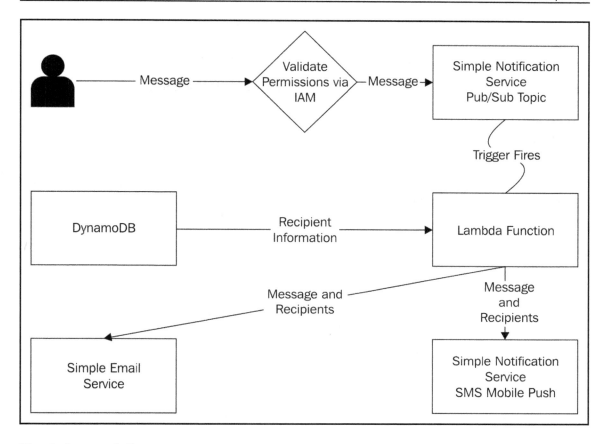

Here's the rough flow:

- A message is published to a topic in the Simple Notification System
- Once the permissions of the caller have been verified, the message is delivered
- Upon message delivery, a trigger is fired, delivering the message from the topic to our function
- Inside the function, we'll query Amazon's **DynamoDB** to get the list of recipients that have signed up, providing either an email address, cell phone number, or both
- All of the cell phone numbers will be sent a text message via **Simple Notification System**
- All the email addresses will be sent an email via **Simple Email Service**

To start building the function, we need to create a Java project. Like many of our other projects, this will be a multi-module Maven project. In NetBeans, click on **File | New Project | Maven | POM Project**. We'll call the `CloudNotice` project.

The project will have three modules--one for the function, one for a test/demo client, and one for a shared API. To create the function module, right-click on the `Modules` node in the project explorer and select **Create new module**. In the window, select **Maven | Java Application**, click on **Next**, and set the project name to `function`. Repeat those steps and create a module called `api`.

Before we go any further, we have to address the fact that, at the time of writing, AWS does not support Java 9. We must, therefore, target Java 8 (or earlier) for anything we will ship to Lambda. To do that, we need to modify our `pom.xml` file like this:

```
<properties>
  <maven.compiler.source>1.8</maven.compiler.source>
  <maven.compiler.target>1.8</maven.compiler.target>
</properties>
```

Modify the POM for both `api` and `function`. Hopefully, AWS will support Java 9 as quickly as possible after its release. Until then, we'll just have to target JDK 8.

With our project configured, we're ready to write our function. AWS Lambdas are implemented as `RequestHandler` instances:

```
public class SnsEventHandler
  implements RequestHandler<SNSEvent, Object> {
    @Override
    public Object handleRequest
      (SNSEvent request, Context context) {
        LambdaLogger logger = context.getLogger();
        final String message = request.getRecords().get(0)
         .getSNS().getMessage();
        logger.log("Handle message '" + message + "'");
        return null;
}
```

Ultimately, we want our function to be triggered when a message is delivered to an SNS topic, so we specify `SNSEvent` as the input type. We also specify `Context`. There are several things we can get from the `Context`, such as the request ID, memory limit, and others, but all we're interested in is getting a `LambdaLogger` instance. We could just write to standard out and standard error, and those messages would be saved in Amazon CloudWatch, but `LambdaLogger` allows us to respect system permissions and the container configuration.

To make this compile, we need to add some dependencies to our application, so we add the following lines to pom.xml:

```xml
<properties>
  <aws.java.sdk.version>[1.11, 2.0.0)</aws.java.sdk.version>
</properties>
<dependencies>
  <dependency>
    <groupId>com.amazonaws</groupId>
    <artifactId>aws-java-sdk-sns</artifactId>
    <version>${aws.java.sdk.version}</version>
  </dependency>
  <dependency>
    <groupId>com.amazonaws</groupId>
    <artifactId>aws-lambda-java-core</artifactId>
    <version>1.1.0</version>
  </dependency>
  <dependency>
    <groupId>com.amazonaws</groupId>
    <artifactId>aws-lambda-java-events</artifactId>
    <version>1.3.0</version>
  </dependency>
</dependencies>
```

We can now start implementing the method as follows:

```java
final List<Recipient> recipients =  new CloudNoticeDAO(false)
  .getRecipients();
final List<String> emailAddresses = recipients.stream()
  .filter(r -> "email".equalsIgnoreCase(r.getType()))
  .map(r -> r.getAddress())
  .collect(Collectors.toList());
final List<String> phoneNumbers = recipients.stream()
  .filter(r -> "sms".equalsIgnoreCase(r.getType()))
  .map(r -> r.getAddress())
  .collect(Collectors.toList());
```

We have a couple of new classes to look at, but to recap this code first, we will get a list of Recipient instances, which represents the numbers and email addresses that have been subscribed to our service. We then create a stream from the list, filtering for each recipient type, SMS or Email, extracting the value via map(), then collecting them in a List.

We will get to `CloudNoticeDAO` and `Recipient` in a moment, but let's finish up with our function first. Once we have our lists, we can then send the messages as follows:

```
final SesClient sesClient = new SesClient();
final SnsClient snsClient = new SnsClient();

sesClient.sendEmails(emailAddresses, "j9bp@steeplesoft.com",
 "Cloud Notification", message);
snsClient.sendTextMessages(phoneNumbers, message);
sesClient.shutdown();
snsClient.shutdown();
```

We have encapsulated two more AWS APIs behind our own client classes, `SesClient` and `SnsClient`. This may seem a bit excessive, but these types of things tend to grow, and this approach puts us in a good position to manage that.

That leaves us with three APIs to look at: DynamoDB, Simple Email Service, and Simple Notification Service. We'll take them in order.

DynamoDB

Amazon DynamoDB is a NoSQL database, very much like MongoDB, which we looked at in `Chapter 9`, *Taking Notes with Monumentum*, though DynamDB supports both document and key-value store models. A thorough comparison of the two, as well as a recommendation as to which to choose, is well outside the scope of our work here. We chose DynamoDB here, since it is already provisioned in the Amazon Web Service, and, thus, easily configured for our application.

To get started with the DynamoDB API, we need to add some dependencies to our application. In the `api` module, add this to the `pom.xml` file:

```
<properties>
  <sqlite4java.version>1.0.392</sqlite4java.version>
</properties>
<dependency>
  <groupId>com.amazonaws</groupId>
  <artifactId>aws-java-sdk-dynamodb</artifactId>
  <version>${aws.java.sdk.version}</version>
</dependency>
<dependency>
  <groupId>com.amazonaws</groupId>
  <artifactId>DynamoDBLocal</artifactId>
  <version>${aws.java.sdk.version}</version>
  <optional>true</optional>
</dependency>
```

```
<dependency>
  <groupId>com.almworks.sqlite4java</groupId>
  <artifactId>sqlite4java</artifactId>
  <version>${sqlite4java.version}</version>
  <optional>true</optional>
</dependency>
```

Before we start writing our DAO class, let's define our simple model. The DynamoDB API provides an object-relational mapping facility, much like the Java Persistence API or Hibernate, which will require a POJO and just a few annotations as we see here:

```
public class Recipient {
    private String id;
    private String type = "SMS";
    private String address = "";

    // Constructors...

    @DynamoDBHashKey(attributeName = "_id")
    public String getId() {
        return id;
    }
    @DynamoDBAttribute(attributeName = "type")
    public String getType() {
        return type;
    }

    @DynamoDBAttribute(attributeName="address")
    public String getAddress() {
        return address;
    }
    // Setters omitted to save space
}
```

In our POJO, we declared three properties, id, type, and address, then annotated the getters with @DyanoDBAttribute to help the library understand how to map the object.

 Note that, while most of the property names match the field names in the table, you can override the property-to-field name mapping as we did with id.

Before we can do anything with our data, we need to declare our table. Remember that DynamoDB is a NoSQL database, and we will use it as a document store just as we did with MongoDB. However, before we can store any data, we have to define **where** to put it. In MongoDB, we would create a collection. DynamoDB, though, still refers to this as a table, and, while it is technically schemaless, we do need to define a primary key, which is made up of a partition key and an optional sort key.

We create the table through the console. Once you've logged on to the AWS DynamoDB console, you will click on the **Create Table** button, which will bring you to a screen like this:

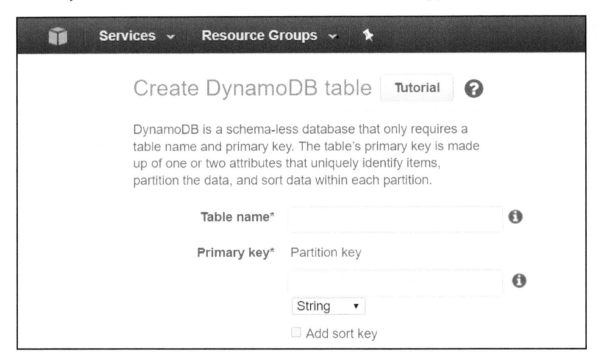

We will name our table `recipients`, and specify `_id` as the partition key. Click on the **Create Table** button and give AWS time to create the table.

We are now ready to start writing our DAO. In the API module, create a class called `CloudNoticeDAO`, to which we'll add this constructor:

```
protected final AmazonDynamoDB ddb;
protected final DynamoDBMapper mapper;
public CloudNoticeDAO(boolean local) {
  ddb = local ? DynamoDBEmbedded.create().amazonDynamoDB()
    : AmazonDynamoDBClientBuilder.defaultClient();
```

```
    verifyTables();
    mapper = new DynamoDBMapper(ddb);
}
```

The local property is used to determine whether or not to use a local DynamoDB instance. This is here to support testing (as is the call to `verifyTables`), which we will explore in a moment. In production, our code will call `AmazonDynamoDBClientBuilder.defaultClient()` to acquire an instance of `AmazonDynamoDB`, which talks to the Amazon-hosted instance. Finally, we create an instance of `DynamoDBMapper`, which we'll use for our object mapping.

To facilitate creating a new `Recipient`, we will add this method:

```
public void saveRecipient(Recipient recip) {
    if (recip.getId() == null) {
        recip.setId(UUID.randomUUID().toString());
    }
    mapper.save(recip);
}
```

This method will either create a new entry in the database, or update an existing one if the primary key already exists. In some scenarios, it might make sense to have separate save and update methods, but our use case is so simple that we don't need to worry about that. All we need to do is create the key value if it's missing. We do so by creating a random UUID, which helps us avoid key collisions should there be more than one process or application writing to the database.

Deleting a `Recipient` instance or getting a list of all of the `Recipient` instances in the database is just as simple:

```
public List<Recipient> getRecipients() {
    return mapper.scan(Recipient.class,
      new DynamoDBScanExpression());
}

public void deleteRecipient(Recipient recip) {
    mapper.delete(recip);
}
```

Before we leave our DAO, let's take a quick look at how we can test it. Earlier, we noted the `local` parameter and the `verifyTables()` method, which exist for testing.

Generally speaking, most people will frown, and rightfully so, on adding methods to production classes just for testing. There's a difference between writing a class that is testable, and adding test methods to a class. I would agree that adding methods to a class just for testing is something that should be avoided, but I am violating that principle a little here for the sake of simplicity and brevity.

The `verifyTables()` method checks to see if the table exists; if the table doesn't, we call another method that will create it for us. While we manually created the production table using the preceding console, we could also let this method create that table for us. What approach you use is completely up to you. Be aware that there will be performance and permissions issues that will need to be addressed. That said, that method looks something like this:

```java
private void verifyTables() {
  try {
    ddb.describeTable(TABLE_NAME);
  } catch (ResourceNotFoundException rnfe) {
      createRecipientTable();
  }
}

private void createRecipientTable() {
  CreateTableRequest request = new CreateTableRequest()
    .withTableName(TABLE_NAME)
    .withAttributeDefinitions(
      new AttributeDefinition("_id", ScalarAttributeType.S))
    .withKeySchema(
      new KeySchemaElement("_id", KeyType.HASH))
    .withProvisionedThroughput(new
      ProvisionedThroughput(10L, 10L));

  ddb.createTable(request);
  try {
    TableUtils.waitUntilActive(ddb, TABLE_NAME);
  } catch (InterruptedException  e) {
    throw new RuntimeException(e);
  }
}
```

With the call to the `describeTable()` method, we can check to see if the table exists. In our test, this will fail every time, which will cause the table to be created. In production, should you use this method to create the table, this call will fail only on the first invocation. In `createRecipientTable()`, we can see how a table is created programmatically. We also wait until the table is active to make sure our reads and writes won't fail while the table is being created.

Our tests, then, are very simple. For example, consider the following code snippet:

```
private final CloudNoticeDAO dao = new CloudNoticeDAO(true);
@Test
public void addRecipient() {
  Recipient recip = new Recipient("SMS", "test@example.com");
  dao.saveRecipient(recip);
  List<Recipient> recipients = dao.getRecipients();
  Assert.assertEquals(1, recipients.size());
}
```

This test helps us verify that our model mapping is correct, and that our DAO methods function as expected. You can see additional testing in the `CloudNoticeDaoTest` class, in the source bundle.

Simple Email Service

To send emails, we will use the Amazon Simple Email Service, or SES, which we will wrap in the `SesClient` class in the `api` module.

 IMPORTANT: Before you can send an email, you have to verify either your sending/from address or domain. The verification process is fairly simple, but how to do that is probably best left to Amazon's documentation, which you can read here: http://docs.aws.amazon.com/ses/latest/DeveloperGuide/verify-email-addresses.html.

The Simple Email Service API is quite simple. We need to create a `Destination`, which tells the system to whom to send the emails; a `Message` that describes the message itself, including subject, body, and recipients; and a `SendEmailRequest` that ties everything together:

```
private final AmazonSimpleEmailService client =
  AmazonSimpleEmailServiceClientBuilder.defaultClient();
public void sendEmails(List<String> emailAddresses,
  String from,
  String subject,
```

```
      String emailBody) {
        Message message = new Message()
          .withSubject(new Content().withData(subject))
          .withBody(new Body().withText(
            new Content().withData(emailBody)));
        getChunkedEmailList(emailAddresses)
          .forEach(group ->
            client.sendEmail(new SendEmailRequest()
              .withSource(from)
              .withDestination(
                new Destination().withBccAddresses(group))
                .withMessage(message)));
        shutdown();
    }

    public void shutdown() {
      client.shutdown();
    }
```

There is an important caveat though, which is in the preceding bolded code. SES limits the number of recipients per message to 50, so we need to take our list of email addresses and process them 50 at a time. We will do that using the getChunkedEmailList() method:

```
    private List<List<String>> getChunkedEmailList(
      List<String> emailAddresses) {
        final int numGroups = (int) Math.round(emailAddresses.size() /
        (MAX_GROUP_SIZE * 1.0) + 0.5);
        return IntStream.range(0, numGroups)
          .mapToObj(group ->
           emailAddresses.subList(MAX_GROUP_SIZE * group,
           Math.min(MAX_GROUP_SIZE * group + MAX_GROUP_SIZE,
           emailAddresses.size())))
            .collect(Collectors.toList());
    }
```

To find the number of groups, we divide the number of addresses by 50 and round up (for example, 254 addresses would get us 6 groups--5 of 50 and 1 of 4). Then, using an IntStream to count from 0 to the number of groups (exclusive), we extract sublists from the original list. Each of these lists is then collected into yet another List, giving us the nested Collection instances we see in the method signature.

Design note: Many developers will avoid using nested `Collection` instances like this, as it can quickly become difficult to understand what exactly the variable represents. It is considered by many to be a best practice in situations like this to create a new type to hold the nested data. For example, if we were to follow that advice here, we could create, perhaps, a new `Group` class that had a `List<String>` property to hold the group's email addresses. We have not done so for the sake of brevity, but that would definitely be a good enhancement to this code.

Once we've **chunked** our list, we can send the same `Message` to each group, and thus fulfill the API contract.

Simple Notification Service

We've already seen the Simple Notification System at work, at least in theory, as that is what delivers the outbound message to our function: a client of some sort publishes a message in a specific SNS topic. We have a subscription to that topic (I'll show you how to create that later) that calls our method with the message for us to deliver. We will use the SNS API now to send text (or SMS) messages to the users who have subscribed a phone number to the system.

With SNS, to send a message to more than one phone number you must do so through a topic to which each number is subscribed. What we'll do then is follow these steps:

1. Create a topic.
2. Subscribe all of the phone numbers.
3. Publish the message to the topic.
4. Delete the topic.

If we use a persistent topic, we will likely get unpredictable results if we have more than one instance of the function running simultaneously. The method that orchestrates all of this work looks like this:

```
public void sendTextMessages(List<String> phoneNumbers,
  String message) {
    String arn = createTopic(UUID.randomUUID().toString());
    phoneNumbers.forEach(phoneNumber ->
      subscribeToTopic(arn, "sms", phoneNumber));
    sendMessage(arn, message);
    deleteTopic(arn);
}
```

To create a topic, we have the following method:

```
private String createTopic(String arn) {
  return snsClient.createTopic(
    new CreateTopicRequest(arn)).getTopicArn();
}
```

To subscribe the numbers to the topic, we have this method:

```
private SubscribeResult subscribeToTopic(String arn,
  String protocol, String endpoint) {
    return snsClient.subscribe(
      new SubscribeRequest(arn, protocol, endpoint));
}
```

Publishing a message is equally simple, as we see here:

```
public void sendMessage(String topic, String message) {
  snsClient.publish(topic, message);
}
```

And finally, you can delete the topic with this simple method:

```
private DeleteTopicResult deleteTopic(String arn) {
  return snsClient.deleteTopic(arn);
}
```

All of these methods are clearly very simple, so the calls to the SNS API could be made directly inline in the calling code, but this wrapper does provide us with a way to hide the details of the API from our business code. This is more important, for example, in createTopic(), where extra classes are needed, but, to be consistent, we'll encapsulate everything behind our own facade.

Deploying the function

We have now completed our function and we're almost ready to deploy it. To do that, we need to package it. AWS allows us to upload either a ZIP or a JAR file. We'll use the latter. However, we have some external dependencies, so we'll use the **Maven Shade** plugin to build a fat jar with our function and all of its dependencies. In the function module, add the following piece of code to the pom.xml file:

```
<plugin>
  <groupId>org.apache.maven.plugins</groupId>
  <artifactId>maven-shade-plugin</artifactId>
  <version>3.0.0</version>
```

```
<executions>
  <execution>
      <phase>package</phase>
      <goals>
          <goal>shade</goal>
      </goals>
      <configuration>
          <finalName>
              cloudnotice-function-${project.version}
          </finalName>
      </configuration>
  </execution>
</executions>
</plugin>
```

Now, when we build the project, we'll get a large file (about 9MB) in the target directory. It is this file that we will upload.

Creating a role

Before we can upload the function, we need to prepare our AWS environment by creating the appropriate role. Log on to AWS and navigate to the **Identity and Access Management Console** (`https://console.aws.amazon.com/iam`). In the navigation pane on the left, click on **Roles**, then click on **Create new role**:

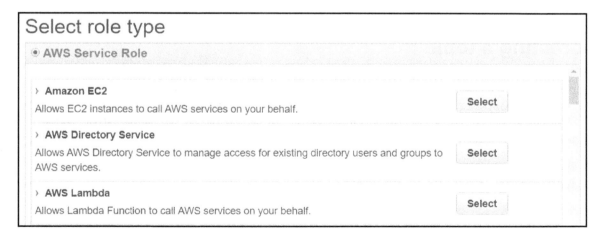

When prompted to select a role, we want to select AWS Lambda. On the next page, we will attach the policies:

Attach Policy

Select one or more policies to attach. Each role can have up to 10 policies attached.

Filter: Policy Type ▼ | Filter | Showing 262 results

		Policy Name ⇕	Attached Entities ⇕	Creation Time ⇕	Edited Time ⇕
☑		AmazonSNSFullAcc...	3	2015-02-06 12:41 CDT	2015-02-06 12:4...
☐		AmazonS3FullAccess	2	2015-02-06 12:40 CDT	2015-02-06 12:4...
☑		AWSLambdaFullAc...	2	2015-02-06 12:40 CDT	2017-05-25 14:0...
☐		AmazonAPIGatewa...	1	2015-07-09 12:34 CDT	2015-07-09 12:3...
☐		AmazonAPIGatewa...	1	2015-07-09 12:36 CDT	2015-07-09 12:3...
☑		AmazonSESFullAcc...	1	2015-02-06 12:41 CDT	2015-02-06 12:4...

Click on **Next**, set the name to `j9bp`, and click on **Create role**.

Creating a topic

To make creating the function and the associated trigger simpler, we will create our topic first. Navigate to the SNS console. Given that not all AWS functionality is always available in every region, we need to choose a specific region. We can do that in the upper-left corner of the web page. If the region does not say N. Virginia, select it--**US East (N. Virginia)**-- from the drop-down menu before continuing.

Once the region is set correctly, click on **Topics** in the left navigation bar, then click on **Create new topic** and specify the name as `cloud-notice`:

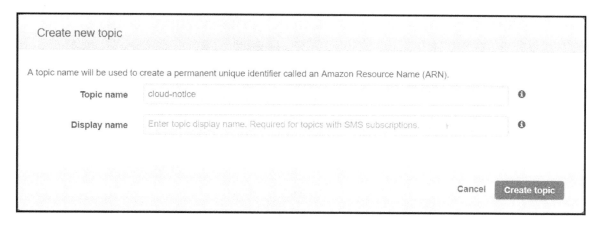

Deploying the function

We can now navigate to the Lambda console and deploy our function. We will start by clicking on the **Create a lambda** function button. We'll be asked to select a blueprint. The only option suitable for a Java-based function is **Blank Function**. Once we click on that option, we are presented with the **Configure Triggers** screen. When you click on the empty square, you will be presented with a drop-down menu, as seen in this screenshot from the AWS console:

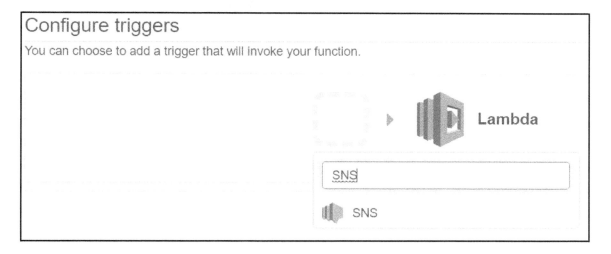

You can either scroll down to find **SNS**, or enter SNS in the filter box as in the preceding screenshot. Either way, when you click on **SNS** in the list, you will be asked to select the topic to which you want to subscribe:

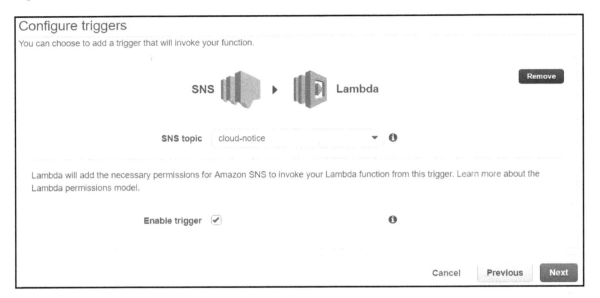

Click on **Next**. We now need to specify the details of our function:

Scrolling down the page, we also need to specify the Lambda function handler and role. The **Handler** is the fully-qualified class name, followed by two colons, and the method name:

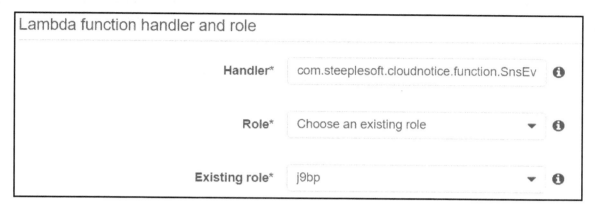

We now need to select the function archive by clicking on the upload button and selecting the jar file created by our Maven build. Click on **Next**, verify the details of the function, and then click on **Create function**.

We now have a usable AWS Lambda function. We can test it using the Lambda Console, but instead we'll build a small JavaFX application to do that, which will simultaneously test all of the service integrations, as well as demonstrate how a production application would interact with the function.

Testing the function

To help test and demonstrate the system, we'll create a new module, called `manager`, in the `CloudNotice` project. To do that, click on the **modules** node in the NetBeans project explorer, then click on **Create New Module...** | **Maven** | **JavaFX Application**. Call the project `Manager` and click on **Finish**.

I have renamed `MainApp` to `CloudNoticeManager`, `FXMLController` to `CloudNoticeManagerController`, and `Scene.fxml` to `manager.fxml`.

Our `Application` class will look a little different than in previous JavaFX applications. Some of the AWS client APIs require that they be shut down explicitly when you are finished with them. Failure to do so means that our application won't fully quit, leaving behind **zombie** processes that must be killed. To make sure we properly shut down our AWS clients, we need to add a cleanup method to our controller, which we'll call from the `stop()` method in our application:

```
private FXMLLoader fxmlLoader;
@Override
public void start(final Stage stage) throws Exception {
  fxmlLoader = new FXMLLoader(getClass()
   .getResource("/fxml/manager.fxml"));
  Parent root = fxmlLoader.load();
  // ...
}

@Override
public void stop() throws Exception {
  CloudNoticeManagerController controller =
    (CloudNoticeManagerController) fxmlLoader.getController();
  controller.cleanup();
  super.stop();
}
```

Now, regardless of whether the user clicks on **File** | **Exit** or clicks on the **Close** button on the window, our AWS clients can be cleaned up correctly.

In terms of layout, there's nothing new to discuss, so we'll not dwell on that aspect here. This is what our manager app will look like:

We have a list of the subscribed recipients on the left, an area for adding and editing a recipient at the top right, and an area for sending a test message at the bottom right. We do have some interesting bindings, so let's take a look at this.

First, in `CloudNoticeManagerController`, we need to declare some containers for our data, so we declare a number of `ObservableList` instances:

```
private final ObservableList<Recipient> recips =
  FXCollections.observableArrayList();
private final ObservableList<String> types =
  FXCollections.observableArrayList("SMS", "Email");
private final ObservableList<String> topics =
  FXCollections.observableArrayList();
```

These three `ObservableList` instances will back the UI controls matching their names. We will populate two of those lists (`type` is hardcoded) in `initalize()` as follows:

```
public void initialize(URL url, ResourceBundle rb) {
  recips.setAll(dao.getRecipients());
  topics.setAll(sns.getTopics());

  type.setItems(types);
  recipList.setItems(recips);
  topicCombo.setItems(topics);
```

Using our DAO and SES client, we fetch any already subscribed recipients, as well as any topics configured in the account. This will get *every* topic, so if you have a lot, this may be a problem, but this is just a demonstration application, so that should be fine here. Once we have these two lists, we add them to the `ObservableList` instances we created earlier, then associate the `List` with the appropriate UI controls.

To make sure the `Recipient` list displays correctly, we need to create a `CellFactory` as follows:

```
recipList.setCellFactory(p -> new ListCell<Recipient>() {
  @Override
  public void updateItem(Recipient recip, boolean empty) {
    super.updateItem(recip, empty);
    if (!empty) {
      setText(String.format("%s - %s", recip.getType(),
        recip.getAddress()));
    } else {
        setText(null);
    }
  }
});
```

Remember that, if the cell is empty, we need to set the text to null to clear out any previous value. Failure to do that will result, at some point, in a `ListView` with **phantom** entries.

Next, we need to update the edit controls when the user clicks on a `Recipient` in the list. We do this by adding a listener to the `selectedItemProperty`, which is run every time the selected item changes:

```
recipList.getSelectionModel().selectedItemProperty()
    .addListener((obs, oldRecipient, newRecipient) -> {
  type.valueProperty().setValue(newRecipient != null ?
      newRecipient.getType() : "");
  address.setText(newRecipient != null ?
      newRecipient.getAddress() : "");
});
```

If `newRecipient` is not null, we set the value of the controls to the appropriate value. Otherwise, we clear the values.

We now need to add handlers for the various buttons--the **Add** and **Remove** buttons above the `Recipient` list, and the `Save` and `Cancel` buttons in the two **form** areas on the right.

The UI control's `onAction` property can be bound to the method in the class by editing the FXML directly, as shown here:

```
<Button mnemonicParsing="false"
  onAction="#addRecipient" text="+" />
<Button mnemonicParsing="false"
  onAction="#removeRecipient" text="-" />
```

It can also be bound to the method by editing the property in Scene Builder, as shown in the following screenshot:

Either way, the method will look like this:

```
@FXML
public void addRecipient(ActionEvent event) {
  final Recipient recipient = new Recipient();
  recips.add(recipient);
  recipList.getSelectionModel().select(recipient);
  type.requestFocus();
}
```

We're adding a `Recipient`, so we create a new one, add it to our `ObservableList`, then tell the `ListView` to select this entry. Finally, we ask the `type` control to request focus so the user can easily change the value with the keyboard, if so desired. The new Recipient isn't saved to DynamoDB until the user clicks on Save, which we will look at in a moment.

When we delete a `Recipient`, we need to remove it from the UI as well as from DynamoDB:

```
@FXML
public void removeRecipient(ActionEvent event) {
  final Recipient recipient = recipList.getSelectionModel()
   .getSelectedItem();
  dao.deleteRecipient(recipient);
  recips.remove(recipient);
}
```

Saving is a bit more complicated, but not much:

```
@FXML
public void saveChanges(ActionEvent event) {
  final Recipient recipient =
    recipList.getSelectionModel().getSelectedItem();
  recipient.setType(type.getValue());
  recipient.setAddress(address.getText());
  dao.saveRecipient(recipient);
  recipList.refresh();
}
```

Since we're not binding the values of the edit controls to the selected item in the list, we need to get the reference to the item, then copy the values from the controls to the model. Once that's done, we save it to the database via our DAO, then ask `ListView` to refresh itself so that any model changes are reflected in the list.

We aren't binding the controls to the item in the list as that leads to a slightly confusing user experience. If we did bind, as the user made changes to the model `ListView` would reflect those changes. It is conceivable that the user would then assume that the changes are being saved to the database when, in fact, they are not. That doesn't happen until the user clicks on **Save**. To avoid this confusion, and the loss of data, we have *not* bound the controls and manage the data manually.

To cancel the change, all we need to do is get a reference to the unchanged model from `ListView`, and copy its values over those in the edit controls:

```
@FXML
public void cancelChanges(ActionEvent event) {
  final Recipient recipient = recipList.getSelectionModel()
    .getSelectedItem();
  type.setValue(recipient.getType());
  address.setText(recipient.getAddress());
}
```

That leaves us with the **send a message** section of the UI. Thanks to our SNS wrapper API, these methods are very simple:

```
@FXML
public void sendMessage(ActionEvent event) {
  sns.sendMessage(topicCombo.getSelectionModel()
    .getSelectedItem(), messageText.getText());
  messageText.clear();
}

@FXML
public void cancelMessage(ActionEvent event) {
  messageText.clear();
}
```

From our desktop application, we can now add, edit, and remove recipients, as well as send test messages.

Configuring your AWS credentials

Those paying very close attention may be asking a very important question--How do the AWS client libraries know how to log on to our account? Clearly, we need to tell them, and we have a few options.

The AWS SDK, when run locally, will check three places for the credentials--environment variables (AWS_ACCESS_KEY_ID and AWS_SECRET_ACCESS_KEY), system properties (aws.accessKeyId and aws.secretKey), and the default credentials profiles file ($HOME/.aws/credentials). What credentials you use is up to you, but I will show you here how to configure the profiles file.

Just like a Unix or Windows system, your AWS account has a root user that has complete access to your system. It would be extremely imprudent to run any client code connected as this user. To avoid that, we need to create a user, which we can do on the **Identity and Access Management** console (https://console.aws.amazon.com/iam).

Once you've logged on, click on **Users** on the left, then **Add user** at the top, the result of which is shown in the following screenshot:

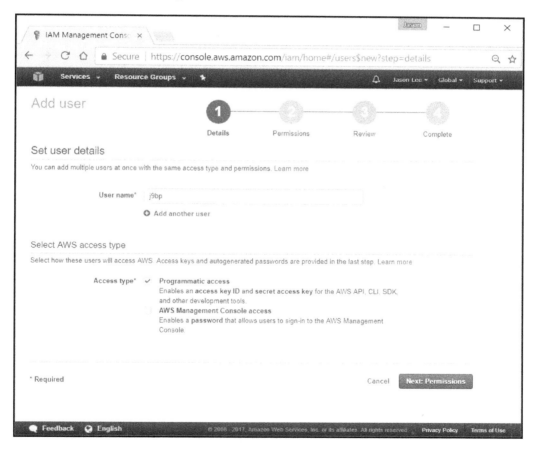

Click on **Next: Permissions** and check the entry in the **Group** list for our role, j9bp. Click on **Next: Review**, then **Create User**. This will take you to the **Add user** screen, which should have a success message box. The important part is the user information listed toward the bottom of the screen. On the right side of this table, you should see the columns **Access key ID** and **Secret access key**. Click on **Show** on the access key to reveal the value. Make a note of both of these, as there is no way to retrieve the access key once you leave this page. If you lose it, you will have to generate a new set of keys, which will break any other application using the old credentials.

	User	Access key ID	Secret access key
●	j9bp	AKIAISQVOILE6KCNQ7EQ	Npe9UiHJfFewasdi0KVVFWqD+KjZXat69W HnWbZT Hide

In a text editor, we need to create the ~/.aws/credentials file. On a Unix system, that may be /home/jdlee/.aws, and on a Windows machine that will be something like C:\Users\jdlee\aws. The credentials file should look something like this:

```
[default]
aws_access_key_id = AKIAISQVOILE6KCNQ7EQ
aws_secret_access_key = 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
```

In the same directory, we need to create another file called config. We'll use this file to tell the SDK which region we want to work in:

```
[default]
region = us-east-1
```

When the AWS clients start up now, they will default to connecting as the j9bp user in the us-east-1 region. Should you need to override that, you can either edit this file or set the environment variables or system properties noted above in the section, *Configuring your AWS Credentials*.

Summary

We've done it! We've created, many of us, our very first AWS Lambda function, and it really wasn't all that difficult. It is a simple application, of course, but I hope you can see how this type of application could be very useful. Using this as a starting point, you can write systems, with the help of a mobile application, to help keep track of your family's location. Using embedded devices such as Raspberry PI, for example, you can build devices to track inventory as it is shipped across the country, reporting location, speed, environmental conditions, sudden drops or impacts, and so on. A piece of software running on a server could constantly report various metrics about the system, such as CPU temperature, free disk space, memory allocated, system load, and so on. Your options are limited only by your imagination.

To wrap up, let's take a quick look back at what we've learned. We learned about some of the various **... as a service** systems that are being offered today, and what **serverless** really means and why it may appeal to us as application developers. We learned how to configure various Amazon Web Services offerings, including Identity and Access Management, Simple Notification System, Simple Email Service, and, of course Lambda, and we learned how to write an AWS Lambda function in Java and how to deploy it to the service. And finally, we learned how to configure triggers that would tie an SNS publish/subscribe topic to our Lambda function.

There's no denying that our application is somewhat simple, and there's no way in the space of a single chapter to make you an expert in all that Amazon Web Services or any other cloud provider has to offer. Hopefully, you have enough to get you going--and get you excited--about writing cloud-based applications using Java. For those wanting to go deeper, there are a number of great books, web pages, and so on to help you delve deeper into this rapidly changing and expanding area. In our next chapter, we'll return from the cloud and turn our attention to another great space for Java developers--your mobile phone.

11
DeskDroid - A Desktop Client for Your Android Phone

We've come at long last to our final project. To close our time together here, we're going to build a very practical application, one that lets us send and receive SMS messages from the comfort of our desktop. There are a number of products on the market that let you do this now, but they typically require a third-party service, meaning your message travels through someone else's servers. For the privacy-minded, that can be a real problem. We'll build a system that is 100% local.

Building the app will cover several different topics, some familiar, some new. That list includes the following:

- Android applications
- Android services
- REST servers
- Server-sent events for event/data streaming
- Data access using Content Providers

There will also be a host of other, smaller tidbits along the way as we finish out our time together on a strong, high note.

Getting started

This project will have two parts:

- The Android application/server (not to be confused with application server, of course)

- The desktop/JavaFX application

The desktop piece is somewhat useless without the **server** piece, so we'll start by building the Android side first.

Creating the Android project

While we have been using NetBeans for most of our work so far, we will again use Android Studio for this piece of the project. While there is some semblance of Android support for NetBeans, as of this writing, the project seems to have stalled. Android Studio, on the other hand, is very actively developed by Google and is, in fact, the official IDE for Android development. I will leave it as an exercise for the reader, if needed, to install the IDE and the SDK.

To create a new project, we click on **File | New Project**, and specify **Application name**, **Company domain**, and **Project location**, as shown in the following screenshot:

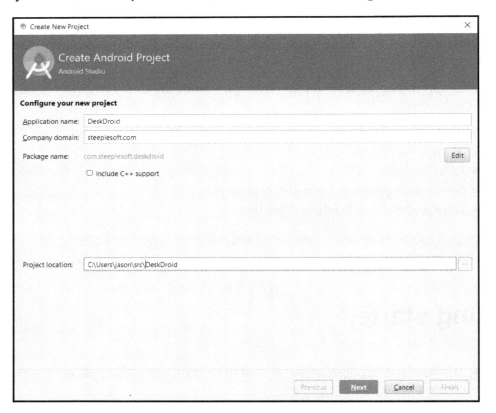

Next, we need to specify the API version we want to target. This can be a tricky choice. On the one hand, we'd like to be on the cutting edge and have all of the great new features that Android offers available to us, but on the other hand, we don't want to target such a new API level that we make the application unusable (read uninstallable) for a larger number of Android users than is necessary. In this case, Android 6.0, or Marshmallow, seems like an acceptable trade-off:

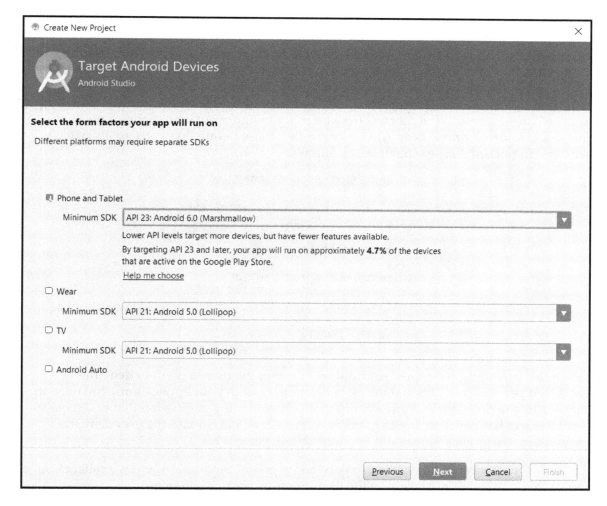

Click on **Next**, select **Blank Activity**, **Next**, and **Finish**, and our project is ready for development.

On the Android side, we are not going to do much in the way of user interface. Once we have finished the project, you will likely have all sorts of ideas of what could be done, which is great, but we won't spend the time here doing any of those. That said, the first thing we really need to do is ask the user for permission to access the text messages on their phone.

Requesting permissions

In earlier versions of Android, permissions were an all or nothing proposition. Starting with Android 6, though, the user is prompted for each permission that the application requests, allowing for the possibility of a user to grant some permissions while denying others. We will need to request some permissions--we need to be able to read and write SMS messages, and we'll need access to the contacts (so we can try to figure out who sent us a given message). Android provides an API for requesting those permissions very easily, which we'll put in our onCreate() method, as follows:

```
public static final int PERMISSION_REQUEST_CODE = 42;
@Override
protected void onCreate(Bundle savedInstanceState) {
  super.onCreate(savedInstanceState);
 // ...
 ActivityCompat.requestPermissions(this,
        new String[]{
                Manifest.permission.SEND_SMS,
                Manifest.permission.RECEIVE_SMS,
                Manifest.permission.READ_CONTACTS
        },
        PERMISSION_REQUEST_CODE);
}
```

When this preceding code runs, Android will prompt the user to grant or deny the requested permissions. This is done asynchronously, so, in your applications, you need to make sure you don't attempt any operation that requires any permission that you request until the user has had a chance to grant the permission (and, should the user deny the permission, the application should degrade, or fail, gracefully).

To allow the application to respond to permission grants, Android provides a callback. In our callback, we want to make sure the user grants us both permissions:

```
@Override
public void onRequestPermissionsResult(int requestCode,
  String permissions[], int[] grantResults) {
    switch (requestCode) {
      case PERMISSION_REQUEST_CODE: {
```

```
        if (grantResults.length != 3
        || grantResults[0] !=
            PackageManager.PERMISSION_GRANTED
        || grantResults[1] !=
            PackageManager.PERMISSION_GRANTED
        || grantResults[2] !=
            PackageManager.PERMISSION_GRANTED) {
            AlertDialog.Builder dialog =
              new AlertDialog.Builder(this);
            dialog.setCancelable(false);
            dialog.setTitle("Error");
            dialog.setMessage("This app requires access
             to text messages and contacts. Click OK
             to close.");
            dialog.setPositiveButton("OK",
             new DialogInterface.OnClickListener() {
               @Override
               public void onClick(DialogInterface dialog,
                int id) {
                  finish();
               }
           });

            final AlertDialog alert = dialog.create();
            alert.show();
        }
     }
   }
}
```

When Android calls back in to our application, we need to make sure that the
`requestCode` is what we specified-- `PERMISSION_REQUEST_CODE`--to make sure that we
only respond to our own requests.

Once we've identified an appropriate response, we make sure that `grantResults` is the
correct length, and that each entry is `PERMISSION_GRANTED`. If the array is too short, or if
either array element is not the correct type, we display a dialog informing the user that both
permissions are required, and then exit the application.

In our example, we are requesting both permissions simultaneously, so we respond to both
simultaneously. If you have a complex set of permissions, for example, if your application
can work with only some of the requested permissions, you can make multiple calls to
`ActivityCompat.requestPermissions`, providing a distinct `requestCode` for each. You
would then need to expand your switch block in `onRequestPermissionsResult()` to
cover each new `requestCode`.

One final word on permissions. Typically, you should always check to make sure that you have the permission needed to perform a given task. You can do that with a method as follows:

```
protected boolean checkPermission(Permissions permission) {
    return ContextCompat.checkSelfPermission(this,
        permission.permission) ==
        PackageManager.PERMISSION_GRANTED;
}
```

In our case, we just don't allow the application to run if we aren't granted the required permissions, so we need not worry about additional permission checks.

Creating the service

The heart of the Android portion of the project is our REST endpoints. We would like these endpoints to be available whenever the phone is on, so we can't use an `Activity` to host them. What we want is a `Service`. The Android documentation defines a `Service` as *an application component that can perform long-running operations in the background, and it does not provide a user interface*. There are three types of Services--`scheduled` (which runs on a schedule), `started` (which can be started explicitly by another application component), and `bound` (which is bound to an application component via the `bindService()` call, and runs until all the bound components are destroyed). Since we want this to be available all the time, we want a started service.

To create the service, click on **File** | **New** | **Service** | **Service**. Enter `DeskDroidService` for the service, uncheck **Exported**, and click on **Finish**. That will get you the following stubbed code:

```
public class DeskDroidService extends Service {
    public DeskDroidService() {
    }

    @Override
    public IBinder onBind(Intent intent) {
        throw new UnsupportedOperationException(
            "Not yet implemented");
    }
}
```

The wizard also updates `AndroidManifest.xml` as follows:

```
<service
  android:name=".DeskDroidService"
  android:enabled="true"
  android:exported="false" />
```

The method `onBind()` is abstract, so it must be implemented. We are not creating a bound service, so we can leave this unimplemented, although we will change it so that it returns `null` rather than throwing an `Exception`. We are, though, interested in when the service is started and stopped, so we need to override these two relevant lifecycle methods:

```
public int onStartCommand(Intent intent, int flags, int startId) {
  super.onStartCommand(intent, flags, startId);
}
public void onDestroy() {
}
```

It's in these methods that we'll place our REST service code. We will once again use Jersey, the JAX-RS reference implementation, which provides a nice way of bootstrapping a server in a Java SE environment, such as what we find ourselves in here in our Android application. We'll encapsulate that logic in a new method called `startServer()` as follows:

```
protected static Server server;
protected void startServer() {
  WifiManager WifiMgr = (WifiManager) getApplicationContext()
   .getSystemService(Service.Wifi_SERVICE);
  if (WifiMgr.isWifiEnabled()) {
    String ipAddress = Formatter.
     formatIpAddress(WifiMgr.getConnectionInfo()
      .getIpAddress());
    URI baseUri = UriBuilder.fromUri("http://" + ipAddress)
     .port(49152)
     .build();
    ResourceConfig config =
      new ResourceConfig(SseFeature.class)
       .register(JacksonFeature.class);
    server = JettyHttpContainerFactory.createServer(baseUri,
     config);
  }
}
```

The first thing we do is check to make sure that we're on Wi-Fi. This isn't strictly necessary, but it seemed to be a prudent precaution to prevent the application from listening for connections, regardless of the network state. If the phone is not on Wi-Fi, there's a good chance the intended laptop is not either. There may be legitimate use cases for allowing the endpoints to listen even on a cellular network, however. Making this restriction configurable is a great candidate for a preferences-driven option.

For this code to work, we need to add this new permission to the manifest:

```
<uses-permission android:name=
  "android.permission.ACCESS_WIFI_STATE" />
```

Once we're sure that we're on Wi-Fi, we look up our IP address, and bootstrap a Jetty-based Jersey server. With a nod to the Venerable Commodore 64, for those of us old enough to remember that computing pioneer, we listen on port `49152` on the Wi-Fi network interface.

Next, we create a `ResourceConfig` instance, providing two feature references that we're interested in--`SseFeature` and `JacksonFeature`. We've already seen `JacksonFeature`; that's what lets us work with POJOs, leaving the JSON concerns to Jersey. What is `SseFeature`, though?

Server-sent events

SSE, or server-sent events, is a means by which we can stream data from the server to the client. Typically, a REST request is very short-lived--make a connection, send the request, get a response, close the connection. Sometimes, though, the REST server may not have all of the data that the client wants at the time of the request (for example, reading data from another data source such as a log file or network socket). So, it would be nice to be able to push that data to the client as it becomes available. That's exactly what SSE allows us to do. We'll look into that in more detail later.

Finally, we start the server instance with a call to `JettyHttpContainerFactory.createServer()`. Since we need to be able to stop the server later, we capture the server instance, and store it in an instance variable. We call `startServer()` from `onStartCommand()` as follows:

```
private static final Object lock = new Object();
public int onStartCommand(Intent intent, int flags, int startId) {
  super.onStartCommand(intent, flags, startId);
  synchronized (lock) {
    if (server == null) {
      startServer();
      messageReceiver = new BroadcastReceiver() {
```

```
        @Override
        public void onReceive(Context context,
          Intent intent) {
            String code = intent.getStringExtra("code");
            DeskDroidService.this.code = code;
            Log.d("receiver", "Got code: " + code);
        }
    };
    LocalBroadcastManager.getInstance(this).
      registerReceiver(
        messageReceiver,
          new IntentFilter(CODE_GENERATED));
    }
  }
  return Service.START_STICKY;
}
```

Notice that we've wrapped our call to `startServer()` in a `synchronized` block. For those that might be unaware, `synchronized` is one of the more basic approaches to concurrent code available to Java developers. The net effect of this keyword is that multiple threads that try to execute this block of code must do so synchronously, or one a time. We do this here so that if we have two different processes attempting to start the server, we can guarantee that at most one is running. Without this block, the first thread could start the server and store the instance in the variable, while a second thread could do the same thing, but its server instance, which gets stored in the variable, fails to start. We would now have a running server with no valid reference to it, so we would be unable to stop it.

We have also registered a `BroadcastReceiver` that listens for `CODE_GENERATED`. We'll come back and explain this later in the chapter, so don't worry about this for now.

Controlling the service state

If we run the application now, our service won't run, so we need to make it such that it will run. We'll do that in a couple of different ways. The first way will be from our application. We want to make sure the service is running when we open the application, especially after it is just installed. To do that, we need to add one line to `MainActivity.onCreate()` as follows:

```
startService(new Intent(this, DeskDroidService.class));
```

When the application is started now, it will guarantee that the service is running. We don't, though, want to require that the user open the application to run the service. Fortunately, we have a way to start the application when the phone starts. We can do that by installing a `BroadcastReceiver` that listens for boot events, as shown here:

```
public class BootReceiver extends BroadcastReceiver {
  @Override
  public void onReceive(Context context, Intent intent) {
    context.startService(new Intent(context,
      DeskDroidService.class));
  }
}
```

The body of the preceding method is identical to our recent addition to `MainActivity`. We do, though, need to register the service, and ask for permission. In `AndroidManifest.xml`, we need to add this:

```
<uses-permission android:name=
  "android.permission.RECEIVE_BOOT_COMPLETED" />
<receiver android:name=".BootReceiver" android:enabled="true">
  <intent-filter>
    <action android:name=
    "android.intent.action.BOOT_COMPLETED" />
  </intent-filter>
</receiver>
```

We now have a service that starts either at device boot or application startup. It does not, however, do anything of interest, so we need to add some endpoints to our server.

Adding endpoints to the server

As covered in Chapter 9, *Taking Notes with Monumentum*, a JAX-RS resource lives in a POJO with certain annotations. To stub out our endpoint class, we can start with this:

```
@Path("/")
@Produces(MediaType.APPLICATION_JSON)
protected class DeskDroidResource {
}
```

We will also need to register this class with JAX-RS, which we do with this line in `startServer()`:

```
config.registerInstances(new DeskDroidResource());
```

Ordinarily, we would pass, say, `DeskDroidResource.class`, to the `ResourceConfig` constructor, like we did with `JacksonFeature.class`. We will be accessing Android resources, and to do that, we're going to need the `Service`'s `Context` instance. There are a number of resources on the internet that will suggest creating a custom `Application` class and storing it in a `public static`. While that does seem to work, it will also leak memory, so, Android Studio, for example, will complain if you try that. We can, however, avoid that by using nested classes. That approach can get a bit unwieldy, but our classes should be small enough that it remains manageable.

Getting conversations

Let's start by adding an endpoint to get all of the conversations on the phone, as follows:

```
@GET
@Path("conversations")
public Response getConversations() {
  List<Conversation> conversations = new ArrayList<>();
  Cursor cur = getApplication().getContentResolver()
  .query(Telephony.Sms.Conversations.CONTENT_URI,
  null, null, null, null);
  while (cur.moveToNext()) {
    conversations.add(buildConversation(cur));
  }

  Collections.sort(conversations, new ConversationComparator());

  return Response.ok(new GenericEntity<List<Conversation>>(
  conversations) {}).build();
}
```

Here is where we see the Android artifacts start to show up--we are going to use a `ContentProvider` to access the SMS data. A `ContentProvider` is a way for an application, or, in this case, an Android subsystem, to expose data to outside consumers in a portable, storage-agnostic manner. We don't care how the data is stored. We simply specify what fields we want, what filters or restrictions we want placed on that data, and `ContentProvider` does the rest.

Using `ContentProviders`, we specify the type of data not by a table name, like we would with SQL, but with a `Uri`. In this case, we specify `Telephony.Sms.Conversations.CONTENT_URI`. We pass several null values to `query()` as well. These represent the projection (or field list), the selection (or filter), the selection arguments, and the sort order. Since these are all `null`, we want every field and every row in the natural sort order for the provider. That gets us a `Cursor` object, which we then iterate over, creating `Conversation` objects, and add them to our `List`.

We create the `Conversation` instances with this method:

```
private Conversation buildConversation(Cursor cur) {
  Conversation conv = new Conversation();
  final int threadId =
    cur.getInt(cur.getColumnIndex("thread_id"));
  conv.setThreadId(threadId);
  conv.setMessageCount(
    cur.getInt(cur.getColumnIndex("msg_count")));
  conv.setSnippet(cur.getString(cur.getColumnIndex("snippet")));
  final List<Message> messages =
    getSmsMessages(conv.getThreadId());
  Set<String> participants = new HashSet<>();
  for (Message message : messages) {
    if (!message.isMine()) {
      participants.add(message.getAddress());
    }
  }
  conv.setParticipants(participants);
  conv.setMessages(messages);
  return conv;
}
```

Each conversation is just a thread ID, message count, and snippet, which is the last message received. To get the actual messages, we call `getSmsMessages()` as follows:

```
private List<Message> getSmsMessages(int threadId) {
  List<Message> messages = new ArrayList<>();
  Cursor cur = null;
  try {
    cur = getApplicationContext().getContentResolver()
      .query(Telephony.Sms.CONTENT_URI,
      null, "thread_id = ?", new String[]
      {Integer.toString(threadId)},
      "date DESC");

    while (cur.moveToNext()) {
      Message message = new Message();
      message.setId(cur.getInt(cur.getColumnIndex("_id")));
```

```
      message.setThreadId(cur.getInt(
         cur.getColumnIndex("thread_id")));
      message.setAddress(cur.getString(
         cur.getColumnIndex("address")));
      message.setBody(cur.getString(
         cur.getColumnIndexOrThrow("body")));
      message.setDate(new Date(cur.getLong(
         cur.getColumnIndexOrThrow("date"))));
      message.setMine(cur.getInt(
         cur.getColumnIndex("type")) ==
            Telephony.Sms.MESSAGE_TYPE_SENT);
      messages.add(message);
   }
} catch (Exception e) {
   e.printStackTrace();
} finally {
   if (cur != null) {
      cur.close();
   }
}
return messages;
}
```

This method, and the processing logic, is mostly identical to that for conversations. The Uri for the ContentProvider, Telephony.Sms.CONTENT_URI, is different, of course, and we specify a filter for the query as follows:

```
cur = getApplicationContext().getContentResolver().query(
   Telephony.Sms.CONTENT_URI,
   null, "thread_id = ?", new String[]
   {Integer.toString(threadId)},
   "date DESC");
```

We do have a slight bit of data analysis here. We need to know which of the messages are the ones we sent and which are the ones we received so that we can display the thread more meaningfully. On the device, the messages we've sent have the type Telephony.Sms.MESSAGE_TYPE_SENT. The values for this field translate roughly to folders (sent, received, draft, and so on). Rather than leaking part of the Android API into ours by sharing the value of the constant, we have a boolean field, isMine, which is true if the message is of type MESSAGE_TYPE_SENT. It is, admittedly, a slightly clumsy alternative, but it works and should be clear enough.

Once we return the list of messages, we iterate over the list, getting a list of the unique participants (which should be only one, since we are dealing with SMS messages).

Finally, we return this `List<Conversation>` to the client using Jersey's POJO-mapping feature as follows:

```
return Response.ok(new GenericEntity<List<Conversation>>(
    conversations) {}).build();
```

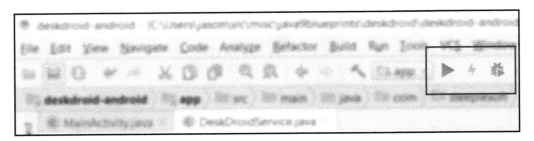

If we click either the run or debug buttons (the large triangle or the triangle-over-a-bug icons in the tool bar), you'll be asked for the deployment target, as seen in this screenshot:

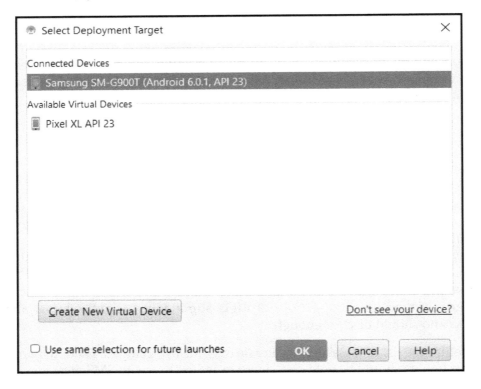

Since we require Wi-Fi, I select my physical device. If you want to configure an emulator with Wi-Fi, that would work as well. Click on **OK**, and after a few moments, the application should start on the device you have selected, and we can make our first REST request as follows:

```
$ curl http://192.168.0.2:49152/conversations | jq .
[
  {
    "messageCount": 2,
    "messages": [
      {
        "address": "5551234567",
        "body": "Demo message",
        "date": 1493269498618,
        "id": 301,
        "mine": true,
        "threadId": 89
      },
      {
        "address": "+15551234567",
        "body": "Demo message",
        "date": 1493269498727,
        "id": 302,
        "mine": false,
        "threadId": 89
      }
    ],
    "participants": [ "+15551234567" ],
    "snippet": "Demo message",
    "threadId": 89
  }
]
```

This preceding sample code shows a conversation I'm having with myself. Too many late nights, perhaps, but you can see where the first message, the oldest message, is marked as mine, which is the one I sent to myself, and the second is where I received it back. Pretty cool, but how do you send a message? It turns out that that's actually quite simple.

Sending an SMS message

To send a message, we will create a POST endpoint that takes a `Message` object, which we'll then pull apart and pass to Android's telephony APIs.

```
@POST
@Path("conversations")
public Response sendMessage(Message message)
```

```
throws InterruptedException {
    final SmsManager sms = SmsManager.getDefault();
    final ArrayList<String> parts =
    sms.divideMessage(message.getBody());
    final CountDownLatch sentLatch =
    new CountDownLatch(parts.size());
    final AtomicInteger statusCode = new AtomicInteger(
    Response.Status.CREATED.getStatusCode());
    final BroadcastReceiver receiver = new BroadcastReceiver() {
    @Override
    public void onReceive(Context context, Intent intent) {
        if (getResultCode() != Activity.RESULT_OK) {
            statusCode.set(
                Response.Status.INTERNAL_SERVER_ERROR
                    .getStatusCode());
        }
        sentLatch.countDown();
    }
    };
    registerReceiver(receiver,
    new IntentFilter("com.steeplesoft.deskdroid.SMS_SENT"));
    ArrayList<PendingIntent> sentPIs = new ArrayList<>();
    for (int i = 0; i < parts.size(); i++) {
        sentPIs.add(PendingIntent.getBroadcast(
            getApplicationContext(), 0,
            new Intent("com.steeplesoft.deskdroid.SMS_SENT"), 0));
    }
    sms.sendMultipartTextMessage(message.getAddress(), null,
    parts, sentPIs, null);

    sentLatch.await(5, TimeUnit.SECONDS);
    unregisterReceiver(receiver);
    return Response.status(statusCode.get()).build();
}
```

There's a lot going on this method. Here is the breakdown:

1. We get a reference to the `SmsManager` class. This class will do all of the work for us.
2. We ask `SmsManager` to divide the message for us. Text messages are, typically, limited to 160 characters, so this will split the message as needed.
3. We create a `CountDownLatch` with a count that matches the number of parts in the message.

4. We create an `AtomicInteger` to store the status code. As we'll see in a moment, we need to change the value of this variable from inside an anonymous class. However, for an anonymous class to access variables from its enclosing scope, those variables must be `final`, which means that we can not have a `final int`, as then we would not be able to change the value. With `AtomicInteger`, though, we can call `set()` to change the value while leaving the instance reference, which is what the variable will hold, unchanged.

5. We create a new `BroadcastReceiver`, which will handle `Intents` broadcast (as we'll see further) when the message is sent. In `onReceive()`, if the result code is not `ACTIVITY.RESULT_OK`, we call `AtomicInteger.set()` to reflect the failure. We then call `sentLatch.countDown()` to indicate that this message part has been processed.

6. With the call to `registerReceiver()`, we let the operating system know about our new receiver. We provide an `IntentFilter` to restrict which `Intents` our receiver has to process.

7. We then create a new `PendingIntent` for each part our message has been split into. This will allow us to react to each part's send attempt individually.

8. We call `sendMultipartTextMessage()` to send the message part(s). Android handles the details of a multipart message for us, so there's no extra effort required.

9. We need to wait for all of the message parts to be sent, so we call `sentLatch.await()` to give the system time to send the message. We don't want to wait forever, though, so we give it a timeout of five seconds, which should be long enough. It is conceivable that some networks may be very slow about sending text messages, so this value may need to be adjusted.

10. Once we pass the latch, we `unregister` our receiver, and return the status code.

Using curl again, we can now test sending a message (be sure to click on `Run` or `Debug` again to deploy your updated code):

```
$ curl -v -X POST -H 'Content-type: application/json'
http://192.168.0.2:49152/conversations -d
'{"address":"++15551234567", "body":"Lorem ipsum dolor sit
 amet..."}'
> POST /conversations HTTP/1.1
> Content-type: application/json
> Content-Length: 482
< HTTP/1.1 201 Created
```

In the preceding `curl` we send some `lorem ipsum` text to our recipient, which gives us a nice, long message (482 total characters for the request payload), which is correctly chunked up and sent to the destination phone number, as indicated by the `201 Created` response status.

We now have a working REST service on the phone, which lets us read the existing messages and send new ones. Interacting with the service with `curl` has worked well enough, but it's time to build our desktop client, and put a nice face on this project.

Creating the desktop application

To build our application, we'll return to NetBeans and JavaFX. As in the previous chapters, we'll create a new Maven-based JavaFX application by clicking on **File** | **New Project**:

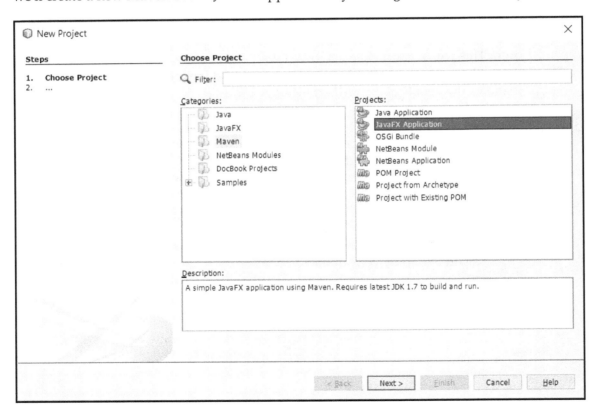

In the next step, call the project `deskdroid-desktop`, verify the package name, and click on **Finish**. While not strictly necessary, let's clean up the naming a bit, changing the controller to `DeskDroidController`, and the FXML file to `deskdroid.fxml`. We'll also need to modify the references to the FXML and the CSS in the controller, and the reference to the controller in the FXML. Click on **Run | Run Project** to make sure everything is wired up correctly. Once the app starts, we can immediately close it so we can start making changes.

Defining the user interface

Let's start by building up the user interface. Here's what the application will look like:

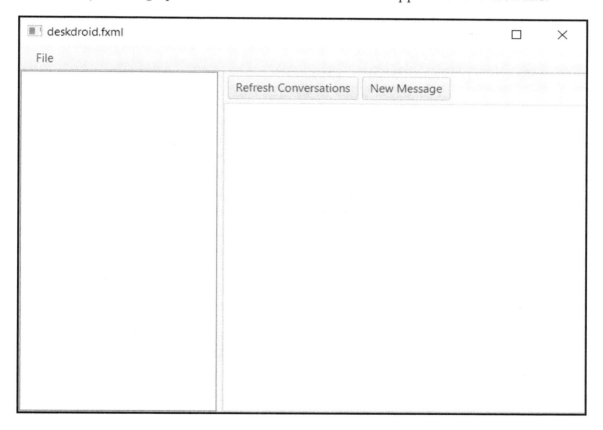

In the preceding screen, we'll have our list of conversations on the left, and we will display the selected conversation on the right. We will add a mechanism for auto-refreshing, but the **Refresh Conversations** will allow for a manual refresh, if needed. **New Message** should be self-explanatory.

We can use Gluon's Scene Builder to build the user interface, of course, but let's take a look at the FXML. We'll start, as usual, with a `BorderPane`, as follows:

```
<BorderPane fx:id="borderPane" minWidth="1024" prefHeight="768"
xmlns="http://javafx.com/javafx/8.0.111"
xmlns:fx="http://javafx.com/fxml/1"
fx:controller="com.steeplesoft.deskdroid.
desktop.DeskDroidController">
```

For the `top` section, we're going to add a menu bar as follows:

```
<MenuBar BorderPane.alignment="CENTER">
  <menus>
    <Menu text="_File">
        <items>
            <MenuItem onAction="#connectToPhone"
                text="_Connect to Phone" />
            <MenuItem onAction="#disconnectFromPhone"
                text="_Disconnect from Phone" />
            <MenuItem onAction="#closeApplication"
                text="E_xit">
                <accelerator>
                    <KeyCodeCombination alt="ANY" code="F4"
                        control="UP" meta="UP" shift="UP"
                        shortcut="UP" />
                </accelerator>
            </MenuItem>
        </items>
    </Menu>
  </menus>
</MenuBar>
```

We'll have three `MenuItems` in the `FileMenu`: `connectToPhone`, `disconnectFromPhone`, and `Exit`. Each menu item will have a mnemonic, as indicated by the underscores. The `ExitMenuItem` has an accelerator key, `ALT-F4`.

We'll put the bulk of the user interface in the `center` section. The vertical split allows us to resize the two sides of the user interface. For that, we use a `SplitPane` as follows:

```
<center>
  <SplitPane dividerPositions="0.25"
    BorderPane.alignment="CENTER">
  <items>
```

With `dividerPositions`, we set the default split at the 25% mark along the horizontal rule. The `SplitPane` has a nested `items` element to hold its children to which we add the left element, `ListView`:

```
<VBox>
  <children>
    <ListView fx:id="convList" VBox.vgrow="ALWAYS" />
  </children>
</VBox>
```

We wrap `ListView` in a `VBox` to make the `ListView` grow and shrink, as needed, more easily.

Finally, let's build the right side of the user interface:

```
<VBox fx:id="convContainer">
  <children>
  <HBox>
      <children>
          <Button mnemonicParsing="false"
                  onAction="#refreshConversations"
                  text="Refresh Conversations">
              <HBox.margin>
                  <Insets right="5.0" />
              </HBox.margin>
          </Button>
          <Button fx:id="newMessageBtn"
              text="New Message" />
      </children>
      <padding>
          <Insets bottom="5.0" left="5.0"
              right="5.0" top="5.0" />
      </padding>
  </HBox>
  <ListView fx:id="messageList" VBox.vgrow="ALWAYS" />
  </children>
</VBox>
```

On the right side, we also have a VBox, which we use to arrange our two user interface elements. The first is HBox, which holds two buttons: **Refresh Conversation** and **New Message**. The second is our ListView for displaying the selected conversation.

Defining user interface behavior

While we can define the structure of the user interface in FXML in all but the most trivial applications, the user interface still requires some Java code to finish defining its behavior. We'll do that now in DeskDroidController.initialize(). We'll start with the left side of the user interface, the conversation list, as follows:

```
@FXML
private ListView<Conversation> convList;
private final ObservableList<Conversation> conversations =
FXCollections.observableArrayList();
private final SimpleObjectProperty<Conversation> conversation =
new SimpleObjectProperty<>();
@Override
public void initialize(URL url, ResourceBundle rb) {
  convList.setCellFactory(list ->
  new ConversationCell(convList));
  convList.setItems(conversations);
   convList.getSelectionModel().selectedItemProperty()
       .addListener((observable, oldValue, newValue) -> {
           conversation.set(newValue);
           messages.setAll(newValue.getMessages());
           messageList.scrollTo(messages.size() - 1);
}) ;
```

We declare an injectable variable to hold a reference to our ListView. JavaFX will set that value for us, thanks to the annotation @FXML. ListView will need a model to display, which we declare as conversations, and we declare conversation to hold the currently selected conversation.

In the initialize() method, we wire everything together. Since ListView will be displaying our domain object, we need to declare a CellFactory for it, which we do with the lambda passed to setCellFactory(). We'll look at ListCell in a moment.

Next, we associate ListView with its model, conversations, and define what is, in effect, an onClick listener. We achieve that, though, by adding a listener to SelectionModel on ListView. In that listener, we update the currently selected conversation, update the messages ListView to display the conversation, and scroll that ListView to the very bottom so that we see the most recent message.

Initializing the message `ListView` is much simpler. We need these instance variables:

```
@FXML
private ListView<Message> messageList;
private final ObservableList<Message> messages =
FXCollections.observableArrayList();
```

We also need these lines in `initialize()`:

```
messageList.setCellFactory(list -> new MessageCell(messageList));
messageList.setItems(messages);
```

And the **New Message** button needs a handler:

```
newMessageBtn.setOnAction(event -> sendNewMessage());
```

`ConversationCell` tells JavaFX how to display a `Conversation` instance. To do that, we create a new `ListCell` child as follows:

```
public class ConversationCell extends ListCell<Conversation> {
```

Then we override `updateItem()`:

```
@Override
protected void updateItem(Conversation conversation,
boolean empty) {
super.updateItem(conversation, empty);
if (conversation != null) {
    setWrapText(true);
    final Participant participant =
        ConversationService.getInstance()
            .getParticipant(conversation
                .getParticipant());
    HBox hbox = createWrapper(participant);

    hbox.getChildren().add(
        createConversationSnippet(participant,
            conversation.getSnippet()));
    setGraphic(hbox);
} else {
    setGraphic(null);
}
}
}
```

If the cell is given a `Conversation`, we process it. If not, we set the cell's graphic to null. If we fail to do that, we'll have unpredictable results when scrolling through the lists.

To build the cell contents, we start by getting the `Participant` and creating the wrapper component as follows:

```
protected HBox createWrapper(final Participant participant) {
    HBox hbox = new HBox();
    hbox.setManaged(true);
    ImageView thumbNail = new ImageView();
    thumbNail.prefWidth(65);
    thumbNail.setPreserveRatio(true);
    thumbNail.setFitHeight(65);
    thumbNail.setImage(new Image(
        ConversationService.getInstance()
            .getParticipantThumbnail(
                participant.getPhoneNumber())));
    hbox.getChildren().add(thumbNail);
    return hbox;
}
```

This is pretty standard JavaFX fare--create an `HBox`, and add to it an `ImageView`. We are, though, using a class we haven't looked at yet--`ConversationService`. We'll look at this later, but for now, it's enough to know that we will encapsulate our REST calls in this class. Here, we're calling an endpoint (that we haven't seen yet) to get the contact information for the phone number at the other end of this conversation.

We also need to create the conversation snippet as follows:

```
protected VBox createConversationSnippet(
  final Participant participant, String snippet) {
    VBox vbox = new VBox();
    vbox.setPadding(new Insets(0, 0, 0, 5));
    Label sender = new Label(participant.getName());
    sender.setWrapText(true);
    Label phoneNumber = new Label(participant.getPhoneNumber());
    phoneNumber.setWrapText(true);
    Label label = new Label(snippet);
    label.setWrapText(true);
    vbox.getChildren().addAll(sender, phoneNumber, label);
    return vbox;
}
```

Using `VBox` to ensure vertical alignment, we create two labels, one with the participants' information, and the other with the snippet of the conversation.

While that finishes the cell definition, if we were to run the application the way it is now, the `ListCell`'s contents would likely be cropped by the edge of `ListView` itself. For example, see the difference between the top list and the bottom list in the following screenshot:

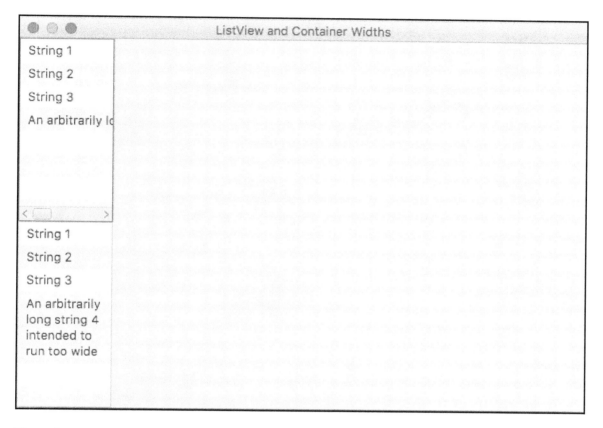

To make our `ListCell` behave as we see at the bottom of the last screen, we need to make one more change to our code, which is as follows:

```
public ConversationCell(ListView list) {
    super();
    prefWidthProperty().bind(list.widthProperty().subtract(2));
    setMaxWidth(Control.USE_PREF_SIZE);
}
```

In our preceding `CellFactory`, we pass in the reference to the enclosing `ListView`.

```
convList.setCellFactory(list -> new ConversationCell(convList));
```

In the constructor, we then bind the preferred width of our cell to the actual width of the list (and subtract a small amount to adjust for the control borders). When rendered now, our cell will wrap just as we expected.

The `MessageCell` definition is similar, and goes as follows:

```
public class MessageCell extends ListCell<Message> {
  public MessageCell(ListView list) {
      prefWidthProperty()
        .bind(list.widthProperty().subtract(20));
      setMaxWidth(Control.USE_PREF_SIZE);
  }

  @Override
  public void updateItem(Message message, boolean empty) {
      super.updateItem(message, empty);
      if (message != null && !empty) {
          if (message.isMine()) {
              wrapMyMessage(message);
          } else {
              wrapTheirMessage(message);
          }
       } else {
          setGraphic(null);
      }
  }
}
```

For *my* message, we create the contents this way:

```
private static final SimpleDateFormat DATE_FORMAT =
 new SimpleDateFormat("EEE, MM/dd/yyyy hh:mm aa");
private void wrapMyMessage(Message message) {
 HBox hbox = new HBox();
 hbox.setAlignment(Pos.TOP_RIGHT);
 createMessageBox(message, hbox, Pos.TOP_RIGHT);
 setGraphic(hbox);
}
private void createMessageBox(Message message, Pane parent,
 Pos alignment) {
   VBox vbox = new VBox();
   vbox.setAlignment(alignment);
   vbox.setPadding(new Insets(0,0,0,5));
   Label body = new Label();
   body.setWrapText(true);
```

```
body.setText(message.getBody());

Label date = new Label();
date.setText(DATE_FORMAT.format(message.getDate()));

vbox.getChildren().addAll(body,date);
parent.getChildren().add(vbox);
}
```

The **message box** is much like the previous conversation snippet--a vertical display of the message, followed by its date and time. This format will be used by *my* messages and *their* messages, so we use `javafx.geometry.Pos` to align the controls to the right or left, respectively.

The *their* message is created this way:

```
private void wrapTheirMessage(Message message) {
    HBox hbox = new HBox();
    ImageView thumbNail = new ImageView();
    thumbNail.prefWidth(65);
    thumbNail.setPreserveRatio(true);
    thumbNail.setFitHeight(65);
    thumbNail.setImage(new Image(
            ConversationService.getInstance()
                .getParticipantThumbnail(
                    message.getAddress())));
    hbox.getChildren().add(thumbNail);
    createMessageBox(message, hbox, Pos.TOP_LEFT);
    setGraphic(hbox);
}
```

This is similar to the *my* message, with the exception that we display the sender's profile picture, if there is one associated with the contact on the phone, which we retrieve from the phone via the `ConversationService` class.

We have a bit more work to do, but this is what the application will look like with data:

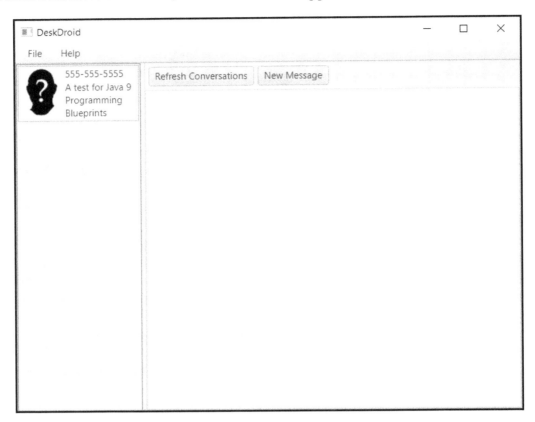

To get the data, we need a REST client, and that is found in `ConversationService`:

```
public class ConversationService {
  public static class LazyHolder {
    public static final ConversationService INSTANCE =
        new ConversationService();
  }
  public static ConversationService getInstance() {
    return LazyHolder.INSTANCE;
  }
  private ConversationService() {
    Configuration configuration = new ResourceConfig()
            .register(JacksonFeature.class)
            .register(SseFeature.class);
    client = ClientBuilder.newClient(configuration);
  }
```

Using the so-called *Initialize-on-Demand Holder* idiom, we create a sort of a poor man's singleton. Since the constructor is private, it can't be called from outside this class. The nested static class, `LazyHolder`, is initialized only when it is finally referenced, which happens on the first call to `getInstance()`. Once that method is called, `LazyHolder` is loaded and initialized, at which point, the constructor is run. The instance created is stored in the static variable, and lives as long as the JVM runs. Every subsequent call will return the same instance. This is important for us, as we have some objects that are expensive to create as well as some simple caching in the class:

```
protected final Client client;
protected final Map<String, Participant> participants =
    new HashMap<>();
```

In the preceding code, we initialize our client instance, registering the `JacksonFeature`, which gets us the POJO mapping we've already discussed. We also register `SseFeature`, a more advanced feature of Jersey that we'll discuss in detail later.

We've already seen the conversation list. That is generated using data from this method:

```
public List<Conversation> getConversations() {
  List<Conversation> list;
  try {
   list = getWebTarget().path("conversations")
            .request(MediaType.APPLICATION_JSON)
            .header(HttpHeaders.AUTHORIZATION,
               getAuthorizationHeader())
            .get(new GenericType<List<Conversation>>() {});
  } catch (Exception ce) {
   list = new ArrayList<>();
  }
  return list;
}
public WebTarget getWebTarget() {
return client.target("http://"
        + preferences.getPhoneAddress() + ":49152/");
}
```

`WebTarget` is a JAX-RS class that represents the *resource target identified by the resource URI*. We're pulling the address for the phone from preferences, which we'll discuss later. Once we have our `WebTarget`, we complete building the URI by appending `conversations`, specify the request mime type, and issue the `GET` request. Note that our request here is somewhat optimistic, as we don't do any status code checking. Should an `Exception` be thrown, we simply return an empty `List`.

The other method we've seen is `getParticipant()`, which is as follows:

```
public Participant getParticipant(String number) {
  Participant p = participants.get(number);
  if (p == null) {
    Response response = getWebTarget()
              .path("participants")
              .path(number)
              .request(MediaType.APPLICATION_JSON)
              .header(HttpHeaders.AUTHORIZATION,
                  getAuthorizationHeader())
              .get(Response.class);
    if (response.getStatus() == 200) {
        p = response.readEntity(Participant.class);
        participants.put(number, p);
        if (p.getThumbnail() != null) {
            File thumb = new File(number + ".png");
            try (OutputStream stream =
                    new FileOutputStream(thumb)) {
                byte[] data = DatatypeConverter
                    .parseBase64Binary(p.getThumbnail());
                stream.write(data);
            } catch (IOException e) {
                e.printStackTrace();
            }
        }
    }
  }
  return p;
}
```

In the last method, we see our cache come into play. When a `Participant` is requested, we look to see if this information has already been fetched. If so, we return the cached information. If not, we can make a request for it.

Much like `getConversations()`, we build a request for the appropriate endpoint, and send the GET request. This time, though, we do check for the status code. Only if the status is 200 (OK) do we continue processing the response. In this case, we ask JAX-RS for the `Participant` instance returned, which `JacksonFeature` happily builds for us from the JSON response body, and which we immediately add to our cache.

If the server found a thumbnail for the contact, we need to process that. The server piece, which we will look at immediately after we finish discussing this method, sends the thumbnail as a base 64-encoded string in the body of the JSON object, so we convert it back to the binary representation, and save that to a file. Notice that we are using try-with-resources, so we need not worry about cleaning up after ourselves.

```
try (OutputStream stream = new FileOutputStream(thumb))
```

We haven't seen the server side of this operation, so let's look at that now. In our Android application in Android Studio, we have this method on `DeskDroidResource`:

```
@GET
@Path("participants/{address}")
public Response getParticipant(@PathParam("address")
String address) {
  Participant p = null;
  try {
    p = getContactsDetails(address);
    } catch (IOException e) {
    return Response.serverError().build();
  }
  if (p == null) {
    return Response.status(Response.Status.NOT_FOUND).build();
  } else {
    return Response.ok(p).build();
  }
}
```

We attempt to build the `Participant` instance. If an Exception is thrown, we return a 500 (Server Error). If `null` is returned, we return a 404 (Not Found). If a participant is found, we return 200 (OK) and the participant.

To build the participant, we need to query the phone contacts. This works in much the same way as the SMS queries:

```
protected Participant getContactsDetails(String address) throws
  IOException {
  Uri contactUri = Uri.withAppendedPath(
    ContactsContract.PhoneLookup.CONTENT_FILTER_URI,
    Uri.encode(address));
    Cursor phones = deskDroidService.getApplicationContext()
    .getContentResolver().query(contactUri,
    new String[]{
      ContactsContract.CommonDataKinds.Phone.DISPLAY_NAME,
      "number",
      ContactsContract.CommonDataKinds.Phone
        .PHOTO_THUMBNAIL_URI},
```

```
            null, null, null);
        Participant participant = new Participant();
        if (phones.moveToNext()) {
          participant.setName(phones.getString(phones
            .getColumnIndex(
          ContactsContract.CommonDataKinds.Phone
            .DISPLAY_NAME)));
          participant.setPhoneNumber(phones.getString(
            phones.getColumnIndex("number")));
          String image_uri = phones.getString(
            phones.getColumnIndex(
              ContactsContract.CommonDataKinds.Phone
                .PHOTO_THUMBNAIL_URI));
          if (image_uri != null) {
            try (InputStream input = deskDroidService
              .getApplicationContext().getContentResolver()
              .openInputStream(Uri.parse(image_uri));
            ByteArrayOutputStream buffer =
              new ByteArrayOutputStream()) {
                int nRead;
                byte[] data = new byte[16384];

                while ((nRead = input.read(data, 0,
                        data.length)) != -1) {
                    buffer.write(data, 0, nRead);
                }

                buffer.flush();
                participant.setThumbnail(Base64
                    .encodeToString(buffer.toByteArray(),
                        Base64.DEFAULT));
            } catch (IOException e) {
                e.printStackTrace();
            }
          }
        }
        phones.close();
        return participant;
    }
```

The preceding is the same type of query and cursor management that we saw earlier with conversations, but there is one exception. If the contact has a thumbnail, the query returns a Uri to that image. We can use ContentResolver to open an InputStream using that Uri to read the contents, which we load into ByteArrayOutputStream. Using Android's Base64 class, we encode this binary image into a String, and add that to our Participant model. We saw the decoding half of this operation previously.

Sending messages

Now that we can see the conversations that we've been having, we need to add the ability to take part in those conversations--to send new text messages. We'll start on the client. We've actually already seen the handler for the New Message button assigned. It is as follows:

```
newMessageBtn.setOnAction(event -> sendNewMessage());
```

What we need to do now is to look at this sendNewMessage() method itself:

```
private void sendNewMessage() {
    Optional<String> result = SendMessageDialogController
        .showAndWait(conversation.get());
    if (result.isPresent()) {
        Conversation conv = conversation.get();
        Message message = new Message();
        message.setThreadId(conv.getThreadId());
        message.setAddress(conv.getParticipant());
        message.setBody(result.get());
        message.setMine(true);
        if (cs.sendMessage(message)) {
            conv.getMessages().add(message);
            messages.add(message);
        } else {
            Alert alert = new Alert(AlertType.ERROR);
            alert.setTitle("Error");
            alert.setHeaderText(
                "An error occured while sending the message.");
            alert.showAndWait();
        }
    }
}
```

The actual dialog is displayed in another window, so we have a separate FXML file, message_dialog.fxml, and controller, SendMessageDialogController. When the dialog closes, we check the return Optional to see if the user entered a message. If so, process the message as follows:

1. Get a reference to the selected Conversation.
2. Create a new message, setting the conversation ID, recipient, and body.
3. Using ConversationService, we attempt to send the message:
    1. If successful, we update the user interface with the new message.
    2. If unsuccessful, we display an error message.

`SendMessageController` works just like the other controllers we've looked at. The most interesting is the method `showAndWait()`. We'll use that method to show the dialog, wait for it to close, and return any user response to the caller. The dialog looks as follows:

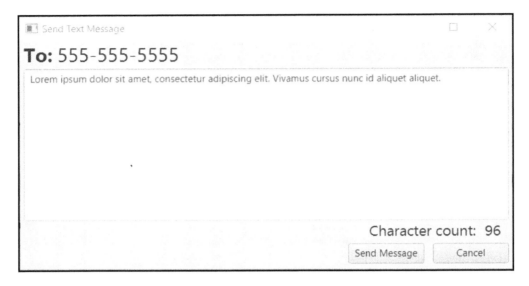

The method looks as follows:

```
public static Optional<String> showAndWait(
  Conversation conversation) {
  try {
    FXMLLoader loader =
        new FXMLLoader(SendMessageDialogController.class
            .getResource("/fxml/message_dialog.fxml"));
    Stage stage = new Stage();
    stage.setScene(new Scene(loader.load()));
    stage.setTitle("Send Text Message");
    stage.initModality(Modality.APPLICATION_MODAL);
    final SendMessageDialogController controller =
        (SendMessageDialogController) loader.getController();
    controller.setConversation(conversation);
    stage.showAndWait();
    return controller.getMessage();
  } catch (IOException ex) {
      throw new RuntimeException(ex);
  }
}
```

The first few lines in the preceding method are what we've normally seen, which is creating the loader and the `Stage`. Before showing the `Stage`, we set the modality, and pass in the current `Conversation`. Finally, we call `showAndWait()`, at which point the method blocks until the user closes the dialog, and then we return the entered message:

```
public Optional<String> getMessage() {
  return Optional.ofNullable(message);
}
```

A Java `Optional` is a *container object which may or may not contain a non-null value*. The value of `message` may or may not be set depending on which button is clicked in the dialog. Using the `Optional`, we can return a, possibly, null value, and handle it more safely in the caller--if (result.isPresent()).

The sending of the message is a simple POST operation in the `ConversationService`, which is as follows:

```
public boolean sendMessage(Message message) {
  Response r = getWebTarget().path("conversations")
    .request()
    .header(HttpHeaders.AUTHORIZATION,
      getAuthorizationHeader())
    .post(Entity.json(message));
  return r.getStatus() == Response.Status.CREATED
    .getStatusCode();
}
```

The client side is simple, but what about the server side? Unsurprisingly, that's where the complexity lies:

```
@POST
@Path("conversations")
public Response sendMessage(Message message) throws
InterruptedException {
  final SmsManager sms = SmsManager.getDefault();
  final ArrayList<String> parts =
    sms.divideMessage(message.getBody());
```

To add the endpoint, we define a new method with the correct annotations. This method will listen on the path `conversations` for POST requests, and expect a `Message` as its payload. The actual work of sending a message is handled by `SmsManager`, so we acquire a reference to the default manager. The next step calls `divideMessage()`, but what's that all about?

Text messages are technically limited to 160 characters. Twitter users are probably somewhat familiar with that already. Twitter limits tweets to 140 characters, leaving 20 characters for the sender's name. While Twitter has stuck hard to that limit, regular SMS users have a better experience. If the message is longer than 160 characters, most modern phones will chunk the message into 153 character segments when sending (with 7 characters for segmentation information used to piece the segments back together), which are merged back into one message on the receiving end if the phone supports it. The `SmsManager` API handles this complexity for us with `divideMessage()`.

Once the message is *chunked*, though, our job gets a little more difficult. We would like to be able to return a status code indicating whether or not the message was sent successfully. To do that, we need to check the status of each chunk of the message, be it one or ten. Sending a text message with `SmsManager`, Android broadcasts an `Intent` with the results. To react to that, we need to register a receiver. Put that all together, and we get this code:

```
final CountDownLatch sentLatch = new CountDownLatch(parts.size());
final AtomicInteger statusCode =
  new AtomicInteger(
    Response.Status.CREATED.getStatusCode());
final BroadcastReceiver receiver = new BroadcastReceiver() {
  @Override
  public void onReceive(Context context, Intent intent) {
    if (getResultCode() != Activity.RESULT_OK) {
      statusCode.set(Response.Status.
        INTERNAL_SERVER_ERROR.getStatusCode());
    }
    sentLatch.countDown();
  }
};
deskDroidService.registerReceiver(receiver,
  new IntentFilter("com.steeplesoft.deskdroid.SMS_SENT"));
ArrayList<PendingIntent> sentPIs = new ArrayList<>();
for (int i = 0; i < parts.size(); i++) {
  sentPIs.add(PendingIntent.getBroadcast(
    deskDroidService.getApplicationContext(), 0,
    new Intent("com.steeplesoft.deskdroid.SMS_SENT"), 0));
}
sms.sendMultipartTextMessage(message.getAddress(), null,
parts, sentPIs, null);
sentLatch.await(5, TimeUnit.SECONDS);
deskDroidService.unregisterReceiver(receiver);
return Response.status(statusCode.get()).build();
```

To make sure that we've received the `Intent` for each message chunk, we start by creating a `CountDownLatch` with a count matching the number of chunks in the message. We also create an `AtomicInteger` to hold the status code. The reason we do this is that we need a final variable which we can access from our `BroadcastReceiver`, but we also need to be able to change the value. `AtomicInteger` allows us to do that.

We create and register a `BroadcastReceiver`, which analyzes the result code on `Intent`. If it's not `Activity.RESULT_OK`, we set `statusCode` to `INTERNAL_SERVER_ERROR`. Either way, we count down the latch.

With our receiver ready, we create a `List` of `PendingIntent`s, one for each chunk, then we pass that, with our list of message chunks, to `SmsManager.sendMultipartTextMessage()`. Message sending is asynchronous, so we call `sentLatch.await()` to wait for the results to be returned. We limit the wait to five seconds so that we don't wait forever. Once the wait time expires or the latch is cleared, we unregister our receiver and return the status code.

Getting updates

So far, we can see all of the conversations, view individual messages in a conversation, and send new messages. What we can't do yet is get updates when new messages arrive on the device, so let's implement that now, starting with the server piece this time.

To get a constant stream of events, we'll use a feature called Server-Sent Events, a W3C specification for receiving push notifications from the server. We enabled this feature in Jersey by registering the `SseFeature` in both the client and server setup steps. To create an SSE endpoint, we specify that the method returns the media type `SERVER_SENT_EVENTS`, and we return an `EventOutput` as the payload:

```
@GET
@Path("status")
@Produces(SseFeature.SERVER_SENT_EVENTS)
@Secure
public EventOutput streamStatus() {
  final EventOutput eventOutput = new EventOutput();
  // ...
  return eventOutput;
}
```

From the Jersey documentation, we learn this:

> *After the eventOutput is returned from the method, the Jersey runtime recognizes that this is a ChunkedOutput extension and does not close the client connection immediately. Instead, it writes the HTTP headers to the response stream and waits for more chunks (SSE events) to be sent. At this point the client can read headers and starts listening for individual events.*

The server, then, keeps the socket to the client open, and pushes data down it. But where does the data come from? The Server-sent Event endpoints create a `Thread` that writes data to the `EventOutput` instance we created earlier. When the `Thread` is finished, it calls `eventOutput.close()`, which signals to the runtime that it is appropriate to close the client connection. To stream updates, our `Thread` looks as follows:

```
final Thread thread = new Thread() {
  @Override
  public void run() {
    final LinkedBlockingQueue<SmsMessage> queue =
      new LinkedBlockingQueue<>();
    BroadcastReceiver receiver = null;
    try {
      receiver = new BroadcastReceiver() {
        @Override
        public void onReceive(Context context,
          Intent intent) {
          Bundle intentExtras = intent.getExtras();
          if (intentExtras != null) {
            Object[] sms = (Object[])
              intentExtras.get("pdus");
            for (int i = 0; i < sms.length; ++i) {
              SmsMessage smsMessage =
                SmsMessage.createFromPdu(
                  (byte[]) sms[i]);
                  queue.add(smsMessage);
            }
          }
        }
      };
      deskDroidService.registerReceiver(receiver,
       new IntentFilter(
         "android.provider.Telephony.SMS_RECEIVED"));
      while (!eventOutput.isClosed()) {
        SmsMessage message = queue.poll(5,
         TimeUnit.SECONDS);
        while (message != null) {
          JSONObject json = new JSONObject()
```

```
                  .put("participant", message.
                  getDisplayOriginatingAddress())
                  .put("body", message.
                  getDisplayMessageBody());
                eventOutput.write(new OutboundEvent.Builder()
                .name("new-message")
                .data(json.toString())
                .build()
                );
                message = queue.poll();
            }
        }
    } catch (JSONException | InterruptedException |
      IOException e) {
        } finally {
            try {
                if (receiver != null) {
                    deskDroidService.unregisterReceiver(receiver);
                }
                eventOutput.close();
            } catch (IOException ioClose) {
                // ...
            }
        }
    }
};
thread.setDaemon(true);
thread.start();
```

As we've seen before, we set up a `BroadcastReceiver`, which we register here and unregister before the `Thread` ends, but this time, we're listening for broadcasts that an SMS message has been received. To make sure our `Thread` isn't in a small, tight, fast loop, which would quickly kill the battery on the device, we use `LinkedBlockingQueue`. When a message is received, we pull the `SmsMessage`(s) from `Intent`, and add them to `queue`. In our while loop, we attempt to `take()` an item from `queue`. If we find one, we process it and any more that might either already be in the queue or be added while we are processing. Once `queue` is empty, we go back to waiting. We have a timeout on `take()` to make sure that the thread can respond to the exit criteria, most notably, the client disconnecting. This will run as long as the client remains connected. Let's look, then, at the client.

We encapsulated the details in `ConversationService.subscribeToNewMessageEvents()` as follows:

```
public void subscribeToNewMessageEvents(
  Consumer<Message> callback) {
    Thread thread = new Thread() {
```

```
@Override
public void run() {
  stopListening = false;
  EventInput eventInput = getWebTarget().path("status")
    .request()
    .header(HttpHeaders.AUTHORIZATION,
     getAuthorizationHeader())
     .get(EventInput.class);
  while (!eventInput.isClosed() && !stopListening) {
    final InboundEvent inboundEvent =
      eventInput.read();
    if (inboundEvent == null) {
      // connection has been closed
      break;
    }
    if ("new-message".equals(inboundEvent.getName())){
      Message message =
        inboundEvent.readData(Message.class);
      if (message != null) {
        callback.accept(message);
      }
    }
  }
};
thread.setDaemon(true);
thread.start();
}
```

In the preceding code, we create a `Thread`, in which we make the call to the SSE endpoint. The return type on the client is `EventInput`. We loop to process each incoming event, which we get as an `InboundEvent`. If it is null, then the connection has been closed, so we break out of our processing loop. If it is not null, we make sure that the event name matches what we're waiting for--`new-message`. If found, we extract the event payload, a `Message`, and call our callback, which we pass in as `Consumer<Message>`.

From the application proper, we subscribe to the status stream this way:

```
cs.subscribeToNewMessageEvents(this::handleMessageReceived);
```

`handleMessageReceived()` looks like this:

```
protected void handleMessageReceived(final Message message) {
  Platform.runLater(() -> {
    Optional<Conversation> optional = conversations.stream()
      .filter(c -> Objects.equal(c.getParticipant(),
      message.getAddress()))
```

```
        .findFirst();
    if (optional.isPresent()) {
      Conversation c = optional.get();
      c.getMessages().add(message);
      c.setSnippet(message.getBody());
      convList.refresh();
      if (c == conversation.get()) {
        messages.setAll(c.getMessages());
        messageList.scrollTo(messages.size() - 1);
      }
    } else {
        Conversation newConv = new Conversation();
        newConv.setParticipant(message.getAddress());
        newConv.setSnippet(message.getBody());
        newConv.setMessages(Arrays.asList(message));
        conversations.add(0, newConv);
    }
    final Taskbar taskbar = Taskbar.getTaskbar();
    if (taskbar.isSupported(Taskbar.Feature.USER_ATTENTION)) {
      taskbar.requestUserAttention(true, false);
    }
    Toolkit.getDefaultToolkit().beep();
  });
}
```

The first step in handling this new message is very important--we pass a `Runnable` to `Platform.runLater()`. If we don't do this, any attempts to modify the user interface will fail. You have been warned. In our `Runnable`, we create a `Stream` of `Conversations`, `filter()` it, looking for a `Conversation` whose participant matches the `Message` sender, then grab the first (and only) match.

If we find the `Conversation` in the list, we add this new `Message` to its list, and update the snippet (which is just the `Conversation`'s last message body). We also ask the `Conversation` list to `refresh()` itself to make sure the user interface reflects these changes. Finally, if the `Conversation` is the currently selected one, we update the message list and scroll to the bottom to make sure the new message shows.

If we don't find the `Conversation` in the list, we create a new one, and add it to the `ConversationObservable`, which results in the `List` automatically updating on the screen.

Finally, we attempt a couple of desktop integration tasks. If `Taskbar` supports the USER_ATTENTION feature, we request user attention. From the Javadocs we learn that, *depending on the platform, this may be visually indicated by a bouncing or flashing icon in the task area.* Regardless, we issue a beep to get the user's attention.

Security

There's one last major piece that we haven't discussed, and that's security. Currently, anybody with the desktop application can, in theory, connect to your phone, see your messages, send others, and so on. Let's fix that now.

Securing the endpoints

To secure the REST server, we will use a filter just like we used in Chapter 9, *Taking Notes with Monumentum*. We'll start by defining the annotation that will specify which endpoints need to be secured, as follows:

```
@NameBinding
@Retention(RetentionPolicy.RUNTIME)
@Target({ElementType.TYPE, ElementType.METHOD})
public @interface Secure {}
```

We will apply this preceding annotation to each secured endpoint (annotations condensed to one line for brevity):

```
@GET @Path("conversations") @Secure
public Response getConversations() {
  ...
  @POST @Path("conversations") @Secure
  public Response sendMessage(Message message)
   throws InterruptedException {
    ...
    @GET @Path("status") @Produces(SseFeature.SERVER_SENT_EVENTS)
    @Secure
    public EventOutput streamStatus() {
      ...
      @GET @Path("participants/{address}") @Secure
      public Response getParticipant(
        @PathParam("address") String address) {
          ...
```

We will also need a filter to enforce security, which we add as follows:

```
@Provider
@Secure
@Priority(Priorities.AUTHENTICATION)
public class SecureFilter implements ContainerRequestFilter {
  private DeskDroidService deskDroidService;

  public SecureFilter(DeskDroidService deskDroidService) {
    this.deskDroidService = deskDroidService;
```

```
    }

    @Override
    public void filter(ContainerRequestContext requestContext)
      throws IOException {
        try {
          String authorizationHeader = requestContext.
           getHeaderString(HttpHeaders.AUTHORIZATION);
          String token = authorizationHeader.
           substring("Bearer".length()).trim();
          final Key key = KeyGenerator.
           getKey(deskDroidService.getApplicationContext());
          final JwtParser jwtParser =
            Jwts.parser().setSigningKey(key);
          jwtParser.parseClaimsJws(token);
        } catch (Exception e) {
            requestContext.abortWith(Response.status(
              Response.Status.UNAUTHORIZED).build());
        }
    }
  }
```

Much like in Chapter 9, *Taking Notes with Monumentum*, we'll be using **JSON Web Tokens (JWT)** to help authenticate and authorize clients. In this filter, we extract the JWT from the request headers and validate it through these steps:

1. Get the signing key from KeyGenerator.
2. Create the JwtParser using the signing key.
3. Parse the claims in the JWT. For our purposes here, this is, basically, just a validation of the token itself.
4. Abort the request with UNAUTHORIZED (401) should the token be invalid.

The KeyGenerator itself looks a bit like what we saw in Chapter 9, *Taking Notes with Monumentum*, but has been modified to use Android APIs in this manner:

```
    public class KeyGenerator {
      private static Key key;
      private static final Object lock = new Object();

      public static Key getKey(Context context) {
        synchronized (lock) {
          if (key == null) {
            SharedPreferences sharedPref =
              context.getSharedPreferences(
                context.getString(
                  R.string.preference_deskdroid),
```

```
                Context.MODE_PRIVATE);
            String signingKey = sharedPref.getString(
              context.getString(
                R.string.preference_signing_key), null);
            if (signingKey == null) {
              signingKey = UUID.randomUUID().toString();
              final SharedPreferences.Editor edit =
                sharedPref.edit();
              edit.putString(context.getString(
                R.string.preference_signing_key),
                  signingKey);
              edit.commit();
            }
            key = new SecretKeySpec(signingKey.getBytes(),
             0, signingKey.getBytes().length, "DES");
          }
        }

      return key;
    }
  }
```

Since we might possibly receive requests from multiple clients at a time, we need to be careful about how the key is generated. To make sure it's done once and only once, we'll use the same type of synchronization/locking we saw in the server startup.

Once we've acquired the lock, we perform a null check to see if the process has already generated (or read) the key. If not, we then read the signing key from SharedPreferences. If it's null, we create a random string (here, just a UUID), and save it to SharedPreferences for reuse next time. Note that to save to Android preferences, we have to get an instance of SharedPreferences.Editor, write the string, then commit(). Once we have the signing key, we create the actual SecretKeySpec that we'll use to sign and verify our JWTs.

Handling authorization requests

With our endpoints now secured, we need a way for the clients to request authorization. To do that, we'll expose a new endpoint, unsecured, of course, as follows:

```
@POST
@Path("authorize")
@Consumes(MediaType.TEXT_PLAIN)
public Response getAuthorization(String clientCode) {
    if (clientCode != null &&
      clientCode.equals(deskDroidService.code)) {
```

```
         String jwt = Jwts.builder()
           .setSubject("DeskDroid")
           .signWith(SignatureAlgorithm.HS512,
           KeyGenerator.getKey(
             deskDroidService.getApplicationContext()))
               .compact();
         LocalBroadcastManager.getInstance(
           deskDroidService.getApplicationContext())
           .sendBroadcast(new Intent(
             DeskDroidService.CODE_ACCEPTED));
       return Response.ok(jwt).build();
     }
     return Response.status(Response.Status.UNAUTHORIZED).build();
   }
```

Rather than require a more complicated authorization system that might require a username and password or an OAuth2 provider, what we'll implement is a simple system that requires only a random number:

1. On the phone, the user requests that a new client be added, and is presented with a random number.
2. In the desktop application, the user enters the number, which the desktop application then POSTs to the server.
3. If the numbers match, the client is given a JWT, which it will send with every request.
4. The JWT is verified each time to make sure the client is authorized to access the target resource.

In this method, we get the number POSTed by the client (which we let JAX-RS extract from the request body), then compare it to the number generated on the phone. If they match, we create the JWT, and return it to the client. Before doing so, we broadcast an intent with the action CODE_ACCEPTED.

Where does the number come from, and why are we broadcasting this intent? We haven't looked at this in detail yet, but in the main layout, activity_main.xml, there is a FloatingActionButton. To this, we attach an onClick listener as follows:

```
       FloatingActionButton fab =
         (FloatingActionButton) findViewById(R.id.fab);
       fab.setOnClickListener(new View.OnClickListener() {
         @Override
         public void onClick(View view) {
           startActivityForResult(new Intent(
             getApplicationContext(),
             AuthorizeClientActivity.class), 1);
```

```
    }
  });
```

When the user taps on the button, the following screen will be shown:

The client will use this information to connect and gain authorization. The `Activity` itself is fairly basic. It needs to present the IP address and code, and then respond to a client connecting. All of this is done in `onCreate()` in our new `AuthorizeClientActivity` class. We get the IP from `WifiManager`:

```
WifiManager wifiMgr = (WifiManager) getApplicationContext().
 getSystemService(WIFI_SERVICE);
String ipAddress = Formatter.formatIpAddress(wifiMgr.
 getConnectionInfo().getIpAddress());
```

Remember that we require that the client be on a Wi-Fi network. The code is just a random, 6-digit number:

```
String code = Integer.toString(100000 +
 new Random().nextInt(900000));
```

To listen for the `Intent` we saw earlier, which indicates that a client has been authenticated (which, presumably, will happen shortly after this `Activity` has been displayed), we register another receiver as follows:

```
messageReceiver = new BroadcastReceiver() {
  @Override
  public void onReceive(Context context, Intent intent) {
    clientAuthenticated();
  }
};
LocalBroadcastManager.getInstance(this).registerReceiver(
  messageReceiver, new IntentFilter(
    DeskDroidService.CODE_ACCEPTED));
```

We also need to tell the `Service` what this new code is so that it can verify it. To do that, we broadcast an `Intent` as follows:

```
Intent intent = new Intent(DeskDroidService.CODE_GENERATED);
intent.putExtra("code", code);
LocalBroadcastManager.getInstance(this).sendBroadcast(intent);
```

We've already seen the other half of this broadcast in `DeskDroidService.onStartCommand()` earlier, where the code is retrieved from the `Intent`, and stored in the service for use by `DeskDroidResource.getAuthorization()`.

Finally, this method, which handles the authentication notice, simply cleans up the receiver and closes the `Activity`:

```
protected void clientAuthenticated() {
  LocalBroadcastManager.getInstance(this).
    unregisterReceiver(messageReceiver);
  setResult(2, new Intent());
  finish();
}
```

With this, when a client connects and successfully authenticates, the `Activity` closes, and the user is returned to the main `Activity`.

Authorizing the client

Up until this point, everything has assumed that the desktop is already connected to the phone. We have enough pieces in place now that we can talk about that in a meaningful manner.

In the application's main `Menu`, we have two `MenuItems`: `Connect to Phone` and `Disconnect from Phone`. The `Connect to Phone` handler looks as follows:

```
@FXML
protected void connectToPhone(ActionEvent event) {
  ConnectToPhoneController.showAndWait();
  if (!preferences.getToken().isEmpty()) {
    refreshAndListen();
  }
}
```

We're going to use the now-familiar `showAndWait()` pattern to display a modal dialog, and to get the response using the new `ConnectToPhoneController`. The user interface is very simple, and is shown in this screenshot:

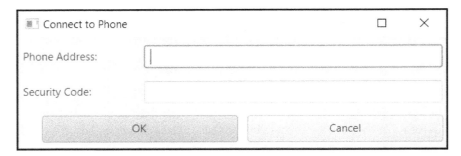

When the user clicks on **OK**, we save the address and the code in the application's preferences, then attempt to authorize against the server, as follows:

```
@FXML
public void connectToPhone(ActionEvent event) {
  String address = phoneAddress.getText();
  String code = securityCode.getText();
  preferences.setPhoneAddress(address);
  final ConversationService conversationService =
    ConversationService.getInstance();

  conversationService.setPhoneAddress(address);
  Optional<String> token = conversationService
    .getAuthorization(code);
  if (token.isPresent()) {
    preferences.setToken(token.get());
    closeDialog(event);
  }
}
```

Notice the use of `Optional<String>` as the return type for `ConversationService.getAuthorization()`. Using `Optional`, as we've discussed before, makes working with potentially `null` values much safer. In this case, if `Optional` has a value present, then we've successfully authenticated. So, we save the token to preferences, and close the dialog.

The actual authentication is handled by `ConversationService`:

```
public Optional<String> getAuthorization(String code) {
    Response response = getWebTarget().path("authorize")
     .request(MediaType.APPLICATION_JSON)
     .post(Entity.text(code));
    Optional<String> result;
    if(response.getStatus()==Response.Status.OK.getStatusCode()) {
      token = response.readEntity(String.class);
      result = Optional.of(token);
    } else {
        result = Optional.empty();
    }
    return result;
}
```

This last method sends the code to the server via a `POST`, and if the status code is `200`, we create an `Optional` with the returned token. Otherwise, we return an empty `Optional`.

Summary

In this chapter, we built a different kind of project. We've had applications that run on Android, and some that run on the desktop. This one, though, runs on both platforms simultaneously. One is no good without the other. That requires that we build things a bit differently to make sure the two are synchronized. While there are a variety of ways to go about this, we chose to use a REST server on the phone, with the desktop acting as a REST client.

By the end of the chapter, we built an Android application that provides not only a user interface, but a background process (called `Service`), and embedded our REST server in the Android application using Jersey and its Java SE deployment option. You also learned how to interact with text (SMS) messages on Android using the system-provided Content Providers and platform APIs, and streaming those messages to the client using Server-Sent Events. We demonstrated how to send messages between processes/threads in Android using `Intent`s, broadcasts, and `BroadcastReceiver`s. Finally, on the desktop side, we built a JavaFX client to display and send text messages, which connects to the REST server on the phone via the Jersey REST client, and we consumed the Server-sent Event stream, updating the user interface as appropriate.

With all of the moving parts, this was probably the most complex of our projects. It was certainly a great way to round out our list of projects. In the next chapter, we'll take a look at what's next for Java, as well as some other technologies that might be good to have on your radar.

12
What's Next?

At last, we have come to our final chapter together. We've built a number of different types of application, attempting to highlight and demonstrate different parts of the Java platform, especially those new to Java 9. As we've discussed, it's impossible to write something with **only** new-in-Java-9 technologies and APIs, so we also saw a variety of interesting items from Java 7 and 8. As Java 9 is finally shipping, it makes sense to look ahead to see what Java's future might hold for us, but it's also wise to look around and see what other languages are offering so that we can decide if our next Java will actually **be** Java. In this chapter, we'll do just that.

We will cover the following topics in this chapter:

- Recapping topics we previously covered
- What we can expect in the future

Looking back

Before looking forward to Java 10 and beyond, let's quickly recap some of the things we've covered in this book:

- The Java Platform Module System, perhaps the largest, most anticipated addition to the platform in this release. We saw how to create a module and discussed its implications on the runtime system.
- We walked through the new process management APIs in Java 9 and learned how to view processes, and even kill them, if needed.
- We looked at some of the major functional interfaces introduced in Java 8, discussing how they could be used, and showing how code might look with and without the lambdas that these interfaces support.

- We discussed Java 8's `Optional<T>` at length, showing how to create instances of the class, the various methods it exposes, and how one might use it.
- We spent a good deal of time building JavaFX-based applications, demonstrating various tips and tricks, working around several **gotchas**, and so on.
- Using the Java NIO File and Path APIs, we walked the filesystem, looking for duplicate files.
- We implemented data persistence using the Java Persistence API, demonstrating how to use the API in a Java SE environment, how to define entities, and so on.
- We built a calculator using the Java 8 Date/Time APIs, exposing the functionality as both a library and a command-line utility.
- As part of that effort, we briefly compared a few command-line utility frameworks (specifically focusing on Crest and Airline), before settling on Crest and demonstrating how to create and consume command-line options.
- While we didn't focus on it in every chapter, we did take a break to discuss and demonstrate unit testing.
- We learned about **Service Provider Interfaces** (**SPIs**) as a means to provide multiple alternate implementations for an interface that can be loaded dynamically at runtime.
- We implemented a couple of REST services, demonstrating not only the basic functionality of JAX-RS, how to deploy it in a Java SE environment, and POJO mapping, but also some more advanced features including server-sent events and securing endpoints using `Filter`.
- We built a couple of Android applications and discussed and demonstrated activities, fragments, services, content providers, asynchronous messaging, and background tasks.
- We saw OAuth2 authentication flows in action, including how to set up credentials using the Google OAuth provider and the Java code necessary to drive the process.
- We discovered JSON Web Tokens, a cryptographically secure way to pass data back and forth between, for example, a client and a server, and saw their very basic use as part of an authentication system.
- We toured the JavaMail API, learning a bit of the history and workings of common email protocols, such as POP3 and SMTP.
- We learned about job scheduling using the Quartz scheduler library.
- We saw how to specify constraints for our data in a declarative manner, then how to validate data in the light of those constraints using the Bean Validation API.

- Changing gears completely, we built a moderately sophisticated application using the feature-rich NetBeans Rich Client Platform.
- We looked briefly at world document databases with MongoDB.
- And we learned about dependency injection and how to use it with the CDI specification.

That's quite a list, and that doesn't cover all of it. One of the stated purposes of the book is to discuss and demonstrate the new features of Java 9. There are almost 100 **Java Enhancement Proposals** (**JEPs**) shipping with the release, making some of them difficult, at best, to demonstrate, but we've done our best.

Looking forward

With Java 9 done, then, the natural question is, **What is next?** As you might expect, the engineers at companies such as Oracle, Red Hat, IBM, Azul Systems, and others have been thinking about this question even while Java 9 was being planned and developed. While it is next to impossible to say what Java 10 will hold with any certainty (remember it took three major releases to get the module system done), we do have several items that are currently being discussed and designed, with the hope of shipping them in the next release. Over the next few pages, we'll explore some of these to get an early look at what our life as Java developers might be like in a couple of years.

Project Valhalla

Project Valhalla is an *incubation grounds for advanced language-VM co-development projects*. It is being led by Oracle engineer, Brian Goetz. As of this writing, there are three planned features for Valhalla. They are value types, generic specialization, and reified generics.

Value types

The goal of this effort is to update the Java Virtual Machine, and, if possible, the Java language, to support small, immutable, **identity-less** value types. Currently, if you instantiate a new Object, it is given an identifier by the JVM, which allows the **variable** instance to be referenced.

For example, if you create a new integer, `new Integer(42)`, a variable with the identity of `java.lang.Integer@68f29546`, but the value of `42`, the value of this variable will never change, and that's all we, as developers, typically care about. However, the JVM doesn't really know that, so it has to maintain the identity of the variable, with all of the overhead that entails. According to Goetz, that means every instance of this object will require up to 24 additional bytes to store the instance. If you have a large array of these, for example, that can be a significant amount of memory to manage and, eventually, to garbage-collect.

What the JVM engineers hope to achieve, then, is a way to **gently extend** the Java Virtual Machine byte code and the Java language itself to support the notion of a small, immutable aggregate type (think of a class with 0 or more properties) that lacks identity, which will result, it is hoped, in "memory-and locality-efficient programming idioms without sacrificing encapsulation". Their hope is that Java developers will be able to create these new types and treat them as just another primitive. If they do their jobs correctly, Goetz says, the feature can be summarized as **Codes like a class, works like an int!**

The current proposal, as of April 2017 (`http://cr.openjdk.java.net/~jrose/values/shady-values.html`), offers the following code snippet as an example of how one might define a value type:

```
@jvm.internal.value.DeriveValueType
public final class DoubleComplex {
  public final double re, im;
  private DoubleComplex(double re, double im) {
    this.re = re; this.im = im;
  }
  ... // toString/equals/hashCode, accessors,
    math functions, etc.
}
```

When instantiated, instances of this type could be created on the stack, rather than the heap, and use much less memory. This is a very low-level and technical discussion, which is far beyond the scope of this book, but if you are interested in more details, I would suggest reading the page linked earlier, or the effort's initial announcement at `http://cr.openjdk.java.net/~jrose/values/values-0.html`.

Generic specialization

Generic specialization is, perhaps, a bit easier to understand. Currently, generic type variables can hold only reference types. For example, you can create a List<Integer>, but not a List<int>. There are some pretty complex reasons why this is so, but being able to use primitives, and value types, would make collections more efficient in terms of memory and computation. You can read more about this feature in this document from, again, Brian Goetz--http://cr.openjdk.java.net/~briangoetz/valhalla/specialization.html. Jesper de Jong also has a good write-up about the complexities of primitives in generic type variables here:

http://www.jesperdj.com/2015/10/12/project-valhalla-generic-specialization/

Reified generics

The term **reified generics** is one that, more often than not, it seems, causes very vocal, animated reactions. Currently, if you declare a variable to be of type List<Integer>, the byte code generated has no real notion of the parameterized type, so it's not discoverable at runtime. If you were to examine the variable at runtime, you would see no mention of Integer. You could, of course, look at the types of each element, but, even then, you can't be sure of the type of the List, as there is nothing enforcing that **only** the Integer can be added to the List.

Java developers have been clamoring for reified generics, or, put simply, generics that retain their type information at runtime since generics were introduced in Java 5. As you might guess, making Java's generics reified is no trivial task, but, finally, we have a formal effort to see if it can be done and, if it can be done, to find a backwards-compatible way that doesn't have, for example, negative performance characteristics.

Project Panama

While not yet targeted for any particular Java release, Project Panama offers some hope for those who use, or hope to use, third-party, native libraries. Currently, the primary way of exposing native libraries (that is, OS-specific libraries written in, say, C or C++) to the JVM is via the **Java Native Interface (JNI)**. The problem with JNI, or at least one of them, is that it requires that every Java programmer who wants to expose a native library to the JVM also become a C programmer, which means not only the C language itself, but also the related build tools for each supported platform.

Project Panama hopes to ameliorate that issue by offering the Java developer a new means of exposing native libraries without needing a deep understanding of the library language's ecosystem, or the JVM's. The JEP for Project Panama (`http://openjdk.java.net/jeps/191`) lists these design goals:

- A metadata system to describe native library calls (call protocol, argument list structure, argument types, return type) and the native memory structure (size, layout, typing, life cycle).
- Mechanisms to discover and load native libraries. These capabilities may be provided by the current `System.loadLibrary` or may include additional enhancements for locating platform or version-specific binaries appropriate to the host system.
- Mechanisms for binding, based on metadata, a given library/function coordinate to a Java endpoint, likely via a user-defined interface backed by plumbing to make the native downcall.
- Mechanisms for binding, based on metadata, a specific memory structure (layout, endianness, logical types) to a Java endpoint, either via a user-defined interface or a user-defined class, in both cases backed by plumbing to manage a real block of native memory.
- Appropriate support code to marshal Java data types to native data types and vice-versa. This will, in some cases, require the creation of FFI-specific types to support bit widths and numeric signs that Java can't represent.

JNI has been available for quite some time, and it's finally getting some long overdue attention.

Project Amber

Project Amber's goal is to **explore and incubate smaller, productivity-oriented Java language features**. The current list includes local-variable type inference, enhanced enums, and lambda leftovers.

Local-Variable Type Inference

As we have seen countless times in this book alone, when you declare a variable in Java, you have to declare the type twice, once on the left-hand and once on the right-hand side, plus a variable name:

```
AtomicInteger atomicInt = new AtomicInteger(42);
```

The problem here is that this code is verbose and repetitive. The Local-Variable Type Inference effort hopes to fix that, enabling something like this:

```
var atomicInt = new AtomicInteger(42);
```

This code is more concise, making it more readable. Notice the addition of the val keyword. Typically, the compiler knows that a line of code, for example, is a variable declaration when it sees `<type> <name> = ....` Since the effort would remove the need for a type on the left-hand side of the declaration, we need a cue for the compiler, which the authors of this JEP propose as var.

There is also some discussion around simplifying the declaration of immutable, or final, variables. Among the proposals are `final var` as well as val, as seen in other languages such as Scala. At the time of writing, no decision that has been made on which proposal will make the final cut.

Enhanced enums

Enhanced enums will augment *the expressiveness of the enum construct in the Java Language by allowing type-variables in enums (generic enums), and performing sharper type-checking for enum constants.* (http://openjdk.java.net/jeps/301). What this means is that enums will finally support a parameterized type, allowing something like this (taken from the JEP at the link mentioned previously):

```
enum Primitive<X> {
  INT<Integer>(Integer.class, 0) {
    int mod(int x, int y) { return x % y; }
    int add(int x, int y) { return x + y; }
  },
  FLOAT<Float>(Float.class, 0f)  {
    long add(long x, long y) { return x + y; }
  }, ... ;

  final Class<X> boxClass;
  final X defaultValue;

  Primitive(Class<X> boxClass, X defaultValue) {
    this.boxClass = boxClass;
    this.defaultValue = defaultValue;
  }
}
```

Note that, in addition to specifying a generic type for each enum value, we can also define type-specific methods for each enum type. This will make it much easier to define a set of predefined constants, but also to define type-safe and type-aware methods for each of the constants.

Lambda leftovers

There are currently two items labeled as leftovers from the lambda work in Java 8. The first is the use of the underscore for unused parameters in lambda declarations. For example, in this very contrived example, all we care about are the Map values:

```
Map<String, Integer> numbers = new HashMap<>();
numbers.forEach((k, v) -> System.out.println(v*2));
```

That results in things like this in the IDE:

```
Map<String, Integer> numbers = new HashMap<>();
// ...
                      Parameter k is not used
numbers.forEach((k, v) -> System.out.println(v * 2));
```

Once the use of the underscore is allowed, this code will look like this:

```
numbers.forEach((_, v) -> System.out.println(v*2));
```

This allows better static checking of unused variables, allowing tools (and developers) to more easily identify such parameters and either correct or mark them.

The other leftover is allowing lambda parameters to shadow variables from the enclosing scope. If you were to try that now, you would get the same error if you tried to redefine a variable inside a statement block--**variable is already defined**:

```
Map<String, Integer> numbers = new HashMap<>();
String key = someMethod();
numbers.forEach((key, value) ->
  System.out.println(value*2)); // error
```

With this change, the preceding code would compile and run just fine.

Looking around

The JVM has supported alternative languages for years. Some of the better known ones include Groovy and Scala. Both of these languages have influenced Java in one way or another over the years, but, like any language, they are not without their problems. Many feel that Groovy doesn't perform as well as Java (though the `invokedynamic` bytecode instruction is supposed to have addressed that), and many find Groovy's more dynamic nature less appealing. Scala, on the other hand, suffers (fairly or not, depending on who you ask) from the perception that it's too complex. Compilation time is also a common complaint. Also, many organizations are quite happily using both, so they are definitely worth considering to see if they will work in your environment and for your needs.

While those may be great languages, we are taking some time here to see what's next, and there are at least two languages that seem to stand out from the crowd--Ceylon and Kotlin. We can't give each of these languages an exhaustive treatment, but, over the next few pages, we'll take a quick look at the languages to see what they offer JVM developers now, and, perhaps, see how they might influence future changes to the Java language.

Ceylon

Ceylon, a language sponsored by Red Hat, first appeared around 2011. Led by Gavin King of the Hibernate and Seam Framework fame, the team set out to solve, at a language and library level, some of the pain points they had experienced over the years in developing their own frameworks and libraries. While they confess to being **unapologetic fans** of the Java language, they also readily acknowledge that the language is not perfect, especially with regard to some of the standard libraries, and aim to fix those flaws in Ceylon. The goals of the language include readability, predictability, toolability, modularity, and metaprogrammability (`https://ceylon-lang.org/blog/2012/01/10/goals`).

One of the biggest differences you are likely to notice when getting started with Ceylon is that the idea of modules is already baked into the language. In many ways, it looks very similar to Java 9's module declaration, which is as follows:

```
module com.example.foo "1.0" {
   import com.example.bar "2.1";
}
```

There is, however, a very obvious difference--Ceylon modules **do** have version information, which allows various modules to depend on different versions of a module that may already be in the system.

There is at least one more rather significant difference between Ceylon and, say, Java-- Ceylon has a build tool built in. While there is, for example, a Maven plugin, the preferred approach is to use Ceylon's native tooling to build and run the project:

```
$ ceylonb new hello-world
Enter project folder name [helloworld]: ceylon-helloworld
Enter module name [com.example.helloworld]:
Enter module version [1.0.0]:
Would you like to generate Eclipse project files? (y/n) [y]: n
Would you like to generate an ant build.xml? (y/n) [y]: n
$ cd ceylon-helloworld
$ ceylonb compile
Note: Created module com.example.helloworld/1.0.0
$ ceylonb run com.example.helloworld/1.0.0
Hello, World!
```

Other than the module system, what might Ceylon offer a Java developer? One of the more immediately useful and practical features is improved null-handling support. Just as we have to do in Java, we still have to check for null in Ceylon, but the language offers a much nicer approach, and it all starts with the type system.

One of the complaints about Scala (whether its truly warranted or not) is that the type system is too complicated. Regardless of whether or not you agree, it seems clear that there's certainly room for improvement over what Java offers (even the Java language architects agree as evidenced by, for example, the proposed local variable type inference proposal). Ceylon offers a very powerful addition to the type system--union types and intersection types.

Union types allow a variable to have more than one type, but only one at a time. Where this comes into play in discussing nulls is that `String? foo = ...`, which declares a variable of type `String` that is nullable, is actually the same as `String|Null foo = ....`

This declares a variable, foo, whose type is either `String` or `Null`, but not both. The ? syntax is just syntactic sugar over the union type declaration (A | B or A or B). If we have a method, then that takes this union type; we know that the variable is nullable, so we need to check it using the following code snippet:

```
void bar (String? Foo) {
  if (exists foo) {
    print (foo);
  }
}
```

Since this is a union type, we can also do this:

```
void bar (String? Foo) {
  if (is String foo) {
    print (foo);
  }
}
```

Note that, once we've tested with `exists` or `is`, we can assume that the variable is not null and is a `String`. The compiler won't complain, and we won't have an unexpected `NullPointerException` at runtime (they actually don't exist in Ceylon as the compiler requires that you be very explicit in your handling of nullable variables). This type of compiler awareness of null and type checks is called **flow-sensitive** typing. Once you've verified the type of something, the compiler knows and remembers, so to speak, the results of that check for that remainder of that scope so you can write cleaner, more concise code.

While union types are either A or B, intersection types are A **and** B. For a completely arbitrary example, let's say you have a method whose parameter must be, say, `Serializable` **and** `Closeable`. In Java, you'd have to check manually by writing the following lines of code:

```
public void someMethod (Object object) {
  if (!(object instanceof Serializable) ||
    !(object instanceof Closeable)) {
    // throw Exception
  }
}
```

With intersection types, Ceylon would let us write this:

```
void someMethod(Serializable&Closeable object) {
  // ...
}
```

If we try to call that method with something that doesn't implement **both** interfaces, or, say, extends one class and implements the other interfaces, then we get an error at **compile time**. That's very powerful.

Before adopting a new language, or even a library, in an enterprise, one often looks to see who else is using it. Are there notable adoption stories? Are there other companies confident enough in the technology to build a production system using it? Unfortunately, the Ceylon website (at the time of writing) is very thin on the details of adoption outside Red Hat, so it's hard to answer that question. However, Red Hat is spending a good deal of money designing the language and building tooling and a community around it, so it should be a safe bet. It is, of course, a decision your enterprise will have to make after careful consideration. You can find out more about Ceylon at `https://ceylon-lang.org`.

Kotlin

Another up-and-coming language is Kotlin. It is a statically-typed language from JetBrains, the makers of IntelliJ IDEA, that targets both the JVM and Javascript. It even has nascent support to compile directly to machine code via LLVM for those environments, such as iOS, embedded systems, and so on, where a virtual machine is not desired or allowed.

Kotlin was started in 2010, and open sourced in 2012, as a means to address some common issues JetBrains was facing in large-scale Java development. Having surveyed the then-current language landscape, their engineers felt that none of those languages adequately addressed their concerns. Scala, considered for years now by many to be the **next Java**, was, for example, deemed to be too slow in compiling, despite having an acceptable feature set, so JetBrains began designing their own, eventually releasing 1.0 in February of 2016.

The design goals of the Kotlin team include expressiveness, scalability, and interoperability. They aim to allow developers to write less code that does more in a clearer fashion via language and library features, and in a language that is 100% interoperable with Java. They have added features such as coroutines to enable Kotlin-based systems to scale quickly and easily.

With all of that said, what does Kotlin look like and why should we, as Java developers, be interested? Let's start with variables.

As you'll recall, Java has both primitive (`int`, `double`, `float`, `char`, and so on) and reference, or **wrapper** types (`Integer`, `Double`, `Float`, `String`, and so on). As we've discussed in this chapter, the JVM engineers are working on ways to ameliorate some of the behavioral and capability differences this dichotomy brings. Kotlin avoids this altogether, as every value is an object, so there's no concern over `List<int>` versus `List<Integer>`.

Furthermore, Kotlin already supports local variable type inference, as well as immutablity. For example, consider the following Java code as an example:

```
Integer a = new Integer(1);
final String s = "This is a string literal";
```

The preceding lines of code could be written like this in Kotlin:

```
var a = 1;
val s = "This is a string literal";
```

Notice the use of the var and val keywords. As discussed earlier with regard to future Java language changes, these keywords allow us to declare mutable and immutable variables (respectively). Also notice that we need not declare the type of the variable, as the compiler handles that for us. In certain situations, we may need to explicitly declare the type, for example, in situations where the compiler might guess incorrectly or when it just does not have enough information to make a guess, at which point, it will stop compiling and present an error message. In those situations, we can declare the type this way:

```
var a: Int  = 1;
val s: String = "This is a string literal";
```

With Java 8, as we've seen, we have Optional<T> to help deal with null values. Kotlin has null support as well, but it's built into the language. By default, all variables in Kotlin are **not** nullable. That is to say, if the compiler can tell that you are attempting to assign a null value to a variable, or if it can't determine whether or not a value might be null (for example, a return value from a Java API), you'll get a compiler error. To indicate that a value is null-capable, you add a ? to the variable declaration as follows:

```
var var1 : String = null; // error
var var2 : String? = null; // ok
```

Kotlin also offers improved null-handling support in method calls. Suppose, for example, you want to get a user's city. In Java, you may do something like this:

```
String city = null;
User user = getUser();
if (user != null) {
  Address address = user.getAddress();
  if (address != null) {
    city address.getCity();
  }
}
```

In Kotlin, that can be expressed in a single line, as follows:

```
var city : String? = getUser()?.getAddress()?.getCity();
```

If, at any point, one of the methods returns null, the method call chain ends, and null is assigned to the variable city. Kotlin doesn't stop there with null handling. It provides, for an example, the `let` function that can serve as a shortcut for if-not-null checks. For example, consider the following lines of code:

```
if (city != null) {
    System.out.println(city.toUpperCase());
}
```

The preceding lines of code become this in Kotlin:

```
city?.let {
    println(city.toUpperCase())
}
```

This could, of course, be written as `city?.toUpperCase()`. What this should demonstrate, though, is the ability to safely use a nullable variable in an arbitrarily large, complex block of code. It's also worth noting that, inside the `let` block, the compiler knows that `city` is not null so no further null checks are necessary.

Hidden, perhaps, in the preceding example is Kotlin's support for lambdas, without which, it seems, no modern language is worth considering. Kotlin does, indeed, have full support for lambdas, higher order functions, underscores as lambda parameter names, and so on. Its support and syntax are very similar to Java's, so Java developers should be very comfortable with Kotlin's lambdas.

The big question is, of course, **Is Kotlin ready for prime time?** JetBrains definitely thinks so, as they have it in use in many of their applications, both internal and external. Other notable users include Pinterest, Gradle, Evernote, Uber, Pivotal, Atlassian, and Basecamp. Kotlin is even officially supported by Google (in Android Studio) for Android development, so it's definitely a production-grade language.

There's much, much more to this great new language, of course, and space won't allow us to discuss all of it, but you can browse through `https://kotlinlang.org` to learn more and see if Kotlin is a good fit for your organization.

Summary

There is much more that can be discussed of course, about Java 10 and these two languages, and the myriad of other projects happening in and around the Java Virtual Machine. After over 20 years of development, Java--the language **and** the environment--is still going strong. In the pages of this book, I've tried to demonstrate some of these great advancements in the language, giving you a variety of starting points for your own projects, sample code to study and reuse, and explanations of various libraries, APIs, and technologies that may be helpful in your day-to-day work. I hope you've enjoyed the examples and explanations as much as I've enjoyed preparing them, and, more importantly, I hope they help you build the Next Big Thing.

Good luck!

Index

serverless Java 21
Social Media Aggregator 18
starting with 22, 27

Q

quarantined 53

R

refresh button
  adding 165, 167
reified generics 435
Rich Client Platform (RCP) 261

S

Scene Builder
  reference 34
security, desktop application
  authorization requests, handling 424
  endpoints, securing 422, 424
server-sent events (SSE)
  about 388
  endpoints, adding to server 390
  service state, controlling 389
serverless 351
serverless computing 353
Service Provider Interfaces (SPIs) 121, 432
service
  building 255, 259
siblings 173
Simple Email Service (SES) 363, 365
Simple Notification Service (SNS) 365, 366
SMTP (Simple Mail Transport Protocol) 222
SMTP RCF
  reference 222
Software as a Service (SaaS) 352
Standard Edition (SE) 59
Sunago
  controller, finishing up 131
  controller, setting up 129
  image, adding for item 133
  Instagram, adding 167
  model class, writing 130
  network, adding 145
  plugins and extensions, using with Service
    Provider Interface 140

plugins, loading 172, 175
preferences user interface, building 134, 137
resource, handling with try-with-resources 141,
  145
setting up 128
starting with 122, 124, 126
Twitter preferences, adding 149
user interface, setting up 127
user preferences, saving 138

T

Test-Driven Development (TDD) 115
testing interlude 115
time-based unit of time 100
timely interlude
  clock 102
  code 103, 113
  duration 100
  period 101
TopComponent 270, 273, 276
Twitter client
  implementing 159, 160
Twitter developer
  registering as 146, 148
Twitter
  adding, to Sunago 145
  logging on 152, 157
  model, adding 157
  OAuth authorization 152, 157

U

user interface
  defining 34, 36
  initializing 37, 39, 41, 44

V

value types
  about 433
  references 434
variable 433

W

work stealing 58
Wrapper library

Z

www.ingramcontent.com/pod-product-compliance
Lightning Source LLC
Chambersburg PA
CBHW081457050326
40690CB00015B/2828